D1448539

Leisure Research in Europe

Methods and Traditions

Edited by

H. Mommaas, H. van der Poel

Tilburg University
The Netherlands

P. Bramham

Leeds Metropolitan University
UK

and

I. Henry

Loughborough University
UK

CAB INTERNATIONAL

CAB INTERNATIONAL
Wallingford
Oxon OX10 8DE
UK

Tel: +44 (0)1491 832111
Fax: +44 (0)1491 833508
E-mail: cabi@cabi.org
Telex: 847964 (COMAGG G)

A catalogue record for this book is available from the British Library.

ISBN 0 85198 773 7

Printed in the UK by Biddles Ltd, Guildford.

Contents

Contributors

Peter Bramham, *Senior Lecturer in Leisure Studies, Leeds Metropolitan University, UK*

Theo Beckers, *Professor of Leisure Studies, Tilburg University, the Netherlands*

Eric Corijn, *Lecturer in Leisure Studies at the Vrije Universiteit Brussel, Belgium, and Tilburg University, the Netherlands*

Ian Henry, *Senior Lecturer in Leisure Studies and Recreation Management, Loughborough University, UK*

Bohdan Jung, *Professor, Research Institute for Developing Economies, Warsaw School of Economics, Poland*

Hans Mommaas, *Senior Lecturer in Leisure Studies, Tilburg University, the Netherlands*

Nicole Samuel, *Researcher, Laboratoire du Changement des Institutions, CNRS, Paris, France*

Roberto San Salvador del Valle, *Lecturer at the Institute of Leisure Studies, Universidad de Deusto, Bilbao, Spain*

Hugo van der Poel, Senior *Lecturer in Leisure Studies, Tilburg University, the Netherlands*

Patricia Van den Eeckhout, *Researcher, Vrije Universiteit Brussel, Belgium*

Preface

This text represents the third book to be published out of the work of the European Consortium for Leisure Studies and Research. *Leisure and Urban Processes: critical studies of leisure policy in Western European cities* was published in 1989 by Routledge, and *Leisure Policies in Europe*, was published in 1993 by CAB International. The primary aim of the Consortium is to bring together European academics working in leisure studies, and to generate literature of a comparative and/or transnational nature for the leisure studies field. One of the major difficulties in such an endeavour is the variation in disciplinary backgrounds, substantive research interests and intellectual traditions which researchers from different national backgrounds bring to the analysis of leisure. This volume has therefore sought to undertake something of an inventory and analysis of the nature of work undertaken in six European nation states, while seeking also to identify ways in which transnational influences have operated in the leisure studies field. By recognising the historically nation-state bound nature of social analysis in this field, the book seeks to provide a platform for analysis which goes beyond such bounds in examining the global-local relations which are so evident in contemporary leisure.

The preparation of this text was greatly aided by bringing many of the contributors together in a seminar held in 1993 in Tilburg. We wish to express our gratitude to the Board of the Faculty of Social Sciences of the Tilburg University / Katholieke Universiteit Brabant, for their financial support for a Consortium seminar on European Leisure Research

Peter Bramham, Ian Henry,
Hugo van der Poel and
Hans Mommaas

April 1996

List of Figures and Tables

Figures

Tables

Chapter 1

Leisure Research in Europe: An Introduction

Hans Mommaas, Hugo van der Poel, Peter Bramham and Ian Henry

All books take a long time to write but this one has taken longer than most. Although the usual reasons behind delays in publications are well known, this particular book has developed a full repertoire of its own. The aim of this introduction is to provide something of an initial history of the development of this text, to examine some of the debates and issues raised in the writing of such a book about leisure research and in so doing to provide an introduction to its contents and the contexts in which this book was conceived and constructed.

The very title of the book resonates with many of the problematics in the text itself; any definitive mapping of both 'leisure' and also of 'Europe' has been and continues to be contested fiercely. All contributors engage with the difficulty of both identifying and translating 'leisure' within nation-state research communities. Indeed, there is a more global, and incomplete determination of concepts; 'leisure' and 'loisir' for example, are not coterminous. 'Loisir' mobilises a different configuration of intellectual networks in France than does 'leisure' in the UK. The historical development and deployment of concepts are mediated by intellectuals - the networks organise and create concepts whilst concepts organise and create networks. This symbiosis becomes more obtuse and tenuous in nation states where leisure research is more or less equated with 'free-time studies'. We will return to these issues in the conclusion which explores the economic, political and cultural debates underpinning concepts not only of 'leisure' but also of 'Europe'.

The book has adopted a broad remit to trace developments in leisure research in different nation states. It does not provide a definitive history of the study of particular leisure sectors, such as the arts, sports, recreation, gambling, tourism and culture. These histories must be found elsewhere, in texts with a narrower focus on particular leisure practices. By way of contrast, this book examines the history of the study of leisure by those researching in different nation-state contexts, as well as examining the cross-fertilisation of ideas within international academic networks. The following chapters examine both the 'forgotten' history of research into 'free time', 'popular culture' as well as mainstream authors who work self-consciously within a national 'leisure studies' tradition and also contribute to international leisure conferences, journals and the like.

Such an exposition is necessary in that it exemplifies one of the central positions of the book itself that history matters and shapes intellectual work. Such a claim has long been central to the sociology of knowledge and to more recent debates about postmodernism and globalisation. Many intellectuals have been reluctant to be drawn into such epistemological and ontological anxieties but they are doubly unavoidable when writing about leisure and the history of leisure research in different nation states.

In line with the 'internationalisation' of modern leisure, there has been a related increase in international contacts between scholars active in the field of leisure studies, in the development of transnational teaching courses on leisure and in the volume of cross-national comparative research within the leisure field (see for example, Bramham, Henry, Mommaas and van der Poel, 1993). Along with this increase in transnational contacts between scholars interested in the study of leisure, there is a growing interest in a cross-national comparison of ways of doing leisure research. This, first of all, with regard to the methods and theories used in the different national research programmes and the results these programmes have produced. In Europe in particular, there is a recognition that the different intellectual, academic and disciplinary traditions within which leisure research has been generated provide a fertile ground for analysis. The lines of development of national traditions, the distinctive schools of thought, their methodologies, historical trajectories, debates and critiques provide the key topics of this book.

When originally drafted, the book set out to provide an overview of the substantive and time-spatial identification of leisure along with an account of how the material for the book was gathered for the chapters. The editors wished to summarise the general perspectives deployed in studying the histories of the various national research traditions and the theoretical pedigree of the questions addressed in the various contributions. In keeping with the need for comparative analysis, we aimed to develop a framework for the evaluation and explanation of developments in leisure research. Such developments would be interpreted as the result of the confluence of global, national and local processes. Of particular contextual interest would be international economic, political and cultural developments, national political, economic, and moral agendas, as well as regional and local cultural responses. How did national intelligentsia interrogate these processes? What were the similarities, differences, silences within their commentaries and research projects? How did different nation states organise and institutionalise research networks at an international, national and local level?

From the outset of the book, substantive chapters were envisaged from the following nation states: Belgium, France, Germany, Hungary, Italy, Netherlands, Russia, Poland, Spain, Sweden, Yugoslavia, United Kingdom.

The contributors were encouraged to address the following areas:
- the styles of research discernible in the national histories of the study of leisure; their theoretical background and academic position, the types of problems addressed, the conceptualisations of leisure and methods of research used, the social, political and moral interests behind them, the sections of the populations investigated
- the contemporary situation with regard to the organisation of research in leisure, the institutions involved, the types of questions addressed, the theoretical questions addressed, the political concerns involved, the disciplines covered
- possible explanations for the historical changes and continuities in leisure research, the relationship between the problematisation of leisure, intellectual traditions and political and social developments
- lessons to be learned from the national traditions in leisure research; the weak and the strong methodological points, the gaps still existing in the research problems addressed, problematic tendencies in the way research is funded.

Given this broad remit, the editors began to approach leisure researchers in different European countries who had expressed an interest in contributing to such a book. Unsurprisingly, professional colleagues linked with the European Leisure Research Consortium provided a strong short list of the first group of likely contributors. Many had already been associated with an earlier volume on leisure policy taken by the same academic publisher, eager to develop an international portfolio of leisure and tourism publications (Bramham, Henry, Mommaas and van der Poel, 1993). The material resources available to professional academic groups, continuities in personnel, joint-curricula, student supervision on ERASMUS[1] exchange programmes, shared theoretical interests, revitalised at international conferences and so on - all provide some necessary although not sufficient conditions for the successful completion of projects. Without this shared transnational resource base many projects never come to fruition and are subsequently hidden from history.

The contexts of intellectual work are rarely innocent, although mostly ignored or dismissed as irrelevant by intellectuals themselves who simply want to get on with the 'real work' of research and data collection. This leaves philosophers to worry about issues such as knowledge and power, the nature of scientific activity, 'reflexivity' and so on. Yet intellectual networks become important configurations within which research topics are developed and data collected. Different networks mediate and contest disciplines, fields of study and research traditions which, at an ideological and institutional level, become more powerful than others as they gain currency within the academy, the state, the economy and in civil society. We are close here to Foucault's notion of 'discursive formations' which define ways of proceeding both in the academic world and in professional practice. It is also clear from the contributions that follow in the book that leisure research networks, discourses and their historical trajectories inside nation states have been shaped by transnational, national and local forces.

The final shape of the contributions, the numbers of chapters, the actual authors from different nation states must also be understood within the confluence of the global, national and local. For example, the contribution from Russia became impossible to complete because of lack of leisure material in the archives of research institutes in Moscow, the unsettled trajectory of the Russian state and other publishing commitments of the author. The contributions from Italy and Sweden were impossible to secure within the publishing time scale as the authors approached were tied into other teaching and research projects. During 1992 more seismic changes were taking place in Yugoslavia which disintegrated as the book was being planned. Reflecting such national changes, the chapter narrowed its focus to leisure research in Slovenia but so fragile was the prospective author's academic position that it became impossible to subscribe to any long-term writing commitment when personal and institutional survival were in doubt. The contribution from Hungary disappeared from the final volume because of the editorial team's failure to secure a chapter from locally-based writers who were in a position to reflect upon national histories of leisure research, rather than those writing in exile. To commission work from the latter would introduce new complications within the global, national and local which were not present, nor theoretically conceived of, in other national contributions. Although the transnational movement of intellectuals is a fruitful area for further comparative research, particularly around issues of detachment and involvement, this collection does not explore this dimension of transnational and comparative research.

Within the original time scale it was hoped to have completed the manuscript by the end of 1992. However, when the writing group met at Tilburg in September 1991 and again alongside the ELRA IV

Conference in Bilbao July 1992, the first drafts generated wide discussion around the recurrent theme about the relation between the national and the international, that is with the relation between the transnational field of leisure studies and the national scientific communities of leisure researchers and even more broadly conceived national histories of the study of leisure. All contributions acknowledged the generic problems of how to write the history of leisure research, whilst trying to come to terms with a particular and neglected history of leisure research in a single nation state.

A European Union of Leisure Scholars?

Rothblatt and Wittrock (1993) map out the great transformations that have taken place around the idea of the university in Europe. They demarcate three major stages: the rebirth of the university at the end of the eighteenth century; its emergence within national legitimations in the late nineteenth century; its reappraisal at the end of the post-war experience. Each fin de siècle seems to generate a reassessment of the university and the place of intellectual thought and research within the restructuring of economic, political, social and cultural formations. As we shall see from the later discussion surrounding postmodern thought, the twentieth century seems to be no exception.

Rothblatt and Wittrock (1993) suggest, rhetorically at least, that European nation states have a clear idea of what the university and scholarly activity should be. European scholars belong to a loosely structured community within Europe, although universities have developed and been shielded within their own national carapaces. Their collection of historical and sociological essays starts to examine the changing relationship in European and American nation states of the configurations of the academy, the state and the market. They emphasise the common themes and different trajectories of the university within Europe and America during the past two hundred years. The contributions proceed to explore then the historical relationship between the state, the market and the academy - the policies and practices surrounding academic scientific research and scholarly activity and their combined relationship with professional practice and vocations in law, engineering and medicine.

If tensions appear between the university ideal (independent, detached scholarly research) and the real demands for useful knowledge to help with social and political projects (whether they be totalitarian, social democratic or ethnocentric), the same tension reasserts itself in newly emerging fields of study within the academy. Leisure, as a topic of scholarly activity within the university, expresses and reflects the similar tensions between the state, the market and the academy. This present book traces the history of leisure research, the emergence of leisure mapped out as an object of study in its own right or in relation to other research topics such as work, family, politics and culture.

The aim of this collection of national case studies is to encourage reflection upon the pace and trajectory of leisure research within nation states, to document the links and exchanges of research with international scholars and to examine the developments of institutional networks around leisure studies and leisure research in Europe.

Faced with such a daunting task, the contributors, all themselves university scholars, focused upon several issues raised by the book. First, there is the fact that knowledge reproduced within the transnational field of leisure studies does not simply reflect the sum of national histories of leisure. There is no comfortable accumulation of knowledge within an international scientific community. This is partly a problem of the established and outsiders, of uneven development, of forms of intellectual positioning and domination. It is partly also a problem of forgotten or neglected histories, a chronic lack of reflexivity, of taking established histories for granted, and of a lack of historical data. Finally, it is partly a problem of language, of markets for books and articles, of the transparency of national and regional cultures for outsiders given the position of languages in the multi-national language system. The dominance of the cosmopolitan language of English has shaped the international discourse around the topic of leisure and leisure studies.

As the subtitle of the book implies, this collection is primarily interested in the dominant and somehow institutionalised styles or traditions of doing research that have existed in different nation states in Europe. Such national research can either be organised in terms of theoretical perspectives, thematic issues, disciplines, methodologies or techniques of collecting data. So it is a matter for the specific national histories what kind of differences and demarcations have dominated the field of research and hence what kind of demarcation will structure the contribution within each chapter. The book's primary interest is in research in which some kind of general attention was paid to 'leisure'. Authors were also encouraged to be reflexive in that they should explain to the reader why they had written or structured the chapter in the way they had, as well as positioning their own writing within national traditions or methods. Consequently, some historical legitimation would be provided for the way in which the history, and the structure of the chapter, had been presented. Each chapter is a reflection of, and simultaneously reflexive upon national leisure research.

Within the individual contributions which make up the chapters of this book, three major traditions or positions emerge as currents and confluences in the international thinking about leisure in Europe. These may be loosely caricatured, both culturally and spatially, as German idealism, French rationalism and British empiricism. German idealism draws upon the philosophy of the social science as conceptualised by Dilthey, Weber and others. The emphasis here is on understanding forms of life, on the meanings embedded within leisure forms and practices but also on spirituality and emotion. Secondly, there is a strong French contribution from analytic philosophy, humanism and rational structuralism drawing upon the works of Dumazedier and Caillois which stress experience and cognition. Leisure is defined as a cultural mission, a human project of self-development and enlightenment. Thirdly, there is the empirical positivism in the UK; research must gather up the facts of leisure time, a sphere of everyday life created with industrialisation.

All three strands of thought provide the carapace within which universities, disciplines and research topics have been organised, legitimated and sponsored. Needless to say the boundaries between these three major currents or traditions are permeable. It is precisely this permeability which encourages intra- and transnational analysis and exploration. It is worth stating from the outset that all three major perspectives are different versions or expressions of a modernist project. They share a common determination of nation states, (and of organic intellectuals) to act as legislators, to map out the universal rational scientific principles from which the nation state can shape distinctively the contours of civil society. Following the concepts of Bauman (1987, 1991), intellectuals in modernity can be seen as legislators, constructing a society which is coterminous with the nation state. Whether enthused by the canons of German 'Bildung' and leisure pedagogy, French cultural 'animation' or British pragmatism and more recently leisure professionalisation, intellectuals have stories to tell about society and recommendations to make in social and economic policy. The history of leisure and leisure studies can be seen as part of this modernising project which starts to lose confidence and direction during the 1980s.

Because of the changing role of the nation state, intellectuals no longer have a powerful legislative function but rather an interpretative one. They are one 'expert' voice amongst a babble of interpreters. They offer a distinctive interpretation of what is going on in the world but one that lacks the political backing of the nation state, which increasingly looks to the market to integrate individuals into social order via consumer culture rather than a common citizenship in a shared polity. Consequently, there are now more books exploring globalisation and mass culture than there are examining leisure. Leisure is presently an unfashionable topic, although we would argue, as do the individual contributions, that it is still a crucial concept to lay bare the problems of transnational analysis and the contested nature of pleasure and culture, given its resonance with Williams' (1981) notion of culture as a 'whole way of life'.

The power of different philosophical positions, of domain assumptions underpinning intellectual activity, of discursive formations should never be underestimated. It is striking that in some countries people are more aware of the history of (the study of) leisure in the USA or England or France or Germany than the history of (the study of) leisure in their own country. The result can be that people take the transnationally established histories, and especially the terms in which these histories are presented, as in a sense mirroring the history of (the study of) leisure in their own country, and hence start to interpret their own history in terms of these established perspectives. In similar vein, modernisation theories of industrialism implied a convergence of political, economic and cultural systems on a global scale, with mature nation states providing the inevitable historical trajectory for emergent states to follow. However, established histories may have hegemonic influence but they do not have universal value. Such histories themselves are in various ways linked to the national-historical circumstances of the countries involved, such as the moment and impact of the process of industrialisation, national activities of political elites, the establishment of something like a separate social scientific field or discourse, the establishment of the welfare state with leisure services as an ingredient at a national, regional and local level. Besides, one should be aware of the fact that what in the transnational field counts as an established history does not necessarily have to have that status in the country of origin.

On the other hand, national histories, however written up, do not develop in isolation. Established histories in the transnational field of leisure studies do influence national histories. Here one can think of students who, when starting to analyse leisure relations in their own country, begin by reading established transnational literature, to take that literature as a sort of vantage point from which to analyse and understand national and local events. Hence, more recent national histories of the study of leisure will no doubt reflect and engage with transnationally established perspectives on leisure, containing for instance references to such established authors as Dumazedier, De Grazia, Parker, Roberts etc. By the same token, traditionally established national leisure research becomes reified and staid with new generations of writers often looking abroad for inspiration and new directions to pursue their studies.

Commonalities in Research

Although national histories have different trajectories and have been influenced to varying degrees by transnational currents of thought, striking commonalities emerge when reading the chapters. All nation states exhibit parallels and continuities within the history of free time or leisure studies as both an intellectual and as a policy project. Leisure and leisure research have been shaped by intellectuals as legislators exploring the emergence and the rational reconstruction of free time as part of modernising projects of nation elites, denominational groups and secular social movements. This shared but differentiated leisure project has fired research into the arts, sports and recreation, the media and tourism as well as into the regulation of unemployment and popular culture.

In the contributions to this text, there are commonalities in theoretical developments such as sociography, American functionalism, neo-Marxism and postmodernism. All have permeated studies in particular historical periods and institutional settings in different nation states. There are also commonalities in research methodologies and techniques of data collection as leisure researchers have systematically immersed themselves in time budget and consumption data, household surveys, interviews, and ethnographies, often replicating research completed elsewhere - on a local, national and international scale. There has also been the similar deployment of techniques of data collection - time budget research, household consumption, leisure participation surveys, ethnographies and so on. The demand for leisure data, usually for policy purposes, has asserted itself within the history of each nation state. Such research initiatives may be inspired by collaboration with other researchers on international projects.

Each individual contribution to this text faces the common problem of writing history, of reconstructing the past and choosing an adequate vantage to make sense of the history of leisure research. Decisions have to made about periodisation and chronologies, the inclusion and exclusion of research, the models and disciplinary perspectives to organise the overview. Authors face the common problem of locating their own work within such a history, whether on a local, national or transnational level. There is the question also of detail - authors have had to make decisions on what to include: local and national background information which may be obvious to informed or indigenous readers.

The common themes within the individual contributions are also sources of difference. Indeed, comparative research sensitises us to such difference (Albrow and King, 1990). The leisure project has different historical trajectories and different enthusiasms and commitments from different intellectuals in different nation states. The actual position of intellectuals within the academy, the state and the economy differs from one nation state to another and changes within different historical periods. The position of Polish intellectuals and of French intellectuals for example, differs greatly. Intellectual life in Spain under fascism is different from academic debates under a democratising regime in the 1980s. The level of detachment and involvement of intellectuals with policy issues, leisure pedagogics and consultancy varies dramatically, as does their career involvement with and commitment to a transnational tradition in leisure studies.

It has been suggested that social research never solves problems but gets bored with them. It is hard to do so with leisure and leisure studies. If intellectuals are free floating, as Mannheim maintains, they are often at sea when it comes to leisure and leisure studies. The maritime metaphor perhaps helps here. There are clearly major tides and currents which have informed social research and the study of leisure, such as German idealism, French rationalism and British empiricism, as well as transatlantic intellectual trade winds. National research agendas may be seen as flotillas of ships navigating these high seas of ideas, whilst dealing with internal changing legislative policy agendas in different historical periods. In leisure studies, certain writers, such as Dumazedier, De Grazia, Parker and Roberts, operate as famous captains of multinational carriers dominating shipping lanes and trade routes, shaping global flows of information, research and sponsorship. Yet there are smaller craft exploring local shorelines, taking cognisance of major fleets riding on the waves of internationally significant research and institutional sponsorship. This book then starts to chart the high seas, to encourage leisure research to be more self-reflexive by comparing histories of leisure research in different nation states.

REFERENCES

Albrow, M. and King, E. (1990) *Knowledge and Globalisation.* London: Sage.

Bramham, P., Henry, I., Mommaas, H. and van der Poel, H. (1993) *Leisure Policies in Europe.* Wallingford: CAB International.

Bauman, Z. (1987) *Legislators and Interpreters.* London: Routledge.

Bauman, Z. (1991) *Intimations of Postmodernity.* London: Routledge.

Foucault, M. (1974) *The Archaeology of Knowledge.* London: Tavistock.

Rothblatt, B. and Wittrock, D. (1993) *The European and American University since 1800.* Cambridge: Cambridge University Press.

Williams, R. (1981) *Culture.* London: Fontana.

NOTES TO CHAPTER 1

[1] ERASMUS was a scheme funded by the European Community to support students' mobility between member states. Its initial goal was that 10% of the total EC population would enjoy direct experience of the programmed exchanges. In 1995 the ERASMUS programme will be superseded by SOCRATES.

Chapter 2

The Prehistory and History of Leisure Research in France

Nicole Samuel

Obviously leisure is a very important contemporary phenomenon in France as in other industrial countries. Indeed, its development has been one of the major events of the last 150 years on the French social scene. During this period, it has become a social right so deeply anchored in our collective mind that it keeps its full impact even now, despite the concomitant acute problem of unemployment. Paradoxically however, it has been - and still is - difficult to establish and maintain leisure research as a legitimate and autonomous field of study. This situation seems to result from several factors among which the following seem the most important. First, in the community of French academics as a whole, leisure is still not considered as a topic 'serious' enough to be tackled by a fully-fledged scholar. This is because of an implicit assumption according to which some spheres of life (for example work, the family, and religion) have more social significance, and should therefore be more important focuses for research, than leisure. Secondly, it follows that in a country where the major part of fundamental research in the social sciences is organised and financed by the state, and where decisions in this respect are made with the advice of commissions of scientists, scholars have never been encouraged to choose leisure as a field of research. Leisure as a topic has never been at the top of priorities for the allocation of funds for fundamental research. Thirdly, among French leisure researchers, there is no agreement on the concept of leisure and as a consequence there is no agreement either on the field to be covered by leisure research. Finally, although it is frequently claimed that leisure should be studied from a multidisciplinary perspective, attempts at doing so have mostly been unsuccessful. All this explains that going into leisure research has often been felt in France to be somewhat of a challenge.

One point needs to be clarified to begin with. As mentioned above, the concept of leisure is still under discussion. From the standpoint of my own field - the sociology of leisure - and as far as my own position is concerned, leisure is not synonymous with free time but is part of the latter. I define free time as a social time (or a socio-cultural time in the terms of P.A. Sorokin) which has several characteristics among which are the following: it is heterogeneous, it brings about transformations in many social processes and it produces new values (Samuel, 1984). As heterogeneous social time, free time is made up of leisure time and also of political and religious time. Whereas the activities pursued in the two latter spheres are mostly oriented to institutions, the ultimate end of leisure activities is self-accomplishment (Dumazedier, 1974: 99). In the first approach, leisure then appears as a set of activities and/or behaviours chosen by each person during his or her free time, within the limits of freedom that socio-cultural determinants allow him or her to have. These activities can be of a physical, intellectual, artistic or social nature while leisure behaviours can include 'non activities' such as rest, relaxation, thinking, day dreaming, etc. As a concept, however, leisure goes beyond this description. As part of free time, it stands at the origin of many transformations of social processes and it produces new values. These values in turn have an influence on other social times such as work time and family time which have long been known as having an impact on leisure time. It is through this process of interaction with the other social times (and especially with work time) that leisure has slowly become a social phenomenon which in its turn could be taken up as a field of research.

The existence of leisure as a social fact was the guiding prerequisite for the emergence of leisure research. But this condition was not sufficient: it was also necessary that a certain social value be linked to leisure (Olszewska and Pronovost, 1982: 300) and that the social sciences be ready to take it up as a field of study. This set of conditions was not met until the period following the Second World War. The present chapter will explain how these conditions came to be fulfilled and how leisure started and developed in France.

The first section will show that, for the major part of the French urban population, leisure did not exist at the beginning of the industrial era: its conquest was a long struggle which was not completed until the 8 hour work day was voted in during 1919, and paid holidays became legal in 1936. The second section will analyse what the social thinkers of the 19th century, some of whom can be considered as the ancestors of leisure research, had to say about leisure. The third section will deal (briefly) with the development of the French social sciences and especially sociology since the turn of the century in order to make it clear how and when it became ready to take up the scientific study of leisure. The fourth section will deal with the birth and growth of leisure research in the French social sciences.

How Leisure Came to Exist as a Social Phenomenon

The beginning of the industrial era was characterised in France, as well as in other industrialising countries, by very long working days combined with work schedules much stricter than they had been in the preceding era of craftsmanship. The average duration of the working day was 13 hours, but 14 and 15 hour work days were quite common and 17 hour work days were not exceptional. During the first part of the 19th century, with the extension of gas lighting, work days became even longer and, in many plants and factories, they were prolonged well into the night. By the middle of the 19th century, it was common for French workers to have a 14 hour work day; night work was quite frequent in very poor environmental conditions. Altogether, around mid-century, in most industrial settings, work was a long daily ordeal with few legal holidays and no paid vacations. Free time and leisure were non existent, perhaps not even as dreams because there was no time for dreaming!

In spite of such hard working conditions, very few claims were laid in favour of a reduction of work time until 1848 and very few legislative steps were taken in this direction. Moreover those in existence were far from being strictly observed. Two main factors can explain this situation: one is of a political and economic nature; the other one is sociological.

From a political standpoint, the whole period between the beginning of the first empire (1804) and the Second Republic (1848) was altogether one of repression and conservatism: labour - and not free time - was encouraged. From an economic standpoint, during this phase of the accumulation of capital, when the emphasis was on production more than on consumption, periods of prosperity called for very intensive work but were followed by periods of recession during which there was unemployment. This meant that each worker was very dependent upon his or her employer. Working conditions, including the length of the work day, had to be accepted by the workers as defined by the decisions of employers. Finally, from a sociological standpoint, the working class which had developed during the first decades of industrialisation was essentially made up of peasants who had little propensity to unite. This was a considerable hindrance to the building up of a movement for free time.

But things started to change around the middle of the century. A consciousness of the working class began to develop and the voice of workers became more firmly expressed through groups which became politically active. A public debate started about the length of the work day. After the Revolution of 1848, on March 2 of that year, Louis Blanc, a member of the new Provisional Government, succeeded in having a decree passed to legalise the 10 hour work day in Paris (11 hours in the provinces). This was a turning point even though this decree was repealed as early as the following September when the New Assembly passed another one which extended the work day limit to 12 hours in factories and manufacturing without even making any provisions for the workshops. But the principle of a legal limit to the length of the work day was now institutionalised. Free time was thus becoming a social right in France and has not since been challenged by the various types of government which have succeeded each other up to the present day.

From 1848 onwards, the growing claim for the reduction of work time first continued to be centred on the length of the work day; it was later extended to the right of a weekly holiday and to a paid vacation. Under the Third Republic, in 1879, Martin Nadaud (1815-1898), a leftist politician who was the author of *The Working Classes in England* (1872) and of *The Workers' Society* (1873) proposed a new law aimed at limiting the work day to 10 hours and the working week to six days, thus combining a reduction of the work day with the right to a weekly day of rest. But this proposal was rejected. The 10 hour work day was not passed until July 4 1912, while a weekly holiday had been decided by the law in 1906. The 8 hour working day was voted for in 1919 and paid leave (congés payés) which had existed on a small scale in some sectors of the French economy, was made legal for all wage earners in 1936, under the leftist government of the Popular Front. Thus gradually free time (including leisure time) had not only become a social right but also a social fact. Leisure was now a social phenomenon concerning a very large part of the population.

Leisure in the Social Thinking of the 19th Century

From this overview, it obviously appears that the French wage earners had to wait a long time until the emergence of non-work time which could be anything more than a mere recovery from the efforts of work.

Starting in the 1830s, the conditions arising from the industrial revolution had been a topic of interest for a number of social thinkers who had become especially preoccupied with the living conditions of industrial workers. Some, often from a socialist perspective, presented an utopian view of society. Others, from a liberal standpoint, suggested practical improvements of the workers' living conditions without deep modifications to the social system. Most thought more in terms of improving the living conditions of workers than in terms of promoting free time and leisure as such. Indeed a frequent underlying theme of both positions was a bitter criticism of idleness which was often associated with leisure.

This can be explained in the following manner. In the 19th century, from an ideological standpoint, work had become the central value of the social system, the value upon which the recent industrial society was founded with the emergence of an increasingly powerful bourgeois class which both distrusted the workers and hated the idleness of the wealthy. The principle of a distinction between productive and unproductive activities had been inherited from the Physiocrats. The economists in the 19th century demonstrated the necessity of an accumulation of wealth through work in order to build up the capital which would allow an economic 'take off' (Lanfant, 1972:33). This anti-leisure philosophy was shared by the Catholics whose religion was dominant in France. They thought that leisure distracted people from religion and encouraged idleness and lazy behaviour: work was a duty to be performed for the sake of the harmonious development of society but also for the sake of individual salvation. There was also a fear among those in power that leisure time could be used to stir political agitation. From such a perspective, the concept of leisure was criticised from the triple standpoint of economics, politics and morality.

All this explains why most sociological thinkers of the 19th century - with important exceptions such as Auguste Comte, Lafargue and Le Play - had little to say in favour of leisure even though they criticised the poor living conditions of workers.

An Utopian View of Society

Such was the case of an early socialist like Saint-Simon (1760-1825). His main principle was that every person should be put to work in a society based on the development of industry. He strongly wished for an improvement of the living conditions of the underprivileged classes but he felt that the laziness of the idle wealthy class was a crime against the growth of the new industrial society. He advocated an industrial state directed by modern science and organised for productive labour by the most capable individuals. The aim of society should be to produce the goods which are useful for life. In his *Nouveau Christianisme* (1825), the cause of the poor took the form of a religion. But little attention was given to leisure in his utopian socialism which strove for an egalitarian society.

Pierre-Joseph Proudhon (1808-1865), in numerous writings, also set forth a society based on justice, freedom and equality. He called himself a socialist, as an opponent to capitalism and private property. But he looked forward to anarchy as an ethical ideal. He bitterly criticised the institutions of capitalism and emphasised the inherent capacity of the working class to organise itself. While he gave the foremost importance to the right for every person to work, his doctrine however always laid the main stress on personal freedom and voluntary association in a society, freed from monopolist property rights. In 1839, in a long essay entitled 'De la célébration du dimanche', he insisted on the necessity of promoting rest from work on Sunday. This was not for religious reasons, but nor was it for the sake of leisure. The author speaks instead of the good influence that a Sunday freed from work would have on public hygiene, on morals, on family ties, and on relationships between urban dwellers. In his next work, there is no mention of the word leisure or even of a synonymous term.

Louis Blanc (1811-1882), a political leader and historian whose ideas were to have a great influence on the development of socialism, founded the *Revue du Progrès*, in which he published his well-known essay 'L'Organisation du Travail'. In this text, he imputed all the social evils to the pressure of competition and demanded an equalisation of wages and the merging of individual interests in the common good, with an economy based on the principle: 'to each according to his needs, from each according to his abilities'. This was to be materialised by the establishment of 'social workshops' , a kind of combined co-operative and trade union in which workmen of all trades united their efforts for their common benefit. In 1843, Louis Blanc joined *La Réforme*, the journal of the extreme left republicans. After the Revolution of 1848, he became a member of the provisional government of the Second Republic. On his motion, on February 25, 1848, the government undertook to 'guarantee work for every citizen'. On 2 March, as already mentioned, he was influential in having a decree passed to legalise the 10 hour work day. Upon his occasion, he declared: 'Not only does too long a spell of manual work deteriorate the worker's health but it also attacks his dignity as a human being by preventing him from cultivating his intelligence'. The implication was that, following the tradition of popular education, the workers should be given an opportunity for education during their non-working time. But there was no emphasis on leisure as such.

These utopian writers all highlighted the poor living conditions of the working class, but the remedies they suggested were centred on the right to work and to do so in better conditions. Even in utopian thinking, leisure still seemed to be a long way off in the future.

There was however a brilliant exception in the person of Auguste Comte. Indeed, leisure plays a positive role in the utopian view of society which Auguste Comte (1798-1857) presented in the second volume of his *Système de Politique Positive* (1824), where he imagined a positivist society in which all material needs would be satisfied. The traditional human activities would be to a great extent replaced by a striving toward the development of feelings and intelligence. Individualistic instincts would weaken to the benefit of altruistic feelings. Intelligence would lose its materialistic motivations and would bloom in the aesthetic sphere. To the development of industry and science would succeed the development of art. Human activity would become primarily aesthetic: games, festivals, the eloquent expression of feelings would become our main activities with a priority given to family or social group life and not the commonweal. Social stratification would no longer be founded on material power but rather on personal merit. Each person would express his abilities in games and in art. Aesthetic competitions would be organised. Such a society would need no industry and would have no army, no theology. It would be regulated by feelings which would command both intelligence and activity (Kremer-Marietti, 1983:31-39). From such a perspective, leisure is seen as a true substitute for work in an ideal society.

Leisure as Pictured in the Research about the Actual Living Conditions of the Working Class

Around 1830, some interest in this topic had been aroused. A working class paper, *L'Artisan*, suggested in October 1830 an inquiry on the subject, but this brought few results. A few systematic studies were however conducted by Gerando, Bigot de Morogues and Villeneuve-Bargimont and especially by Louis-René Villermé (1782-1863) whose thinking - far from utopian - was tied in to social action. As a physician and a statistician, this author was a member of the Academy of Medicine and of the Academy of Moral and Political Sciences. In 1832, the latter entrusted him with the task of studying the living conditions of the poor. Among other reports, he published in 1840 a study on the living conditions of workers in textile manufacturing (Villermé, 1971) which remained famous and which resulted very quickly in the promulgation of a law limiting the work of children in manufacturing. In his text, while honestly observing the difficult living conditions of the workers, Villermé clearly wanted to refute the current opinion of the 'pessimistic' socialists by showing that these conditions, although far from good, had never been better and had even improved since the previous generation (Villermé, 1971:290). According to him, whatever free time the workers had should be filled by educative occupations (Villermé, 1971:210), thus avoiding the absolute idleness of Sunday and other non-working days. For indeed this idleness was the reason which attracted them to the taverns and to a state of drunkenness (Villermé, 1971:208). In other words, Villermé distrusted leisure which he considered as the source of the main evil of society: drunkenness. Moreover, he sought that the educative activities he advocated (learning to read and to write) would only be desirable if they were combined with an ethical and religious training (Villermé, 1971:255-256).

A similar distrust of leisure - and for similar reasons - was expressed by several other authors belonging to liberal circles. For example, Adolphe Blanqui (1798-1854), a liberal economist who was the brother of the socialist Auguste Blanqui, criticised in the following terms the decree of 1848 which momentarily introduced the 10 hour work day: 'The sterile leisure that (the law) created for the working populations only encouraged their physical and moral intemperance, the taverns and the clubs' (Guerrand, 1963:49). In the following decades, some liberal thinkers continued to establish a link between leisure and drinking with an insistence on the necessity of organising leisure time activities to prevent the workers from visiting the taverns too often. Such were the cases for Armand Audiganne (1814-1875), a liberal economist and for Auguste Cochin (1823- 1873), a liberal catholic who wanted leisure activities to be regulated; they also urged business leaders to become interested in the leisure activities of their employees in order to have a better control over them.

Voices in Favour of Leisure

But the idea of the legitimacy of leisure slowly appeared on the scene. For example, Louis-Marthurin Christophe (1800-1881), known as Moreau-Christophe, a General Inspector of Prisons, was interested in the underprivileged people who were in jail. He was also a scholar and, in 1849, he published a book about the right to idleness in Greek and Latin antiquity, making the point that the Latin word for leisure (otium) was not a synonym for 'desidia' (laziness), or for 'segnitia' (apathy) or for 'pilgritia' (sloth) or for 'inertia'. Moreau-Christophe underlined the fact that all these words had a negative connotation which indeed was not the case for 'otium' (Dommanget, 1977:44).

This idea made progress in the following decade and by 1860 the notion that leisure could be a legitimate field of human activity was gaining ground. For example, in 1861, Maurice Cristal, a music critic who also did some work on social economics, wrote a pamphlet entitled *Les Délassements du Travail*. Still denying any weakness for laziness or idleness, he nevertheless insisted on the fact that relaxation (leisure?) was legitimate when it compensated the effects of work. He also introduced the interesting idea that the economists were wrong in being concerned only with production, competition and salaries while they should take 'relaxation' into account. Against this background, a conservative writer, Frederic Le Play (1806-1882) and a socialist author Paul Lafargue (1842-1811) shed new light on the question of leisure.

Frederic Le Play contributed some valuable information about the leisure expenditure of the working class in several European countries. He had started his study of society with the family and industry and had moved on to theories about relations between the worker and industry, the people and leaders, and the best functions of government. His focus was the family budget which, after recounting income and its sources, expenses and their uses, then covered work, moral attitudes, and the relations between the worker, employer and society. His doctrine was founded on a social system based on the family, religion and property. In *La Méthode Sociale* (Le Play, 1989), we find a summary and a justification of the categories the authors chose to study the life style of workers and their budgets (Chapter XII, p. 290). Expenses are classified in the following sections: food, lodging, clothes, moral needs, recreation and health, domestic industries, debts, taxes and insurance. The argument was based on the primacy of work in any society. But 'recreation' was studied in section 4 and a concession made to the fact that work should not absorb all the energy of body and soul: 'Keeping up the right balance between all his faculties requires for man to practice periodically physical and intellectual exercises, essentially distinct from labour proper' (Le Play, 1989:362). From his studies on the European worker, Le Play concluded that such recreational activities varied with the climate, except birthdays, weddings and religious celebrations which were popular everywhere. According to his own scale of values, the best types of recreation were 'the pleasures of intelligence, linked with the family and neighbourhood relationships' (Le Play, 1989:365). Communal reading, listening to stories, musical and literary associations offered such opportunities. From the results of his study of workers' life in different countries, Le Play quotes the winter social evenings with neighbours in France and Spain, the public lectures offered to workers in Paris and other western big cities. He saw in such 'recreations' the possible starting point of new institutions which would improve the well-being of workers. Two conclusions are interesting. First, the methodical study of recreational activities chosen by the people in different countries could suggest useful patterns for action in the future. Secondly, the programme of the primary schools should contain elements which, although useless for the pupils' future professional work, would later encourage them to enjoy 'moral' types of recreation. Perhaps this was the starting point of education for leisure!

But Le Play had introduced a theory of the cyclical changes in society which was contrary to the popular evolutionary ideas of progress held by Comte, Spencer and later Durkheim. Besides, he predicted the future weakness of France and western society. This explains why he was not widely accepted in his time. Little attention seems to have been paid to his observations and suggestions about what he called 'recreation' .

As for Paul Laffargue, in his pamphlet entitled *The Right to Laziness* (1880), he criticised the work ethic which he described as leading workers to accept alienation and he suggested solutions to the problem of the dire living conditions of the working class. First, the idle wealthy people should all be put to work. This would bring down by a maximum of three hours, the average length of the work day. Secondly, ignoring the strong emphasis which was usually put on production, Lafargue suggested an increase of consumption on the part of the workers. Under the new circumstances, the latter would enjoy good food and good wine while entertainment (shows and theatre plays) would continually be at their disposal in order to protect them for boredom. Leisure would become an integral part of every day life.

Lafargue's pamphlet was widely distributed and by 1900 it has been translated into many languages. It was well received among French socialist leaders and well known by the deputies who were Lafargue's colleagues at the Assembly. But he gave his readers an utopian image of leisure without seeming to realise that the latter was beginning to take shape as a social fact. He was concerned with leisure as it should be, from his perspective, in an ideal socialist society and not with leisure as it was developing in his own country in the latter part of the 19th century.

A New Impulse to Popular Education

In this climate, the reduction of working time came to be seen in many circles as a necessity not only for physical recovery but also for spiritual and intellectual development. A new impulse was given to the movement for popular education which had been strong in France since the end of the 18th century (Pronovost, 1983:140-146). This movement existed and developed under the various forms of government of the 19th century (Poujol, 1981; Darmon, 1972; Mandrou, 1975; Agulhon, 1978). Over time, it became increasingly active: in 1862, an important group of trade unionists returning from a study trip in England claimed the right to attend evening school. Jean Macé (1815-1894) founded the 'Magasin d'Education et de Recreation' in 1864 and the *Ligue de l'Enseignement* in 1886. In 1898, the 'Universities of the People' were created in a secular spirit. A Federation of 'Institutes for the People' was started in 1903 under the influence of Marc Sangnier (1873-1950), editor of *Le Sillon*, a famous catholic paper. Even though these endeavours were of short duration they contributed to spread the idea that leisure time could be used for intellectual development.

In the meantime, leisure had also come to be promoted on a large scale as a tool for physical and personal improvement: in 1894, for example, Pierre de Coubertin (1863-1937), renovator of the Olympic games, organised the first Congress for the development of sport.

How the Social Sciences Slowly Came Round to the Study of Leisure

At the end of the 19th century, the Republican government, somewhat anxious about the strength of the workers' movement, felt the need for information about the working class. It became interested in the social sciences which were coming into fashion (Cuin and Gresle, 1992:

I.70). This was a help to the universities and to research. This also resulted in the creation (1891) of an 'Office of Employment (Office du Travail), which depended upon the Ministry of Commerce and Industry and was to be a tool for social investigations bearing principally on the working class. The private sector was also becoming more interested in social research. For example, Jules Siegfried, a Protestant who was the Minister of Commerce in 1892-1893, supported several private initiatives. In 1894, he helped create a 'Social Museum' (Musée social) which was an Institute for Applied Research on behalf of employers, with an interest in the study of the working class. Until this experience came to an end in 1897, several studies were undertaken about British trade unionism, conducted by Paul de Rousiers and Paul Bureau. These disciples of Le Play brought changes to the latter's method and extended their observations to the workshops and the townships in an attempt to combine statistics and monographs. But they were more interested in work than in leisure.

Around this time, the term 'social sciences' seems to disappear to the benefit of the term 'sociology' , under the impulse of René Worms (1869-1926), with the creation of the *Revue Internationale de Sociologie* (1893), of the Institut International de Sociologie (1894), of the Paris Society of Sociology (1895) while Durkheim (1868-1917) and his group launched *l'Année sociologique* in 1896. Among the Durkheimians, subgroups were created to take charge of specific subjects which were very broad in perspective. There were for example: General Sociology, Sociology of Religion, Economic Sociology, Social Morphology, Moral and Juridical Sociology. The time was not ready for the Sociology of Leisure and not even for the Sociology of Work !

Although the success of the Durkheimian school was very impressive on the intellectual scene, the progress of sociology as an academic discipline remained slow: by 1914, only four Professorships existed for the field (Cuin and Gresle, 1992:I.84).

After the First World War, during the 1920s, the Durkheimian group (in spite of the leader's death in 1917) remained powerful (viz. the creation of the French Institute of Sociology by Mauss in 1924; the publication of the second series of *L'Année sociologique* between 1925 and 1927 and so on). New fields were taken up by the Durkheimians (psychology, economics, human geography) while Durkheim's perspective and methodology spread in all the disciplines of the social sciences (Cuin and Gresle, 1992:II.7).

But this influence weakened in the 1930s: among other reasons, no leader emerged to succeed Durkheim and also Durkheimian sociology was accused of being 'governmental' and conservative (Cuin and Gresle, 1992:II.10). Two other groups had been active before the war: the one around René Worms, who died in 1926, had practically disappeared while the Le Playsian school, in spite of an abundant production, had lost most of its impact.

By the start of the Second World War, French sociology had experienced a decline, in part because the dominant Durkheimian sociology had remained too speculative and had been incapable of widening its field of investigation to contemporary social reality, of which leisure was a part.

After the Second World War, France went through a thirty year period of prosperity ('les trentes glorieuses'), first marked by the efforts of reconstruction, and this in spite of the political turmoil due to the wars in Indochina and in Algeria; the student uprising and the workers' strike in 1968 were quite unexpected. The post-war reconstruction efforts included a new impulse to sociology, mostly thanks to the individual initiatives of three people: Jean Stoetzel (1910-1987), Georges Gurvitch (1894-1965) and Georges Friedmann (1902-1977). Gurvitch was instrumental in the launching of the *Cahiers Internationaux de Sociologie* and in the creation of the Centre for Sociological Studies (1946) where Dumazedier was to start his group on the sociology of leisure. Friedmann was the Director of the CES until 1952 and encouraged this initiative of Dumazedier. Many other developments took place and by 1958 the institutionalisation of sociology had been completed.

The Development of Leisure Research

It was at this point that leisure research appeared in the social sciences and especially in sociology. In the late 1940s and in the 1950s, several French sociologists had become interested in this topic. At first however, it was not considered as an independent field of research but as an appendix of the sociology of work or as an element of the sociology of everyday life (Raymond, 1964).

The Sociology of Leisure as an Appendix of the Sociology of Work

For Georges Friedmann, leisure was a complement or a compensation for work which, in his opinion, was becoming increasingly alienating and frustrating as a consequence of industrialisation. The remedies he suggested were the improvement and the enrichment of work but also the use of leisure to re-establish a good equilibrium of life. 'Good' music and literature as well as a selective use of the radio and of TV were advocated for this purpose. This outlook was related to the idea, expressed by some social thinkers of the 19th century, that leisure could counterbalance the negative effects of work. It was also connected with the preoccupation for leisure which had been strong in the politics of the Popular Front in 1936. His first important work *La Crise du Progrès* was published during the same year. The second one *Problèmes humains du Machinisme industriel* came out in 1945.

His outlook changed and this was explored in *La Puissance et la Sagesse* (1970): Friedmann no longer believed that leisure could be 'active' and could be the condition and the opportunity for human development. He arrived at the conclusion that his contemporaries had become as alienated in their leisure as they were in their work.

For Friedmann, the study of leisure was part of the sociology of work. But he made leisure a well-defined category of social analysis. This was an important step which was a prerequisite for the development of a sociology of leisure 'per se'.

According to Pierre Naville (1904-1993), also a sociologist of work, automation could have a favourable part to play in the future: there would be more free time for workers and leisure might become an important aspect of a new industrial society (Naville, 1957). Jean Fourastié, an economist interested in sociological problems, also emphasised new openings for leisure following the drastic reduction of working time which he felt was bound to take place in the future (Fourastié, 1965). While both Naville and Fourastié had their own sociological perspective on leisure, they did not consider it, any more than Friedmann had, as a specific field of research. As a consequence, for about a decade, the sociology of leisure mostly developed as part of the sociology of work. In the words of Pierre Naville, written in 1957: '... the field of sociology of work extends to what is its negation: non work, the area of free activities' (Naville, 1957:489). Like the social thinkers of the 19th century, Naville seems careful not to use the word 'leisure'!

The Sociology of Leisure as Part of the Sociology of Everyday Life

During the 1950s, other authors recognised the sociological importance of leisure but felt it should be studied as an element of everyday life (vie quotidienne). This was the standpoint of Michel Crozier (born in 1922) when he analysed the leisure of lower rank civil servants as a life style (Crozier, 1955: 1959). This was also the standpoint of Henri Lefebvre (1905-1991), a marxist sociologist who believed that, in the industrial setting, everyday life, including leisure could be only a source of alienation. But, according to him, each citizen, spontaneously and in his/her own way, is bound to criticise his/her everyday life. This criticism, itself a part of everyday life, takes place within leisure time and through leisure (Lefebvre, 1957) which is defined as 'le non quotidien dans le quotidien', leisure being a key to understanding everyday life. This was Lefebvre's perspective when he conducted research in new French towns and in the Parisian suburbs (Lefebvre *et al.*, circa 1960).

The Sociology of Leisure from an Anthropological Perspective

Also in the 1950s, other social scientists underlined the interest of studying leisure as the expression of the deep motivations and trends of human behaviour. This was part of the outlook of two authors who were mentioned in the preceding sections: for Paul Naville, leisure was an outlet for libido (Naville, 1957:28); for Henri Lefebvre, the image of sexuality broke away from everyday life and belonged to leisure while leading to the secret of the former: dissatisfaction and frustration (Lefebvre, 1957:43). Another social scientist, Edgar Morin (born in 1921), pointed out the emergence of a new culture which included the mass media. The latter were described as not only channels of a new type for the diffusion of traditional culture but also as a means of expressing the existence of a new type of human being who was the result of industrial society. In this new culture, leisure was of great influence as in the case of the cinema (Morin, 1956). Another important contribution to the anthropological study of leisure was brought by Roger Caillois (1913-1978). This author - who had founded the College of Sociology in 1938 with Georges Bataille and Michel Leiris and whose writings encompass a very wide spectrum of topics - studied games as a total phenomenon related to the whole sum of human activities and ambitions: 'Le jeu est un phénomène total. Il intéresse l'ensemble des activités et des ambitions humaines' (Caillois, 1957:335). Leisure time is presented as a prerequisite for games (1957:22) which have the following characteristics: they are not compulsory, well circumscribed within time and space, regulated by specific rules, fictitious and uncertain in their outcome. Caillois also suggested a classification of games in four categories: 'âgon' (games of competition such as sports); 'alea' (games of chance); 'mimicry' (games of imitation) and 'ilinx' (games leading to vertigo and suddenly and temporarily annihilating reality (Ibid.: 51-57). Each category in turn covers a spectrum: at one pole, the organising principle ('paidia') is one of freedom, entertainment, carelessness, improvisation; at the other pole, the organisation principle ('ludus') is one of discipline and strict rules (Ibid.: 75-90). Games are explained as resulting in most cases of the combination of these two elements, distributed across each of the above mentioned categories. Such combinations appear at varying degrees in every civilisation, expressing the deepest trends of the group of human beings concerned. If games are factors and images of culture, it follows that to a certain extent a civilisation (and within a civilisation, a period of time) can be characterised by its games (Caillois, 1955:35). Again we find here the idea that leisure activities - games in this case - provide a leading thread to understand society. As for Roland Barthes (1915-1980), his anthropological perspective on contemporary society came from de Saussure's remarks (Saussure, 1955) about the development of a science of signs (semiology). According to Barthes, our society has a very low degree of semiologic consciousness. As a result signs can constantly be suggested as natural without being identified as what they really are: the historical products of the ideology prevailing in our society (Barthes, 1960). Therefore, in order to understand the latter, Barthes suggests a systematic analysis of signs some of which belong to the realm of leisure, like tourist guide books. This was also the angle from which Henri Raymond and Nicole Haumont studied group holidays. They analysed this phenomenon not only in terms of activity but also in terms of signs, showing tourism as a semiological system, as a set of signs transmitting an image of the world which in turn influences everyday life through a symbolic opposition between the latter and vacation time. Leisure thus analysed is seen as an expression of a new culture but it is the meaning of this culture as a whole which is the ultimate object of the study: the analysis of leisure is only a tool to reach this end (Raymond, 1960, 1963, 1964; Haumont, 1962).

The Sociology of Leisure as an Autonomous Field of Research

In the meantime, Joffre Dumazedier, born in 1915, was fighting for this goal. When he returned to civilian life, after his maquis experience, Jean Guehenno, who was the National Director for Popular Education, appointed him Inspector General of Popular Education. In 1947, he started working in the unit of Experimental Psychology led by Henri Wallon (1879-1962). The next step in 1953, was his integration in the National Centre for Scientific Research, a government agency dedicated to fundamental research in all disciplines. His candidature had been supported by Georges Friedmann and Jean Fourastié. He participated in the research seminar on the Sociology of Work and Leisure directed by George Friedmann who, as seen above, had an interest in leisure. Other participants were Michel Crozier, William Grossin, Alain Touraine and Roland Barthes. In the same year, he started a research group on leisure per se (Equipe de Sociologie du Loisir et de la Culture Populaire). In 1956, during the Third World Congress of Sociology in Amsterdam, he suggested that a special committee on the Sociology of Leisure should be formed within the framework of the International Association of Sociology. This was done in 1961. A first official meeting was held during the Fifth World Congress of Sociology in Washington, D.C. (September 1962). This Committee still exists (Research Committee on Leisure or R.C. 13) and Dumazedier was to be its Chair until 1974. Meanwhile, in 1968 his research group at the National Centre for Scientific Research took the name of 'Group of Sociology of Leisure and Cultural Patterns' . In 1984, following his retirement, it became the 'Group of Study of Social Times, Ages and Cultural Patterns' under my own leadership. Various factors, the most important one the lack of interest in leisure in a period of growing unemployment on the part of sponsoring institutions, led to its dissolution in 1988. A new group, studying social times, including leisure time, had been started by Roger Sue at the University Paris V in the Department of the Sciences of Education. In 1962, the year when he founded his research group on leisure, Joffre Dumazedier published *Toward a Civilisation of Leisure'* which stood as a declaration of independence for the sociology of leisure in France. Dedicated to Georges Friedmann, this book nevertheless claimed that it was misleading to define leisure merely by contrast to work:

> Contemporary leisure is defined by contrast not just to
> one's job but to all of the ordinary necessities and
> obligations of existence and it must be remembered that
> they who have and use leisure regard it as part of the
> dialectic of daily living, where all elements operate and
> interact
>   (Dumazedier, 1967:14).

So at this early stage of Dumazedier's contribution, we find one of his fundamental ideas: there is an interaction between all the components of daily life, including leisure which indeed is influenced by other components but also has an influence on them. This is not surprising since he sees leisure as 'the very central element in the life-culture of millions upon millions of workers' (Ibid.:3). The definition he suggested for leisure was both to become famous and to be bitterly criticised, among other things for being too 'psychological' (e.g. Lanfant, 1972:242).

> Leisure is activity - apart from the obligations of work,
> family and society - to which the individual turns at will,
> for either relaxation, diversion of broadening his
> knowledge and his spontaneous social participation, the
> free exercise of his creative capacity
>   (Dumazedier, 1967:16-17).

From Dumazedier's perspective, leisure has three main functions: relaxation, entertainment, development. But a warning is uttered about the ambiguity of leisure which can also have a negative function of driving people to a selfish evasion from social participation (Dumazedier, 1967), especially under the influence of cultural industries. The main goal of leisure is to provide every member of society access to culture. This can be achieved though 'cultural action'. The latter, as seen by Dumazedier, does not involve replacing mass culture by an elitist culture for all (which anyway would be impossible!). It would instead aim at promoting, in the whole society, values which are carried by leisure, especially those linked to the development of everyone's personality of creativity, thus leading to a wider social participation in the cultural and even to the scientific developments of contemporary life. Adult education, life long education and self education - in which Dumazedier was interested and in which he had been involved especially since the founding of *Peuple et Culture* (1945) - are shown as very efficient means to this end. Such 'cultural action' in turn will enhance, on the societal level, cultural development, distinct from economic and from social development but combining with them in the move to a 'better' society. Cultural development was linked by Joffre Dumazedier to the idea of cultural planning, understood in its French definition (i.e. as based on an advisory, rather than a regulatory, approach). Dumazedier relates such planning to the idea of a prospective sociology of leisure in which international comparisons would play an important role (Dumazedier and Ripert, 1966; Dumazedier and Samuel, 1976; Dumazedier, 1974, 1988). His contribution is of primary importance since he was the first scholar in France to establish leisure as an autonomous field of sociological research, a social phenomenon of its own, distinct not only from work but also from other spheres of life, and also endowed with a relative independence from political and social contingencies. He has often been criticised for bringing his own ideology into his research. But it may be argued that every researcher does so. Besides it is unquestionable that Dumazedier always thought in terms of providing empirical testing for his hypotheses.

Leisure Research in the Group of Sociology of Leisure and Cultural Patterns and Later in the Group of Sociology of Social Times

In the 1960s, Dumazedier's group on Sociology of Leisure and Cultural Patterns focused its work on the relations between leisure and social stratification, giving special attention to the relation between leisure and the level of education (Dumazedier and Ripert, 1966). It also studied the relations between leisure and urban space (Dumazedier and Imbert, 1964). With the arrival of the 1970s, topics of study were the relations and interactions between leisure and work, between leisure and family life, between leisure and religious worship, and political activity. There was again interest in the impact of the level of education on leisure: it was shown that participation in voluntary leisure associations could to a certain extent compensate for a low level of education and raise the level of leisure activities and leisure experiences (Dumazedier and Samuel, 1976, 1st part, chapter 3). During the same period, a study was conducted in a middle-sized French town (Annecy) on the problems arising between the local government and the leaders of voluntary associations. This analysis emphasised the development of a 'cultural power' (mostly made up of these leaders) which stood as an important pressure group actually participating in local decisions concerning leisure programmes and cultural life in general, as well as urban planning (Dumazedier and Samuel, 1976: Chapter 8). On the same local scene, it was shown that an 'educational society' was in the making: local institutions (such as

churches, trade unions, firms, political parties) were increasingly
taking up educative functions, through the organisation of training
sessions which often consisted of leisure activities designed to have a
training impact (Dumazedier and Samuel, 1976: Chapter 8). This
analysis of the educative function of local institutions during leisure
time led to a study of the use of the latter for individual or collective
self-training (auto-formation) (Dumazedier, 1980). Another direction
of research was the study of cultural resistance coming from
subcultures in a situation of dependence in their relations with the
dominant culture in the French society. With this problem in mind,
M.J. Parizet has studied popular cultures in search of self-expression
through leisure activities (Parizet, 1978). In the 1980s, a study started
by Dumazedier in the 1960s about the use of free time in the
development of urban areas of developing countries, especially in
Brazil, resulted in several publications (Dumazedier, 1981; Lima de
Camargo, 1982). The diachronic study of the development of leisure
time was another topic of research as well as the question of values
connected with leisure, their strengthening as a consequence of the
extension of free time and of the weakening of the leisure ethic, and
the impact on other spheres of life (Samuel, 1981). This concern led
to the study of leisure from the angle of social time and to the
analysis of the symbolic structure of the latter (Samuel, 1982; Samuel
and Romer, 1981).

> Results obtained from a secondary analysis of existing
> documents and from freshly-collected empirical data
> showed the priority of leisure in the use of free time newly
> gained from a reduction of work time and from the
> reduction of time needed for domestic chores
> (Brochard *et al.*, 1987).

The research undertaken on social time led to a book published in
1984 showing how leisure time gradually became social time in the
full meaning of the expression as defined in our introduction (Samuel
with Romer, 1984). It also led to a follow up study of leisure and
culture in the town of Annecy showing that, in the three decades that
had passed since Dumazedier had started studying this local scene,
leisure time had developed a growing importance in the symbolic
structure of social time as experienced by a representative sample of
the population (Samuel and Romer, 1981). At the moment, the study
of leisure as social time is continued by Roger Sue in his above-
mentioned unit of research which he recently established at the
University Paris V (Sue, 1991). Still another direction of research has
been directed towards comparative studies of leisure. This had been
an interest of Dumazedier as early as 1963 (Dumazedier, 1963). Later
the topic was analysed from a theoretical standpoint (Samuel, 1980)
and a paper on the state of the art in comparative studies of leisure
was presented at the World Congress of Sociology in Madrid in 1990

(Hantrais and Samuel, 1992). Throughout the whole period from 1962 until 1988 a seminar on the Sociology of Leisure was held once a month.

Other Developments

Sub-fields of the sociology of leisure were developing in the meantime. This was the case for the sociology of tourism (Lanfant, 1991; Lanquar, 1978, 1981), for the sociology of art (Bourdieu and Darbel, 1969), for the sociology of sport (Magnane, 1965; Bouet, 1968; Brohm, 1976; Malenfant, 1977; Pociello, 1981; Leziart, 1989; Vigarello, 1978), for the sociology of voluntary associations (Lanfant, 1972; Ion, *et al.,* 1974; Gaudibert, 1967; Dumazedier and Samuel, 1976; Simonot, 1974; Besnard, 1978; Poujol, 1981) and for the sociology of the non-profit sector (Malenfant, 1980, 1982; Sue, 1982). But social scientists from disciplines other than sociology seem to have taken comparatively little interest in leisure except as far as the history and geography of tourism are concerned.

The history of tourism has been a focus of attention especially the research of Marc Boyer, Professor at the University of Lyons II. His book, *Tourism* emphasises the role of the imitation of higher social class patterns in the development of mass leisure (Boyer, 1972). Among many other publications from Boyer, there is a history of thermalism in the Savoie region as well as several studies concerning the history of paid leave in France (Boyer, 1960, 1964, 1972, 1990). Some of this historian's studies have a sociological connotation. A valuable contribution to the history of tourism has also come from geographers like Bernard Barbier (Barbier, forthcoming) and from some sociologists.

In the field of geography, the first approach to leisure was about tourism. As early as 1942, Maximilien Sorre studied holidays in terms of huge migrations. In the 1960s, research done at the Centre for Higher Studies on Tourism, which was part of the Institute of Geography, followed the same trend and often demonstrated holidays as answering the need to escape from the urban environment (for example Burnet, 1963). Geographers have also analysed the ecological transformations which result from this flight from the cities (from Hublin, 1963 to Dewailly and Flament, 1993). The first doctoral thesis on tourism dates back to 1969. In 1971, the French National Committee on Geography founded a Commission on the Geography on Tourism. By that time, mass tourism had become well established and there has been a continued expansion of research in the field during the last two decades. French geographers have mainly studied tourism in France but have also done research in various Mediterranean countries, in the Austrian Tyrol, in Eastern Europe and in the Third World. The research on tourism had been influenced by the general French perspective on geography. In the words of Bernard Barbier: 'In each area they studied, (the geographers who discovered tourism in the 1960s and 1970s) tried to uncover the causes and structures of tourism and to see how this activity had given rise to particular landscapes or even how it had created new regions' (Barbier, 1984).

According to Professor Barbier, the French geographical tradition explains the regional focus of the French geography of tourism. In the 1980s geographers of tourism extended their interest to the geography of leisure as testified by the doctoral thesis of Joël Mirloup (Mirloup, 1981) and by the proceedings of the Conference of Angers in 1983 on 'Geographic Approaches to Leisure' (Norois, 1983). At this conference, Professor Barbier explained how French geographers widened their interest from tourism and urban to peri-urban leisure, often focusing on leisure as an organiser of space but also on the geography of the types and forms of leisure activities (Barbier, 1983).

At the moment, an interdisciplinary approach to the study of tourism is advocated by several specialists in the field. For there is a growing awareness of tourism as a global fact which can no longer be studied from the vantage point of a single discipline (Bonneau, 1988). For example, such an interdisciplinary approach includes the contribution of specialists of foreign languages (University of Toulouse II).

Conclusion

During the last decades, several factors have been favourable to the development of leisure research. Documentation centres of leisure have been set up. The first one was established in the 1950s within the framework of Dumazedier's group. The largest one is the Centre for Higher Tourism Studies founded in Aix-en-Provence by Professor René Baretje and includes a wide spectrum of publications not only on tourism but more generally on leisure. In the 1970s, reports supplying information on leisure were published by the Planning Committee (Commissariat Général du Plan, 1970, 1971, 1976). A comprehensive description of leisure activities and facilities was written in 1974 (Coronio and Muret, 1974). Debates took place among scholars and among non-specialists about the conclusions of books pertaining to leisure (Charpentreau, 1967; Bensaid, 1969; Emmanuel, 1971; Jeanson, 1973). The leading Institute on Statistics has conducted two national surveys on leisure activities (INSEE, 1967, 1987). This was also done by the Ministry of Culture (Ministère de la Culture, 1973, 1989).

Surveys on sporting activities have also been carried out on representative samples (Garrigues, 1988; Irlinger *et al.*, 1988).

National time-budget studies (INSEE, 1974-1975, 1985-1986) and household-budget studies (CREDOC, enquête annuelle) have shown the important part leisure plays in the time and in the finances of the French population. During the early period of the socialist government of François Mitterand, who came to power in 1981, it seemed that special attention was going to be given to the field of leisure, following the socialist tradition of the Popular Front in 1936. A Ministry of Free Time was created and several journals were launched on free time (if not on leisure!). But the Ministry was of short duration. Some claimed that it was not accomplishing enough; others felt that it cost too much money. The journals promptly disappeared. Under the impulse of Jack Lang, the Minister of Education and Culture, more attention was given to artistic creation than to leisure policy. With the economic crisis deepening with the rise of unemployment, priority had been increasingly given to research connected with work, employment and current economic and social problems: education, family, life in the city and in the suburbs, immigration, and so on.

But the idea spontaneously developed that leisure could be therapeutic in a (momentarily!) ailing society. This was the perspective indicated in a recent report of the Social and Economic Council (a deliberative institution which has influence on political decisions) in which leisure was presented as a means of social integration for young people (CES, 1991). Decision makers also have to solve practical problems about leisure programmes and this is why several Ministries have been and are sponsoring studies on various aspects of leisure time. Leisure is also recognised as a social need (CES, 1990) and this is also an encouragement to sponsor empirical research on leisure.

Consequently, as a final assessment, it may be said that the scientific study of leisure is fostered by the acuteness of some social problems to the solution of which it may bring a partial solution.

Paradoxically, while the status of leisure as an autonomous field of research has been well established in the past, it seems to be threatened in the present situation. In what may be considered as a turn to an anthropological perspective and perhaps as the result of one of these intellectual fashions which frequently dominate the French scene, several authors take the perspective of a comprehensive sociology which does not study leisure as a specific field but as a part of daily life in the new 'social totality' of post-modern societies (Lipovetsky, 1987; Yonnet, 1985; Maffesoli, 1985). Joffre Dumazedier, in his *Cultural Revolution of Free Time*, still insists on the relevance of a sociological study of leisure 'per se' which he opposes to the institutionalist as well as to the comprehensive theories concerning this social phenomenon.

REFERENCES

Agulhon, M. (1978) *Le cercle dans la France bourgeoise 1810-1848, Etude d'une mutation de sociabilité.* Paris: Armand Colin.

Barbier, B. (1983) 'La géographie des loisirs urbains et péri-urbains'. *Norois*, No. 120, Octobre-Décembre, 591-596.

Barbier, B. (1984) 'The geography of tourism in France: Definition, scope and themes'. *Geo Journal*, vol. 9, No. 1, 47-53.

Barbier, B. (forthcoming) 'Le temps libre et le tourisme au XXème siècle'. *Encyclopédie italienne.* Paris: Editions Universitaires.

Baretje, R. (1965-1991) (one volume per year). *Bibliographie touristique*, vols 1-129. Aix en Provence. Centre des Hautes Etudes Touristiques. Collection Etudes et Mémoires.

Baretje, R. (1969) *Le phénomène de concentration dans le tourisme moderne.* Aix en Provence: CHET. Collection Les Cahiers du tourisme, série C.

Barthes, R. (1960) *Mythologies.* Paris: Le Seuil.

Bensaid, G. (1969) *La culture planifié?* Paris: Le Seuil.

Besnard, P. (1978). *L'Animation socio-culturelle.* Paris: PUF, Collection Que sais-je?

Bonneau, M. (1988) 'Intervention à la réunion du 22 Septembre sur la formation supérieure et la recherche en matière de tourisme.' Compte rendu: Ministère du Tourisme.

Bouet, M. (1968) *Signification du Sport.* Paris: Editions Universitaires.

Bourdieu, P. & Darbel, A. (1969) *L'Amour de l'art. Les musées européens et leurs publics.* Paris: Editions de Minuit.

Boyer, M. (1960) 'Contributrion à l'Histoire du Thermalisme en Savoie de 1860 à 1914' . *Actes du 85ème Congrès des Sociétés savantes.* Paris: Imprimerie Nationale: 391-394.

Boyer, M. (1964) *Les vacances des Français, leur évolution.* Aix en Provence: CHET. Collection Etudes et Mémoires, No. 3.

Boyer, M. (1972) *Le Tourisme.* Paris: Le Seuil.

Boyer, M. (1990) '1936 et les vacances des Français', *Mouvement social*, no. 150, 35-45.

Brochard, C. *et al.* (1987) *L'Impact des changements de régime temporel sur la vie des salariés.* Paris: Ministère du Travail et CNRS/IRESCO.

Brohm, J.-M. (1976) *Critiques du Sport.* Paris: Editions Christian Bourgeois.

Burnet, L. (1963) *Villégiature et Tourisme sur les côtes de France.* Paris: Hachette.

Caceres, B. (1973) *Loisirs et Travail du Moyen-Age à nos jours.* Paris: Le Seuil.

Caillois, R. (1955) 'Les jeux dans le monde moderne'. *Profils*, No. 13: 33-43.

Caillois, R. (1957) *Les jeux et les hommes*. Paris: NRF. Collection Idées.

Charpentreau, J. (1967) *Pour une politique culturelle*. Paris: Editions Ouvrières, Collection Vivre son temps, No. 13.

Commissariat Général du Plan (1970) *Les transformations du mode de vie. Mobilité et coûts de l'adaptation. Temps et espaces de loisirs. Problèmes du 3ème âge*. Paris: Armand Colin. Collection Plan et Prospective.

Commissariat Général du Plan (1971) *Rapports des Commissions du 6ème Plan 1971-1975*, Loisirs, 191 p. Activités sportives et socio-éducatives, 242 p. Action sociale, 223 p., Affaires culturelles, 104 p. Paris: La Documentation française.

Commissariat Général du Plan (1976) *Rapport du groupe: Culture*, 127 p., *Rapport du groupe sectoriel d'analyse et de prévision: Arts, créations, loisirs*, 95 p., *Rapport du groupe: Tourisme et loisirs*, 105 p., Préparation du 7ème Plan. Paris: La Documentation française.

Comte, A. (1851-1854) *Système de Philosophie positive ou Traité de Sociologie instituant la religion de l'humanité*. Paris: L. Mathias, 4 volumes.

Conseil économique et social (CES) (1990) *L'évolution et les perspectives des besoins des Français et leur mode de satisfaction*. Paris.

Conseil économique et social (CES) (1991) *Le développement personnel et l'intégration des jeunes par les loisirs*. Paris.

Coronio, G. and Muret, J.P. (1974) *Loisir, du mythe aux réalités*. Paris: Centre de Recherche d'urbanisme.

Crozier, M. (1955) *Les activités de loisir et les attitudes culturelles. Petits fonctionnaires au travail*. Paris: CNRS.

Crozier, M. (1959) 'Employés et petits fonctionnaires parisiens. Note sur le loisir comme moyen de participation aux valeurs de la petite bourgeoisie'. *Esprit*: Juin 1959: 934-954.

Cuin, C.-H. and Gresle, F. (1992) *Histoire de la Sociologie*. Paris: Editions La Découverte, Collection Repères, 2 volumes.

Darmon, J.-J. (1972) *Le colportage de librairie en France sous le second Empire, grands colporteurs et culture populaire*. Paris.

Dewailly, J.-M. and Flament, E. (1993) *Géographie du Tourisme et des Loisirs*. Paris: SEDES.

Dommanget, M. (1977) 'Préface' au *Droit à la Paresse* de P. Lafargue. Paris: Maspéro.

Dumazedier, J. (1952) 'Ambiguités du loisir et dynamique socio-culturelle'. *Cahiers Internationaux de Sociologie*. No. XXIII: 75-76.

Dumazedier, J. (1962) *Vers une civilisation du loisir.* Paris: Le Seuil.

Dumazedier, J. (1963) 'Contenu culturel du loisir ouvrier dans six villes d'Europe' . *Revue française de Sociologie,* V: 12- 21.

Dumazedier, J. and Imbert, M. (1964) *Espace et loisir dans la société d'hier et de demain.* Paris: Centre de Recherche sur l'Urbanisme, 2 volumes.

Dumazedier, J. and Ripert, A. (1966) *Loisir et Culture.* Paris: Le Seuil.

Dumazedier, J. (1967) *Toward a Society of Leisure.* New York: Free Press.

Dumazedier, J. (1974) *Sociologie empirique du loisir.* Paris: Le Seuil.

Dumazedier, J. and Samuel, N. (1976) *Société éducative et Pouvoir culturel.* Paris: Le Seuil.

Dumazedier, J. (1980) *Vers une socio-pédagogie de l'auto-formation.* Cahiers du Centre national de Pédagogie des Sèvres.

Dumazedier, J. (1981) *Lazer e teoria de la decision na sociedad brasileira.* San Paullo: CESC.

Dumazedier, J. (1988) *Révolution culturelle du temps libre 1968-1988.* Paris: Klincksieck.

Emmanuel, P. (1971) *Pour une politique de la culture.* Paris: Le Seuil.

Fourastié, J. (1963) *Le grand espoir du XXème siècle.* Paris: Gallimard, Collection Idées.

Fourastié, J. (1965) *Les 40.000 heures.* Paris: Laffont.

Friedmann, G. (1946) *Problèmes humains du machinisme industriel.* Paris: Gallimard.

Friedmann, G. (1967) *Où va le travai! humain?* Paris: Gallimard, Collection Idées (1st edition, 1950).

Friedmann, G. (1976) *Le travail en miettes. Spécialisations et loisirs.* Paris: Galllimard, Collection Idées (1st edition, 1956).

Friedmann, G. (1970) *La Puissance et la Sagesse.* Paris: Gallimard.

Garrigues, P. (1988) *Evolution de la pratique sportive des Français de 1967 à 1984.* Paris: INSEE; Série M, 134.

Gaudibert, P. (1967) *Action culturelle, intégration et/ou subversion.* Paris: Casterman (3rd edition).

Guerrand, R. (1963) *La conquête des vacances.* Paris: Editions ourvrières.

Hantrais, L. and Samuel, N. (1992) 'The State of the Art in Comparative Studies of Leisure'. *Loisir et Société,* vol. 14, no. 2: 381-398.

Haumont, N. (1959-1962) *Enquêtes sur les villages de vacances et sur le camping.* Paris: Centre de Sociologie Urbaine.

Hublin, A. (1963) *Etude sur les villages de vacances.* Aix en Provence: CEST.

Ion, J., Miege, B. and Roux, A.-N. (1974) *L'appareil d'action culturelle*. Paris: Editions ouvrières.

INSEE (1967) 'Enquête sur les pratiques de loisir des Français', fr. Debreu, Pierre, 'Les comportements de loisir des Français', *Economie et Statistique*, no. 51, Décembre 1973 et Debreu, Pierre, *Les comportements de loisirs de Français*, Collections de l'INSEE M 25, aôut 1983.

INSEE (1987-1988). 'Enquête sur les comportements de loisir des Français', cf. Dumontier, F. and Valdelievre, H. (eds) *Consommation Modes de Vie*, no. 1/1989.

INSEE (1974-1975) Enquête 'Emplois du Temps' (unpublished).

INSEE (1985-1986) Enquête 'Emplois du Temps' (unpublished).

Irlinger, P., Louveau, C. and Metoudi, M. (1988) *Les pratiques sportives des Français*. Vincennes: Institut National du Sport et de l'Education Physique (INSEP). Laboratoire de Sociologie.

Jeanson, F. (1973) *L'action culturelle dans la cité*. Paris: Le Seuil.

Kremer-Marietti, A. (1983) 'Les avatars du concept de loisir dans la société industrielle et dans la philosophie sociale' *Oisiveté et loisirs dans les sociétés occidentales du 19ème siècle*. Adeline Daumart (ed.). Abbeville: Paillart, 1983.

Laffargue, P. (1977) *Le droit à la paresse*. Paris: Maspero (1st edition: 1880).

Lanfant, M.-F. (1972) *Les théories du loisir*. Paris: PUF, Collection Le Sociologue.

Lanfant, Marie-Françoise (1991). *Le tourisme international reconsidéré: milieu exclu, tiers exclu?* Aix en Provence: CHET, Collection les Cahiers du Tourisme.

Lanquar, R. (1978) *Le tourisme social*. Paris: PUF, Coll. Que sais-je?

Lanquar, R. (1981) *Sociologie du tourisme et des voyages*. Paris: PUF, Coll. Que sais-je?

Lefebvre, H. (1957) *Critique de la vie quotidienne*. Paris: L'Arche. (Voir 'Travail et loisir dans la vie quotidienne' : 37-52 et 'Fêtes' : 214-226.)

Lefebvre, H. (1962) *Introduction à la modernité*. Paris: Ed. de Minuit.

Lefebvre, H. *et al.* (1960) *Enquête interdisciplinaire sur la banlieue sud de Paris*. Paris: Institut de Sociologie Urbaine.

Le Play, F. (1989) *La méthode sociale. Abrégé des ouvriers européens*. Paris: Klincksieck.

Leziart, Y. (1989) *Sport et dynamique sociale*. Paris: Actio.

Lima de Camargo, O. (1982) *Le loisir et le sous-développement*. Thèse de Doctorat. Paris: Université Paris V.

Lipovetsky, G. (1987) *L'Empire de l'éphémère. La mode et son destin dans les sociétés modernes*. Paris: Gallimard.

Maffesoli, M. (1985) *L'Ombre de Dyonisos*. Paris: Méridiens / Anthropos.

Maffesoli, M. (1979) *La conquête du présent. Pour une sociologie de la vie quotidienne*. Paris: PUF, Coll. Sociologie d'Aujourd'hui.

Magnane, G. (1965) *Sociologie du Sport. Situation du Sport dans la sociétés contemporaine*. Paris: Gallimard.

Malenfant, C. (1977) *L'économie du sport en France. Un compte satelite du Sport*. Paris: Cujas.

Malenfant, C. (1980) 'Sport and the voluntary non profit sector of the economy: Franco / North American comparisons.' Halifax: *Proceedings of International Seminar on Comparative Physical Education and Sport*.

Malenfant, C. (1982) *Le secteur non marchand demain*. Paris: ADRAC.

Mandrou, R. (1975) *De la culture populaire au 17ème et 18ème siècle*. Paris: Stock.

Ministère de la Culture (Département des Etudes et de la Prospective) (1973) *Les pratiques culturelles des Français*. Paris: La Documentation française.

Ministère de la Culture (Département des Etudes et de la Prospective) (1989) *Nouvelle enquête sur les pratiques culturelles des Français en 1989*. Paris: La Documentation française.

Mirloup, J. (1981) *Les fonctions touristiques et de loisirs en Loire moyenne. Contribution à l'étude de l'aire de loisirs* des Parisiens.Thèse de doctorat. Orléans: ASCESI.

Morin, E. (1956) *Le cinéma ou l'homme imaginaire. Essai d'Anthropologie Sociologique*. Paris: Ed. de Minuit.

Naville, P. (1957) *Le Nouveau Léviathan*. Paris: Marcel Rivière. (voir 2nd vol., of vol. 2, last chapter: 'Travail et non travail.').

Naville, P. (1962) 'Recherches de la France, 8 émissions sur le loisir' par H. Raymond and H. Portnoy, RTF, France III, .

Norois (1983) No. 120, 'Approaches géographiques du loisir. Actes des journées organisées à Angers par la Commission française de Géographie du Tourisme et de la Recréation.'

Olszewska, A. and Pronovost, G. (1982) 'Current problems and perspectives in the sociology of leisure. In T. Bottomore *et al.* (Eds), *Sociology, the State of the Art* (pp. 299-321).London: Sage.

Parizet, M. J. (1978) 'La culture, terrain d'affrontement'.*Projet*, no. 128.

Pociello, C. (1981) *Sports et Société. Approche socio-culturelle des pratiques*. Paris: Vigot.

Poujol, G. (1981) *L'éducation populaire: histoire et pouvoirs*. Paris; Editions ouvriéres.

Pronovost, G. (1983) *Temps, culture et société*. Sillery:Presses de l'université du Quebec.

Proudhon, P.-J. (1839) 'De la célébration du dimanche,considérée sous les rapport de l'hygiène publique, de la morale,des relations de famille et de cité'. *Oeuvres complètes de Proudhon*. Paris: Marcel Rivière, 1926.

Raymond, H. (1960) 'L'utopie concrète: recherches sur unvillage de vacances' . *Revue française de Sociologie*, 1, 322-333.

Raymond, H. (1963) 'Les vacances'. *Arts*, 22 mai.

Raymond, H. (1964) 'La sociologie du loisir en France: Résultats et perspectives' . *Information sur les sciences sociales*, vol. III, mars.

Saint-Simon, C. H. de Rouvroy (1969-70) *Oeuvres complètes*, 6 vol. Paris: Marcel Rivière

Samuel, N. (1980) *La méthode comparative dans l'histoire des sciences sociales*. Paris: Université Paris V.

Samuel, N. (1981) *Etapes de la conquête du temps libre en France: 1780-1980*, avec la collaboration de M. Romer. Paris: ADRAC.

Samuel, N. (1982) 'Loisir, valeurs et structure symboliqquedes temps sociaux' . *Loisir et Société*, vol. V, no. 2.

Samuel, N. (1984) *Le temps libre, un temps social*, avec la collaboration de M. Romer. Paris: Klincksieck, Coll. Les Méridiens.

Samuel, N. (1992) 'Le loisir, temps social' . *Projet*, no.229, 7-15.

Samuel, N. and Romer, M. (1981) *Mobilité de fin de semaine et représentation du week end*. Paris: Institut deRecherche sur les Transports.

Saussure, F. de (1955) *Cours de linguistique générale*. Paris: Payot, 33 (Quoted by H. Raymond, 1964:18).

Simonot, M. (1974) *Les animateurs socio-culturels*: *Etude d'une aspiration à une activité sociale*. Paris: PUF.Sorre, Maximilien (1942). Les migrations humaines. Paris: Flammarion.

Sue, R. (1982) *Vers une société du temps libre*. Paris: PUF.

Sue, R. (1991) 'Contribution à une sociologie historique duloisir' . *Cahiers Internationaux de Sociologie*, vol. XC1:273-299.

Vigarello, G. (1978) *Le corps redressé*. Paris: Delarge.

Villermé, L.-R. (1971) *Etat physique et moral des ouvriersemployés dans les manfactures de coton, de laine et de soie*. Textes choisis et présentés par Yves Tyl. Paris: Union Générale d'Editions 10/18.

Yonnet, P. (1985) *Jeux, modes et masses: 1945-1985*. Paris:Gallimard.

Zeldin, T. (1979) *France 1848-1945: Politics and Anger*. Oxford: Oxford University Press.

Chapter 3

Leisure Research in Post-war Poland

Bohdan Jung

Scope and Limitations of the Study

The task of summarising and evaluating over 45 years of leisure research in post-war Poland is a difficult one not only because of the recent discontinuity in its development, but also because of the author's direct involvement in the field and other limitations of which the reader must be made aware.

This interpretation of leisure research in Poland does not represent a truly multidisciplinary perspective. Instead, it is biased towards sociological and economic studies. It also draws from published work, especially from books that summarise empirical studies or theorise on leisure and referenced journals. Such an approach underplays the role and quality of conference papers and articles that popularise the leisure problematics both at home and abroad. It also underplays the role of people who have made a great contribution to the popularisation of leisure problematics in Poland and have made Polish leisure research known in the West[1]. Since research leading to publication of books in Poland was more likely to be subject to censorship and ideological control than specialised publications with a lesser circulation, this approach also tends to over-represent the 'official' vision of leisure research of its time, as endorsed by the authorities of a communist country. While being a limitation, this may, on the other hand, present the Western reader with an opportunity to see how ideological control in Poland (despite 'statisation' of science in general) was not fully enforced.

The second limitation in the scope of this chapter has to do with the organisation of research in Poland. This organisation has so far prompted little interdisciplinary dialogue. Lack of common language and methodology, apparent during the various leisure conferences, resulted not only in little cross-fertilisation and hermetic, specialised language, but also in completely different research agendas which were supported with research grants from the various ministries which financed the academic and research institutions. In consequence of this compartmentalisation of leisure research, the body of studies carried out in academies of physical education in Poland is missing from the presented picture, as is the research on tourism. In fact, the picture of leisure research in Poland might have looked much different had it been told from the perspective of these academies, which were more focused on active physical recreation and education of trainers, tourist guides and recreation professionals, as well as on physical and psychological effects of sports and recreation on the individual.

The interpretation of the post-war history of leisure research in Poland is also incomplete due to the character of changes taking place in Poland since 1989, the scope and pace of which causes a discontinuity in nearly all aspects of life. This discontinuity is a consequence of the efforts to dismantle the communist system in Poland. This process, seen as part of the systemic transformation taking place throughout Central and Eastern Europe, has a number of consequences for the financing, priorities and organisation of research. The rapid change in the country's political, social, cultural and economic scene has made many of the traditional topics of interest obsolete. On the other hand, the pace of changes over the 1989-93 period was such that no major studies attempting to capture the changing social (not to mention leisure) scene have to this day been completed. This feeling of vacuum and transition does not make the evaluation of the past days of leisure research in Poland any easier.

Organisation of Leisure Research

The character of leisure research in Poland in the post-war years was largely determined by the institutional framework created by the state. The history of this research reflects the functioning of science and education geared to the needs of the command economy and central planning, yet independent enough to establish occasionally its own research agenda. The presence of the state continues four years after the collapse of communist rule in Poland, with the state acting as financial sponsor, contractor and publisher for most research. The reform of Polish higher education and research, far from being completed, has not shaken the existing structure of leisure research sufficiently to claim that a new institutional framework was created after 1989. As a consequence, the ensuing description of the compartmentalised leisure research continues to apply to the present day.

The bulk of leisure research undertaken in Poland was carried out in four types of institutions: the Polish Academy of Sciences, public (state-owned) universities, Academies of Physical Education and the so-called 'branch institutes', which act as research centres for the various ministries and government agencies. The activities of the Polish Academy of Sciences were entirely financed by the state. Its objectives were to enhance 'pure' research, develop new methodologies of research, and to elaborate topics of particular interest to Poland's future development. The Polish Academy of Sciences (PAN) is divided into disciplinary sections, which are broken down into institutes and departments. Within the section for social sciences, there exists the Institute for Philosophy and Sociology (IFiS). Within this institute, there used to be (in the 1970s) a department of sociology of leisure, which in the early 1980s was transformed (a significant change) into the department of research on social inequality. Within the same institute, there was also a department dealing with cultural participation and sociology of culture, which has survived to the present day. These two departments/research centres were the mainstay of sociological leisure research in Poland. In mid-1970s, the PAN has set up an interdisciplinary project called 'Polska 2000' (Poland 2000) the objective of which was to plot scenarios of the country's future at the outset of the next millennium. This project also examined the future of leisure and culture from a multi-disciplinary perspective. Another inter- and multi-disciplinary project set up by the Polish Academy of Sciences dealt with changes in consumption patterns and lifestyles of the Polish society. Although far from occupying the centre stage, leisure, considered together with cultural participation, was present in the study.

In Polish universities which had sociology, social psychology, cultural studies or economics departments, leisure was occasionally the topic of dissertations (the so-called degree-oriented research) or projects. Given the diversity of themes and approaches, it is difficult to apply some common denominator to these forms of leisure research. The theme of the impact of mass culture on Poland (more concern with cultural participation than recreation, tourism, sports or semi-obligations) and its relation to the country's rapid urbanisation and industrialisation in the post-war years seemed to dominate. This research can also be described as fairly atomised and individualistic, with no forum for exchange of ideas on how to enhance the study of leisure and trace the progress of other leisure scholars. Under these conditions, narrow disciplinary approaches prevailed, creating research themes and methodologies which were difficult to reconcile even within closely related departments of the same universities or institutes.

The situation was somewhat clearer in universities which specialised in economics. They usually had a specialised department of tourism economics which carried some research on spatial dimensions of tourist infrastructure, management of tourist facilities, master plans for development of local tourism etc. Compared to research interests of the sociology of leisure, for whom mass culture and cultural participation were the main subjects of interest, these departments were not concerned with the phenomenon of leisure in other ways than an occasional venture into the subject of incentive tourism and organised vacations sponsored and financed by state-owned firms for their employees.

The above research centres and universities were organised, financed and controlled entirely by the Ministry of Education. However, the next set of institutions which were also important contributors to leisure research in Poland - the Academies of Physical Education - were jointly financed by the Ministry of Education and the State Office on Physical Education and Tourism (a junior ministry within the structure of the Polish government, previously known under the names of the Central Committee for Physical Education and Tourism, State Committee on Youth and Sports) and subordinate to the latter. While the focus of these schools was on ensuring leadership and education in sports, these schools also had departments which specialised in physical recreation, sociology of sport, therapeutic recreation, and more rarely, tourism. Beside studies carried out for educational purposes and degree-oriented research, these institutions were also involved in projects commissioned by their branch ministry. The preoccupation of these studies with the physical aspects of recreation is the reason for excluding this type of research from being presented in this chapter.

Similar subordination to the more applied interests of a given government agency characterises two other Polish research centres in which leisure research has been taking place: the Institute of Culture (financed by and subordinated to the Ministry of Culture) and the Institute of Tourism (a branch of the aforementioned State Office for Physical Education and Tourism). The former had a specialist department for the study of cultural participation and economics of culture, the latter even had a department for the study of the leisure of the Polish population (which is no longer active). The Ministry of Labour and Social Relations had its own research institute that dealt, among others, with the consequences of reduction in work time in the public sector. It must be stressed that these institutions did not collaborate with each other and failed to undertake joint projects focused on leisure, even though a discussion forum on problems of leisure and urban planning was informally active among the Warsaw academic community in the late 1970s. Strangely enough, the initiative for this forum came from the Polish Association of Urban Planners, which acted as the official affiliation for the forum.

As in any centrally planned economy, in Poland to this day, there functions a powerful Central Statistical Office (GUS), which has had local branches collecting statistics throughout Poland. This office, which is entirely financed by the state, has carried annual household studies on huge representative samples of the Polish population, conducted national time-budget surveys, published annual yearbooks of culture, sports, tourism and recreation. The information gathered by GUS (particularly by its department of social statistics) was the empirical backbone of all leisure research in Poland. The mammoth scale of statistical research, the facilities and funds available were envied by many Western statistical services and quite unrivalled in what even the richest Polish universities could hope to receive as grants for social or economic research. Unless the studies required very specialised sets of data, it became customary for these institutions to perform a secondary analysis of statistics collected by GUS.

Until 1990, the research money available to academic institutions and institutes was granted through the system of commissioned projects approved by the Ministry of Education and financed from the state budget. In theory, the Ministry of Education and the Planning Commission were charged with the co-ordination of research topics on a national scale and assuring that they matched the country's priorities. In practice, the selection process of research projects, both those suggested 'from below' by the various research centres and those assigned 'from above' by government agencies was superficial; factors such as good personal contacts with the Ministry mattered more than the actual project. Once commissioned for an initial period of five years, the project was generously funded and likely to be extended. In social sciences, projects lasting for over a decade were not uncommon and additional sums of money could easily be made available if the grant was likely to face cost overruns. In particular, the 1970s were the years of easy, 'soft' financing of research projects, which from the outset were designed to supplement wages of the underpaid researchers. In the social sciences there was no follow-up on the recommendations of the project nor implementation of its conclusions or policy directives. The bulk of the research was not published.

The system of distributing state money for research was changed in 1990, when the State Research Committee was set up. Research grants started to be given on a more competitive basis, with applications from all disciplines accepted twice a year and graded by anonymous reviewers. However, the introduction of the new system was coupled with a crisis in Poland's public finance and much less money was available for research. State priorities for commissioned research were narrowed to a handful of topics such as cancer research and economic reforms. The ambitious projects on leisure, comparable to those undertaken in the 1970s, stood no chance of selection. While for the first time since the pre-war days there emerged sources of external funding which were alternative to grants commissioned by the state (such as foundations and private sponsors), topics related to leisure were again well outside of all priorities established by these institutions.

Unity of Divided Time[2]

The presentation of main issues taken up in Polish leisure research starts with the theme of relations between work time and free time. In his influential two books, which were often quoted in leisure research, Danecki (1967, 1970) offers a number of reasons for making the work-leisure relationship such a crucial subject for Polish leisure studies. The first one was ideological and had to do with Marxist perception of the future of work. In the writings of 'young' Marx, he places much faith in the possibility to make paid labour more humane by creating a new (socialist, then communist) mode of production based on social ownership of the means of production. Bringing an end to capitalist exploitation, this mode of production also overcomes the alienation of labour and production characteristic of capitalism. Social time ceases to be sharply divided into alienated, exploited and depersonalised work time, and on the other hand, free time which has to compensate for work in terms of human development, sense of life, and the reproduction of 'man' as a cultural and physical human being. Thus, in Marx's eyes, the division between work time and free time is mainly a capitalist product, whereas the new mode of production is to integrate (assure unity of) divided time by subordinating both of these times to the goal of human development.

Danecki took up Marx's reasoning and explored the mutual feedback between work time and free time under socialism, presented in schematic form adapted from Marx (Danecki, 1970:63) - see Figure 3.1. To reconcile work and leisure, both had to be treated jointly from the perspective of their contribution to human development. With respect to the issue of 'humanisation' of work, Danecki refused those suggestions made by Western sociologists and philosophers who attempted to contrast the idealism of 'young' Marx with a more pragmatic and production-oriented 'old' Marx (Danecki, 1970:59-62). He maintained that all (i.e. both work and leisure) time had to be made free and that shortening work time and transforming its character are only partial solutions to the freeing of time for enjoyment and self-development (Ibid: 54-58).

While the above argument may suggest an orthodox Marxist approach taken by one of the forefathers of Polish sociological research on leisure, the rest of his argument is of a different character. Together with Wnuk-Lipinski, another prominent author in the field of Polish leisure studies, he argues that the existence of real socialism in Poland creates a special set of conditions which call for much effort to integrate work with leisure (Wnuk-Lipinski, 1972). These conditions can virtually be boiled down to the fact that the new social, political and economic system in the post-war years did not succeed in overcoming the alienation of production and labour. This failure is attributed by Danecki to the copying of most primitive Fordist techniques of production and socialism's shortcomings in the organisation of work (Danecki, 1970:146). While some of the sources of alienation in post-war Poland can be traced back to the acquisition of production techniques which depreciate work in industry (depersonalised, fragmented, standardised, routine - Danecki, 1967), his argument hints at the post-war system's capacity to generate its own sources of alienation of work, which will be more and more active as Poland advances on the path of 'socialist industrialisation' (Danecki, 1967:42). These include poor organisation of work, unrealistic planning, politically-motivated investment decisions, state policy of keeping wages and consumption low (lower respect for poorly paid work, necessity to look for jobs in grey and black economy, overtime work), much time lost on commuting, and poor development of services which forces households to spend much time on family and home obligations and so on.

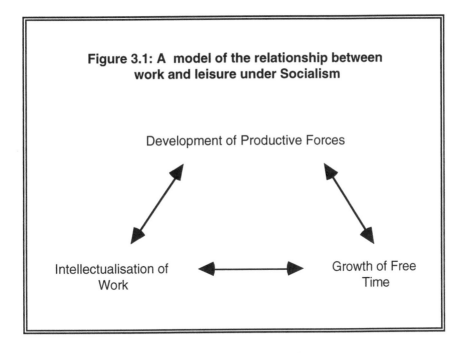

Figure 3.1: A model of the relationship between work and leisure under Socialism

While Danecki concentrates on production techniques and organisation of work, other authors (Toeplitz, quoted by Jasinska, 1978:249) write about 'the loneliness of individuals under the new political (communist) system' and this system's inability to fulfil the need for stability, privacy and consumption aspirations (Ibid.).

The vision of 'pathologies of free time' under socialism (mainly youth hooliganism and vandalism - Danecki, 1970:34) is seen as yet another consequence of alienated work in post-war Poland. Danecki quotes Moore (*Man, Time and Society*, John Wiley and Sons, London,

1963) to state that 'Free time is a problem when work time is a problem' (Ibid:37). Alienation sanctions the split between *homo ludens* and *animal laborans*. Alienated labour has to be compensated for by ostentatious consumption and possession of material goods, which are a feature of alienated leisure (Danecki, 1967:68-69). To remedy the situation, Polish researchers approaching the field of leisure from a sociological perspective (Wnuk-Lipinski, Szczepanski, Kloskowska, Suchodolski) agreed that state policy must seek to integrate transformations of both work and free time. This policy must stress the teaching of the importance of culture (Szczepanski, 1967), with cultural (humanistic) values being seen as a counter-balance to alienation. The state must also guarantee a 'socially indispensable amount of free time' (Danecki, 1967:29).

Polish research on the 'unity of divided time', which was prominent in the leisure field in the 1960s and early 1970s also concluded that the dilemma of choice between the vision of civilisation of work and civilisation of leisure is a false one, since the only worthwhile goal is to strive for creation of a 'universal man' (sic) (Danecki, 1970:97), who 'would both like and know how to make use of his free time' (Pohorille, 1982). Personality development of such an individual could only take place when both work time and leisure time are simultaneously transformed. However, there was general recognition that the prevailing character of alienation makes this project a matter for the distant future.

Democratisation of Culture and Recreation

The research on the apparent failure to de-alienate both work and leisure under real socialism in Poland has been carried out in close dialogue with another major theme of leisure research - the democratisation of free time. The underlying question which Polish sociologists, economists and statisticians tried to answer was whether the post-war political system had been successful in giving equal access to culture and recreation and actively stimulating the underprivileged to wider participation in leisure activities. In contrast to the theoretical theme of 'unity of divided time', this research topic was mostly dealt with through empirical studies, of which there was an abundance in Poland in the late 1950s and the early 1960s.[3]

The historical roots of leisure research centred on the problem of democratisation; social stratification could be traced to the study of workers' free time conducted in the years 1925-26 by the Social Economy Institute of the Warsaw School of Economics (Kaminski, 1965). The data compiled from this study, together with latest pre-war (1938) statistics on cultural participation were often used as basis for comparison with the post-war period.

The main thrust of research on democratisation of culture went into fact-finding. Studies were conducted to establish the impact of age, income, education, socio-professional group, place of dwelling, size of the family, and sex (Wnuk-Lipinski, 1972,1981; Skórzynski, 1965; Kloskowska, 1980; Adamczuk, 1978; Milic-Czerniak, 1985). These studies were largely based on time-budget statistics gathered in Poland by the Central Statistical Office, as well as leisure statistics compiled annually by this institution[4]. These national statistics, especially time series for post-war years, were the standard reference point for smaller studies that focused specifically on some professional group or strata. Such research included the study of peasants' leisure (Jagiello-Lysiowa, 1960; Lapinska, 1972; Jastrzebska-Smolaga, 1977) or workers' leisure (Pietraszek, 1963; Malanowski, 1962; Rosner, 1966; Siemienski, 1961; Turowski and Kubejko, 1959; Wojska, 1960; Plucinska, 1960; Nowakowski, 1958; Bokszanski, 1976). Much attention was also given the role of culture and recreation in the lives of the new intelligentsia, especially that of working class and peasant origin (Dziecielska, 1959; Kowalewska and Kowalewski, 1959; Kowalewski, 1962), university graduates (Kadzielska, 1960, Izydorkiewicz, 1960) or professions (such as journalists - Dziecielska, 1962). The publication and timing of these studies are related to the political situation in Poland. October 1956 marks the beginning of the years of 'thaw' and de-Stalinisation of the countries political and social life, when researchers were more free to explore the real image of the post-war society.

The picture which emerged from both national and more specific cases studies was that of, on the one hand, a great civilised leap towards mass culture and recreation (Kloskowska, 1980; Czajka, 1974; Wnuk-Lipinski, 1981), expressed by the rapidly growing numbers of people reading books, listening to the radio, watching TV, attending theatre, going to the movies, leaving on holidays etc.[5] On the other hand, there was evidence that the boundaries of class belonging and social stratification were as strong as ever and that distinct class and strata patterns of leisure participation prevailed (Skórzynski, 1965; Kaminski, 1965; Kobus-Wojciechowska, 1973; Wnuk-Lipinski, 1972). The research on graduates of philosophy, sociology and social sciences faculties even prompted its author to conclude that 'life of the participants of this study, who are part of the country's new intelligentsia, is again closed, like prior to 1939, within the bounds of the ghetto of intelligentsia' (Kadzielska, 1960). This confirmed Danecki's fear that mass leisure, while raising the 'common denominator' of cultural and recreational participation throughout the society, would not be able to override the bounds of class and social stratification even in a socialist society (Danecki, 1970:102).

More general conclusions about the post-war political system's ability to provide a much more egalitarian access to culture and recreation, but failure to bridge the gap between cultural competence and social reproduction of participation patterns, based on the individual's positioning on the ladder of social stratification also gave rise to more specific issues which emerged from this research. These included such problems as the lack of adequate leisure infrastructure in the rural areas and small towns, which was often quoted as the main reason behind youth's flight into the big cities (Kloskowska, 1980; Pohorille, 1982; Suchodolski, 1977) or the demonstration effect generated by those leading in 'cultural consumption' (Kaminski, 1965; Skórzynski, 1965). As practical measures to enhance more democratic access to leisure, attempts were made to advocate the role of education for leisure (Kaminski, 1965; Wojnar, 1977; Przeclawski, 1960)[6], draw up normative systems of leisure infrastructure and provision (Podoski, 1977; Strak, 1988), give equal rights to paid holidays to white and blue collars (Strzeminska, 1976; Penc, 1978), pursue an egalitarian income policy to prevent consumption from becoming a factor of social distinction and prestige (Szczepanski, 1977, 1981) or continue to subsidise provision of leisure goods and services (Pohorille, 1976, 1982). Much attention was also given to the impact mass media, especially television, had on traditional patterns of cultural 'consumption' (Czerwinski, 1971; Kloskowska, 1980).

Pursuit of an Alternative Model of Consumption and Lifestyle

The third of the great themes characterising Polish leisure research in the post-war period was related to the ideological goal of creating the system's specific model of consumption and lifestyle which would serve as an alternative to the capitalist one. Considerations on this topic tended to be both normative and heuristic. The differences between disciplinary approaches were also more distinct, with the sociologists tending to outline desired evolution of *lifestyles* and economists analysing *models of consumption* and means to shape them to the desired ends.

Sociologists and economists dealing with relations between leisure and lifestyle in post-war communist Poland were favoured with a unique opportunity. After communists gained full political control of the country towards 1948, they were calling on intellectuals to help them to build a new society, free from exploitation, based on rationality and science, not subject to materialistic morality and mentality of the petty bourgeois (Milosz, 1989). Theoretically, intellectuals could devise (with blessing of the communist party) a whole integrated package of social, educational, cultural or economic measures which would be given the rank of state policy to create the new society. This great social project was readily embraced by many intellectuals. This support and commitment to the creation of a new society were not necessarily signs of support for the doctrine and practice of the teachings of Marx, Lenin or Stalin, but rather the consequence of disenchantment with pre-war Poland and atrocities of war (Milosz, 1989).

The role given to leisure in this great social project was quite essential. Free time was referred to as the most essential issue in social development, a criterion of progress (Penc, 1978). Wnuk-Lipinski (1972:36) writes about leisure time as presenting 'a golden opportunity for shaping social consciousness' and improving the level of general (mass) culture. This logic is clearly laid out in the theoretical and methodological chapter which prefaces his analysis of the 1968-69 national time budget study:

> In the capitalist system ... the producers of mass culture are dominated by the urge to 'adjust' to tastes and preferences of the customers ... which results in a far reaching trivialisation in the production of mass culture. In the socialist system, where the system of mass media is not subject to commercial goals, priority is given to the policy 'active shaping' of the preferences of the customers, hence the opportunity to popularise the most valuable (from the perspective of the criteria of socialist culture) products of 'elite culture', which therefore become elements of mass culture
> (Ibid: 22; translated from Polish by the author)

In contrast to the capitalist system, in which the means have outstripped the ends, the planned system of development of the socialist economy was to offer the possibility to chart cultural goals and provide the means to achieve them (Suchodolski, 1979). Danecki writes that 'only socialist planning is capable of reconciling growth in material welfare with extension of time free from work' (1970:260). Kloskowska sees 'the historical opportunity to shape the image of mass culture free from commercial pressures' (1980:398). As part of the new 'full socialist life', cultural participation was to become an intrinsic value (Szczepanski, 1977), as opposed to its instrumental use to achieve social advancement noted in the earlier studies of Kaminski (1965) and Skórzynski (1965). The new socialist lifestyle and model of consumption were to be characterised by supremacy of 'being' over 'having', 'horizontal' social bonds (based on solidarity, friendship and co-operation) rather than 'vertical' ones (subordination, competition), creativity and innovation rather than conformism, active rather than passive leisure pursuits and attitudes to life (Sicinski, 1978; Suchodolski, 1977; Szczepanski, 1977).

While grandiose schemes were propagated, research on lifestyles and models of consumption resulted in a number of more specific studies focused on leisure, the importance of which has not been undermined by the collapse of communism in Poland after 1989.

These include such research problems as the sociological perception of living standards, which include the (now neglected) notion of sustainability of lifestyles, including leisure patterns (Wnuk-Lipinski, 1981), the already mentioned need of education for leisure and tourism (Wojnar, 1977; Przeclawski, 1960; Kaminski, 1965), the forecasting of future demand patterns for leisure (Pohorille, 1982; Rakowski, 1976), including the minimum and optimum availability of free time, the role of reference groups, consumption elites and demonstration effects in the diffusion of leisure patterns (Szczepanski, 1981; Kaminski, 1965; Danecki, 1967). The role of mass media in the creation of personality patterns among youth and the social perception of those engaged in luxury consumption during their leisure time were also the object of separate analysis and research projects (Jasinska and Siemienska, 1978).

Despite an important ideological content in the research on the alternative model of consumption and lifestyle, the studies also unveiled the obvious failure of totalitarian control over the Polish society's discretionary time, as well as the decline in social support for ascetic and frugal lifestyles propagated under the early years of communism (Danecki, 1970:236). Despite the official campaign aimed at discrediting social groups excelling in ostentatious luxury consumption (Jasinska, 1978:254), the evolution of new needs in the sphere of leisure and acknowledgement of such phenomena as moral obsolescence, fun morality and job ethic had to be incorporated even into highly moralising and idealistic visions of the future society.

Economics of Longer Weekends

While throughout the 1970s (a period of relative prosperity in Poland, brought about by easy to obtain and inexpensive Western credits and a relatively liberal political regime) sociologists debated about the growing individualisation and privatisation of leisure behaviour, as well as complained about the low level of culture of Polish holiday makers and lack of 'cultivated' patterns of passing free time, the economists were discussing the planned and orderly way to cope with new, more differentiated demand, which called for a new allocation of capital between collective and individual provision of goods and services (Pohorille, 1982). In this discussion, they were soon joined by social policy makers concerned with the need and opportunities to give longer periods of discretionary time to the Polish working population (Strzeminska, 1988).

In fact, in early 1976 Poland was one of the last communist European countries to have no free Saturdays (Strzeminska, 1976; Penc, 1978). First non-working Saturdays (one per month) were introduced on an experimental basis in 1976 on days designated by the state administration. When 'Solidarity' was created, one of its first demands was to make all Saturdays free from work. Under the pressure of strikes, the authorities gave in, then reiterated during the period of martial law, allowing for two Saturdays off per month. In the 1980s a forty-two hour working week became the norm in the state sector (accounting for 90% of the country's industrial output). With the coming of market reforms, the problem of shorter working hours became less relevant with rapid expansion of the private sector, introduction of Sunday trading etc. Anxious to take advantage of new business opportunities, both the self-employed and the employees of private companies were glad to extend their work time to gain extra profits or supplement their wages with overtime and bonuses.

The main concern of Polish economists at the outset of the shortening of the working week in the 1970s was how to adjust a relatively rigid and bureaucratic machine of the command economy to shorter work time. This was analysed from both the supply and demand side. One of the early preoccupations (and areas of research) was with the impact of the shorter working week on the output of state-owned enterprises. The general assumption was that given low levels of productivity in Poland, shorter working hours would lead to an overall fall in the country's national product (Penc, 1978; Strzeminska, 1976). Even when no fall in output was envisaged, calculations of foregone output have been made (Otto, 1974). This gave ground to deliberations on what this foregone additional production could have contributed to the country's economy given low levels of income and persistent shortages in Poland (Pohorille, 1976; Rakowski, 1976; Rosner, 1975). Among economists, extending time free from work was seen as threat to the country's future welfare (Jung, 1986). They argued that growth in the productivity of labour would have to precede the shortening of work time (Penc, 1978; Otto, 1985; Strzeminska, 1976). The *ex-post* research carried after work time was significantly shortened in Poland in 1976 and 1981 showed that their worries were not justified. As various studies have shown, productivity of labour has gone up to compensate for shorter work time (as in the West when longer weekends were introduced) (Strzeminska, 1988).

Another set of dilemmas that were on the agenda of leisure studies in Poland had to do with the ability of the country's underinvested cultural, recreational and tourist infrastructure to cope with additional demand caused by the extra leisure time (Strzeminska, 1976 > 1988; Pohorille, 1982; Szczepanski, 1977; Penc, 1978). Under the conditions of constant shortages of goods and services, some studies expressed concern that growth in what was meant to be leisure time would in fact be diverted to more time spent on queuing (Wnuk-Lipinski, 1981). Under realities of the planned economy, expansion of the infrastructure had to be a carefully planned operation, prepared years in advance and financed entirely from the state budget, as most

of the leisure provision was offered at token prices from state-run institutions as part of the so-called 'collective consumption'.

Arguments were also put forth that shortening the work week was possibly the most expensive and least efficient form of increasing time available for leisure to the country's population. Whereas from comparative studies it was clear East European countries in general (and Poland in particular) were lagging behind Western Europe in reduction of work time (Strzeminska, 1988), some researchers argued that a much simpler and cheaper method of reducing work time would be to increase the number of days of paid leave (Penc, 1978), lower the retirement age (Pohorille, 1982) or develop various time-saving services to help to cut down considerable time spent on household obligations (Ibid.). These measures were presented as alternatives to shortening the work week. The economists complained about the lack of 'weekend culture' in Poland and no tradition of established weekend patterns of leisure (Penc, 1978). However, as the national time-budget study on the first year of non-working Saturdays (1976) showed, distinct leisure patterns of longer weekends were quick to evolve. Co-operative and private agencies soon moved in to expand leisure infrastructure, especially as this period in Poland coincided with an increase in living standards, the beginnings of mass car ownership and clear growth in both domestic and foreign tourism (Sicinski, 1978).

Perspectives

Rather than attempt to evaluate subjectively the contributions made by individual authors, it is both easier and, perhaps, more enriching to make an overview of Polish leisure studies as a whole. If these studies were presented from a chronological perspective, then the late 1950s to mid-1960s could be described as the period of conceptualisation of the leisure phenomenon and fact-finding. Starting roughly in mid-1960s, this was followed by fascination with huge empirical studies (time budget, household behaviour, cultural participation etc.), all carried out on representative national samples of tens of thousands of inhabitants. While some of these studies continue to be performed annually by the Central Statistical Office, they no longer capture the minds of the researchers and publishers to the extent they used to until late 1970s.

The 'empirical phase' of leisure studies in Poland coincided with the realisation that after post-war reconstruction and the grim years of Stalinism, the newly industrialised and urbanised Polish society was beginning to enjoy some measure of comfort and stability. The country's march towards mass culture and recreation was confirmed by each new study. The preoccupation of researchers was with the dynamics and scope of these phenomena, rather than their causes and sustainability. Some hailed this expansion in nearly all forms of leisure participation as the sign of a new, alternative, lifestyle and model of consumption, free from capitalist commodification, advertising and commercialisation (Kloskowska, 1980).

The economic and political crisis that started to emerge in the late 1970s changed this picture. In the leisure field, there were signs of saturation with large empirical studies, or to be precise, no attempt to develop a deeper interpretation of their results. This feeling was well captured by one of Poland's top sociologists of culture, who accused researchers involved in this massive gathering of data of succumbing to a 'statistical fetish', which resulted in a lack of critical studies on cultural participation (Czerwinski, 1985). As the quest for meaning became the key issue in Polish sociology of leisure, more semiotic and anthropological approaches to the study of culture (and leisure practices) have found their way into the books published in the 1980s (Zadrozynska, 1983; Kloskowska, 1983; Szczepanski, 1981; Tarkowska, 1992). Critical approach to the sustainability of the cultural boom experienced in Poland until the late 1970s was also expressed in the works of the prestigious POLAND 2000 Committee, which pointed to the converging ideological and infrastructural crisis of Polish culture (Czerwinski, 1986).

From the perspective of 1995, it looks as if the best days of Polish leisure research are over. Leisure has never played a major role in Polish sociology or economics; leisure studies have never assumed an identity of their own. Leisure was at best an annex to studies on the sociology of culture or lifestyles, or an element of economic debate on shortening work time or forecasting consumption (Luszniewicz, 1966). The following reasons could be given to support the claim that the best days of leisure research in Poland are over:

- the loss of institutional affiliations (departments of sociology of leisure, or other units with distinguishable leisure problematics, have disappeared from the Polish Academy of Sciences, research institutes and universities);
- the volume of work on leisure published in Polish is much smaller than in the 1965-75 period;
- despite the formation of the Polish Leisure Association, the body of researchers dealing with culture and recreation is highly atomised and fragmented, there is no forum (such as a journal) for exchange of ideas and polemics; the existing pattern of research can at best be described as chaotic (see: Delbaere *et al.*, 1993);
- the role of leisure (seen from a perspective other than that of an expanding market segment) is clearly downplayed in the era of economic and political reforms in Poland[7];
- the financial support for leisure research, already minimal in relation to the 1970s, is rapidly dwindling and research institutions live on a year-to-year basis, under constant threat of disappearance.

There is a handful of newer publications on leisure, which appeared in Poland in the late 1980s and early 1990s. Lack of an adequate time perspective makes it difficult to identify research issues common with the earlier studies. One identifiable and homogeneous theme characterises a few recent publications of the Institute of Culture (research outpost of the Ministry of Culture). These take up the problematics of commercialisation of culture and cultural policy in a market economy, drawing heavily on the West European experience (Golinowska, 1991, 1992; Chelminska, 1993). Another research theme taken by this institute is the role of culture in the life of contemporary Poles (Adamczuk, Koprowska, 1991; Gawda, 1991). A series of publications entitled *Around the post-modern breakthrough* was initiated by a theoretical study of post-modern interpretation of modern culture (Zeidler-Janiszewska, 1992).

Nearly 20 years of studies and research projects on the evolution of consumption patterns were summarised in a study which sees leisure time as the time during which most important consumption decisions of the household are made (Cieloch *et al.*, 1992). Some efforts were also made to produce books that could be used for future students of leisure studies in Poland (Winiarski, 1989; Jung, 1989). The impact of the Polish crisis on leisure patterns has also been analysed (Jung, 1990). There is no way to assess the volume of work going on in the offices of consultants and promotion agencies springing up throughout Poland. Assessments of the various segments of the country's leisure market (some very creative in the methodological sphere), feasibility studies for hotels, amusement parks and golf courses have replaced the debates on the humanistic role of leisure and alternative lifestyles. On the other hand, disenchanted intellectuals are harbouring a grudge against the cultural consequences of the laissez-faire and monetarist model of economic reforms taken in 1989 (Miedzyrzecki, 1991). They ponder about the demise of the intelligentsia (biggest leisure consumers), the spreading of 'nouveau-richism', the collapse of Polish culture under pressure of imports from the West, the new commodification and commercialisation of life. These issues need some more time for analysis and publication, but they are likely to assume a key role in the future studies on leisure.

REFERENCES

Adamczuk, L. (1978) *Budzet czasu mieszkanców Polski* (Time budget of Poles). Warszawa: GUS.

Adamczuk, L. and Koprowska, T. (eds) (1991) *Kultura a zycie codzienne Polaków* (Culture and everyday life of Poles). Warszawa: Instytut Kultury.

Bokszanski, Z. (1976) *Mlodzi robotnicy a awans kulturalny* (Cultural advancement of young workers). Warszawa: KiW.

Chelminska, M. (1993) *Warunki rozwoju kultury na szczeblu lokalnym* (Conditions for development of culture at the local level). Warszawa: Instytut Kultury.

Cieloch, G. Kuczynski, J. and Rogozinski, K. (1992) *Czas wolny - czasem konsumpcji?* (Leisure time - the time of consumption?). Warszawa: PWE.

Cwiakowski, M. (1967) *Problemy spoleczne wolnego czasu* (Social problems of leisure). Warszawa: Wyd.Zwiazkowe CRZZ.

Czajka, S. (1974) *Z problemów czasu wolnego* (On problems of leisure). Warszawa: Instytut Wydawniczy CRZZ.

Czerwinski, M. (1971) *Telewizja wobec kultury* (Television and culture). Warszawa:Wydawnictwa Artystyczne i Filmowe.

Czerwinski, M. (1985) *Kultura i jej badanie* (Culture and its study). Wroclaw: Ossolineum.

Czerwinski, M. (1986) 'Przejawy patologii w sferze kultury (dysfunkcje w dzialaniu niektórych instytucji kulturalnych w Polsce)' (Signs of pathology in the sphere of culture: disfunctions in the operation of some cultural institutions in Poland) in: *POLSKA 2000. Zagrozenia spoleczne i warunki oraz srodki ich przezwyciezania* (POLAND 2000. Social constraints, conditions and means of overcoming them). PAN, Ossolineum, 'Polska 2000' Series, Vol.2

Danecki, J. (1967) *Czas wolny. Mity i potrzeby* (Leisure time. Myths and needs). Warszawa: KiW.

Danecki, J. (1970) *Jednosc podzielonego czasu. Czas wolny i czas pracy w spoleczenstwach uprzemyslowionych* (Unity of divided time. Leisure and work time in industrial societies). Warszawa: KiW.

Delbaere, R., Fleming, I., Gomez Marroquin, I. and van der Duim, R. (1993)*European directory of free-time and tourism: Pologne -Lettonie*. Bruxelles: LORETO.

Dziecielska, S. (1959) Jak organizuje swój wolny czas inteligencja miasta powiatowego (How intelligentsia from a county town organises its leisure time), *'Przeglad Zachodni'*, No.2, pp.110-126.

Dziecielska, S. (1962) *Sytuacja spoleczna dziennikarzy polskich* (Social situation of Polish journalists), Series: *On the Working Class and Intelligentsia* ed. by J.Szczepanski, Warszawa.

Federacja Konsumentow (1983) *Konsumpcja i rynek w dobie kryzysu* (Consumption and market at time of the crisis). Warszawa: PTE.

Gawda, W. (1991) *Nierównosci w kulturze Polaków i Rosjan* (Inequalities in the culture of Poles and Russians). Warszawa: Instytut Kultury.

Golinowska, S. (ed.) (1991) *W poszukiwaniu nowych zródel i form finansowania kultury. Studia z krajów o gospodarce rynkowej* (In search of new sources and forms of financing culture. From the experience of market economies). Warszawa: Instytut Kultury.

Golinowska, S. (ed.) (1992) *Komercjalizacja w kulturze. Szanse i zagrozenia* (Commercialisation in culture. Opportunities and threats). Warszawa: Instytut Kultury.

Izydorkiewicz, T. (1960) Praca zawodowa i pozycja spoleczna absolwentów wydzialu matematyczno-przyrodniczego Uniwersytetu Lódzkiego (Work careers and social position of graduates of the mathematical and natural science faculties of the University of Lódz). Series: *Education and Social Position of the Intelligentsia*, Vol.2, Lódz.

Jagiello-Lysiowa, E. (1960) Zawód rolnika oraz wolny czas w swiadomosci starszego i mlodszego pokolenia wsi (Profession of a farmer and the perception of leisure among older and younger generations living in the countryside). *'Wies wspólczesna'*, No.12.

Jasinska, A. and Siemienska, R. (1978) *Wzory osobowe socjalizmu* (Personality patterns under socialism). Warszawa: Wiedza Powszechna.

Jastrzebska-Smolaga, H. (1977) 'Bariery wyzwalania czasu wolnego w rolnictwie' (Barriers to free time in agriculture). *Wies Wspólczesna*, No.2.

Jung, B. (1986) Discretionary Time as an Object of Economic Analysis . *OEkonomica Polona*, No.2.

Jung, B. (1989) *Ekonomia czasu wolnego* (Economy of free time). Warszawa: PWN.

Jung, B. (1990) 'The impact of the crisis on leisure patterns in Poland'. *Leisure Studies*, No.9.

Kadzielska, K. (1960) Studia, praca zawodowa, zycie spoleczne i kulturalne bylych studentów socjologii, filozofii i nauk spolecznych (Studies, work careers, social and cultural life of former students of sociology, philosophy and social science), Series: *Education and Social Position of the Intelligentsia*. Vol.2, Lódz.

Kaminski, A. (1965) *Czas wolny i jego problematyka spoleczno-wychowawcza* (Leisure time, its social and educational problematics). Wroclaw: Ossolineum.

Kloskowska, A. (1980) *Kultura masowa. Krytyka i obrona* (Mass culture. Critique and defense). Warszawa (2nd edition):PWN.

Kloskowska, A. (1983) *Socjologia kultury* (Sociology of Culture). Warszawa: PWN.

Kobus-Wojciechowska, A. (1973) Ilosc czasu wolnego i formy jego spedzania (Quantity of leisure time and forms of spending it), in: K.Slomczynski and W.Wesolowski (eds.), *Struktura i ruchliwosc spoleczna* (Social structure and mobility). Wroclaw.

Kowalewska, S. and Kowalewski, Z. (1959) Inteligencja techniczna klasy robotniczej (Technical intelligentsia derived from the working class). Series: *Education and Social Position of the Intelligentsia*, ed. J.Szczepanski, Vol.1, Lód.

Kowalewski, Z. (1962) *Chemicy w Polskiej Rzeczypospolitej Ludowej. Studium o pozycji spolecznej i kulturalnej inteligencji technicznej* (Chemists in People's Poland. Study on social and cultural position of technical intelligentsia). Warszawa.

Lapinska, K. (1972) *Wies uprzemyslowiona a problem czasu wolnego* (Industrialised village and the problem of leisure). Wroclaw.

Luszniewicz, A. (1966) *Problemy gospodarowania czasem* (On problems of managing time). Warszawa: PWE.

Malanowski, J. (1962) *Robotnicy Warszawskiej Fabryki Motocykli* (Workers of the Warsaw Motorcycle Plant). Warszawa.

Miedzyrzecki, A. (1991) Dyktatura czy dialog? (Dictatorship or Dialogue?). In: *Gazeta Wyborcza*, 18.III. 1991.

Milic-Czerniak, R. (1985) *Zróznicowanie struktury dobowego budzetu mieszkanców Polski 1982* (Differentiation in the structure of the daily use of time of Poles in 1982). Warszawa: IFiS PAN.

Milosz, C. (1989) *Zniewolony Umysl* (Captive Mind). Kraków: KAW.

Nowakowski, S. (1958) Hotel robotniczy na tle procesów urbanizacji i industrializacji (Worker's hostel as seen against the background of urbanisation and industrialisation processes). *'Przeglad Socjologiczny'*, Vol.XII, pp.32-71.

Otto, H. (1974) *Problemy skracania czasu pracy. Aspekty spoleczne i ekonomiczne* (Problems in shortening work time. Social and economic aspects). Warszawa: PWN.

Otto, H. (1985) *Z teorii i praktyki czasu wolnego* (On theory and practice of leisure). Radom: WSI.

Penc, J. (1978) *Spoleczne-ekonomiczne uwarunkowania skracania czasu pracy* (Socio-economic determinants of shortening work time). Warszawa: KiW.

Pietraszek, E. (1963) Urlop wypoczynkowy robotnika w Polsce w okresie miedzywojennym (Workers' vacations in pre-war Poland) in: D.Dobrowolska (ed.) *Robotnicy na wczasach w pierwszych latach Polski Ludowej* (Workers on holiday in the first years of People's Poland). Wroclaw.

Plucinska, M. (1960) 'Budzet czasu i sposoby spozytkowania czasu wolnego uczniów technikum ekonomicznego dla pracujacych'. *'Kwartalnik Pedagogiczny'*, No.3, , pp.185-90.

Podoski, K. (1977) 'Infrastruktura spoleczna a system wartosci' (Social infrastructure and the value system) in: B.Suchodolski (ed.) *Kultura polska a socjalistyczny system wartosci* (Polish culture and the socialist value system). Warszawa: KiW.

Pohorille, M. (1976) Cena czasu wolnego a konsumpcja dóbr i uslug (The price of leisure time and consumption of goods and services). *Ekonomista,* No.1.

Pohorille, M. (1982) *Tendencje rozwoju konsumpcji. Postulaty i uwarunkowania* (Trends in development of consumption. Postulates and determinants). Warszawa: PWE.

Przeclawski, K. (1960) Socjologia wychowania i turystyki (Sociology of education and tourism). *Ruch turystyczny,* No.1.

Rakowski, M. (1976) 'Efektywnosc wzrostu czasu wolnego a programowanie wzrostu spoleczno-gospodarczego' (Effectiveness of growth in leisure time and programming of socio-economic growth). *Materialy Instytutu Planowania,* No.5.

Rosner, J. (1966) 'Budzety czasu robotników budujacych Zaklady Azotowe w Pulawach' (Time budgets of workers constructing a fertilizer plant in Pulawy). *'Biuletyn IGS',* No.3/4.

Rosner, J. (1975) Prognoza czasu pracy i czasu wolnego do 1990 (Prognosis of work and leisure time up to the year 1990) in: *Przeslanki perspektywicznej polityki spolecznej* (Determinants of a prospective social policy). POLSKA 2000, Vol.II, Warszawa.

Sicinski, A. (ed.) (1978) *Styl zycia. Przemiany we wspólczesnej Polsce* (Lifestyle: Changes in contemporary Poland). Warszawa: PWN.

Siemienski, M. (1961) *Z badan nad dzialalnoscia kulturalno-oswiatowa w Nowej Hucie. Budzet czasu pracownika a mozliwosci jego uczestnictwa w dzialalnosci kulturalno-oswiatowej* (On cultural and educational activities in Nowa Huta. Time budget of an employee and his possibilities to participate in cultural and educational activities). Wroclaw.

Skórzynski, Z. (1965) *Miedzy praca a wypoczynkiem* (Between work and leisure). Ossolineum, Wroclaw: IFiS PAN.

Strak, M. (1988) *Kultura, polityka, gospodarka* (Culture, politics and the economy). Warszawa: PWE.

Strzeminska, H. (1976) *Czas pracy i jego skracanie. Etapy - metody -efekty* (Work time and its reduction. Stages - methods - effects). Warszawa: PWE.

Strzeminska, H. (1988) *Czas pracy i czas wolny w polityce spolecznej* (Work time and leisure time in social policy). Warszawa: PWE.

Suchodolski, B. (1979) Rozwój kultury i wyksztalcenia a model konsumpcji - problemy i perspektywy (Development of culture and education versus the model of consumption - problems and perspectives). *Gospodarka Planowana,* No.6.

Suchodolski, B. (ed.) (1977) *Kultura polska a socjalistyczny system wartosci* (Polish culture and the socialist value system). Warszawa: KiW.

Szalai, A. (ed.) (1972) *The Use of Time*. The Hague: Mouton.
Szczepanski, J. (1981) *Konsumpcja a rozwój czlowieka. Wstep do antropologicznej teorii konsumpcji* (Consumption and human development. Introduction to the anthropological theory of consumption). Warszawa: PWE.
Szczepanski, J. (ed.) (1977) *Badania nad wzorami konsumpcji* (Studies on consumption patterns). Ossolineum, Wroclaw:IFIS PAN.
Tarkowska, E. (1992) *Czas w zyciu Polaków. Wyniki badan, hipotezy, impresja* (Time in Poles' Life. Results of research, hypotheses, impressions). Warszawa: IFIS PAN.
Turowski, J. Kubejko, E. (1959) 'Hotel robotniczy jako srodowisko spoleczne' (Workers' hostel as a social environment). *'Przeglad Socjologiczny'*, Vol.XIII, No.1, pp.106-136.
Winiarski, R.W. (1989) *Wstep do teorii rekreacji (ze szczególnym uwzglednieniem rekreacji fizycznej* (Introduction to the theory of recreation (with special focus to physical recreation). Wyd.Skryptowe nr.100, Kraków: AWF.
Wnuk-Lipinski, E. (1972) *Praca i wypoczynek w budzecie czasu* (Work and Leisure in the Time Budget). Ossolineum, Wroclaw: IFiS PAN.
Wnuk-Lipinski, E. (1981) *Budzet czasu - struktura spoleczna -polityka spoleczna* (Time Budget - Social Structure - Social Policy). Ossolineum, Wroclaw: IFiS PAN.
Wojnar, I. (1977) Czlowiek wielowymiarowy - postulaty wychowania humanistycznego przez sztuke (Multidimensional individual -postulates for humanistic education through art) in: B.Suchodolski (ed.), *Kultura polska a socjalistyczny system wartoci* (Polish culture and the socialist value system). Warszawa: KiW.
Wojska, Z. (1960) Z badan nad problematyka wolnego czasu mlodocianych pracowników fizycznych, mieszkanców hotelu robotniczego (On the problematics of leisure of young manual workers living in a workers' hostel). *'Kwartalnik Pedagogiczny'*, No.3, pp.179-84.
Zadrozynska, A. (1983) *Homo faber i homo ludens* (Homo faber and homo ludens). Warszawa: PWN.
Zeidler-Janiszewska, A. (1992) *Oblicza postmoderny. Teoria i praktyka uczestnictwa w kulturze wspólczesnej* (Face of the post-modern. Theory and practice of participation in contemporary culture). Warszawa: Instytut Kultury.

NOTES TO CHAPTER 3

[1] This applies in particular to Olszewska, who chaired the Research Commission 13 (Sociology of Leisure) of the International Sociological Association, a contributor to, and participant in, many international conferences, and Erdman, who was the president of the European Leisure and Recreation Association (ELRA), as well as founder and first chairman of the Polish Leisure Studies Association.

[2] The title of this section is derived from the title of a much-quoted book by Danecki (1970).

[3] To give an example of the growing popularity of such research, one may quote the example of Skórzynski's book *Between work and leisure* (1965), one of the earliest empirically-based studies on leisure participation in Poland. He quotes as source of inspiration and base of secondary analysis the following studies devoted entirely to leisure:

Table 3.1: Leisure surveys in Poland

1957	Vacations and holidays of the inhabitants of Warsaw	City authorities, Warsaw
1958	How we spent our free time (administered through local press)	Polish Academy of Sciences (PAN)
1958	Time budget of the inhabitants of Warsaw	Public Opinion Pollsters
1958	Free time of the inhabitants of Pruszków (near Warsaw)	PAN/UNESCO project
1960	Leisure pursuits of the Polish urban population	Public Opinion Pollsters

Source: Skórzyñski, 1965:11

[4] The first time budget study on a large sample in Poland was run in 1965 in the historical town of Torun (the birthplace of Copernicus) as part of an international UNESCO project under supervision of A.Szalai. The findings from Poland, together with data gathered in 11 other countries were published in the book *The Use of Time* (Szalai, 1972). In 1968-69, a time budget study was conducted nation-wide on a representative sample of some 50000 Poles. The study was repeated in 1976 and in 1984, but in the case of leisure these studies were not fully compatible as some categories of leisure activities were successively dropped or added to the list.

[5] Growth in sports participation was perceptibly slower. While the statistics testifying to a huge increase (compared to the pre-war days) in Poles' participation in various leisure pursuits were largely biased towards institutionalised participation, the expansion in the number of people participating, in the leisure infrastructure, and in the time spent on these activities was impressive and continued until late 1970s.

[6] The traditional high interest of Polish leisure researchers in (and even overvaluation of) education as the leading factor in the acquisition of cultural competence and full enjoyment of leisure was derived from empirical evidence. Under conditions of low wages, little differentiation in incomes and subsidised provision of many leisure goods and services, education played the key role in stratification of cultural and recreational participation (Skórzynski, 1965:105). In fact, researchers were quoting evidence of a gap perceived by the workers and peasants, who after the war found themselves faced with unprecedented opportunities to access all forms of leisure, but 'lacked the necessary *preparation* to make use of them' (Kaminski, 1965:139).

[7] The 1989-93 period in Poland was one of economic hardship (a drop in living standards, high unemployment, polarisation of wealth), of newly discovered consumer pleasures in abundance in shops, but also of the omnipresence of the consumerist message flowing from advertising and ostentatious consumption of the new elites. Leisure time without material wealth to enjoy it has become much less attractive and more likely to be traded for overtime work or informal occupations in the grey and black economy.

Chapter 4

The Study of Free Time and Pleasure in the Netherlands: The End of the Legislator

Hans Mommaas

Introduction

To study social reality from a 'trans-temporal' or 'trans-spatial' perspective has one indisputable advantage. It produces a strong awareness of the contextual character of things. Because of a change of context, the self-evident becomes problematic and in need of clarification. Related to that, and before presenting a picture of the history of the study of leisure in the Netherlands, two things have to be made clear.

First there is the concept of leisure. In Dutch there is no equivalent for the concept as such. Whereas in various languages some sort of differentiation does exist between leisure and free time - like in French *loisir* and *temps libre*, in German *Muße* and *Freizeit*, in Spanish *ocio* and *tiempo libre* -, in Dutch one has to make do with *vrijetijd*. Consequently, the connotations associated with leisure, leisure time and free time on one side and *vrijetijd* on the other will 'vary differently' within the respective language communities. As far as vrijetijd is concerned, much depends on context. Sometimes the term refers to free time proper, to a temporal zone or enclave, which in a variety of possible ways is associated with notions of freedom. But more often than not, that connotation becomes inextricably interwoven with another field of interpretations, referring more to the symbolic meaning of activities. For instance, visiting a ballet-performance no doubt is a form of *vrijetijdsbesteding*. Except for the professional critic, visiting ballet-performances will take place within that temporal enclave in which workers do not have to work, caretakers do not have to take care or students do not have to study. Nevertheless, in another sense, to typify visiting ballet-performances as a form of *vrijetijdsbesteding* is quite problematic. It implies levelling it with 'popular' pastimes such as visiting a disco, watching television or reading tabloids. The moment the concept of *vrijetijd* became part of Dutch public discourse, it also formed part of strategies of cultural inclusion and exclusion. In those cases, *vrijetijd* implied the pleasurable and relaxing, in contrast with the educated, the refined, the cultivated or the civilised.

Secondly, there is the question of what is presented in this contribution under the heading of 'the history of the study of leisure'. There are at least two ways of handling this problem. The first would be to formulate beforehand some strict operational definition of the phenomenon, which can then be used as an unambiguous yardstick to demarcate our subject matter. The second would be to leave the matter open to history and see how the notion of free time was constructed in the research itself. Both strategies are not without problems. Following the first option one runs the risk of excluding research which contemporaries nevertheless would have regarded as dealing with free time. Following the second option one treats history as self-evident and disregards one's own role in its demarcation and reconstruction.

A solution might be to see things from a more processual point of view. Studying the history of the study of free time - 'what is historically produced as such' - at one and the same time involves choosing a position in the current conceptual debate around free time - 'what is presently regarded as such' - and vice versa. Both sides feed one another. The ongoing debate around the conceptualisation of free time should constantly be informed by research dealing with the history of the phenomenon. At the same time historical research into the constitution of free time should always be informed by ongoing conceptualising debates.

There is no need to go into these debates at this point, suffice to say that in this contribution, the history of the study of free time in the Netherlands will be (re)presented along five lines of demarcation and interpretation. First this text does not restrict itself to studies presented as research on free time proper. It also deals with analyses which, in a more indirect way, can be said to have involved free time or free time-related issues. Hence in the Netherlands, as elsewhere, extensive research has been carried out with regard to people's everyday life. Often, in that research, attention has also been paid to the pastimes, amusements and pleasures involved. This sort of research, most of the time presented under other labels than those of the study of free time (e.g. 'culture', 'everyday life', 'pleasure'), is nevertheless taken into account. Secondly, excluded is research that focused upon some particular free-time sector. We will not be dealing with for example, the history of the study of sports, the study of tourism, media studies, the study of recreation or the study of cultural participation as such. The focus will be on research which in one way or another dealt with people's free time, pleasures or pastimes in a more encompassing way. Thirdly, the focus will be on research that can be regarded as exemplars of major episodes in the history of the study of free time in the Netherlands. Consequently, our focus will be more on change than on continuity and more on that minority of research done within the field of social theory than on the majority of research more involved with (national/local) administrative or moral-political issues.[1] Fourthly, given the author's own disciplinary background and interest, it can not be avoided that this overview will probably be slightly biased towards research developed within the area of sociology or social theory. Finally, the studies involved will not be analysed as, in a sense, representing a self-evident outside reality called free time. Rather than questioning the research history on the progress that is made in the *explanation* of an external reality, the focus will be more on the involvement of academics in the *construction* of that reality. How and why did academics involve themselves with the topic and what sort of representation did they give of it, based on what sort of intellectual and/or social theoretical sentiments and within what sort of societal circumstances.

Research projects can be differentiated variously. For example, they can be classified with regard to the theories and methods used, the problems with which they concern themselves, the parts of the population the research is targeted at or the moral conventions or political affiliations inevitably implicated. More often then not, these characteristics show some interdependency in the sense that one can discern schools, phases or episodes of research, distinguishable by some specific mixture of the above. The same is true for the history of the study of free time in the Netherlands. For most of this century having no self-generated history - at least not one comparable to vested disciplines such as sociology, human geography or psychology, based on a significant institutional framework with its own academic chairs, graduate courses and research programmes - the history of the study of free time looks rather erratic, more strongly influenced by 'external' administrative or policy agendas than by 'internal' academic considerations. On the other hand, in the course of time there also developed something like a relatively self-reliant line of research, based upon a growing number of research publications, with every new researcher involved referring to the work of others. It was not until the early 1970s that academics started to regard themselves as part of a domain of 'leisure research'.

Broadly conceived one can distinguish between five episodes in the history of Dutch academic attention for free time. First there is a period of public inquiries or 'proto-research', lasting from the last quarter of the former century until the 1930s. Secondly, one can distinguish a period of so called 'sociographic research' lasting from the early 1930s until just after the Second World War. Thirdly, there is a post-war period in which a more 'hermeneutic', 'personalist' or 'idealist' outlook dominated, lasting until the second half of the 1950s. A fourth period was dominated by 'modern sociology', imported from the US, and lasted from the late 1950s until the second half of the 1970s. For want of a better perspective, a last period can be typified as a period of fragmentation and multi-paradigmatic pluralisation, beginning somewhere in the late 1970s and stretching well into the 1990s.

The structure of the following text follows this periodisation. It is a periodisation which reflects not only wider societal transformations (especially the institutionalisation of industrial capitalism and the growth and demise of post-war 'social modernism'), but also the response to those by specific generations of academics, given their own biographies, settings and interests.

Free Time and Modernity (1900-1940)

In the Netherlands modern industrial capitalism and hence the modern phenomenon of free time developed rather late. Whereas in the UK the struggle for a shortening of the working day goes back as far as the first half of the 19th century and the first law on working hours was established as early as 1847 (Weaver, 1988), by that time, in the Netherlands, industrial production did not amount to much. Dutch society was still dominated by a conservative, estate-like cultural climate, not so much based on the dominant position of a rural feudal aristocracy proper, but on that of an urban mercantilist-patrician class. It would last until the last quarter of the 19th century, before an industrialisation of some comparable importance would develop, and until 1919 before a law was established which would regulate working hours for the general male working population (Diederiks, 1987; Karsten, 1989).

Nevertheless, when looked upon from the perspective of the constitution of free time proper, developments followed similar trajectories. Industrialisation went along with the establishment of an increasingly concentrated and labour-dependent work force. At the same time the operational logic of industrial capitalism stimulated the spread of a modern time-based instead of product- or task-based model of labour organisation (Thompson, 1967). This time-based organisation of labour not only changed production relations, it also changed the entire structure of the everyday life of labourers. Labour became gradually differentiated from the rest of local life, which amongst other outcomes resulted in the emergence of a time-spatially differentiated enclave called free time.

The latter did not amount to much in the beginning. Industrialisation and proletarianisation went along with a severe attack on the time labourers formerly could spend off the job. The pace of work became dominated by machine-technology and regulated by a strict surveillance, based on Taylorist and Fordist doctrines (depending in turn on favourable labour market conditions). The celebration of 'Saint Monday' was actively discouraged, together with other activities formerly embedding labour activities in local culture (e.g. talking, singing and drinking during work). According to an inquiry held by the Dutch labour inspection in 1900, in the midst of Dutch industrialisation, the average working day was still 11 hours long, and one third of the factories had working days of 12 hours or more (Beckers, 1983:53). As Marx had already noticed, industrial-capitalist production in itself does not set limits to the length of the working day. Free time had to be (re)gained by politico-economic struggle and regulated by nation-state interventions.

In turn, this restructuring of the everyday life of a growing amount of people changed the whole time-spatial fabric of pleasure and entertainment, educational reform and political organisation. The free time to be (re)gained from the production process became the time-spatial locus of not only folk culture and popular pleasures, but also of popular education, political organisation and religious celebration. This explains the paradoxical character that would mark the history of the socialist and progressive liberal reformist involvement with free time from say 1890 onwards, an involvement very much responsible for the early free time-oriented inquiries and research projects. On the one hand, free time symbolised a victory over capitalist or production interests, a time captured to study, to cultivate and to organise. In that sense to (re)gain some free time from the production process did form a pre-condition for the constitution of a respectable labour movement and a respectable national citizenry (the latter often seen as a precondition for the former). On the other hand however, there were no guarantees to preclude labourers from spending their (re)gained free time on, for example, traditional folklore with its local-regional customs, 'rough' pleasures and 'inward' orientations. That was considered objectionable because it not only threatened the legitimacy and authority of the cultivated lifestyle of the cultural elites themselves, but also endangered the formation of a respectable socialist movement and enlightened citizenry, integrated in a nationalised rational-moral culture (Westen, 1990). Hence, Dutch socio-liberal and socio-democratic reformers were confronted with a complicated task. Besides, from the end of the 19th century onwards, their nationalisation, emancipation and enlightenment projects were endangered by denominational elites, striving for a maintenance of their control over regional populations vis-à-vis centralising state policies, secularised enlightened concerns and socialist organisations, that is vis-à-vis 'modernism' (Stuurman, 1983).

The educational concern with popular culture was based upon a well established Dutch reformist tradition. Already from 1784 onwards, several Dutch towns had their own local branches of the so-called *Maatschappij tot Nut van het Algemeen* (Society for Public Welfare). These societies were dominated by members from middle class cultural backgrounds, opposing a still dominant classicist intellectual orientation amongst men of letters, arguing instead for a nationalised popularisation of 'useful' science (Mijnhardt, 1988).[2]

The result of all this is clear: where labourers regained some freedom from the production process, their free time became the object of civilising, educating, cultivating or moralising concerns, initiated by progressive liberal, socialist or denominational interests. In organisational terms, these interests were based upon a typical Dutch patchwork of local/regional societies, foundations, clubs, associations, unions and the like, competing amongst each other for public authority and financial resources.

Labourers' Free Time

Until the Second World War, the interests in and explorations of people's pastimes in every sense reflected the above mentioned developments. At first the research took the form of public inquiries, initiated either by the early workers' unions, by philanthropic or educational progressive liberal or socialist movements, by state agencies or by parliamentary committees. For instance in 1907 the Dutch socialist workers' union analysed the arguments employers used against a shortening of the working day. The research report concludes that the arguments are of a totally political nature. There are no production or market-related obstacles hindering a decrease of working hours. On the contrary, experiences elsewhere pointed at a possible increase in productivity. But what would become of the free time (re)gained?

In 1923, due to a request from the International Labour Organization in Geneva, at that time preparing the 1924 International Conference on 'The Problem of Free Time' (see Beckers and Mommaas, Chapter 8), the Dutch labour inspection investigated the use labourers made of their recently (re)gained free time. Central were the questions of whether the decrease in working hours had resulted in an increase in drunkenness or whether it had stimulated the worker's intellectual and spiritual development (Arbeidsinspectie, 1924).

In line with this moral concern, in 1927, in the midst of the 'roaring twenties', a 'Commissie inzake Volksvermaken' (Committee concerning Folk Pleasures) organised an inquiry concerning people's behaviour at dance-halls and fairs. The committee was founded by the so-called 'Tucht-unie' (Union for Moral Discipline), a public initiative of conservative liberals. The results were brought to the attention of Dutch parliament, which in turn led to the founding of three state committees investigating people's behaviour in parks, dance-halls and cinemas. The reports were published around 1931. In the report on dancing it says:

> Often the modern dance - the step, foxtrot, shimmy, Charleston, etcetera - is given a rather sexual character. Some influence for the better can not result from it'
> (cit. in Wouters, 1990:155).

The source of this endangerment of Dutch sexual morality - the topic really at stake here - was, of course, America. But what could one expect from a country inhibited by 'incoherent masses', integrated only on the level of the 'instinctive' (ibid:157).

Normally, these and other inquiries were based upon interviews conducted with local spokespersons. Administrators, politicians, philanthropists or unionists - usually from upper middle-class backgrounds - had talks with local policemen, employers, union leaders, social workers and the like - and thus with their class fellows. The latter were expected to have a well-informed and unbiased overview of reality, in contrast with the illiterate workers themselves.

An academic involvement with the topic of free time marks the beginning of a second phase. In 1934, in the midst of an economic crisis, the Dutch social scientist and social democrat J.P.Kruijt published an article in a special issue of the journal *Volksontwikkeling* (Popular Education) titled: 'Arbeid en vrije tijd als sociologies probleem' (Labour and free time as sociological problem). The article presents a mixture of Durkheimian, Marxian and Weberian explanations for the historical and geographical variation in free time. The analysis is still dominated by a typical 19th century evolutionist perspective. Mirroring a general way of seeing things, free time is perceived as the correlate of labour or work, the amount of which has to be explained in terms of a nation's labour-productivity and 'work-ethic'. Hence, free time is seen as a phenomenon only conceivable of in relation to people 'working', and thus to men (Kruijt, 1934:39).

Together with J. Blonk, another social scientist, Kruijt was preparing a nation-wide research project. That project aimed at an examination of the free time behaviour of organised labourers. The project was initiated by the 'Instituut voor Arbeidersontwikkeling' (IvAO: Institute for Labourers' Education), an organisation founded in 1924 by the social-democratic movement. Its aim was to organise educational activities and cultivated pleasures in order to enhance labourers' pastimes. The IvAO wanted to know why the majority of organised labourers did not participate in its activities (Beckers, 1983).

The results of this first nation-wide academic survey into free time were published in 1936. By that time, the project was taken over by the aforementioned 'Maatschappij tot Nut van 't Algemeen' (Society for Public Welfare). The research was based upon 621 questionnaires and 226 time budgets. Labourers' free time activities were classified along 17 categories, clearly reflecting a middle class perspective, concerned with a demarcation of the civilised and the popular, the serious and the pleasurable.[3] The conclusions are reassuring. The increase in free time has resulted in:

> a growing involvement of fathers with their children, a
> strengthening of family ties, a decrease in alcoholism, a powerful
> expansion of educational work amongst grown-ups, the
> spreading of the daily press amongst the lowest social layers, an
> exodus on foot or by bicycle to the countryside, a strong
> expansion of many branches of sports, an enormous increase of
> social life
> (Blonk *et al.*, 1936:73)

Nevertheless, it was noticed that one third of the organised labourers still did not touch a book, a fact clearly proving that work remained to be done. Moreover, competition from commercial culture, such as from cinemas, dance halls, sport events and the radio increased.

The researchers not only based their conclusions on observations and opinions from local spokesmen, they also actually posed questions to the labourers concerned. But then, of course, this project was aimed at more enlightened fractions of the Dutch labour force.

This was not the only occasion in the 1930s that academic researchers studied people's free time. Both Blonk and Kruijt belonged to the so-called sociographic school, founded by S.R. Steinmetz, professor at the Municipal University of Amsterdam. Steinmetz's original teaching commitment concerned geography and ethnology, with a special dedication to the East-Indian archipelago (the location of a Dutch colony). He propagated a mixture of sociology, ethnology and geography labelled 'sociography'. In methodological terms, doing sociography implied describing the situated life of local communities in all its material, physical, geographical, demographic, social and moral details. The research was based upon all kinds of sources. These included historical travel reports, newspaper archives, regional novels, memorial books, police reports and local statistics. Besides one could have talks with local spokesmen (mostly men) like police-officers, priests, welfare workers and union officials or make observations of local habits and customs. Speaking to the local labour population itself was considered unscientific. According to Steinmetz, the *primus inter pares* of sociography, it took a learned mind to observe things properly (Steinmetz, 1942).

As exemplars of what he had in mind with his sociography, Steinmetz himself referred to studies like those of the Lynds (*Middletown*, 1929 and *Middletown in Transition*, 1937), Thomas and Znaniecki (*The Polish Peasant in Europe and America*, 1918), Seebom Rowntree (*Land and Labour, Lessons from Belgium*, 1910) and to *The New Survey of London Life and Labour* (1930) (Steinmetz, 1942:37). As far as models of empirical research were concerned, Steinmetz and his sociographic school were clearly inspired by the Anglo-American social survey tradition.

Within the various sociographic studies carried out in the 1930s as independent academic research projects, researchers frequently also paid attention to local pastimes. For example, in 1929, the above mentioned sociographer Blonk published his PhD on Enschede, a town in the East of Holland, dominated by textile industries. He devoted some 185 pages to the everyday life of local textile workers. Classified under headings such as 'Morals and Morality', 'Alcoholism', 'Intellectual Development' and 'Pleasures', a vivid and very detailed picture was painted of how labourers spend their time off the job.[4] Blonk is rather concerned about the poor quality of local free time. He relates that, amongst other things, to the influence of particularistic political or denominational interests:

> There is almost no denominational or political group, or besides its inescapable brass band, string band and choir it also has its theatre or reciting club. The complaint of professional players that these clubs threaten their existence is yet no evidence of the artistic enjoyment these dilettantes bring. In many cases they have missed a good example, or had their plays judged by a standard, not independent of secondary considerations.
> (Blonk, 1929:345)

Overall, Blonk's conclusion is rather clear and straight forward: in Enschede the beneficial is still covered by the pleasurable (Blonk, 1929).

Civilisation and Evolution Theory

The attention given to the developmental level of people's free time activities, to such things as the attendance of lectures and visits to libraries, to drinking, sexual and gaming habits, and to the common respect for public authority, was more than just a product of morally prejudiced minds. The dichotomies in terms of which free time activities were classified - such as those of relaxation and effort, pleasure and spiritual advancement, emotion and reason - and the evaluation of developments in terms of growth, refinement, elevation and education, these not only expressed some 'external' political or economic interest. At least for the researchers involved things also worked the other way around. In the prevalent rationalist intellectual climate of those days, shared as much amongst progressive liberals as amongst social democrats, political and moral standpoints had to be based upon rational-scientific knowledge (Jonker, 1988). Scientific knowledge was considered a pre-condition for reaching true virtue, real enjoyment, authentic aesthetic sensitivity, honest moral judgement and hence genuine progress. A strong relation existed between the theoretical orientations of the social scientists involved, their modernist stance in matters of social development and their interest in, and involvement with, the projects of popular education and labour emancipation.

For Steinmetz, sociography not only involved a nuanced description of the situated life of social communities. His intellectual ambitions reached much further. Sociographic research was part of a project, in the end aimed at the formulation of a general theory of human civilisation. Inductive classifications and comparisons of situated community life should in the end lead to an explanation of types and stages of civilisation. Civilisation here involved a rationally formulated, empirically traceable and scientifically explainable phenomenon. It depended upon two indications: '(...) of the possession of which much depends, which more than anything else influences social and cultural life entirely' (Steinmetz, 1942:115). These involved 'the nature of thinking' and 'the nature of the means of sustaining life'. Both functioned as an indicator of the place of a people on the developmental axis connecting and differentiating 'natural' and 'cultural' societies.

Dutch sociography was one of many 20th century heirs of a colourful 19th century social-evolutionist tradition.[5] Steinmetz was not uncritical about evolutionist works such as those of Darwin (*Origin of Species*, 1859), Spencer (*Social Statics*, 1850), Bachofen (*Das Mutterrecht*, 1861), Tylor (*Primitive Culture*, 1871) and Ferguson (*Primitive Marriage*, 1865). He especially criticised too reductionist a use made of the organic analogy and of naturalist arguments. Nevertheless, the project of sociography evolved within the broader framework of social evolutionism, very much inspired by the work of Spencer.

Popular education and rational science shared a common interest. Both aimed at a national recognition of the virtues of rationalist reasoning, a recognition on which the very public legitimacy and status of national science itself depended (Bauman, 1987; Gellner, 1983). The scientists themselves shared the strong conviction that once people were freed from the burdens of local folklore and classical religious thought, and enriched with the salvation of scientific knowledge, they would be convinced not only of the truth-claims of that knowledge, but also of the virtues of the civilising project based on it, with its political aims, social classifications, aesthetic values and moral rules. Social reformism thus formed an important resource base for the researchers concerned, as much in financial as in cultural terms. Evolution theory in a sense closed the circle in this rationalising power-knowledge syndrome. It delivered a scientific rationale for the civilising offensive concerned and the public status of the intellectuals involved.[6]

Post-war 'Moral Panic' (1945-1955)

On first sight it seems as though not much changed in the post-war research on free time. Activities remained to be classified and evaluated in terms of a developmental narrative. However, outward appearance is deceptive here. The common descriptions and typologies conceal a fundamental change in perspective and problematic.

First, something changed with regard to the populations on which the research was targeted. Whereas in pre-war years industrial labourers were the prime target of research, in post-war years these were exchanged for others. After 1919, working hours had become regulated by law. Because of that, the issue of the length of the working day was gradually replaced from the domain of economic conflict to that of politics - which in Holland meant coalition politics. Besides, because of successful denominational policies, labourers' free-time had become integrated in a 'pillarised' social structure. The various denominational blocks had developed their own vertically integrated social 'pillars', with their own educational institutions, newspapers, health care services, broadcasting organisations, political parties, youth- and women's organisations, workers unions and free time associations, the latter ranging from athletics and football to scouting and pigeon flying. Liberal interests had become marginalised under denominational pressures and the social-democratic movement was forced to develop into a sort of 'pillar' of its own. This more or less precluded the constitution of a nationally shared labour-class culture, transcending the denominational structure. Hence the issue of labourers' free time was resolved, or better perhaps, dissolved, economically as well as culturally.

Secondly, the economic and cultural institutionalisation of labourers' free time went along with what can be typified as a 'generalisation' of the issue. Although the notion of free time remained associated with a condition of non-work, it became gradually dissociated from its specific relation to the world of labour and looked upon as a general condition of life. Whenever fractions of the population gained some freedom vis-à-vis the realms of production, education or care - as in the case of post-war youth liberating itself from pre-war 'pillarised' youth organisations - those developments became addressed in terms of a free-time problem. Central was the question whether or not people would be able to make a satisfying use of the freedoms gained or whether they would lapse into selfish, passive, hedonistic postures.

But, most important of all, something had also changed in the evaluation of free time. Whereas pre-war investigations and evaluations were essentially characterised by a positive stance towards modernisation, in post-war research strong anti-modern sentiments surfaced. As such the research mirrored a moment of increased moral anxiety. That mood was first of all fed by the various disintegrating effects of the war: neighbourhoods being bombed, the deportation of large sections of the population, schools confiscated, youth experiencing violence as a normal part of life, families disrupted, women gaining more independence, movements born out of the resistance wanting to democratise established social and political relations. But also various post-war developments were endangering Dutch segmented cultural integration. There was first of all the rapid re-industrialisation of the Dutch economy, stimulated both by the post-war decolonisation and by the Marshall Plan. Along with that a rapid urbanisation of Dutch landscape took place, partly encouraged by a post-war population boom, partly by modernising aspirations amongst planning agencies and authorities. And last but certainly not least, there were the de-stabilising effects of new commercial pleasures, a more permissive sexual morality and mass consumer culture, brought initially to Holland by the American and Canadian liberators. According to the established denominational elites, these developments threatened Dutch 'pillarised' hegemony. As a result, something of a 'moral panic' developed amongst leading politicians, social scientists and ecclesiastical representatives (e.g. Galesloot and Schrevel, n.d.; De Liagre Bohl and Meershoek, 1989).

Central to this cultural nervousness was the metaphor of 'massification'. For those involved, modernisation equalled a levelling of culture to the average, the victory of passion and nature over reason and culture. As a result, the population, transformed into a mass of disintegrated personalities, living their lives on the level of the instinctive, could easily fall victim to the rages and fads of mass culture and mass politics. Massification was thought of as being responsible for the pre-war uprising of fascism and massification also threatened Dutch pillarised consensus and solidarity, deemed necessary for a successful regeneration of the national economy. In 1954, a report of the Ministry of Social Work suggests:

> Because of the increasing concentration of the population, the increasing complication of the social structures, the urbanisation and industrialisation process, massification, secularisation and so

many other causes that lately capture attention, the family increasingly runs the risk of disorganisation and resulting adjustment disturbances. The necessity exists, at least for more severe forms of anti-social behaviour, to create an apparatus that gradually takes up the fight, treatment and prevention.
(cit. in Van Wel, 1988:112).

'Unsocials' and Mass Youth

These 'anti-modernist' sentiments induced two post-war series of research projects. One was concerned with the *verwildering van de massajeugd* (degeneration of mass youth). The other series formed part of a policy aimed at the 'cultivation' or 'normalisation' of life of the so called *onmaatschappelijken* ('unsocials').[7]

The studies aimed at 'degenerate' or 'mass' youth were initiated in 1948 by a Department of the Dutch Ministry of Education, Arts and Science called 'Vorming Buiten Schoolverband' (Education Outside School). The administrators involved were concerned about post-war youth, spending more time loitering, visiting cinemas and cafes, than within the established 'pillarised' youth organisations. The Ministry wanted to explore the 'spiritual well-being' of mass youth. The research programme involved no less than seven research institutes, evenly spread amongst the three main social 'pillars' of Dutch society.

More than one hundred (!) local research reports were written, situated all over the Netherlands, in urban as well as in rural areas. In all these reports, free time behaviour was amongst the aspects investigated. After all, the degeneration of mass youth best revealed itself in the domain in which youth behaved 'freely'.

Again, in line with pre-war sociographic research, most reports were based upon observations, on talks with local spokesmen such as priests, policemen, teachers, social workers and on analyses of written material such as local newspapers, historical regional novels, memorial books and the like. Only one of the research institutes directly interviewed youth itself and their parents. Otherwise, posing personal questions to working class youth was considered 'improper' (Dresen-Coenders, 1991).

The observation reports contain detailed descriptions of the daily life of youth, although pictured in what to us appear as rather moralising terms. An impression is given of how local youth spent its evenings and weekends; their 'hanging around' and frequenting dancing, cinemas, cafes, clubs; the sort of films, books, music they watch, read or listen to; the clothes they wear, and the topics they talk about with friends and parents. A report on youth in Utrecht recounts:

Here one can also find the same characteristics: free time
activities evolve uncontrolled and unbounded. On weekly
evenings, most of the time, youth can be found in their own
neighbourhood, on the streets or sometimes at home, listening to
the *Bonte Dinsdagavondtrein* (a popular radio play: HM), or
playing cards. On Saturday and Sunday evening, boys and girls
go into town, hanging around on the *Neude* or the *Vredenburg*
(two squares in Utrecht: HM) or visiting the cinema. On those
occasions a lot of sweets are eaten. On Sunday mornings they
prefer to sleep in, in the afternoon many of them visit a football
match or go into town. There is no question of any choice here,
they just go to the movies (at least once a week), being attracted
by the excitement and sensation offered. (...) They do not do
much reading, only cheap novels, westerns and detectives or
stories like from *De Lach* or *Okido* (popular comic strips: HM).
These books are passed on from hand to hand: little use is made
of the library. They do not spend much time in the open air,
only when swimming in the natural swimming pool or the
Merwedekanaal.
                (Bronnenboek, 1952:67)

   The studies of the so called 'unsocials' were initiated by local
governments and provincial welfare agencies. From 1945 onwards
until 1966 some 180 (!) observation reports were published. In
practice, the projects aimed at those marginalised sections of the
labour class that did not live their lives according to privatised middle
class standards, with a steady job and career, inward-oriented family
relations, a clean, well-inhabited and well-used home, with well-ironed
clothes awaiting their proper destination in the wardrobe, well-washed
windows, a clean step etc. Because of their 'maladjusted' behaviour,
those concerned did not fit into the moral fabric of the public
housing estates built in great numbers during the fifties and sixties,
with their images of future-oriented tidiness and neatness, dominated
by a family-centred and consumerist life style, accompanied by rising
middle-class expectations. Hence these families presented a problem
for local government and public housing agencies.
   In some 15 research reports, free-time activities were amongst the
indicators used to analyse people's level of maladjustment. In
Maastricht, one of the researchers concerned, H.P.M. Litjens,
observed:

The men rather like fishing. Besides, a large amount of attention
is devoted to pigeon flying. This is sometimes seen as a disaster
for the families involved because it is expensive and it increases
the shortage of living space. Some keepers of pigeons do not
hesitate to use entire rooms as dovecote, while their families do
not have enough living space already. In general the men are not

very active in their free time. They spend quite some time in cafes and especially in the summer they populate the streets, grouping together, or sitting in front of their homes.
(Litjens, 1953:156)

To finish this presentation of post-war research on free time, the following quotation, taken from *Maatschappelijke verwildering der jeugd* (Social degeneration of mass youth), one of the three main reports on mass youth published in 1952, clearly shows how leisure behaviour was used as an indicator of the socio-cultural disease plaguing post-war morality:

Degenerated youth lives in a world which can be called exceedingly formless. The purposelessness of its world expresses itself in the inability to give form: its appearance is covered in ready-to-wear film clothing or being totally neglected; attitude and movement express no inner orientation: one leans, hangs, loiters, etc. Often, there is an excess of restless, purposeless motion. (...) Also voice and articulation expresses a hollow emptiness: one howls, one roars, one chats as an endless drivel, one screams and screeches, one whines and nags. (...) The gesticulations are without grace, inadequate, now dull then excessive. (...) one wobbles and jumps in a boogie-woogy, rumba, samba, but one no longer knows the personal liberating and joyful character of the jump or dance. Thus (...) develops a human, adjusted to living in a chaos of stimuli, addressed to the senses (...) but that will not penetrate. Their stamina for noise, for blazing light, bright colours, sharp tastes, etc. is unimaginable.
(cit. in Van Wel, 1988:113)

'Kulturwissenschaft' and Personalism

In a sense one could say that Dutch social theory mirrors the geographical position of its formulators, situated in between three major political and cultural powers; Germany, France and the United Kingdom. Not so much exporting new ideas, but balancing and reworking theories taken from abroad, Dutch intellectuals 'borrow' from a variety of neighbouring intellectual traditions such as French rationalism, German idealism and English empiricism. In line with this in the pre-war period a Dutch branch of social idealism developed, based upon the German tradition of the *Kulturwissenschaften*. Before the war however, the orientation remained confined to introductory textbooks on either sociology or *Kulturgeschichte* (cultural history) (see e.g. Bouman, 1938, 1940; Bierens de Haan, 1939).

The idealist outlook on Dutch life in those years becomes clear from the following quotation, taken from a famous textbook titled *Gemeenschap en maatschappij* (Community and Society), published in 1939:

> Also outside the company, during people's free time - through radio and cinema, in sports and traffic or through the mass-production of goods and houses - mechanisation, mass and organisation dominate life. Only a few small spaces are left for personal realisation: especially in the countryside - as long as that is not also dominated by impersonal powers - and outside society, in the community of the family, in various cultural communities, or - for those who have been able to preserve that - in the sphere of personal life (Bierens de Haan, 1939:309).

This quotation captures rather well the cultural mood and moral passions of the 'personalist' orientation, which surfaced in Dutch post-war research on free time. In a pre-war Dutch text-book on sociology, Bouman, himself an adherent, traces the tradition to the romantic-irrationalist writings of philosophers like Rousseau, Hamann, Herder and Goethe (Bouman, 1938:156). In terms of social thought, the turn of the century was significant for the so-called 'generation of 1890', with authors like Bergson, Dilthey, Sorel and Weber. What these and others within the tradition of the *Geisteswissenschaften* had in common is their intellectual reaction against 19th century mechanistic naturalism and utilitarianism, against social-Darwinism and the related optimistic belief in progress and civilisation (Jonker, 1988). Mechanic rationalism neglected issues of human consciousness, of morality and culture. It treated human culture as subjected to the same sort of laws of explanation as nature. Instead, cultural reality had to be 'interpreted' (*verstehen*). Central were Tönnies' concerns about the transformation from *Gemeinschaft* to *Gesellschaft*, Weber's notion of the *Entzauberung der Welt* and Simmel's thesis of the dissociation of objective and subjective culture. One shared a feeling of despair, of excitement and catastrophe, of crisis, dismantling and weakening. Modernity was looked upon with some concern, or with an overtly critical eye. It would result in a passive mass of individuals lacking a real personality, institutional bonds or inner needs, victims of the technical rationality of mass- production, the free market and democratised mass politics. The cinema, newspapers, before the war the radio and after it the television, these all exposed people to the dangers of the world writ large:

> Because of this, the people whose life formerly was enclosed within the boundaries of an enclosed existence, now get involved in all what the world offers, in pleasure and diversion, in knowledge and new opinions, in everything that happens, in all the rumours and the multiplicity of social life. It is obvious that

this makes man different, whether he lives on the countryside or not; he has become involved in the massive, the stirring and the superficial totality of modern social life.
(Bierens de Haan, 1939:171-2)

It was this worried culturalist or personalist tradition that dominated the post-war study of free time and culture. The classifications used to describe and analyse people's free time activities mirrored a concern for cultural and personal integration. Central were dichotomies such as those between culture and pleasure, personality and instinct, inner conviction and outward orientation, individual and society, form and passivity.

However irrational the mood, nevertheless this orientation was based upon firm rationalist assumptions. Social order was thought to be based upon a common culture, in turn depending on culturally integrated personalities and a healthy socialisation, bound together by a clear notion of good and evil, the cultivated and the vulgar. The one relied on and defined the other. A weak cultural integration resulted in a distorted socialisation, and thus in dependent personalities, deprived of a notion of direction and inner motives, and vice versa.

Looked at from the perspective of its public economic and cultural resource-base, this episode in the study of free time was linked to three programmes (see Michielse, 1978). First, it was related to an alternative sort of popular education. In contrast with the rationalist educational programme of the Popular Universities, which was based on notions of enlightenment and aimed at the distribution of scientific knowledge, a more irrational, romantic or tradition oriented educational practise had come into being, inspired by the German model of 'Kulturbildung' and based within the 'Volkshogeschool' (Popular High School). The first one had opened in 1932. The programmes celebrated local folklore, the community and harmonic personalities (Ibid:122). Secondly, this personalist outlook was well in line with post-war moral concerns amongst denominational elites, anxiously trying to control their own regions and 'pillars'. Thirdly, the orientation coincided with so-called personalist-socialism. This was a programme of socialist reform, shared by members of the Dutch social-democratic movement, aiming at the construction of a new socialist personality, based on ideals of pure, undefiled communal life.

The members of these various programmes saw their projects and positions threatened by the coming of new times. Mass media, mass markets and mass communications had opened up the conditions on which traditional cultural elites could thrive as authorities of knowledge, morality and taste. Due to an increase in the flow of information, products and images, they no longer could monopolise the mediation between the here and there, the present and the future.[8]

Social Modernism and the Welfare State (1955-1975)

Post-war developments were rather ambivalent and it is not surprising that in the Netherlands they have been the object of some debate amongst historians (see e.g. Blom, 1988; Messing, 1988; De Liagre Bohl and Meershoek, 1989). Central is the question whether or not the post-war period can be characterised in terms of a restoration, or in terms of a renewal (Dieleman, 1991).

Perhaps this is not an either-or issue. Maybe the post-war reconstruction of Dutch society was so successful because it could rely on a firmly institutionalised culture of consent, based on a solid co-operation between the various denominational and social-democratic elites (the doctrine of pacification-democracy) and on a consensus-based economic policy (the doctrine of corporatism). During the first post-war period, economic policies were primarily targeted at economic growth, re-industrialisation and full employment. At least until the early 1960s, this resulted in Holland becoming a European enclave of low labour costs. It was upon this economic, political and cultural foundation that the Dutch post-war welfare state, together with its consumer culture, became established.

Of course, the increase in cultural restlessness, against which denominational elites had reacted in so panic a fashion, did not take place over night. Pre-war generations had already experienced Hollywood films, the products of the Ford Motor Company and early jazz music with its mundane, city-centred culture of pleasure. But in one way or another, although they were the cause of some moral concern, their general impact remained confined. These modern pleasures could still be managed and controlled by all kinds of local/regional licensing and censoring strategies. Besides, most of these pastimes were still reserved for the better-off. Pre-war Americanisation was still very much a restricted phenomenon, embedded in prevailing production-oriented and pillarised cultural relations. That all changed rather rapidly in the post-war years. The signs of a new time were carried to Holland by the American and Canadian liberating forces. For the average Dutch woman the new times were symbolised by nylon stockings, for men by cigarette-blends like Lucky Strike and Roxy, for youth by chewing gum, jeans, jazz, Dixieland, the jitterbug and the American Armed Forces Network (Van Elteren, 1990).

But that was just the beginning. In the fifties and sixties the Dutch consumer market was flooded by newly conserved food products and mass produced cars, by new streamlined vacuum cleaners, washing machines, refrigerators and, last but not least, televisions. Consumer culture spread, aided by American-imported mass-communication, mass-production, mass-marketing strategies and mass-oriented super stores (Ours, 1985).

Modernisation equalled enlargement of scale. Places like Manhattan or Chicago, with their high-rise buildings, broad avenues, grid-like street pattern, busy traffic, functional lay-out and restless mobility started to form the ultimate ideal alongside which Dutch urban planners became active. Cities became looked upon as bodies or systems, a policy instrument, the spatial parts of which could be structured and planned in terms of differentiated functions such as those of work, traffic, living and recreation (Van der Cammen and De Klerk, 1986).

The conditions for a consumer culture to develop were there. Especially during the sixties Dutch loans rose rapidly and affluence increased. Besides, the establishment of the five-day working week and the inclusion of the right to paid holidays in collective labour agreements, for some signalled the beginning of something like a leisure society (see Beckers, 1983). As far as the division of labour was concerned, not only did the number of people working in the agricultural sector further decrease, but also the number of people working in the industrial sector gradually started to decline. Instead the amount of white collar workers, active in service and administration sectors increased rapidly. Many were the references made to Burnham's idea of the 'managerial revolution' or to Riesman's notion of the coming into being of the 'post-industrial society'.

As far as state policies were concerned, Bell's notion of *The End of Ideology* mirrored the belief that former class, or pillar-based, ideological controversies had lost their importance in Dutch post-industrial society. Thanks to a growth of affluence, class conflicts would diminish. And thanks to mass democracy, a pluralist and Fabian state-apparatus would develop, based upon the notion of the self-reliant citizen. Future policies could focus on a fair and equal redistribution of economic and cultural resources, enhancing a generalised sort of well-being. This redistribution could become something of a technical issue. The specific targets would be set by consensus-oriented politics and the knowledge needed to do the job would be delivered by social scientists. The programmes could be carried out by a growing professionally-trained functionary elite, less involved with traditional moral-ideological concerns, occupying an expanding state-bureaucracy and a growing number of public institutions generated to do the job.

At first, this 'rationalisation' or 'de-politicisation' of politics did not endanger Dutch denominationally segmented social structure. Although pillarised segregation lost much of its emotional charge and would in time lose much of its effects on everyday life - in line with a general secularisation of Dutch society - nevertheless the Dutch welfare state developed along structures already established at the beginning of the century, based upon the so-called 'subsidiarity principle', the doctrine of 'autonomy in one's own circle'. Quangos and public initiatives came to dominate the Dutch model of the welfare state and the central state took care that it did not intervene in the more substantive social and cultural rights of the various denominational blocks.

Within this context, also the issue of free time became 'de-politicised'. Free time was regarded less and less as something actively to be defended against production interests or as a domain of cultural reform and reproduction. Instead it became looked upon as a realm of individual choice and consumption, be it that such individual consumption was expected to take place in the 'natural' context of the nuclear family and was beset with a growing number of social programmes organising what was called 'equal access'. Class-based subcultures became looked upon as remnants of the past, the result of some sort of 'cultural lag', expected to be disappearing soon thanks to an increase in affluence and status aspirations. Whenever free time was problematised, it was either in terms of an uneven distribution of economic and cultural resources (based upon the doctrines of equality of opportunity or the spreading of culture) or in terms of possible cognitive disabilities, caused by a lack of educational preparation, precluding people from spending their free time satisfactorily (Beckers, 1983). In either case however, the hidden assumption was that when people would have sufficient resources and adequate knowledge, they would most certainly share the goals and interests of the generalised middle class citizen, a model in which ballet dancing and classical music quite evidently ranked higher than the jitterbug or Dixieland.

Social Differentiation of Free Time

This new phase of increased 'modernism' can easily be traced to the research on free time. In the winter of 1955/56, following a national representative study on radio listening and free time, the Dutch 'Centraal Bureau voor de Statistiek' (Central Bureau for Statistics) initiated an ambitious project to study the free time activities of the Dutch population writ large. Responsible for this project were two sociologist, P. Thoenes and C. Lammers, both belonging to a post-war generation of sociologists aiming at what they themselves proclaimed as a 'modernisation' of Dutch social theory and research. The study is legitimated as follows:

> it is evident, that a society which changes quickly is quickly unknown and that such a lack of knowledge is unacceptable in a society, which is more and more ordered along centrally established viewpoints. Where transformations are evident and ordering inescapable, extensive practical research is a first necessity
>
>   (Centraal Bureau voor de Statistiek, 1957:5)

The research project involved a survey and time-budget analyses amongst a national representative sample of 7200 people, supplemented with 3300 interviews amongst smaller sub-categories of the population and 250 in-depth interviews. In the latter case, the interviewers also observed people's interiors and social relations. Thus, a combination of quantitative-correlational and qualitative-narrative research methods was used.

The project resulted in 10 reports dealing separately with, e.g. 'the spending of evenings and weekends', 'visiting cinemas', 'reading habits', 'club activities', 'visiting theatres and concerts', 'making music', 'social class and free time', 'religious belonging and free time' and 'age and free time'. The aim was to get a simple and straight forward national representative overview of free-time behaviour, predominantly to have an impression of how various sections of the Dutch population made use of an increasing number of publicly financed free-time provisions, such as in the domain of the media, sports, recreation and culture, and how the differentiations and developments involved could be explained.

The introduction of television in Dutch society necessitated new research. In 1957 the CBS published a research report on 'School Youth and Television', in 1958 followed by 'Visiting Entertainment and the Ownership of Television' and in 1960 by 'Radio, Television and the Spending of Free Time'. In 1962-63 a second national research project was initiated, which however, from a theoretical and methodological point of view, had a much smaller scope. The study nevertheless marks the first attempt in the Netherlands to investigate underlying dimensions of free-time behaviour through cluster analysis (see CBS, 1966).

This series of CBS-studies signalled the beginning of a productive episode in the history of the Dutch study of free time and a new phase in social theory in general; an episode in which the study of free time became dominated by applied correlational survey research, developed in the context of an evolving welfare state and its various public institutions. Central was the issue of the social differentiation of free-time behaviour and the relation between that differentiation and the social distribution of economic and cultural resources.

In Amsterdam, at the 'Sociografische Werkgemeenschap' (Sociographic Working Community), three studies were organised with regard to free time related issues, commissioned by the municipality of Amsterdam. Two dealt with youth and free time and one with changes in how labourers spend their weekends, due to the implementation of the five-day working week. Local government wanted to know what consequences the lengthening of compulsory education and the introduction of the five-day working week would have on the free time activities of youth. Was there a need for subsequent provisions and how were public subsidies to be allocated? In *Jeugd en vrije tijd in Amsterdam* (Youth and Free Time in

Amsterdam), the main focus was on the relation between the working and living environment of different categories of youth and their attitude towards free time and free time behaviour. The spatially situated character of the study mirrored the sociographic background of the institute. Otherwise, the study followed the canons of modern correlational survey research (see Heinemeijer, 1959).

In 1968, the sociologist R. Wippler published his doctoral thesis on *De sociale determinanten van het vrije tijdsgedrag* (The Social Determinants of Free Time Behaviour). It was based upon a study done in 1965 for the provincial government of Groningen and for the *Nederlandse Maatschappij van Nijverheid en Handel* (Dutch Society for Industry and Trade). Both wanted to know the need for recreational facilities in Groningen and what factors influenced that need. The recreational activities were studied in the context of peoples' more general free-time behaviour. A factor analysis was used to differentiate the various activity patterns. Fifteen dimensions of free time behaviour were correlated with fifty background variables, concerning, for example, the sort of work people did (at stake were the famous congruency and contrast hypotheses), their level of education, social class etc. Education appeared to have the strongest differentiating power.

In Utrecht, from the second half of the 1960s onwards, a group of sociologists chose free time as their primary object of study. In 1969 Kamphorst and Spruijt published an article propagating a *value free* approach to free time. This however did not preclude them from also arguing in favour of a programme for free time education; youth had to learn to choose and to enjoy its free time, instead of just being preoccupied with work (Kamphorst and Spruijt, 1969). In 1971 Kamphorst published the result of a survey, commissioned by the municipal theatre of Utrecht, investigating how the local population spent its evenings (Kamphorst and van Besouw, 1971). One of the conclusions is that free-time behaviour has become too differentiated to try and summarise it in terms of meaningful patterns by way of factor analysis (Ibid:23).

Stratification and Functional Analyses

This modernist phase in Dutch free time research was originally initiated by members of a new generation of social scientists, that had received their academic education in post-war years. For them, the classification of people's activities along distinctions such as those between the active and the passive, the cultivated and the vulgar, culture and pleasure, expressed situated status aspirations. Free time behaviour became less regarded as the expression of a level of civilisation or of a level of cultural integration and more as the expression of existing socio-cultural inequalities.

In one of the first national surveys on free time, undertaken by the 'Centraal Bureau voor de Statistiek' (Central Bureau for Statistics), Thoenes typifies 'passive recreation' as 'a perhaps slightly dubious term' (CBS, 1957a:27). And in the research on youth and free time in Amsterdam, the attitudes towards free time are no longer regarded as an expression of a level of degeneration or massification, but as an indication of the 'cultural structure' of the areas involved.

What had taken place was a relativist transformation in the relation between science and morality. The social ontology of political and denominational elites became the object of what was called a scientific 'demythologisation'.

From the perspective of the intellectual field involved, this relativist turn in the social analysis of free time can be linked to two mutually related developments: (a) a turn towards American sociology and (b) a growing interest in issues of social stratification.

For a post-war generation of sociologist, social theory from the land of the former occupier had lost its attractiveness. German idealist social thought, as well as the tradition of sociography, became regarded as a remnant of the past, as a product of a particularistic European tradition, as 'classical' social theory. Instead, North America appeared to be not only the home of nylon stockings and Lucky Strikes, but also the place were a totally new, more open, and truly 'scientific' brand of sociology had developed, a type of sociology also better attuned to the task of constructing a modern, more open, socially mobile and rationally planned society. The Dutch post-war field of social theory gradually became dominated by the intellectual triangle of Parsons, Merton and Lazarsfeld. Central were various versions of functional analyses, coupled with a methodology derived from the basic model of the experiment. As far as free time was concerned, what dominated the academic field was an analysis of the functional relation between free-time behaviour and various social and/or psychological characteristics. This could be based on 'strong' versions of functionalism (with the notion of function used as an explaining device in itself) or on 'soft' versions (in which functional relations are seen as relations of correspondence, in need of a further causal explanation).

Part of American functionalism formed a neo-evolutionist outlook on social history. Social evolution was interpreted in terms of a succession of stages of increasing differentiation and integration, in the course of which societies increased their adaptive capacity and thus their control over their natural and cultural environment. On top of this history of 'modernisation' there was of course America, with its flexible and mobile labour market, secularised, rationalised and individualised culture, democratised politics, its educational revolution and open stratification structure (Turner and Turner, 1990).

It is this issue of the social stratification of Dutch society which captured 'modern' sociological attention in post-war Holland

(Gastelaars, 1985; Jonker, 1988). But then, this provided those concerned with a new intellectual and public platform, linking new intellectual interests to new public concerns and resources. Dutch society had to be 'modernised', freeing itself from the last remainders of a stratification system based upon particularistic values and prestige relations. Subcultural deviancies from main stream middle-class standards were looked upon as belonging to a 'proletarian rearguard', soon to be integrated in a self-evident march towards value pluralism and social mobility.[9]

Within this perspective, there was no space any longer for rules concerning the correct style or the correct way of spending one's free time, thus hindering social mobility by monopolising educational or cultural resources. Parsons himself typified the cultural elitist critique of writers like Ortega Y Gasset and T.S. Eliot on 'modern' society as a sign of a further secularisation, now not only affecting religious thought, but also classical social theory itself (Parsons, 1977:194). Modernisation needed a more open and plural value system, based upon generalised notions of rationality, democracy, equality of opinion and individual responsibility.

The only scientific foundation left in the evaluation of people's behaviour was the notion of functional integration, related to the project of modernisation itself. The value pluralism promoted was far from absolute and still based on solid scientific certainties. Central was the problem of the relation between a changing economic structure, leading towards a more consumption-oriented society, and the general value-structure. In his study on the 'Social Determinants of Free Time Behaviour', Wippler (1968) defined free time as a social problem in so far as the value pattern of a society was not adjusted to its social structure. In America, he noticed, a traditional ascetic value system was replaced by a more hedonistic one. This mirrored a transformation in the social structure of America, from production to consumption. In the latter case adhering to Puritanism would lead to social frictions. In that same line of thought Kamphorst and Spruijt (1969) argued for a leisure-education programme, freeing youth from its preoccupation with work.

In relation to this change in social theory, a transformation had occurred in the social position and orientation of the researchers concerned. Whereas in previous periods they had linked their intellectual projects to 'public reason' and the edification of a well-informed public, during the post-war years their orientation moved towards the state. Either based upon Merton's model of social engineering with its ideal of functional rationality, or upon Mannheim's model of the *freischwebende Intelligenz* with its ideal of substantive rationality, social scientists placed themselves above political discourse, on the level of an expanding state functionary. Both were involved with the fulfilment of the new generalised needs of the middle-class citizen, thus enhancing the citizens individual freedom of choice, that is as far as such freedom would not endanger generalised social interests (Thoenes, 1962, see also Bauman, 1987). For social scientists the primary task was to investigate the stratified leisure needs of the population and the stratified use made of facilities and provisions. Both were important to legitimate policy decisions, based as much on 'what the system needs' as on 'what the people want'.

The Crisis of 'Social Modernism' (1975-1990)

As elsewhere in Western Europe, in the Netherlands the 1970s signalled a gradual change in the optimism and reassurance with which the welfare state had been given shape in the decades preceding. That is not to say that the ongoing expansion of welfare programmes came to an abrupt halt. On the contrary, in later analyses of the period, authors somewhat surprisingly take notice of the fact that the 1970s still showed a steady increase in collective expenditure on public facilities (education, recreation, sports, culture, health care etc.) until well into the beginning of the 1980s (Schuyt, 1991). This despite the fact that in 1975 unemployment passed the symbolic figure of 200,000 and despite a general awareness of the structural character of the problems concerned. The 'pillarised' structure within which the Dutch model of the welfare state had been given shape, with its many semi-public, denominationally segmented and corporatist institutions, had developed a strong dynamic of its own. It had produced an 'administrative solidarity', supported by numerous pressure groups (sometimes referred to in terms of a 'fifth power') having their own connections with public bureaucracy (Jolles and Stalpers, 1978). Besides, national income and the average purchasing power of Dutch citizens were still rising. Given this, an overall confidence in and reliance on the problem-solving capacities of the welfare state and its institutions kept on dominating public thought.

Yet, at the same time, the private sector slowly started to reclaim some of its lost public prestige. Fierce debates took place concerning the role of labour costs in labour-market policies. Captains of industry wrote angry public letters to central government, complaining about their public image and asking for a state-enforced loan fix in order to strengthen their international competitiveness. Based on an increase in the demand on public expenditure, such as for public health and social security, more and more questions were raised with regard to the 'manageability' of the welfare state (SCP, 1984). The levelling of income inequalities, the post-war product of corporatist redistribution policies, slowly came to a halt (Ibid.).

This situation of 'deferred confidence' lasted until the beginning of the 1980s. A second economic crisis hit Dutch society and unemployment figures started to rise above 800,000. Job-decline in the traditional industrial sectors increased rapidly, while job-growth in the service sector stagnated. For the first time since the war the average purchasing power, as well as the average amount of free-time related goods per household, were in decline and income inequalities started to rise (Ibid.). This time a drop in national income and a further increase in collective expenditure (due to a growing demand on social security programmes: SCP 1992) resulted in a restructuring of the welfare-state order. Attention shifted from the North-West European model of the welfare state (using the German or Swedish model as primary points of orientation) to the Anglo-American model of the neo-liberal state (Reaganomics and Thatcherism). Privatisation, commercialisation, decentralisation, deregulation and retrenchment became the benchmarks of policy narratives, thus expressing the decline of the problem-solving capacities of a national state faced with a global restructuring of the economy.

As much within as between the various leisure policies, public support shifted from programmes aimed at 'equal access' and 'well-being', to programmes striving for economic gains and 'public response'. This implied, amongst other things, a relative shift in public support from sports and recreation towards arts and tourism. The responsibilities for welfare-oriented policies (social security, social work, sports and recreation) became relatively decentralised to lower levels of government, while central government held a firm interest in leisure policies thought of as beneficiary to the economy (e.g. the arts and tourism) (Van der Poel, 1993; Bevers, 1993).

On the level of local government this decentralisation of welfare-oriented policies, accompanied by a stagnation of central government funds, implied an increase in budgetary problems. As far as major cities were concerned, that budget was already under growing pressures from the 1970s onwards. This was due to a further de-industrialisation of the local economy, rising unemployment figures and uneven suburbanisation processes, with middle-class families moving out to surrounding towns, weakening the city's economic resource base (WRR, 1990). City-governments developed a more active economic policy, trying to attract economic capital, labour opportunities, purchasing power and higher-income groups. The result was that cities found themselves increasingly competing amongst each other, not only regionally or nationally, but more and more also transnationally, with city-representatives travelling all over the world, to try and lure new businesses and tourists to town (e.g. Kreukels, 1993).

Cities became the focus of fresh public attention, a second post-war 'urban renaissance'. This was carried along by the growing necessity for city-governments to position themselves on business, housing, tourist and consumer markets, as well as by the purchasing power and lifestyle interests of more affluent sections of the population (fractions of the so-called new middle class and the 'early retired'). Part of this repositioning or 'face-lifting' strategy was a growing interest in leisure and culture. This expressed itself not only in a 'beautification' of the inner city, but also in a refurbishment of the leisure and cultural infrastructure, (re)building restaurants, hotels, museums, theatres, pavement cafés, waterfronts, festivals and shopping areas, all given shape according to the latest fashions in architecture and consumption (Mommaas and Van der Poel, 1989; Burgers, 1992).

Pluralisation and Fragmentation

Despite increasing economic problems, the 1970s and 1980s turned out to be a 'Golden Era' for Dutch academic free-time research. Linked to a continuous administrative interest in people's use of a range of free-time facilities, a small but steady stream of public research funds had developed. Together with the ongoing expansion of Dutch universities, based upon a steady increase of students, and the expansion of an administrative functionary involved with issues of free time, this formed an important resource base for the establishment of something like an self-reliant free time research and policy profession. In 1976, this resulted in, and was further enhanced by the formation of the 'Interuniversitaire Werkverband Vrijetijd' (Inter-university Working Group on Free Time), an initiative bringing together Dutch and Flemish scholars active in free time research. In 1982 the IWV launched its own journal, *Vrijetijd en Samenleving* (Leisure and Society).

In institutional terms, free time research during these years was dominated by several centres of research, each functioning around specific key-persons and based upon specific policy-links, and each developing its own research identity.

At the State University of Utrecht, Kamphorst and his team changed their research agenda: socio-demographic variables no longer sufficed to explain a pluralised domain of leisure. Instead, attention was directed to personal biographies. By 1983, several quantitative-correlational research projects culminated in *Vrijetijdsgedrag in het perspectief van socialisatie* (Free-time behaviour in the perspective of socialisation) (Kamphorst en Spruijt, 1983). This PhD focuses on the relation between the age at which a certain activity is learned and the continuation of that activity during the life course. In later years attention shifted towards qualitative in-depth research, resulting in the construction of a so-called 'life cylinder model', incorporating the various factors influencing the formation of leisure interests during the life course (Kamphorst, 1991).

At the same time, correlational research kept on playing a substantial role. In 1973 the 'Sociaal en Cultureel Planbureau' (Social and Cultural Planning Bureau) was established, a quasi-independent research and planning institute for central government, focusing on issues of public welfare. From 1975 onwards the SCP would publish the results of a nationally representative time budget analyses, held every five years.

The data continued to be used to study the social differentiation of free time and free-time behaviour. However, the former functional approach was gradually replaced by a more individualised perspective based on theories of the allocation of time and money, derived from, for example, Linder (1968) and Becker (1976) (see Ganzeboom, 1984, 1988). During the second half of the 1980s, Wim Knulst, the sociologist mainly responsible for analysing the SCP-data, had recourse to rational choice theory (Knulst, 1989). Based on Bourdieu (1984), special attention is given to the role of cultural competence in mediating social class and leisure. In addition the author drew upon the work of Berlyne (1971) and Scitovsky (1976).

Knulst explicitly legitimised this shift to a more individualised approach, by pointing at the condition of a more open and plural society. People's activities had become less dictated by collective norms or institutional constraints. Instead, leisure behaviour should be interpreted as the result of the interrelation between the relatively stable preferences and competencies of individuals and changing temporal and financial circumstances (see Knulst, 1990, 1991).

As these developments have already indicated, during the late 1970s and especially the 1980s, the academic interest in issues of free time and culture went along with an increase in, and a pluralisation of, social theoretical interests. First a pluralisation takes place with regard to the conceptualisation of free time as such: along more objectivist or positivist definitions of free time, more detailed attention is given to the *construction* of free time. Secondly, a pluralisation occurs concerning methodology: alongside ongoing quantitative research, more detailed attention is given to the hermeneutic dimension of leisure, to the images, meanings and sign-values attached, and hence to qualitative research. Thirdly, after some fifty years of involvement with free-time *behaviour*, new attempts are made to analyse free-time developments from a more institutional, historical and spatial perspective.

During the second half of the 1970s the dominance of quantitative survey research, itself associated with a technical-instrumental approach to social reality, became challenged by the human geographer Beckers, in those days working at the Agricultural University of Wageningen. Amongst others stimulated by the research of Rhona Rapoport in the London borough of Brent, by German Critical Theory, and by the early structurationist ideas of Anthony Giddens, Beckers opted for a more theory-informed qualitative approach, studying people's recreational behaviour in the context of their biography and situated living conditions, couched within an action-research model. In line with these ideas, a study was carried out in two socially contrasting neighbourhoods in the city of Breda. The study, commissioned by the 'Rijksplanologische Dienst' (National Planning Service), examined the recreational relevance for women of their living environment (see Van 't Eind *et al.*, 1981). In 1983 Beckers published his PhD, the result of a first attempt to analyse the institutional history of the public organisation of Dutch recreation and free time from the beginning of the 20th century onwards.

Beckers' attempts to move Dutch recreational and free-time studies in a more theoretically informed direction were followed in 1985 by a conference, organised at Tilburg University, entitled 'Everyday Life, Leisure and Culture'. A large delegation of British researchers, working in the fields of cultural and leisure studies, was invited to Holland. The conference was organised by the 'Centrum voor Vrijetijdskunde' (Centre for Free Time Studies - a joint venture between Tilburg University and the 'Nederlands Wetenschappelijk Instituut voor Toerisme' (Dutch Scientific Institute for Tourism, a polytechnic in Breda). It was aimed at a theoretically better informed, historically and institutionally oriented approach to leisure. Inspired by what was happening in British leisure studies - culminating in the 1980s LSA/BSA debate (see Bramham and Henry, Chapter 7) - the central idea was that leisure should not be studied as a reality 'sui generis', but as a socially constructed practice, chronically embedded within people's everyday life. Besides, the critique of authors like Gouldner, Elias and Giddens with regard to the 'orthodox consensus' in social theory in general, were thought of as highly applicable also to the 'conventional wisdoms' in Dutch leisure studies. Central was the critique that the study of free time had become encapsulated in the dualism between actor and structure. Free time was regarded as situated on the individual side of social reality, as a realm of individual freedom and choice, identity and self-realisation, the other side of which was the realm of structures, that is of constraints, alienation and suppression. As a result, issues of power and conflict disappeared from view. Looking for alternatives, inspirations were drawn from such diverse intellectual fields as British social history and cultural studies (e.g. the works of Stuart Hall c.s.), 'constructivist' human geography (Pred, Thrift c.s.), Giddens' structuration theory, Elias' figuration theory and Bourdieu's theory of social space (Mommaas and Van der Poel, 1984; Meijer, 1985). Free time became represented, not as an empty time-space, individually to be filled with discrete activities, but as embedded within *relations* or *interdependencies*, involving dimensions of culture and pleasure, distinction and identity, freedom and control, power and conflict.

Looking back, it seems as though the conference was propitiously planned. It took place at a turning point, not yet fully appreciated at the moment of the conference itself (although there were already some signs pointing at what later would more widely be labelled 'the postmodern condition'; see Featherstone, 1986, Mommaas, 1986,

Wynne, 1986). In the second half of the, 1980s, the 'new realism', and the restructuring of welfare policies was accompanied by a shift in public and academic leisure discourse. Free time became 'trivialised' as an area of cultural reproduction or redistribution, while at the same time more significant as a domain of economic revitalisation. Related to the growing importance of cities as agents of economic development, and city spaces as instruments of economic policy, this restructuring of the leisure discourse was accompanied by a reappraisal of the urban environment as a leisure space, that is as a space of not so much edification or redistribution, but as a space of consumption (of goods as much as of signs, images and fantasies), of 'cultural' tourism, architectural design, 'delightful' flanerie and sociability.

In the sphere of leisure research, the results were fourfold. First, attention was extended from conventional leisure fields such as sports and recreation to popular culture, lifestyles, consumption and tourism. Secondly, a relative shift in attention took place from rural to urban issues, from research related to the use and planning of outdoor recreation facilities to research aimed at the use and planning of an urban infrastructure of culture, consumption and pleasure. Thirdly, apart from sociology and pedagogics or youth studies, also geography, economics and, to a lesser degree, psychology became involved in the study of leisure, due to inter alia an increasing interest in leisure marketing and leisure management. Fourthly, there was a growing involvement of academic researchers with issues of leisure and free time not seeing themselves primarily as 'free-time researchers' but as involved in an expanding variety of related fields such as 'media studies', 'cultural studies', 'tourism studies', geography of tourism, anthropology of tourism, sociology of consumption, communication studies, urban studies, regional economics and so on.

When taken together, these developments implied a growing academic attention for free time or free-time related issues, while at the same time leading to something of a fragmentation of the self-proclaimed field of leisure studies. A brief and incomplete summary of ongoing research activities can illustrates this.

At the Department of Human Geography of the University of Amsterdam research is developed into people's time-spatial behaviour. Following the work of the Scandinavian geographer Hägerstrand, daily life is analysed as a path through time and space, the result of the interaction between people's life projects and institutional and spatial constraints. Attention is focused on the relation between the time-spatial use people make of the city, the type of household they live in, and their place of residence within the city (e.g. Vijgen and Van Engelsdorp Gastelaars, 1986). Building on this work, special attention is also given to the time-spatial significance of free time for women, being trapped between labour and household duties (Karsten and Droogleever Fortuijn, 1988; Karsten, 1992).

At the University of Groningen, the economic geographer Greg Ashworth and his team specialise in conceptual and substantive issues of city-marketing, urban tourism and heritage planning, building on research done in the UK and the Netherlands (e.g. Ashworth and Voogd, 1988, 1990; Ashworth and Turnbridge, 1990). Amongst others, the question is raised of whose heritage is being conserved and marketed, and who exactly is losing and gaining in the process (Ashworth, 1991).

At the Centre for Recreation and Tourism Studies of the Agricultural University of Wageningen, the human geographer Adrie Dietvorst explores the concepts of 'casco-planning' and of 'tourist-recreational complexes', resulting in a model for tourist-recreational product development, thought of as better attuned to the permanent transformation of tourist-recreational resources (e.g. Dietvorst, 1992). Partly in co-operation with the so-called Staring Centre, the Wageningen tradition of planning-oriented recreational research is continued, applying a variety of theoretical orientations ranging from Giddens' structuration theory (Anderson and De Jong, 1987) and environmental psychology (e.g. Klinkers, 1993), to Habermas' theory of the lifeworld (Lengkeek, 1992, 1994), versions of rational choice theory, and MacCannell's and Leipner's constructivist theories of tourism (Dietvorst, 1992).

At the Department of Social Sciences of Utrecht University the urban sociologist Jack Burgers co-ordinates a research programme involving various research assistants from various universities, working on case studies on the changing leisure function of inner cities. Attention is amongst others focused upon festivals (Boogaarts, 1992, Jókövi, 1992), the inner city as a homosexual space (Duyves, 1992), the role of the arts and pleasure in city development (Hitters, 1992; Kingma, 1992), the ethnography of pavement cafes (Oosterman, 1992) and the transformation of the relation between the public and the private (Burgers and Oosterman, 1992).

In 1986, an independent masters degree course on free-time studies was established at Tilburg University. Based on an increasing number of students and an expanding staff, in the years to follow, a multidisciplinary research programme has developed. Part of the energy is focused on the development of course material, on a codification and evaluation of the field of study and its history, and on conceptual and social theoretical issues (see e.g. Beckers and Van der Poel, 1990; Beckers and Mommaas, 1991). Topics dealt with concern amongst others the conceptualisation of free time and free-time behaviour (Mommaas and Van der Poel, 1984/85; Mommaas, 1993; Van der Poel, 1993), theories of leisure and lifestyle (Goossens, 1992; Mommaas, 1990), and the changing character of leisure and leisure research under conditions of late modernity (Mommaas, 1993; Van der Poel, 1993). In addition attention moves to empirical research: from the study of leisure policies (Van der Poel, 1993), the post-war transformation of youth cultures (Van der Heuvel, 1993), the changing role of leisure in urban restructuring (Mommaas, 1993; Mommaas and Van der Poel, 1989) and the imagery of the leisure experience (Goossens, 1993), to the flexibilisation of labour and free time (Beckers and Raaijmakers, 1991; Breedveld, 1995), the social significance and regulation of gambling (Kingma, 1991), the European leisure and tourism market (Gratton, 1991; Richards, 1994), sustainable tourism (Van der Straaten, 1992) and the construction of touristic city images (Dahles, 1993).

In the second half of the 1980s the IWV was transformed into the much broader 'Vereniging voor de Vrijetijdssector' (Union for the Free Time Sector), organising not only researchers and administrators, but also marketeers and managers, sharing free time as their primary object of concern. The transformation of the IWV into the VVS reflected a growing professionalisation of the leisure sector, something which partly can be related to a growing interest in topics of leisure and tourism marketing and management on the level of Dutch polytechnics.

Conclusion

Above, a by no means exhaustive reconstruction has been given of the historic trajectory of the study of free time in the Netherlands. That trajectory has been situated in between wider political-economic developments, and paradigmatic and institutional transformations in academia itself. In the course of time, every now and then, social scientists, mediating between wider institutional developments and the internal dynamics of their discipline, have turned people's pastimes into their object of concern. The focus of attention in this chapter has been on when and why they did so, and how they have subsequently reconstructed what elements of social reality into what sort of free time research questions.

Looking back at the above reconstruction, a first conclusion must be that for most of its history, the research of people's pastimes in the Netherlands was done by researchers who did not situate themselves in some sort of independent free-time oriented research profession. Most of them more or less stumbled upon the topic because of external policy agendas. For others, the study of people's pastimes formed part of more wider sociological or pedagogical research questions, dealing with, for example, civilisation, cultural integration, social stratification or the modern. It is only very recently that something of an independent line of research has developed, with researchers seeing each other as situated in a more or less shared field of research.

Nevertheless, when overlooking this discontinuous history, there are still some overall trends discernible. As such, the history of Dutch research on free time delivers an interesting historical cross-section of the way in which Dutch social scientists have involved themselves with national culture, and on what cultural and economic resource bases they build their judgmental authority.

Looked upon from a long-term perspective, the history can be said to involve an increasing appreciation for the complexity, heterogeneity and/or contextuality of free-time practices. That is not to say that all along, researchers have replaced general, law-like or objectivist explanations for interpretative methods, situated narratives and/or contextualised concepts, on the contrary. Nevertheless, also within the framework of correlational research, there is an increasing concern for pluriformity, for the complexity of social determination, and for 'agency'. Think here for instance of the increasing popularity of rational-choice theory, and of the growing attention for Bourdieu's notion of cultural competence (although often reduced to an isolated explanatory variable and thus totally disconnected from Bourdieu's relational theoretical framework).

Partly, this increasing appreciation of diversity and contextuality can be related to the internal logic of disciplinary fields, to the process in which subsequent generations of academics have tried to situate themselves in the academic field by criticising the hidden assumptions of predecessors, this according to the constant, but also permanently shifting academic 'doxa' (Bourdieu) of rationalism.

In the end, and rather paradoxically, this ongoing rationalisation (in the sense of *Entzauberung*, not in the sense of instrumentalism) seems to have robbed social researchers of the last objectivist foundations on which to ground their judgements of, and integrated interest in, people's free-time behaviour. From a cultural point of view, within academia, free time has become trivialised. And just at that moment at which something of an independent free-time research profession seemed to develop, founded upon the integrated and collective project of cultural participation, free time is under the pressure again of becoming fragmented into a variety of other topics (e.g. consumer studies, cultural studies, tourism studies, sport studies, time studies).

It is in this sense that recent developments can be said to indicate a move beyond former sentiments of scientific 'modernism' (Lyotard, 1986), or of instrumentalist 'legislation' (Bauman, 1987), and to express and sustain notions of an increasing cultural and epistemological ambivalence (Bauman, 1991) or reflexivity (Giddens, 1991).

However, at the same time, such an internal, self-sustaining or evolutionary interpretation will not suffice. In order to understand the internal dynamics involved, one at least has to relate these to wider societal transformations. First, there are those events which have produced the differential cultural and economic resources, actively incorporated by generations of researchers into distinctive research practices. In addition, one obviously also has to take into account the developments which have been responsible for changes in the object of study itself, thus forcing/enabling more open interpretations.

In very general terms, in the above, three institutional domains have been taken into consideration. First, there is the expansion and subsequent transformation of public social policies (the permanent construction/transformation of the social), based upon differential political coalitions and distinctive interventionist rationalities. Changes cited have included those from a public social reformism, based on a varying mixture of rational-enlightened and confessional-integrative patronage, to a standardised-democratic, state-bureaucracy based social Keynesianism or 'modernism', to a present-day consumer oriented neo- or social-liberalism. Secondly, there is a category of elements linked to changes in the sphere of production. Here, one could very generally summarise things by pointing at the gradual shift from the late 19th century establishment and subsequent maturation of a mass-manufacture based economy, to the expansion and subsequent domination of a service-based economy, the latter functioning in a globally more open and interdependent environment. This has been linked to issues such as changes in the organisation and division of labour, changes in class formations, and changes in the distribution of wealth and income. Thirdly, attention has been paid to the periodic opening up (in Giddens' terms: disembedding and re-embedding) of existing cultural spaces, beyond former boundaries of inclusion and exclusion. This can be linked to periodic increases in social and spatial mobility, the further 'mediatisation' of culture (from cinema, to national radio and television broadcasting, to global satellite and cable transmission), and the permanent and simultaneous expansion/implosion of the market within people's everyday lives. The latter can be kept responsible for separating more and more elements from the flow of everyday life, and turning them into the object of an itself globalising discourse of stylised consumption, personal choice and individual needs (e.g. with the help of psychology-based market research).

In the end, the result has been that scientists can no longer base their evaluation of people's pastimes upon some independent or privileged access to social reality or the future. The study of free time as such, consisting of a *mélange* of correlational, ethnographic and historical-institutional analyses, has stepped down from the realm of social science to that of social analysis. In accordance with Bauman, its new specialism is that of the translation/mediation between various cultural traditions and social situations:

> With pluralism irreversible, a world-scale consensus on world-views and values unlikely, and all extant Weltanschauungen firmly grounded in their respective cultural traditions (more correctly: their respective autonomous institutionalisation of

power), communication across traditions becomes the major problem of our time.
(Bauman, 1987:143)

In a certain sense, Richard Johnson, then Director of the Centre for Contemporary Cultural Studies at Birmingham, had already signalled something like that in his contribution to the 1985 conference in Tilburg when he stated:

There is a need for practical and theoretical mediation between the different agents that, together, have the means to change social circumstances more permanently. It is only as enablers of such alliances, as representing one group to another, that we have the right, in my opinion, to speak with any authority other than our personal voice. For youth workers, cultural researchers and leisure providers this is not going to be an easy lesson to learn!
(Johnson, 1987:217)

But whereas in Johnson's case the mediating role of social analysis was still based upon a clear collective project, a project which also informed the sort of analyses done and which provided some coherent links between the various investigations of leisure practices, the question is whether something similar still can be said to exist in today's study of free time. Is there something else, apart from an institutional space created by the academic training of a leisure profession, which integrates today's leisure studies? If so, what is its integrating research programme? And what is the role of the concept of leisure or free time in that programme? Or are these questions which have become slightly outdated, not just because the object of study has lost its integrating rational foundation, but also because the question for integration as such has become somewhat old fashioned?

REFERENCES

Anderson, E.A. and de Jong, H. (1987) *Recreatie in een veranderende maatschappij. Dl. 2: een casestudie.* Wageningen: Werkgroep Recreatie, LUW.

Arbeidsinspectie (1924) *Het gebruik van den vrijen tijd door de arbeiders*, Centraal verslag der arbeidsinspectie over 1923, Dep. van Arbeid. 's-Gravenhage: Handel en Nijverheid.

Ashworth, G.J. (1991) *Heritage Planning. Conservation as the Management of Urban Change.* Groningen: Geo.

Ashworth, G.J. and Turnbridge, J.E. (1990) *The Tourist-Historic City.* London: Belhaven.

Ashworth, G.J. and Voogd, H. (1988) Marketing the City: Concepts, Processes and Dutch Applications. *Town Planning Review*, vol. 59, 1, pp. 65-80.

Ashworth, G.J. and Voogd, H. (1990) *Selling the City: Marketing Approaches in Public Sector Urban Planning*. London: Belhaven.

Bachofen, J.J. (1980) *Das Muterrecht*. Frankfurt am Main (orig. 1861): Suhrkamp.

Bauman, Z. (1987) *Legislators and Interpreters*. Cambridge: Polity Press.

Bauman, Z. (1991) *Modernity and Ambivalence*. Cambridge: Polity Press.

Becker, G.S. (1976) *The Economic Approach to Human Behavior*. Chicago, Ill: The University of Chicago Press.

Beckers, T. (1983) *Planning voor vrijheid. Een historisch-sociologische studie van de overheidsinterventie in rekreatie en vrije tijd*. Wageningen:Vakgroep Sociologie, Landbouwhogeschool Wageningen.

Beckers, T. and Mommaas H. (eds) (1991) *Het vraagstuk van den vrijen tijd. 60 Jaar onderzoek naar vrijetijd*. Leiden: Stenfert Kroese.

Beckers, Th. and van der Poel, H. (1990) *Vrijetijd tussen vorming en vermaak. Een inleiding tot de studie van de vrijetijd*. Leiden: Stenfert Kroese.

Beckers, T. and Raaijmakers, S.F.J.M. (1991) *Tijd-ruimtelijke dynamiek: onderwerpen voor onderzoek*. Den Haag: PRO-Voorstudie 30.

Berlyne, D.E. (1971) *Aesthetics and Psychobiology*. New York: Meredith, Appleton-Century-Crafts.

Bevers, T. (1993) *Georganiseerde cultuur. De rol van overheid en markt in de kunstwereld*. Bussum: Coutinho.

Bierens de Haan, J. (1939) *Gemeenschap en maatschappij, een analyse van sociale verhoudingen*. Haarlem:Tjeenk Willink.

Blom, J.H.C. (1988) 'Nederland onder Duitse bezetting 10 mei 1940 - 5 mei 1945', in: Boogman, J. *et al. Geschiedenis van het moderne Nederland. Politieke, economische en sociale ontwikkelingen*. Houten: De Haan, pp. 481-516.

Blonk, A. (1929) *Fabrieken en Menschen. Een sociografie van Enschede*. Enschede: Tubantia.

Blonk, A., Kruijt, J.P and Hofstee, E.W. (1936) *De besteding van de vrije tijd door de Nederlandse arbeiders*. Amsterdam: Nutsuitgeverij.

Boogaarts, I. (1992) 'Food, fun, and festivals', in: J. Burgers (ed.) *De uitstad. Over stedelijk vermaak*. Utrecht: Van Arkel, pp. 119-133.

Bouman, P.J. (1938) *Van renaissance tot wereldoorlog. Vier eeuwen Europese cultuurgeschiedenis*, Paris, Amsterdam.

Bouman, P.J. (1940) *Sociologie*. Antwerpen/Nijmegen.

Bourdieu, P. (1984) *Distinction, a social critique of the judgement of taste*. London/New York: Routledge and Kegan Paul.

Bovenkerk, F. (1984) 'Haveman en Van Doorn over de ongeschoolde arbeider', in: *Sociodrome*, vol. 1, pp. 3-9.

Breedveld, K. (1995) '*Measuring Flexible Working-Time. Challenges from the Dutch Case*', in: *Statistics in Transition*, vol.2, no.4, pp. 645-662.

Bronnenboek (1952) Behorende bij het rapport betreffende het onderzoek naar de geestesgesteldheid van de massajeugd, Staatsdrukkerij- en uitgeverijbedrijf, 's-Gravenhage.

Burgers, J. and Oosterman, J. (1992) 'Het publieke domein. Over de sociale constructie van openbare ruimte'. *Amsterdams Sociologisch Tijdschrift*, vol. 19, 1, pp. 3-22.

Burgers, J. (ed.) (1992) *De uitstad. Over stedelijk vermaak.* Utrecht: Van Arkel.

Cammen van der, H. and Klerk de, L.A. (1986) *Ruimtelijke ordening. Van plannen komen plannen.* Utrecht/Antwerpen: Het Spectrum.

Centraal Bureau voor de Statistiek (1957) *Vrije-tijdsbesteding in Nederland. Winter 1955/'56, Deel 8, Sociaal milieu en vrije-tijdsbesteding.* Zeist:De Haan.

Centraal Bureau voor de Statistiek (1958) *Vrije-tijdsbesteding in Nederland, Winter 1955/'56, Deel 1, Methodologische inleiding.* Zeist 1957: De Haan.

Centraal Bureau voor de Statistiek (1966) *Vrije-tijdsbesteding in Nederland 1962-'63, Deel 8, Een samenvattend overzicht: karakteristieke patronen.* Zeist: De Haan.

Dahles, H. (1966) *The Social Construction of Mokum*, Paper presented at the LSA/VVS Conference 'Internationalization of Leisure Studies'. Tilburg (manuscript): Dec.

Dahles, H. (1993) 'De sociale constructie van Amsterdam', in: *Volkskundig Bulletin*, vol. 19, 2, pp. 161-180.

Darwin, C. (1955) *The Origin of Species by Means of Natural Selection.* Chicago (oorspr. 1859):Encyclopaedia Britannica.

Diederiks, H.A. (1987), *Van agrarische samenleving naar verzorgingsstaat : de modernisering van West-Europa sinds de vijftiende eeuw.* Groningen: Wolters-Noordhoff.

Dieleman, A. (1991) '*Tussen restauratri en veinieushing*', in: Th. Beckers and H. Mommaas (eds) *Het vraagstuk van den vrijen tijd. 60 Jaar onderzoek naar vrijetijd.* Leiden: Stenfert Kroese.

Dietvorst, A.G.J. (1992) 'Een model voor toeristisch-recreatieve produktontwikkeling', *Vrijetijd en Samenleving*, vol. 10, 2/3, pp. 21-29.

Dietvorst, A. (1994) 'Dutch Research on Leisure, Recreation and Tourism: a Review', in: C.P. Cooper and A. Lockwood (eds) *Progress in Tourism, Recreation and Hospitality Management*, Vol. 5. Chichester:Wiley, pp. 54-88.

Dresen-Coenders, L. (1991) 'Moderne jeugd en vrijetijd', in: Th. Beckers and H. Mommaas, *Het vraagstuk van den vrijen tijd. 60 Jaar onderzoek vrijetijd.* Leiden: Stenfert Kroese, pp. 115-121.

Duyves, M. (1992) 'Openbaar ruimtegebruik naar homoseksuele voorkeur in Amsterdam', in: J. Burgers (ed.) *De uitstad. Over stedelijk vermaak.* Utrecht:Van Arkel, pp. 73-100.

Eind, A. van 't, ter Veer, M. and Beckers, T. (1981) *Huisvrouwen, uit of thuis.* Wageningen:*Dl.* 2, Landbouwhogeschool, Vakgroep Sociologie Westers.

Elteren, M. van (1990) 'I'm free and I do what I want', in: G. Tillekens (red.), *Nuchterheid en nozems, de opkomst van de jeugdcultuur in de jaren vijftig.* Muiderberg: Coutinho, pp. 165-185.

Featherstone, M. (1986) 'Lifestyle and Consumer Culture, in: E. Meijer (ed.) *Everyday Life; Leisure and Culture.* Tilburg: Centre for Leisure Studies, pp. 157-169.

Galesloot, H. and M. Schrevel (eds.), (no date) *In fatsoen hersteld. Zedelijkheid en wederopbouw na de oorlog.* Amsterdam z.j: Sua.

Ganzeboom, H. (1988) *Leefstijlen in Nederland. Een verkennende studie.* Rijswijk: Sociaal en Cultureel Planbureau.

Ganzeboom, H. (1984) 'Tien jaar sociale en culturele rapporten', in: *Vrijetijd en Samenleving,* vol. 2/4, pp. 401-438.

Gastelaars, M. (1985) *Een geregeld leven. Sociologie en sociale politiek in Nederland 1925-1968.* Amsterdam: Sua.

Gellner, E. (1983) *Nations and Nationalism.* Oxford:Basil Blackwell.

Giddens, A. (1991) *Modernity and Self-Identity.* Cambridge: Polity Press.

Goossens, C. (1991) Het fenomeen leefstijl: suggesties voor marktonderzoek, in: *Jaarboek van de Nederlandse Vereniging van Marktonderzoekers* 91-92. Haarlem: De Vrieseborch, pp. 121-155.

Goossens, C. (1993) *Verbeelding van Vakanties.* Tilburg: Thesis.

Gratton, C. (1992) *Cultural Tourism in European Cities: A Case-Study of Edinburgh.* Paper presented at 'De Nederlandse Geografendagen' Nijmegen, November.

Gratton, C. (1991) *Leisure Markets in Europe.* Paper presented at the Conference 'Sport and Leisure Scotland 1991', Glasgow, (Manuscript) Tilburg.

Heinemeijer, W.F. (1959) 'De sociologische bestudering van de vrije tijd', in: *Sociologische Gids,* vol. 6/2, pp. 89-109.

Heuvel, M. van der (1993) *Von Patronaat tot Soos.* Tilburg: TUP.

Hitters, E. (1992) 'Particulier initiatief en lokale cultuur', in: J. Burgers (ed.) *De uitstad. Over stedelijk vermaak.* Utrecht: Van Arkel, pp. 133-155.

Johnson, R. (1987) *'Leisure Studies as Cultural Studies',* in: E. Mejer (ed.) *Everyday Life; Leisure and Culture.* Tilburg: Centium voor Vryitydstande, pp. 297-220.

Jókövi, E.M. (1992) *The Production of Leisure and Economic Development in Cities.* Paper presented at the International Conference on 'European Cities: Growth and Decline', The Hague, April.

Jókövi, M. (1992) 'De economische betekenis van stedelijk vermaak', in: J. Burgers (ed.) *De uitstad. Over stedelijk vermaak.* Utrecht: Van Arkel, pp. 101-119.
Jolles, H.M. and Stalpers, J.A. (1978) *Welzijnsbeleid en sociale wetenschappen.* Deventer: Van Loghum Slaterus.
Jonker, E. (1988) *De sociologische verleiding. Sociologie, sociaal-democratie en de welvaartsstaat.* Groningen: Wolters-Noordhoff/Forsten.
Kamphortst, T.J. (1991) 'Vrijetijd en biografie', in: Th. Beckers and H. Mommaas (eds.) *Het vraagstuk van den vrijen tijd. 60 Jaar onderzoek naar vrijetijd.* Leiden: Stenfert Kroese, pp. 255-265.
Kamphorst, T.J. and Spruijt, E. (1969) 'Vrije tijd en vrijetijdsbesteding; analyse en herorintatie', in: *Mens en Maatschappij,* vol. 44/2, pp. 82-100.
Kamphorst, T.J. and Spruijt, E. (1983) *Vrijetijdsgedrag in het perspectief van socialisatie.* Utrecht: Rijksuniversiteit Utrecht.
Kamphorst, T.J. van Besouw, m.m.v. L.J.M. (1971) *De avondbesteding van de Utrechtse bevolking.* Utrecht (Mededelingen van het Sociologisch Instituut van de RUU, nr.72): Rijksuniversiteit Utrecht.
Kamphorst, T. and Withagen, J. (1976) *Register van vrijetijdsonderzoek.* Amsterdam: Noord-Hollandse Uitgevers Maatschappij.
Kamphorst, T. and Withagen, J. (1984) *Register van vrijetijdsonderzoek.* Amsterdam: Band 2, KNAW/SWIDOC.
Karsten, L. (1989) *De achturendag: arbeidstijdverkorting in historisch perspectief 1817-1919.* Groningen: RUG.
Karsten, L. (1992) *Speelruimte van vrouwen. Zeggenschap over vrijetijd en vrijetijdsbesteding.* Amsterdam: Sua.
Karsten, L. and Droogleever Fortuijn, J. (1988) 'Combining Tasks in Everyday Life', *The Netherlands Journal of Housing and Environmental Research,* vol. 2, pp. 107-122.
Kingma, S. (1991) 'De legitimiteit van het kienen en bingo of de smaak van de noodzaak', in: D. Kalb and S. Kingma (eds) *Fragmenten van vermaak. Macht en plezier in de 19de en 20ste eeuw.* Amsterdam:Rodopi, pp. 125-155.
Kingma, S. (1992) *The Renaissance of the Nijmegen Waterfront 1992. A Political Economy of Pleasure in the Netherlands.* Paper presented at the Conference 'Theory, Culture and Society', Pittsburg, August.
Kingma, S. (1992) *Gaming Policy, Casino's and Internationalisation.* Paper presented at the LSA/VVS Conference 'Internationalization and Leisure Research', Tilburg, December.
Klinkers, P. (1993) *Het Landschap en zijn Recreatief Imago.* Wageningen: Rapport 250, Staring Centre-DLO.

Knulst, W. (1989) *Van vaudeville tot video, Een empirisch-theoretische studie naar verschuivingen in het uitgaan en het gebruik van media sinds de jaren vijftig.* Rijswijk: Sociaal en Cultureel Planbureau, Samsom, Alphen a/d Rijn.

Knulst, W. (1991) 'Vrijetijd, een kwestie van kiezen of delen', in: Th. Beckers and H. Mommaas (eds) *Het vraagstuk van den vrijen tijd. 60 Jaar onderzoek naar vrijetijd.* Leiden: Stenfert Kroese, pp. 265-275.

Kossmann, E.H. (1978) *The Low Countries 1780-1940.* Oxford: Oxford Un. Press.

Kreukels, T. (1993) 'Stedelijk Nederland: de actuele positie vanuit sociaal-wetenschappelijk perspectief', in: J. Burgers *et al.* (eds) *Stedelijk Nederland in de jaren negentig.* Utrecht: Van Arkel, pp. 9-39.

Kruijt, J.P. (1934) 'Arbeid en vrije tijd als sociologies probleem', in: *Volksontwikkeling*, vol. 15, pp. 33-46.

Lash, S. and Urry, J. (1987) *The End of Organized Capitalism.* Cambridge: Polity Press.

Lengkeek, J. (1992) 'Clubs, between lifeworld and system', *Loisir et Societé/Society and Leisure*, vol. 14, 2, pp. 447-464.

Lengkeek, J. (1994) *Een meervoudige werkelijkheid.* Wageningen: Mededelingen van de Werkgroep Recreatie, 20.

Liagre Bohl de, H. and Meershoek, G. (1989) *De bevrijding van Amsterdam. Een strijd om macht en moraal.* Zwolle: Waanders.

Linder, S.B. (1968) *The Harried Leisure Class.* New York: Columbia University Press.

Litjens, H.P.M. (1953) *Onmaatschappelijke gezinnen; sociologisch onderzoek naar de onmaatschappelijkheid te Maastrich*t. Assen: Van Gorcum.

Lynd, R.S. and Lynd, H.M. (1929) *Middletown, a study in American culture.* New York: Harcourt, Brace and World.

Lynd, R.S. and Lynd, H.M. (1937) *Middletown in Transition, A Study in Cultural Conflict.* New York: Harcourt, Brace and Comp..

Lyotard, J. (1986) *The Postmodern Condition: A Report on Knowledge.* Manchester: Manchester UP.

Manicas, P.T. (1987) *A History and Philosophy of the Social Sciences.* Oxford: Basil Blackwell.

Meijer, E. (1985) 'Inleiding tot de conferentiebundel', in: E. Meijer (red.), *Alledaags leven; vrijetijd en cultuur*, Conferentiebundel, Centrum voor Vrijetijdskunde, Tilburg, pp. 1-35.

Messing, F. (1988) 'Het economische leven in Nederland 1945-1980', in: J. Boogman *et al. Geschiedenis van het moderne Nederland. Politieke, economische en sociale ontwikkelingen.* Houten: De Haan, pp. 517-561.

Michielse, H.C.M. (1978) *De burger als andragoog. Een geschiedenis van 125 jaar welzijnswerk.* Meppel: Boom.

Mijnhardt, W.W. (1988) *Tot Heil van 't Menschdom. Culturele genootschappen in Nederland, 1750-1815*. Amsterdam: Rodopi.

Mommaas, H. (1986) 'Everyday Life; Leisure and Culture. Closing Address to the Conference', in: E. Meijer (ed.) *Everyday Life; Leisure and Culture*, Centre for Leisure Studies, Tilburg, pp. 57-72.

Mommaas, H. (1990) *Leisure, Culture and Lifestyle - The Works of Veblen, Weber and Simmel*. Paper presented at ISA Conference Madrid, Manuscript, Tilburg.

Mommaas, H. (1992) 'The City and Cultural Diversity, Mixing the Local and the Global'. *Vrijetijd and Samenleving*, vol. 10, 4, pp. 31-45.

Mommaas, H. (1993) *Moderniteit, vrijetijd en de stad. Sporen van maatschappelijke transformatie en continuiteit*. Utrecht: Van Arkel.

Mommaas, H. and van der Poel, H. 'Naar een sociologie van de vrijetijd? I: De omschrijving van het probleem, een evaluatie', in: *Vrijetijd en Samenleving*, vol. 2/4, PP. 475-506.

Mommaas, H. and van der Poel, H. (1984) 'Naar een sociologie van de vrije tijd? II: Vrijetijd en tijdsbesteding als product van sociaal handelen', in: *Vrijetijd en Samenleving*, 1985-3/1, pp. 9-44.

Mommaas, H. and van der Poel, H. (1989) 'Changes in Economy, Politics and Lifestyles: An Essay on the Restructuring of Urban Leisure', in: P. Bramham, I. Henry, H. Mommaas, and H. van der Poel (eds) *Leisure and Urban Processes*. London: Routledge, pp. 254-276.

Nationaal Instituut, (1946) *De toekomst der Nederlandse beschaving* (Conference report, Nijmegen, 28-30 augustus 1946), S.p.

Oosterman, J. (1992) *Parade der passanten. Over vertier, de stad en de terrassen*. Utrecht: Van Arkel.

Oude Engberink, G. (1987) *Minima zonder marge 1983-1986*. Rotterdam: GSD.

Ours, J.C. van. (1985) *Gezinsconsumptie in Nederland 1951-1980*. Meppel: Krips Repro.

Parsons, T. (1951) *The Social System*. The Free Press of Glencoe, Ill.

Parsons, T. (1977) *The Evolution of Societies* (ed. J. Toby). Englewood, Cliffs N.J: Prentice Hall.

Poel, van der, H. 'Media Policy in Europe; Compromising between Nationalism and Mass Markets'. *Leisure Studies*, vol. 10/3, pp. 187-202.

Poel, van der, H. (1991) 'Leisure Policy in the Netherlands', in: P. Bramham, I. Henry, H. Mommaas, and H. van der Poel (eds) *Leisure Policies in Europe*. Wallingford: CAB International, pp. 41-71.

Poel, van der, H. (1993) *De modularisering van het dagelijkse leven*. Amsterdam: Thesis Publishers.

Richards, G. (1994) 'Cultural Tourism in Europe', in: C.P. Cooper and A. Lockwood (eds) *Progress in Tourism, Recreation and Hospitality Management*. Vol. 5, Chichester: Wiley, pp. 99-115.

Roediger, D.R., and Foner, P.S. (1989) *Our Own Time: a History of American Labor and the Working Day.* New York:Greenwood Press.

Rowntree, B.S. and Lavers, G.R. (1952) *English Life and Leisure.* London: Longmans, Green and Co..

Schuyt, C.J.M. (1991) 'Op zoek naar het hart van de verzorgingsstaat', in: C.J.M. Schuyt, *Het hart van de verzorgingsstaat.* Leiden: Stenfert Kroese, pp. 3-19.

Scitovsky, T. (1976) *The Joyless Economy, an Inquiry Into Human Satisfaction and Consumer Dissatisfaction.* London: Oxford University Press.

Sociaal en Cultuur Planbureau, (1992) *Sociaal en cultureel rapport 1992.* Rijswijk: Sociaal en Cultureel Planbureau.

Sociaal en Cultuur Planbureau, (1984) *Sociaal en cultureel rapport 1984.* Rijswijk: Sociaal en Cultureel Planbureau.

Sociaal en Cultuur Planbureau, (1976) *Sociaal en cultureel rapport 1976.* Rijswijk: Sociaal en Cultureel Planbureau.

Spencer, H. (1851) *Social Statics, or the Conditions Essential to Human Happiness Specified and the First of them Developed.* London: Chapman.

Steinmetz, S.R. (1942) *Inleiding tot de sociologie.* Haarlem: De Erven F. Bohn.

Straaten, van der, J. (1992) 'Milieu-aantasting en toerisme', *Vrijetijd en Samenleving,* vol. 10/2-3, pp 85-97.

Stuart Hughes, H. (1988) *Consciousness and society. The reorientation of European social thought 1890-1930.* Brighton: Harvester Press.

Stuurman, S. (1983) *Verzuiling, kapitalisme en patriarchaat: aspecten van de ontwikkeling van de moderne staat in Nederland.* Nijmegen: Sun.

Thoenes, P. (1962) *De elite in de verzorgingsstaat.* Leiden: Stenfert Kroese.

Thomas, W.I. and Znaniecki, F. (1918) *The Polish Peasant in Europe and America.* New York: Knopf.

Thompson, E.P. (1967) 'Time, Work-Discipline and Industrial Capitalism', in: *Past and Present,* vol. 38, pp. 56-97.

Turner, S.P. and Turner, J.H. (1990) *The Impossible Science. An Institutional Analysis of American Sociology.* London: Sage.

Tylor, E.B. (1903) *Primitive Culture: Researches into the Development of Mythology, Philosophy, Religion, Language, Art, and Custom,* vol. 1. London: John Murray.

Vijgen, J. and van Engelsdorp Gastelaars, R. (1986) *Stedelijke bevolkingscategorieën in opkomst.* Amsterdam: Nederlandse Geografische Studies 22, UvA.

Weaver, S. (1988) 'The Political Ideology of Short Time: England 1820-1850', in: G. Cross (ed.) *Worktime and Industrialization. An International History.* Philadelphia: Temple University Press, pp. 77-102.

Wel van, F. (1988) *Gezinnen onder toezicht. De Stichting Volkswoningen te Utrecht 1924-1975.* Amsterdam: Sua.

Westen, M.G. (ed.) (1990) *Met den tooverstaf van ware kunst. Cultuurspreiding en cultuuroverdracht in historisch perspectief.* Leiden: Martinus Nijhoff.

Wetenschappelijke Raad voor het Regeringsbeleid (1990) (Netherlands Scientific Council for Government Policy), *Institutions and Cities: the Dutch Experience.* Reports to the Government, nr. 37, Revised Edition, The Hague.

Wippler, R. (1968) *Sociale determinanten van het vrijetijdsgedrag.* Assen: Van Gorcum.

Wouters, C. (1990) *Van minnen en sterven. Informalisering van omgangsvormen rond seks en dood.* Amsterdam: Bert Bakker.

Wynne, D. (1986) 'Living on 'The Heath', in: E. Meijer (ed.) *Everyday Life; Leisure and Culture.* Tilburg: Centre for Leisure Studies, pp. 125-133.

NOTES TO CHAPTER 4

[1] For a more detailed overview of free time and recreational studies see Kamphorst and Withagen (1976, 1984). For an alternative recent account see Dietvorst (1994).

[2] Bauman (1987) and others have made clear that this reformist concern was not just aimed at the introduction of a population, lagging behind in a patchwork of local folklore, into the civilized 'etiquette' of the new national citizenry. That would not be without danger. What was at stake was the creation of a national hegemony, legitimating the triumph of reason over passion, culture over nature, speech over violence. In the post-feudal order of the citizenry, authority no longer had to be based upon prestige, force, proprietorship or estate, but on reason.

[3] For instance, the categories included: hobbies (e.g. taking care of plants and dogs just for fun); listening to the radio; attending lectures, instructive meetings, museums or excursions; visiting theatres, cinemas, concerts or festive meetings; going to balls and dancings; frequenting cafes, for company or play; strolling around streets, markets etc.; visiting or receiving relatives, friends or neighbours *without* the purpose of playing games; visiting or receiving relatives, friends or neighbours *with* the purpose of playing games; visiting church and engaging in other religious duties.

[4] Attention is given to such things as the sort of clubs existing, their members and activities; to the books lent in the various local libraries and the sort of literature involved; to the artistic activities in the region, the quality of local performances and the public behaviour during those performances; to the interest for educational meetings

and lectures organized by the local workers union or the local 'Popular University'; to the contents and popularity of local newspapers and to local pastimes such as the keeping of small birds, drinking, sports and dancing.

[5] Mandelbaum, who made a study of social evolutionism, pictured its influence in that century stating: 'Even for those who did not regard social evolution as part of a single evolutionary process, and even when its truth was not taken to be a corollary of Darwin, it was widely believed, that the only scientifically correct way of understanding man's history was through the use of comparative methods, in which societies were seen as representing stages in human development' (Mandelbaum 1971:95 cited in Manicas 1987:71).

[6] Or as Bauman (1987:111) formulated it, through evolution theory the 'collective experience of a category cast in a "gardener" relation to all other categories, was recast as a theory of history'.

[7] 'Anti-social' would, I suppose, be the proper English translation. However, the notion of anti-social behaviour presumes some active stance against social order. The problem here was in a certain sense even worse. These people were considered not to have any commitment whatsoever with the prevailing social order. Hence they were addressed as 'un-socials'.

[8] Or as Bierens de Haan had stated in 1939: 'Railway, automobile, flying machine have made man extremely mobile and the world smaller. Press and telephone, radio and cinema make disappear all distance and continuously bring impressions and messages from all over the world. (...) Modern man continuously comes into contact with the most diverse opinions, with fragments of various cultures or culturelessness. The latest news and what is happening all over the world, political opinions and the demagogues of parties, the suggestions of advertisement and the banalities of the masses, all constantly penetrate his consciousness, at least if he doesn't consciously close himself off from it.' (Bierens de Haan 1939:170)

[9] Or as one of the leading sociologist expressed the mood later: 'Of course, against progress there is decline, one has to do with unbridgeable differences. But that was not popular in those days. Things of a subcultural character, we even linked that with notions of racism, with heredity, it was a reactionary notion' (Van Doorn in Bovenkerk 1984:8).

Chapter 5

Leisure Research in Spain

Roberto San Salvador del Valle

Introduction

The image of Spain is often connected with tourism, holidays, feasts as well as with a long history of unemployment. Leisure, in its many forms and shapes, has a long tradition in the country, particularly recently in Spain's quest for a distinctive national identity within the broad process of Europeanisation. However, leisure studies as a field of analysis, as such, represents a recent development and presents different problems in relation to both elements of this term, *leisure* and *studies*. On the one hand, leisure researchers, linked to the so-called *animación sociocultural*, maintain a holistic approach to present reality, which is defined as stagnant and isolated from the European context. On the other hand, other leisure researchers are looking for new scenarios with the objective of connecting Spanish experiences with those of other European countries, in an active and transnational way. This is the main struggle in the Spanish leisure studies between the old *action-reflection model* of animation and the new reality-research option of leisure studies.

There is always the question of appropriate terminology. There are two words used to refer to leisure: the leisure word itself ('ocio') and the term free-time ('tiempo libre'). There is a conceptual ambiguity between them which has resulted in authors presenting contradictions and exhibiting a lack of conceptual accuracy.

The term, leisure, has two different meanings. It is associated with its Latin root, opposed to 'tripalium' or 'nec-otium' and connected with the idea of gratuity, non-work and freedom. On the other hand, this term carries a pejorative meaning as shown in adjectives such as leisurely ('ocioso') and nouns such as 'ociosidad', which weakens a rigorous approach to its contexts and nature. The Dictionary of Spanish Royal Academy of Language offers two meanings of leisure: as residual time from work and as entertainment in works of wit ('obras de ingenio').

The term free time can also be understood from two perspectives: as compensatory residual time and as time connected with the idea of freedom. The former is mainly as result of the economic forces and the latter stems from the socio-cultural animation movement. The terms reflect two different traditions which reveal several conceptual developments: passive and restorative leisure as opposed to liberated and liberating leisure.

Another two terms have been frequently used in academic debate are 'recreación' and 'solaz'. Both of these have wholesome positive meanings in reference to the cessation of working, the use of time in a pleasant, recuperative way. While 'solaz' which really describes a pleasant state, is hardly ever used, 'recreación' has somehow become narrowed down to refer to activities capable of bringing relaxation (in close connection to extracurricular activities and outdoor activities) and therefore, can be considered as carrying a functional meaning.

In direct reference to the Latin, there are two more terms: 'lo lúdico' often referring to behaviour, from 'homo ludens', and frequently used in sociological and anthropological perspectives. This can relate to a world of activities, patterns and human dimensions located in the area of the gratuitous, of play and of celebration.

Table 5.1 Leisure concepts and terminology

'TIEMPO LIBRE'	Residual time in relation to work Liberation or subversion
'SOLAZ'	Use of time in a pleasant way Non-activities
'RECREACION'	Use of time in a pleasant way Activities of relaxation Outdoors and extra-curricular activities
'LO LUDICO'	Behaviour (Homo Ludens) Socio-anthropological focus Gratuitous /play / celebration
'OCIO'	'Tripalium' (work) 'Otium' (non-work) 'Nec-otium' / Negocio (business)

There is the general situation of research in Spain which is characterised by frail institutional, theoretical and methodological networks, particularly in areas related to the topic of leisure. In fact, the situation of research in Spain deserves some attention. During the last decades, the attempt to foster further scientific research was centred in a response to three urgent needs: to increase the amount invested in these tasks, to achieve a general restructuring of the organisational infrastructure, and to back the researchers from both the social and the institutional levels.

A brief history shows that there was a continuous tradition of high level research in Spain, but this was only maintained by individuals and small groups rather than institutions. In the period immediately after the Civil War there was the prospect and the beginning of a new focus for research. This was government-led and loaded with ideological undertones and was clustered in centres joined under the CSIC (Superior Council of Scientific Research). Work at the university level, in the voluntary sector and at the level of commercial industries hardly existed.

However, this period was short lived and large projects were limited to a group of centres, characterised by inadequate financing, staffed by researchers on low salaries undervalued by a society which saw no connection between their academic work and the social issues, concerns and policies of state formation.

Even during the expansion years of the 1960s, the situation did not change much. Only 0.3% of the PIB was dedicated to research; the bulk spent in salaries for the already reduced number of people employed. Besides, the researchers were scattered among several ministries with little co-ordination among themselves, or with the centres, or with universities and industry.

The panorama of research, carried out by small teams against a general backdrop of lack of money and organisation, as well as a high level of dependence on foreign technology, also characterised the transition years, when other tasks were considered priorities on the political agenda. There was a need to develop a consensus and to approve the Constitution, start the process of regional decentralisation ('autonomías'), and set in motion key institutions. As well as this, there were urgent tasks such as setting into operation the economic system and stimulating industrial development and revitalisation.

Research was postponed until 14 April 1986 when the Law of *'Fomento y Coordinación General de la Investigación Científica y Técnica'* was passed. The following year witnessed the Decree whereby different Plans were formulated. The first Plan for Research was initiated in 1988 and was set for the period 1988-91. Besides the importance given to the training of researchers and the co-ordination of resources, three areas were marked as priorities: agricultural food products and natural resources, technology of production and communications, and (of more relevance for leisure) the quality of life.

In this brief panoramic view of the history of the situation, a further point needs to be taken into consideration; when talking about Spain one needs to have in mind that it is a State of Autonomies. They, too, have their own research programmes and their systems to support research conducted at the university level since industry has had very little impact. Furthermore, the evidence shows that there is also an imbalance in research profiles among the regions of Spain. In the 1970s the term 'las dos Españas' was coined. There was the rural and the urban, the interior and the periphery, the prosperous and the poor, and this was demonstrated clearly in research patterns. In fact, this is one of the major difficulties when mapping out the major trends and developments in a vast and varied country.

In the 1990s, with one of the fastest rates of economic growth and with a clear pattern of a 'dual society', regional differences are still apparent. While Catalonia, Basque Country, Cantabria, Aragón, Madrid and the Balearic Islands keep up the European face, the remaining eleven Autonomies have been considered as priority regions in Europe for development, together with parts of Italy, Greece and Ireland (Objective 1, 1989-91).

When we turn to leisure research two further points need consideration. There has been, until very recently, an absence of an autonomous and structured science in relation to leisure. Even in concrete scientific fields

> it was not until the end of the eighties that the sociological
> study of leisure and sport began to acquire in Spain a
> certain autonomy as academic areas and fields of social
> research
>   (García Ferrando, 1990).

This situation could be extrapolated to other disciplines and topics. Furthermore, leisure was not only an area which was not articulated as a specific field of research but was also outside Spanish research themes which responded, for a long time, to very established theoretical patterns and discourses, connected predominantly to traditional areas of research. Leisure was clearly outside the mainstream.

This chapter then does not deal with leisure research in its strict sense. It rather broadens the domain of leisure. It is an attempt to trace how the topic of interest emerges and comes together as a result of the contribution of these groups whose thought and research contributed to the evolution of issues and debates. This can only be achieved if leisure is seen and understood in the context of the cultural patterns and beliefs of society and its systems of relations. These are not only bound by space but by time; hence this chapter looks at the historical evolution of the major periods along four main lines of analysis:

    a) the historical context with particular emphasis on factors
       influencing leisure and leisure policies
    b) the changing patterns of leisure practices
    c) the general framework of research and thought
    d) the location of leisure research and thought.

The belief that context is crucial for an exploration of the deep structures of leisure, where thought and meaning can be traced, is reinforced in the case of Spain, where the succession of political systems has had a decisive impact, not only on behavioural patterns but also on systems of thought. Much of the discussion that follows focuses on the general 'Weltanschauungen' of intellectuals, primarily within the academy, as these provide a platform from which leisure research has developed.

Historical Evolution (1876-1982)

1876-1936: Leisure as a Tool for Regeneration

Institutionally speaking this period manifests itself in diverse systems from the Restoration of the monarchy to the short-lived experience of the Second Republic, 1931-1936. Different successive political systems shaped the nation state over a period of six decades, during which time modern Spain embarked on a slow process of recovery after the collapse of the colonial era in the last years of the nineteenth century.

Each political moment implies a further break in the political as well as the social framework of twentieth century Spain; a fragmentation that will lead to the Civil War, proof of all the contradictions and conflicts generated during these decades.

With the advent of industrialisation and the urbanising process of the traditional agrarian society, new social phenomena and new ideological formulations were fostered in the midst of reactionary ultra-conservative responses. Socialism, fundamentally from the Basque Country, Asturias and Madrid, and anarchism, to be found mainly in Catalonia and Andalucia, became two natural responses from the new workers' movement growing up around the mines and factories:

> In this way, workers concentrated in certain districts, which
> meant that they lived in an environment in which class
> connotations were palpable, facilitating the creation of
> bonds of solidarity and understanding.
> (Castells, 1989).

The middle class progressively broke with the aristocracy, haute bourgeoisie and landowners, opposing liberal democratic postulates, at times of a Republican federalist nature, and more oligarchic 'caciquil' manifestations, characteristic of the Restoration. A sector of the Catalan and Basque bourgeoisie clashed head on with the motley centralist structures of the State, giving rise to nationalist ideological bodies.

The process of urbanisation sped up according as the industrialisation phenomenon itself evolved, and trade and services increased in magnitude. The development of urban centres was accompanied at the time by the birth of strong migratory trends in the interior of the Iberian Peninsula, which have continued up until very recently. This enormous growth of cities had logistical consequences on the quality of life, health, subsistence levels and so on of the urban population.

Traditional Catholic populist culture also dominated the leisure time of the majority of social classes. Whereas the elitist leisure of the aristocracy and haute bourgeoisie was linked to visiting thermal spas, the seaside and casinos, the lower classes combined new manifestations of tavern leisure with rural cultural traditions. It is a time of the fusion of rural roots and urban fashions, of the aristocratic-bourgeois, of hygienist paternalism and the workers' 'vindictive' action.

However, the profound socio-economic transformations brought about deep changes in all classes. The masses set out on their own with their independent press, popular reading and modest cultural projects. The middle classes became fragmented and differentiated: some moving towards the rationalist and liberal elitism (*Institución Libre de Enseñanza* and the *Novecentismo* of 1913), others towards nationalist and anti-liberal elitism; some embracing a democratising populism, others a nihilistic or crypto-anarchist populism.

Yet, the intensity of the conflicts gave rise to nothing less than an authentic cultural revival which some people have not hesitated in naming the Silver Age of Spanish Culture. In the beginning, the cultural revival was outside the domain of politics and economic production, but the effects became clear in the following decades (e.g. Second Republic). The nascent freedom of assembly and speech, along with those of universities and of the press, in the years from 1881 to 1883, were a driving force for cultural progress. The concept 'espacio generacional' enables us to appreciate four generations overlapping in cultural creation:

- that of 1868: Costa, Giner de los Ríos o Menéndez Pelayo.
- that of 1898: Unamuno, Machado o Menéndez Pidal.
- that of 1913: Ortega y Gasset, Azaña o Eugenio d'Ors.
- that of 1927: García Lorca, Alberti o Dalí.

Alongside the generational differences, there also existed regional differences, in which Catalonia stood out in respect of its cultural production and vitality at this time (though the Basque Country, Andalucia and Galicia were extremely active and fertile regions).

The polemical meeting between tradition and modernism was to be found in research subjects. It was the creation of a scientific spirit which gave palpable results despite the pre-industrial Spain that was dominant: Ramón y Cajal, Hinojosa, Torres Quevedo or Menéndez Pelayo. The conflict between traditionalists, backed by the Minister of Public Works and Economy, Marqués de Orovio, in opposition to

Giner de los Ríos and Azcarate, led to the removal of the latter from their chairs. They then founded the *Institución Libre de Enseñanza* in 1876.

Table 5.2 Leisure and research in Spain 1876-1936

HISTORICAL CONTEXT	• Restoration of the Monarchy (1876-1931) • Second Republic (1931-1936) • Industrialisation and Urban Development • Migratory Flows • Rural Agrarian Areas • New social and ideological phenomena • Socialism and Trade Unions • Reactionary and Conservative responses • Liberal Democratic and Republican Federalist trends • Nationalism of minorities (e.g. Basque Country)
LEISURE PATTERNS	• Catholic populist traditional leisure activities • Aristocratic leisure: thermalism, seaside and casinos • Hygienist paternalist leisure activities • Workers' leisure activities
RESEARCH FRAMEWORK	• Tradition against Modernism / Rationalism • Regenerationism: The problem is Spain • 1931 League of Political Education
LEISURE STUDIES	• Does not exist as an autonomous discipline • Speculative and philosophical approaches • Aspects: non-formal education and cultural development

In the golden years of the Canovite period, traditionalists and institutionalists wrestled intellectually and politically in a more polite fashion. Yet, the first attempts to go further were focused on a teacher of the *Institución Libre de Enseñanza*, Joaquín Costa. The concept of 'regeneracionismo' was born, followed by a whole series of ideological and cultural manifestations that revealed a new expression of reform of Spanish society when symptoms of colonial collapse were beginning to be felt. The influence of his person and thinking are evident even in the lines of the speeches at the Republican Parliament.

His great plans for transformation at times take on overtones of national surgery which turn them into the instruments both of dictators and republicans. The year 1898 made thinkers dwell on the remedies for Spanish misfortunes. Interestingly, regenerationism found a responsive audience in both traditionalists and reformists. It especially influenced the generation whose backbone was the year 1898 and whose protagonists were born between 1860 and 1875.

In 1913, a manifesto *Calling for a League of Political Education* appeared. The said manifesto was signed by important names who spoke of more competent and democratic politics, unrelated to the traditional parties and the monarchy. However, a double perspective was in fact presented: 'the rise of the masses' (Azaña) which inevitably led to the alliance with the masses, and 'the rebellion of the masses' (Ortega y Gasset) which necessarily meant an alliance with the conservative sector. These reflections were spread by cultural magazines like *España'* (1915-24) and *Revista de Occidente* (1923-) as well as by newspapers like *El Sol*, publishers like Calpe or by the work of the Residencia de Estudiantes (linked to the I.L.E.).

Up to the end of the Second Republic despite all its conflicts, traditional culture, the rationalist thinking of intellectual minorities and the popular culture of the masses coexisted in Spain. These ideological battles concentrated on the relative weight of tradition or reason in creation, action, communication of ideas, and on socio-cultural conceptions and practices.

Studies about leisure as such were non-existent in this period. Authors would not recognise an autonomous discipline called leisure studies. Furthermore, leisure suffered from attacks that related it to what was 'perverse and plebeian'. Nevertheless, in the depth of their thinking we can glimpse the outlines of a concept of leisure, under the headings of culture or education. It is a concept of a distinctive speculative and philosophical nature, but which, with time, becomes an instrument for regeneration, of controversial political use, according to which philosophical approach evaluates practice.

The more intellectual magazines, *Boletín de la Institución Libre de Enseñanza and Revista de Occidente* (1877-1931), took up articles in which different aspects of leisure were dealt with. Many much-quoted authors contributed works of great interest: Eugeni d'Ors, Miguel de Unamuno, José Ortega y Gasset, Francisco Giner de los Ríos o Gregorio Marañon. Together with books of essays and newspaper or magazine articles, it is essential to take into consideration the literary work of writers who shaped intellectual thought over a long period: the Generation of 1868, the Generation of 1898 and the Generation of 1927.

The preoccupation with 'the problem of Spain' was the cornerstone of these decades. National reflections developed with cultural and intellectual dimensions which, though they cannot be classified as studies or research on leisure, can be considered as the roots of subsequent research work. They were writers caught up in themselves and the country they lived in, preoccupied with the context in which they lived and with its transformation or conservation. In many of them we can find pages of fresh philosophical reflection, but with clear implications for practice, on problems which today we contemplate from the developing discipline of leisure studies.

1939-1959: Leisure as a Culture of Submission

Spain had just emerged from a triennial war. Years of fratricidal fighting had resulted in upheaval and endless problems for Spanish society and in the messianic intervention of the army within national borders it sought to protect. The Civil War resulted in the victory of Franco. Amongst the different families that made up the military coup against the legal Republic, the more authoritarian forces controlled political, social and economic power during the first two decades. It was a time of isolation, of economic autarchy, of moral degradation of the war and its consequences. It extended ten years of friendly complicity with the fascist regimes of Europe to an unwavering anti-Communist servility in the Cold War period.

Table 5.3: Leisure and research in Spain 1939-1959

HISTORICAL CONTEXT	• Civil War (1936-1939) • First Francoist Period (Authoritarianism) • Authoritarian and imposed customs • International isolation (except from fascist regimes)
LEISURE PATTERNS	• Indoctrination and Escapism • 'The Spirit of National Movement' • Supporting leisure: sport, education, culture
RESEARCH FRAMEWORK	• Spanish Intellectual Neo-Thomism • National Catholic ideology • Internal dissidence and exile
LEISURE STUDIES	• Not recognised and structured • Preoccupation with 'leisure aspects'

The climate of absurd censorship bordered on the ridiculous when the bare chests of the boxers in the press had to be hidden under painted tee-shirts or the word 'thigh' was omitted from literary works. In general, civil society was not familiar with the work of the dissident intellectuals who turned their backs on the propagandistic culture of the regime: 'Intellectuals have known no other period in which their social influence was so restricted'.

Francoism tried to promote political demobilisation, yet, at the same time, it wished to create a supporting culture. Nevertheless, this was an extremely complicated task since the 'other' Spain constituted a real ferment of intellectuals, poets and historians. Only a handful of the faithful remained in the cultural institutions and universities of the regime. The official culture amounted to a certain virile neo-imperialism, military virtues and Tridentine Catholicism, a melting pot, stirred by the universities with the Law of 1943 - whose deans had to be Falangist militants and members of the Superior Council of Scientific Research (1939). There were writers who, from an internal silence, showed their opposition to the budding regime.

Leisure became a double instrument of indoctrination and evasion. The regime, through sport, culture and education, sought to control a demobilised society. The citizenship saw in leisure, a refuge or escape from a terrible reality, as reflected in the stories *La Familia de Pascual Duarte* (Cela, 1942) and *El Jarama*. Occasionally, both met on the terraces of football grounds. From here, one supported the 'Spanish fury' that beat the enemy in a spectacle marked by nationalist overtones. Along with football, the cinema revealed the contradictions of a system which hurled paint at the screens showing *Gilda*, while the parish priest called for the censoring of even the most chaste kisses. It was similarly the time for great sports and folk demonstrations and for movements associated with or close to the regime (including the Catholic Church, when in the first phase which followed official doctrine).

We are dealing with the growth of a certain Spanish intellectual neo-thomism: a state education infused with religion (catholic doctrine), political education (The National Movement's Spirit) and physical education (military values). The more integrative philosophy regained importance, while heterodoxy was persecuted in order to prove its falseness.

We can refer to only very few individuals; those who survived the Civil War remained firmly in exile, their works were reissued whilst new ones were published that maintained the republican line. In Spain itself, within the gregariousness imposed by the Francoist institutions, intellectuals placed themselves at the service of the Spirit of the Movement. Only the aforementioned dissidents reveal any kind of critical reflection on the time in which they lived.

The works of this period that referred to aspects of leisure have suffered from the passage of time, complicated by the divisions amongst intellectuals between supporters and dissidents of the regime, whether living in Spain or in exile. The ideologies of the regime's supporters concentrated on anything that resonated with native values: sport, education and culture. Sport still had hygienist elements and in addition the interesting creation of populist masses who were easily fostered by the regime. Although few and far between, the articles and works referring to the matter locate leisure in this context.

Education regained its darker, more integrative and ideological tones. The achievements of the first three decades of the century were forgotten and contemporary works lost a possibly more interesting vision from the point of view of leisure. Works and articles exhibited a miserable futility.

Culture was the sphere of indoctrination, of repressed minds and of controlled and dirigible associationism. Although from a committed Falangist-corporatism, we can appreciate certain significant efforts and developments as regards leisure sectors.

At home, dissidents sought to avoid theoretical, thematic and methodological impoverishment as best they could, whereas some of the great figures in exile kept alive the tiny flame of dissent, while waiting for new generations of researchers to be formed. From this grey period we can mention some names of interest: Julio Caro Baroja, Francisco Ayala, José Ferrater Mora, María Zambrano, Enrique Gómez Arboleya, Pedro Laín Entralgo, Julián Marías o Víctor García Hoz.

We cannot as yet speak of studies on leisure recognised and structured as such, but we can speak of the preoccupation of these philosophers, pedagogues, psychologists, anthropologists or sociologists, with topics whose subsequent systematisation will locate them within the interdisciplinary framework of leisure studies. The relationship between work and leisure, the origin of the 'fiesta', the sociology of everyday life, the role of culture or youth and leisure are important topics of interest. Such approaches as yet insignificant from the point of view of leisure per se permit their reading into an overall leisure discourse.

1959-1975: Leisure as an Instrument of Development and Subversion

From 1959, Spanish society embarked on what is considered the most spectacular process of socio-economic change in its history. A extraordinary development occurs: rapid industrialisation, the rural exodus, the exorbitant growth of cities and the avalanches of tourists face to face with the agrarian, old, dry and sad Spain which freezes the soul of poets and strikes the conscience of the regenerationist intellectuals.

The historical irony is great in that Franco's regime was a victim of the very social and economic process it had promoted. During this period, there is growing influence of Europe and increasing economic interdependency. In 1972, the Minister of Information and Tourism, Alfredo Sánchez Bella, assessed what had occurred in Spain since the Civil War with the following words: 'Thirty six years have passed and that uninhabitable broken Spain, promised by the Red Side, is a glad Spain with a thousand dollars per capita.'

The philosophies on which the 'Spirit of National Movement' had rested were exhausted: national-syndicalism, tridentine Catholicism, Hispanic imperialism, anti-communism, organic democracy, Carlism and traditionalism. Economic growth became the central preoccupation of the new Opus Dei's technocrats who had come to power using a new dry dull jargon, a long way from J.A. Primo de Rivera's rhetoric. We are now approaching the 'twilight of ideologies' in the middle of pragmatic development.

At the end of the fifties Spain had collapsed into deep economic crisis. It was necessary to change course in order to break with the former doctrinaire approach. In July of 1959, the Minister of the Economy, Ullastres presented the *Plan de Estabilización*, with the intention of reorganising, liberalising and rationalising the Spanish economy. Yet, though the economy was reorganised and became stronger, forced emigration occurred due to rising domestic unemployment and declining purchasing power of citizens. On the other hand, the devaluation of the peseta gave rise to a spectacular boom in the tourist industry, which from then on would play a key part in the social and economic transformation of the country. It is the time for the postscript 'Spain is different'. In effect, it could be said that at the beginning of the seventies Spain was not so much an under-developed country, but a badly-developed one. It experienced important regional imbalances, a significant process of emigration to Europe, and a depopulation of the interior of the country with a significant rural exodus.

It was about to witness the contradiction posited by important figures of the regime (Ullastres, López Rodó or López Bravo) who, whilst responsible for the changes, shared traditional Christian values (as members of Opus Dei), while their political actions led society closer towards consumerism, permissiveness and modernity. All this generated quite a number of psychological and sociological upsets. The Spain in Gerald Brennan's papers gave way to a society in which education was made public, the Press Law was drawn up in 1966, the Religious Freedom Law appeared in 1967, social security and health insurance were developed, industrial disputes became more common, non-vertical syndicalism reappeared and mass consumption grew.

We were witnessing important changes in lifestyles. Spanish households welcomed television, as well as the refrigerator and the telephone; the car became popular and modified Sunday's social function, giving rise to weekend trips and excursions; the second-holiday residence became an established part of bourgeois desires. Leisure practices were changing quickly.

The authoritarian family and religious culture suffered from the impact of a society that had both tourism and consumerism: permissiveness in the family, in education, in fashion and music trends. It was always confined within the borders of a system reluctant to open the floodgates of political freedom.

Leisure, viewed as a 'supporting culture' by the regime's leaders and experienced as an evasion or escape from the crude post-war reality by a great number of people, became in synthesis the face of submission during the early years of Francoism. Nevertheless, the changes produced by the Opus Dei's members, aimed at the assimilation of leisure into a general model of social development, succeeded in fostering consumption levels beyond all previous expectations.

However, in this uncoordinated growth in consumption, changes occurred in the quality and direction of Spanish lifestyles. This gave rise to 'subversive' leisure, outside the traditional norms of the regime, which slowly sought out spaces of cultural, political and social freedom in harmony with the economic trends of liberalisation. Tourism, television, access to outdoor recreation or the car led to something more than just material goods. Leisure time was also turned into space for vindication and militancy.

Leisure was a subversion bred in factories, university halls, street protests, but also under the protection of sacristies that had broken with an ultra-conservative and obsolete regime. Leaders and groups were formed in the spaces of leisure and from a militant social commitment, finished up in the political quest for democratic transition.

As economic structures changed, intellectual communities were not left untouched. In 1951, Joaquín Ruiz Giménez took charge of the Ministry of Education. With the support of internal dissidents like Antonio Tovar, Laín Entralgo or Dionisio Ridruejo, he reinstalled numerous professors who had been expelled from the university sector. The universities were modernised and de-dogmatised. The Vertical Students' Union (S.E.U.) lost its traditional control. By 1956 democratic liberalism and socialism had infected the university student movement, giving rise to the demand to hold a free congress of students, backed by the circle of intellectuals 'Tiempo Nuevo'. Student protests increased in the universities and Ruiz Giménez was dismissed. Nevertheless, the new young university was under way. The protests continued with the succeeding ministers, Jesús Rubio and Lora Tamayo. The problems were not only of a political nature, students and lecturers alike demanded a university with proper means and one abreast of the times. Neither the replacement of the minister by Villar Palasí nor his General Law of Education of 1970 could put a stop to the upheavals taking place in one of the instruments of opposition to the regime.

For the first time there emerged a Marxist school of thought in Spain with Manuel Sacristán and Tierno Galván in a state of secrecy, mocking censorship. In 1963 the magazine *Cuadernos para el Diálogo* appeared under Joaquín Ruiz Giménez's leadership. Many figures, political, social, syndicalist and intellectual militants, found in this journal a place for critical reflection and debate.

A certain empiricism invaded all academic disciplines. A raging criticism of the system can be found behind the escalation in facts and tables. Writing about the social reality with the help of facts was in itself subversive. The university became imbued by the theoretical and methodological trends of post-war Europe. The publishing houses fought their way through ideological censorship and undertook the translation of important works in all fields of knowledge. Despite the resistance of the 'Francoist Bunker', the scientific community fought its way through to Western Europe: its schools, themes and methods.

Studies on leisure have yet to gain autonomy, as an independent paradigm of research, though even disciplines like sociology are in the process of establishing a natural role in the scientific community in Spain. However, aspects which we now consider cornerstones in studies on leisure were the object of unusual interest at this time (for example leisure policies, leisure marketing or leisure time-budgets).

For the first time, intellectuals were faced with enough physical and intellectual space to develop not only speculative exercises on leisure but also to carry out descriptive and explanatory works on social realities. Similarly, works were oriented to theoretical and methodological reformulations in the light of foreign trends. Psycho-pedagogy sought new ways both within and outside the educational system. Sociology evolved by observing a vibrant human laboratory of social practices. History witnessed the establishment of new historiographic perspectives and tendencies. Philosophy struggled to recover its freedom of thought. Economics was interested in the new sources of wealth coming from non-working hours. Anthropology rediscovered historical spaces of Spain without the shackles of a stifling traditionalist ideology. Literature reflected social denunciation in its novels, theatre and poetry.

All the above disciplines recovered their protagonism in the transformation of what was a contradictory regime. Aspects of leisure were analysed autonomously or within areas of traditional disciplines (social agogy, history of the workers' movement, sociology of sport or cultural anthropology).

Within the new focus of research, socio-cultural animation and community development were probably two areas of great importance in the promotion of leisure studies. There was a convergence between the new liberating agogies (for example P. Freire), the citizenship movements from the working-class suburbs and the ecumenical spirit of Vatican II, in a wide range of socio-cultural and political initiatives. Social movements and institutions, for example free-time schools, started from the premise of method-action-reflection-action, had developed theoretical formulations on different aspects of leisure, reflected in documents of internal use or in *fanzines* (organs of expression of the movements), usually unrelated to the academic scientific community.

On the other hand, we can appreciate the development of new fields of interest that were based on development itself, the improvement in living conditions and consumption, tourism and sport. Such topics were the focus of studies and work, carried out from diverse disciplines and viewpoints. It was the golden age for studies, analysis and definitions.

1975-1982: Leisure, Towards a Discipline in Democratic Normality

With the appointment of the Prince Juan Carlos of Bourbon as his automatic successor, it was General Franco's intention to leave everything all sewn up ('todo atado y bien atado'). However, after some squabbling within the regime between the 'aperturistas' and the more reactionary members, the model of political transition conceived by the young politician Adolfo Suarez (ex-general secretary of the Movement) prevailed, with the steady hand from the Spanish King Juan Carlos I and of the President of the Royal Council at the helm.

The Law of Political Reform, the dissolution of the Francoist Parliament, the legalisation of the Communist Party and the organisation of the first democratic elections were milestones in the democratisation of the State. The Constitution of 1978 improved civil society, with a parliamentary monarchy, a two-chamber system, organised according to territories by means of a system of autonomous regions governed by their own special laws ('Estatutos de Autonomía').

The period 1977-82 of governments of Unión de Centro Democrático (U.C.D.), a party made up of several parties around Adolfo Suárez, culminated in the disappearance of the said political party and the unsuccessful Coup of 23 February 1981.

On the 28 October 1982, the historic Partido Socialista Obrero Español won the elections by an absolute majority. A decade of socialist omnipotence then began, only trimmed by the weight of Basque and Catalan nationalisms in their communities and the autonomous governments of Aznar's Partido Popular (the new right-wing party).

Democratisation gets under way timidly amid the clash of sabres and the resistance of some socio-economic forces reluctant to change. However, since the failure of the last reactionary attempt to overthrow the government on the night of 23 February 1981, the Spanish state had made its way in the international community and the European Community (1986). It can be said that Spain was now truly taking part in the European project moving into postmodern scenarios without passing modernity.

With the beginning of the process of democratisation, a deep transformation had taken place in the Spanish society. During the first stage, coinciding with the second half of the decade, the profound world economic crisis shook traditional productive structures. Leisure took second place in the face of the revaluation of work as a scarce resource. Unemployment, on the other hand, signified *enforced* leisure time for a significant percentage of citizenship, particularly among young people.

All the associations and initiatives related to socio-cultural animation faced an important identity crisis after the democratic first steps. The political parties absorbed social protagonism, and, in many cases, mediated the action of the socio-cultural animation. The roots of many political leaders were to be found in the socio-cultural movements, associations and initiatives.

The arrival of the Socialists in central government introduced socio-cultural expressions close to post-modern thinking, after some years of optimism about the transformation of the age-old evils of the state. Society, split by having or not a job, continued to be fragmented by the different forms of emerging leisure patterns.

Sport shared space with a countless number of traditional sports and many others of a new kind. Culture was shattered into a thousand pieces, with different forms and manifestations. Recreation formulas were multiplied and applied in practice. Tourism was transformed from 'sun and sand' to new generational and social expressions. Non-formal education discovered new ways of working. Important advances in technology transformed audio-visual culture creating new consumer patterns and activities during leisure time. New industries related to leisure were developed and leisure began to be considered, in its different forms, as a first-class source of wealth.

The integration process of handicapped people was analysed in relation to leisure and disabilities. An increasing target-segment in the population involved the third age, the elderly who required new initiatives for their leisure time. Women took to the streets in a decisive fashion in democratic Spain, taking part in many leisure activities formerly denied to them. The regeneration of urban spaces and the rural areas development became subjects with interesting interventions for leisure.

The state, regional and local institutions started to take part in shaping all these fields through the use of leisure policies. The fragmentation of practices implied the diversification of social models and lifestyles.

Although for the political and legal sphere, 1975 marks the beginning of a new process towards a liberal regime, for the world of research, academic normalisation had started at the end of the sixties and now continued its course. At that time, there were a series of characteristics which all academic disciplines shared in Spain. They all were responsive to imperative social demands which aimed to recover knowledge on aspects that had been studied in a biased or fraudulent way under the ideologies of the former regime. The new autonomous framework resulted in the extension of centres of intellectual and academic activity in places far from the traditional centres of Madrid and Barcelona. Moreover, there was a notable increase in research of a local nature which compared theses or findings for all states with national identities. There was also an important diversification in themes related to the incorporation of new centres of interest and new communities of research. These began to clarify schools, theoretical and methodological approaches within the cloudy Spanish intellectual map of the sixties.

Some disciplines, such as sociology or pedagogy, attained levels of development inconceivable in the former period, due to the social demand for answers to policy questions and preoccupations. The university once again turned its attention to activities related to research, putting aside its political militancy, in a process of identification with the international academic community. In addition, an infinite number of magazines and organs of communication sprung up at the service of intellectuals and researchers.

Studies on leisure shared the same characteristics. Although it was not until the 1980s that diverse disciplines related the term 'leisure' to academic specialisation (leisure agogy, sociology of leisure or cultural policies), aspects of leisure are treated with a certain rigour and depth.

Following the very fruitful years of the sixties and early seventies in socio-cultural animation outside the university, there was a crisis of re-adaptation to the new socio-political situation. Public participation through animation policies, which were often run by professionals from this very world, provoked a necessary reorientation. Free-time schools and other non-academic centres of thinking opened up new ways of reflection on the accumulated experience of the 1960s and 1970s.

Intellectuals witnessed a profound diversification in topics, which corresponded to the sociable leisure activities present in the new Spanish society. Likewise, theoretical and methodological approaches became more complex and sophisticated.

The number of works dedicated to the theory of leisure and free time increased, along with those which were directed at policies applied to leisure sectors, lifestyles, culture and art, mass media, urban regeneration and leisure spaces, tourism and recreation, sport, health, socio-cultural animation and community development, women, elderly people, children, youth and leisure-work-unemployment.

These theoretical approaches were for the most part placed within a diffuse and eclectic framework. The main currents of contemporary thinking have come to Spain with the limitations imposed by censorship and secrecy. The said currents have been read in a partial and incomplete fashion and their practical applications have sometimes been altered. There are many authors whose works cannot be classified under broad theoretical labels such as neo-positivism, Marxism, historicism, vitalism, existentialism, personalism, psychoanalysis, nihilism, structuralism or the Frankfurt School.

It is difficult to say which are the defining lines between the legacy of authors and schools. Except for very special cases, we must speak rather of the weight of a shared background (university, city or autonomy) or the personal relations (professor-disciple or the same generation) in the works of Spanish authors.

Table 5.4: Leisure and research in Spain, 1959-1975

HISTORICAL CONTEXT	• Second stage of Francoism (Technocracy) • Spectacular socio-economic growth • Second industrialisation / rural exodus • Development of metropolitan areas • The National Movement exhausted • 'OPUS DEI' - technocrats and economic growth • Consumption patterns • Poor quality economic and social development • Regional imbalances • Emigration to Europe • 'Desertisation' in the Spanish interior • Non Democratic political evolution
LEISURE PATTERNS	• Tourism: *'lo extranjero'* • TV /car / weekend / summer holidays • Consumerism and escapism • Liberalisation trends • Subversive leisure: vindication and militancy
RESEARCH FRAMEWORK	• 1951-56. Joaquín Ruíz Giménez. Minister of Education - new young university development • Theoretical and methodological trends of post-war Europe • Growth of empiricism (facts, tables and figures)

LEISURE STUDIES	• Aspects of leisure studies within traditional disciplines: focus on tourism, lifestyles and consumption
	• Relevant aspects of lesiure policy and studies:
	   Sociocultural animation and community development;
	   ('action-reflection-action' Method);
	   Pedagogía de la Liberación (P.Freire);
	   Social Movements;
	   Ecclesiastical Spirit of Vatican II'
	   Political parties developing (in secrecy)

Table 5.5: Leisure and research in Spain, 1975-1994

HISTORICAL CONTEXT	* Political reform (1975-1977) * Democratic transition. Adolfo Suarez. UCD (1977-82) * Socialist hegemony. Felipe González. PSOE (1982-94) * Dissolution of Francoist power (1976) * Legalisation of the Communist Party (1977) * Constitution of 1978 * The Coup of 23 February 1981 * Socialist Party election success (1982) * Nationalist majorities in Basque Country and Catalonia * Socioeconomic crisis (1973...) * Admission to European Community (1986)
LEISURE PATTERNS	* Takes second place in employment revaluation process *Phenomenon of enforced leisure (young unemployed, retired, and housewives) * Democratisation and Democracy * Public sector and private sector growth in leisure provision * Professionalism and voluntary sector * Fragmentation of traditional cultural patterns and new expressions of leisure interests
RESEARCH FRAMEWORK	* Normalisation process: theories and methodology * Imperative social demands * New communities of research (state of Autonomies)
LEISURE STUDIES	* Specialisation within disciplines (e.g. Leisure Agogy or Sociology of Leisure) * Non-university studies (crisis of readaptation) * Leisure education in Elementary School (*'líneas transversales'*) * Leisure training in university curricula (Tourism, Social Work and Social Education) * Leisure training in postgraduate degrees (Leisure Studies, Tourism Administration or Cultural Management)

Contemporary Leisure Research (1982-1994)

As has been suggested earlier, in the Spanish case, there is not an autonomous disciplinary formation devoted to the study of leisure as a subject of inquiry. Furthermore, in many cases, the traditional disciplines register leisure as a specific and segmented meaning within their own partial concerns. Even when leisure is taken into consideration, it is never seen in its richness but rather it is more narrowly limited to sport, tourism or culture.

The cause of this state of affairs must be located in the whole ambience of Spanish thought in this decade. This can easily be extrapolated to the limited impact of research in relation to leisure (San Salvador, 1993):

a) the permeability among the theoretical models of representation of the reality in the majority of authors;

b) the presence of schools founded more on the relationship between professor-disciple and geographical location, than on the structuring of theoretical guidelines;

c) the mixture of methodologies within the same author or school;

d) the subjection of the research project to themes which are defined by social and economic problems.

Theoretical Permeability and Eclecticism

There is no doubt that in the tradition of Spanish thought in the present century, there are various philosophical trends which coexist and influence its formation in significant ways. Despite considerable differences in themes, there are many authors who have drawn inspiration from Christian humanistic thought, sometimes providing a liberal interpretation, while at other times arguing from neo-scholastic metaphysics. For some analysis takes a more individualist perspective, for others analysis is more socially oriented.

These approaches often link with analytic philosophy which has developed a degree of autonomy during the last two decades. While neo-Marxism, which permeates a considerable number of works, has undergone considerable methodological development. Nihilism also has special relevance in the whole context of Spanish thought, perhaps greater than the impact of other systems of interpretation. This is possibly, though not uniquely, the origin of weaknesses in analytic thought in the Spanish case.

All these theoretical models are present at the moment in leisure research. But it is impossible to take the risk to locate the different authors within a particular trend. It can be said with certainty that the majority of leisure researchers develop their activity without a militant, definite or exclusive commitment to one of the above mentioned systems. The presence of humanistic, analytic, neo-marxist, nihilistic or postmodern references is something general to researchers. They are not all present at the same time but the majority of the researchers suffer from the convergence of elements from several perspectives or, at least, have suffered phases under diverse influences. The distinctive trends themselves are fading.

Leisure studies in Spain experience this atmosphere of eclecticism and permeability. Even the most significant works to emerge do not allow any rigid classification, and we risk being denounced by the author for the definition given to his/her personal intellectual allocation. Within the scarce number of authors who have written about leisure theory in the last decade only Zorrilla positions himself within the structuralist perspective. The others are clear examples of a diverse pattern of influences (Racionero, 1983; Cuenca, 1992; Munné, 1988; Pedró, 1984).

Schools and Methods

It is difficult to speak of schools of thought in Spain. The strange examples that appear surround consecrated authors, with the relation professor-disciple as the dominant feature of research circles. Within this framework, the research focus of the teacher is followed by interpretations from the disciples (both orthodox or heterodox). On some occasions the initial common point between both the professor and neophyte fades, diverging even so far as adhering to the same theoretical framework, and yet the sense of school continues.

The other clustering factor at work could be the simple geographical location of a group of researchers. Both the location of the university or the research centre or the region where they work can be decisive to generate a sense of belonging to a common school. This is sometimes reinforced by the presence of a professor, as well as by theoretical or methodological common approaches to social reality.

In the field of leisure it is more difficult to refer to schools of thought. At the geographical level, the only specific Leisure Studies Institute is located in the University of Deusto (Basque Country), but there are also an important group of research centres which have specialised in discrete leisure aspects. If it is difficult to speak of specific researchers on leisure, it is even more difficult to locate them within a distinctive school.

In terms of methodology, the present situation similarly does not allow for any clear categorisation. After the first qualitative or speculative attempts, the majority of the studies tend to be trapped within the research problem analysed from more eclectic methods of analysis (Conde, 1987). Again, as was the case with theory, methodological principles abandon their pure state to end up in the hands of the researchers who adapt them to the demands of the problem studied. Inductive or qualitative methods all are mediated by the nature of the analysed subject matter or the research objectives to be pursued. There is no methodological framework in the strictest sense, and method is seen again as at the service of the rest of the elements of the research.

Bearing in mind the above caveats, it can be argued that leisure research in Spain is generally close to quantitative methodologies, saturated by statistical tables and other quantitative tools. The scientific community, however, seems to be moving towards some kind of equilibrium (Ruiz Olabuenaga, 1989). There is also a trend which systematises work in the tradition of socio-cultural animation from the 1960s and 1970s.

Thematic Subjection

Taking into account theoretical frameworks of interpretation, schools and methodological differences, we can pose the question, which is the decisive discriminating factor for the scientific corpus in relation to leisure? The answer is that thematic priority determines the orientation of leisure research works themselves. There is a high level of dependence of research on themes which demand urgent analysis at the present time.

This element of contemporaneousness, which can give new and accessible insights into social reality, can also degenerate into a dependence on the economic or political demands of the time, driven by the concerns of the sponsoring organisation providing research funds.

Atomisation rather than a body of researchers, individualism rather than schools, theoretical eclecticism rather than theoretical frameworks, thematic fragmentation and dispersion rather than global understanding find concrete expression in this issue of thematic subjection. Yet five major topics do emerge from current leisure studies.

a) Everyday life, lifestyles and consumption

In this sense, the appearance of a strong line of research which revolves around the everyday life, the different modes and styles, the patterns and motivations are a reply to the need to diversify consumption research and to develop traditional socio-anthropological studies (Piñuel, 1987; Gil Calvo, 1988; Zorrilla, 1990).

The sociology and psychology of leisure devote a great deal of attention to the analysis of identifiable social groups and their modus vivendi (Ruiz Olabuenaga, 1989; González Moro, 1990). Leisure time exhibits segmentation and the research work into leisure at the present moment reinforce this fragmentation. What is a matter

Table 5.6: Leisure Research Sources in Spain

REGIONS (Comunidades Autónomas)	LEISURE STUDIES	CULTURE POLICIES AND MANAGEMENT	TOURISM AND OUTDOOR RECREATION	SPORT	SOCIO CULTURAL ANIMATION AND COMMUNITY DEVELOPMENT
Andalucia			Univ. Málaga	UNISPORT	Esc. Animación Andalucia
Aragón					Univ.Zaragoza
Asturias		Univ. Oviedo			
Baleares			Univ. Baleares		
Canarias			Univ. La Laguna Univ. Las Palmas		
Cantabria			Univ. Santander		
Castilla-León					Univ.Pontificia Salamanca
Castilla - La Mancha					
Cataluña		CERC Univ.Barcelona	CETT Univ.Barcelona EADA		Univ.Autónoma Univ.Barcelona IMAE Escola l'Esplai
Extremadura					
Galicia					Univ. Santiago
Madrid		Mtrio.Cultura Univ.Complutense	Secr. Gen. Turismo EOT Univ.Complutense Univ. Politécnica	INEF CSD	Mtrio.Asuntos Sociales Univ.Autónoma UNED CIS-REIS CIRES
Murcia					
Navarra					
País Vasco	Univ.Deusto	Univ.Deusto Univ.País Vasco	Univ.Deusto	IVEF-UPV Univ.Deusto	EDE Univ.Deusto Univ.País Vasco
País Valenciano			ITVA	Univ.Valencia	Grupo Dissabte
Rioja, La					

of concern is how motivation, expenditure and cultural patterns attempt to fit leisure time into daily life (Setién, 1993; Elzo *et al.*, 1992).

b) The feast as a popular expression

There exists at the heart of the Mediterranean world a pre-industrial festive inheritance which is rich in meaning (Caro Baroja, 1986, 1992). Anthropologists have devoted volumes to search into pre-industrial leisure patterns, but they have now begun to look at almost post-industrial festive patterns, linking in some way with this trend, but creating a new entity (Cuenca, 1994). The interest in the feast and festival is connected with the discontinuities in organised and normative time. The feast offers a key to the understanding of the interpretation of social reality for anthropologists, sociologists and educationalists (Gil Calvo, 1991).

In fact, one of the primary avenues for the understanding of leisure is along the path of anthropological research in relation to communication and celebration. In fact, reflection into the meaning of leisure in a country such as Spain needs to take into consideration what Gil Calvo describes as one of the characteristics of Mediterranean countries 'el furor festivo' (the intense popular capacity to celebrate everything) - a characteristic which the peoples from the Iberian Peninsula seem to possess in abundance due to a combination of elements: climatic conditions which allow for outdoor performances, a past Latin inheritance which mixed with the imaginative Muslim world and the catholic emphasis on community values, bearing the imprint of the baroque Counter-reformation. Gil Calvo considers that:

> In the European division of cultural labour, it has been
> historically allowed to the Spanish people the task of
> specialising full time in all forms of techniques of
> celebrations: carnivals, Easter processions, 'Sanfermines',
> 'Fallas', 'romerías' and all sort of expressions of popular
> culture, from the dance in the village square to the ritual of
> going drinking from bar to bar.

In order to explore the meaning of leisure as a particular form of communication, that is to say communication in the sphere not only of the social but also in the public realm, it is necessary to delve into the Ortega's thought (*El hombre y la gente*, 1972). The public is characterised as spectacle which is for and about society itself, since there is no such thing as a private feast; leisure time spent in feasts is always public.

In this general context of investigation into the patterns and symbolism of feast celebration in Spain, Caro Baroja' thought deserves special mention in his attempt to analyse the seasonal cycle of Spanish celebrations and their connections with particular ways of life. Other authors too have followed this tradition and have researched into the collective dimension of the festive rituals. They function as a regenerating and reaffirming source of social order or as its transgression and subversion as authors discover the feast's secret rationality.

c) Socio-cultural animation and community development

Socio-cultural animation which had developed during the sixties and seventies as a distinctive practice, was by the eighties gaining in academic profile. The changes produced by social movements in the transition years from subversive to democratic leisure have special relevance in the realms of animation and community development. A field traditionally fed by the voluntary sector embarked on a process of professionalisation.

There are also the processes of institutionalisation and academisation: the entrance of socio-cultural animation and community development into the universities through the Educational Sciences Faculties (with the degree in Social Education) (Quintana, 1986)

With its various approaches, socio-cultural animation gradually moves towards systematisation, although maintaining numerous elements within the methodology of action-research-action. Within this generic framework, there is a clear concern for certain social groups: marginal groups, ethnic minorities, handicapped people or unemployed. Others based their research on sectors of the population which demand policy answers: children and youth (Toharia, 1990; Zarraga, 1989), the elderly (Castro, 1990; Bazo, 1990) and women (IM, 1990). Of equal relevance was the research around popular and non-formal education directed towards specific social segments of thepopulation (Trilla and Puig, 1987).

d) Leisure policies and management

There are several aspects of leisure which are of special interest in the last decade and grow from new democratic developments, even as far as rediscovery of the territorial space, with the birth of the Autonomous Communities and the process of self-government and decentralisation that this implies. Fields of leisure in their various manifestations become the object of study along different dimensions of policy and management.

Within the field of culture: the evolution of cultural policies are observed with great interest (Fernández Prado, 1991); policies are analysed under the central-local tensions (Fossas, 1990); and there are attempts to reflect on the consequences on different models of managerial skills (Ibar and Longás, 1992; Díaz, 1992).

In the arena of sport: there is growing attention towards themes of social demand, planning and policies; some authors have studied the relation between the sport policies and sport for all; other researchers have analysed issues around the new sport expressions (Cagigal, 1990; Coca, 1994; García Ferrando, 1990).

In the case of tourism, which is of great significance for the Spanish economy: there is a great deal of attention devoted to the problem of the tourism crisis and its necessary redefinition; adequate plans and prospects are sought as well as new forms analysed - ecotourism, agrotourism, cultural tourism and time-sharing are very intensively studied topics (Díaz, 1987; Bayón, 1991; Fernández Fuster, 1991).

e) Leisure and socio-economic regeneration

The concern for an improvement in the fields of policy or management, for example, involving touristic, cultural or urban questions, links with definite socio-economic preoccupations for the revitalisation of certain areas. In the field of the urban space, the void left by the previous regime highlights the need to explore this question which was inadequately tackled during the chaotic development of the sixties. Urban leisure spaces are contemplated in the context of Urban Plans and from the quality of life research projects (Valenzuela, 1987; González, 1990; Cuenca, 1994).

Besides, the leisure industries, particularly, those of touristic, recreational and cultural nature, are objects of special attention in so far as they are discovered as capable of generating social and economic goods (Bustamante and Zallo, 1988; Zallo, 1988; Montaner, 1991). Another important topic in this field is linked to the Spanish integration in the European Union and its impacts (CEP, 1991). Europeanisation is also analysed from the point of view of the impact of new technologies in the leisure framework (Castilla, 1988; Rispa, 1985).

Finally, the role of sponsorship, in relation to leisure, culture, mass-media and sports, is the origin of an interesting batch of research projects (Corredoira, 1991; Cervera, 1992).

Conclusions: Light and Shadow

Shadow

In conclusion to this introductory history of the study of leisure in Spain, we can affirm that there is something of a balance between the light and shadow. As a healthy exercise in future optimism we shall start by recapitulating the shadows, before moving on to the highlights among such inherited obscurity.

As regards the aforementioned studies, the conflict over terminology, as explained earlier in the chapter, has abated. The profound pejorative weight given to everything related to leisure, the linguistic imprecision between concepts such as leisure and free time, as well as the lack of wide space for our existence, has made the development of leisure studies difficult.

Both historic and contemporary reality in Spain has not favoured the development of a field for any type of creative activity. The absence of democratic sources, other than of brief periods of time, has impeded a permanent development of the social context wherein all investigative labours incubate. The socio-political context has conditioned the future of the world of investigation in general and leisure in particular.

As a result, there has been an absence of the minimum of infrastructures for the proper development of investigative and research activity. Other preoccupations have occupied intellectuals in contemporary Spain. The studies related to the diverse aspects of leisure have suffered general sterility.

Within traditional academic disciplines, leisure has barely asserted any certain degree of autonomy. Even those recent contributions to the study of leisure have exposed its contradictory limits and contents. There is no presence of an autonomous discipline within Spanish consciousness, dedicated to the study of leisure. We can not count on a bounded and well-defined field where questions and answers are directed with relation to leisure.

The same can be said of the typical theoretical systems deployed. However, there do exist important figures in the field of theoretical reflection, but perhaps due to the lack of awareness about them in the international community, they have made little impression beyond the Pyrenees. This is even more so in the field of leisure, where the theoretical elaboration has always been a subsidiary footnote to greater questions.

In the framework of leisure studies, there are masters of thought, instigators of theories and reflections, but rarely have they been able to nourish schools of thought. The common ground has been achieved fundamentally by the professor-disciple bond, by close, every-day relationships, rather than by common frameworks of ideas. Methodologies fail to transcend the standard patterns of the scientific community living from experiences and elaboration from within the Spanish peninsula.

Throughout its history, the investigations and studies, which concern the generic framework of leisure, have not been amenable to organisation into subjects or aspects which could have constituted rationales for institutes or schools of research. Coexistence and contemporaneousness determine the scope of the thematic borders; historical circumstance frames the pulse of the preoccupations of leisure studies. Without being a negative aspect in itself, it does carry secondary effects, reflected in the slant which leisure investigations take. If historical trends have been part and parcel of understanding leisure for a greater part of the twentieth century, the demands of contemporary life have resulted in similar sifting and partialisation of leisure topics.

Finally, despite the great expanse of intellectual aridity, there have been rich oases of thought and investigative unrest. Alongside the desert have grown fertile intellectual fields. These are seedbeds that, despite austere conditions have yielded their fruit in the last decades. In Spain, leisure studies does not have a long history but it does have a fertile and undiscovered prehistory.

Lights

The present moment casts a timid light over so much darkness. Its own historical texture has generated an important theoretical capital. The theory of leisure has printed itself in the pages of regenerationism and modernism. The Mediterranean tradition of leisure has left residues, tastes stamped on intellectuals throughout the Spanish twentieth century. The pompous history of Spain in the last century has proved to be a good spawning ground for reflection in the face of necessity.

The opening of democratic horizons has supposed a qualitative change and drawn definitive support from some pre-existing tendencies in the world of investigation. Leisure studies can be found in a distinct and emerging framework, free of mortgages and dependencies.

The public and private policy demands introduce a deepening of consciousness of a little-known field of study between leisure, culture, sports, recreation, tourism, health and community development.

Leisure has achieved a letter of acceptance from traditional academic disciplines, including those who had actively resisted any consideration of 'something not very serious' such as leisure.

The path towards the autonomy of leisure studies can be seen in the not-too-distant decades. Only the sclerotic movement of public and academic institutions slow down what is a social necessity.

Eclecticism invades theories and methodologies. We are living and experiencing moments of relativity in the ideological arena. The democratic succession, united to international actions and policies, has permeated Spanish reality. Not even scientific anger has remained untouched, provoking the fusion of theories and methods, challenging the negative appraisal of non-direction, but also experiencing the relief from the 'anti-dogmatism' which finds opportunities to progress by synthesis.

There is the appearance of highlights of undoubted significance in the panorama of leisure studies in Spain. There emerge points of investigation surrounding themes or concrete studies, but also holistic approximations to the reality of leisure. For the first time, we can speak of interdisciplinary perspectives researching into leisure in its varied manifestations.

Aspects of leisure have been diversified in the last decade. The very segregation of society based on styles, modes and different manners has provoked the multiplication of points of attention on the part of investigators into social reality. There are many pathways opened, and there will be fruitful research in the coming decade.

Some have suggested that the restructuring of the state into autonomies has had negative impacts, with a lack of co-ordination or atomisation of the scientific community at many levels. On the positive side, it allows us to build a discipline from the most simple levels of analysis. The dissection of the pluri-national reality of the Spanish state allows us to build theoretical systems most concordant with the situation over which they maintain jurisdiction. Besides multiplying the numbers of research and policy projects, there is a growing awareness of the reality of leisure in Spain.

Finally, democracy has brought with it the total incorporation of Spain in the international community, and consequently, the same processes apply in the world of investigation and research. Leisure Studies have travelled important paths in Europe and the World. The democratisation of Spain has permitted access to these international processes. But, on the other hand, it may also allow the recuperation of Spanish thought within the international community. The restoration of authors and thoughts, also in leisure studies must be reassessed at the heart of a young new discipline. This chapter has been an introduction to leisure research in Spain, which as an introduction reveals the prehistory of what, even now, is a discipline of the future.

REFERENCES

Bayón Mariné, F. (1991) *Ordenación del turismo*. Madrid: Síntesis.

Bazo, Mª.T. (1990) *La sociedad anciana*. Madrid: CIS - Siglo XXI.

Borja, J. *et al.* (eds) (1990) *Las grandes ciudades en la década de los noventa*. Madrid: Sistema.

Bustamante, E. and Zallo, R. (eds) (1988) *Las industrias culturales en España*. Madrid: Akal.

Cagigal, J.Mª. (1990) *Deporte y agresión*. Madrid: Alianza -CSD.

Caro Baroja, J. (1986) *La estación del amor fiestas populares de mayo a San Juan*. Madrid: Taurus.

Caro Baroja, J. (1992) El estío festivo (fiestas populares de verano). Barcelona: Círculo de Lectores.

Castells, M. (1989) *The Information City*. Oxford: Blackwell.

Castilla, A. (1988) ' Ocio y tiempo libre en la actualidad', in Castilla, A. and Díaz, J.A. (eds) *Ocio, trabajo y nuevas tecnologías*. Madrid: Fundesco.

Castro, A. de (1990) *La tercera edad, tiempo de ocio y cultura*. Madrid: Narcea.

Cembranos, F. *et al.* (1988) *La animación sociocultural: una propuesta metodológica*. Madrid: Popular.

Centre d'Estudis de Planificació (1991) *El sector cultural en España ante el proceso de integración europea*. Madrid: Ministerio de Cultura.

Cervera, E. (dir.) (1992) *El patrocinio empresarial de la cultura en España*. Madrid: Ministerio de Cultura.

Coca, S. (1994) *El hombre deportivo*. Madrid: Alianza.

Conde, F. (1987) 'Una propuesta de uso conjunto de técnicas cuantitativas y cualitativas en la investigación social', in *Revista Española de Investigación Social (REIS)*, 29, Madrid.

Congreso de Animación Sociocultural. Intervención transformadora en una sociedad en crisis (1989) Vitoria: Gobierno Vasco.

Congreso Interacció 94: ponencias y comunicaciones (1994) Barcelona: Diputación de Barcelona.

Congreso Internacional de Deporte para Todos. Aspectos económicos (1990) Vitoria.

Corredoira, L. (1991) *El patrocinio*. Barcelona: Bosch.

Cuenca, M. (1992) 'El ocio, un nuevo marco para el desarrollo de las humanidades', in *Letras de Deusto*, vol. 54, pp. 235-251.

Cuenca, M. (1993) 'Ocio y futuro. Del homo ludens al homo festus', in *Letras de Deusto*, vol. 59, pp. 239-260.

Cuenca, M. (1994) 'La fiesta, realidad de ocio. Elementos de análisis y reflexión', in *Letras de Deusto*, vol. 63, pp. 169-193.

Cuenca, M. et al. (1992) *El ocio en el área metropolitana de Bilbao*. Bilbao: Universidad de Deusto.

Díaz, A. (1992) *Gestión sociocultural. La eficacia social*. Madrid: Comunidad de Madrid.

Díaz, J.R. (1987) *Geografía del turismo*. Madrid: Síntesis.

Elzo, J. et al. (1992) *Euskalerria en la encuesta europea de valores*. Vitoria: Gobierno Vasco-Universidad de Deusto.

Fernández Fuster, L. (1991) *Geografía general del turismo de masas*. Madrid: Alianza.

Fernández Prado, E. (1991) *La política cultural: ¿qué es y para qué sirve?*. Gijón: Trea.

Fossas, E. (1990) *Regions i sector cultural a Europa*. Barcelona: Generalitat Catalunya.

García Ferrando, M. (1990) 'Sociología del ocio y del deporte', in Giner, S. (ed.) *Sociología en España*. Madrid: CSIC.

García Ferrando, M. (1990) *Aspectos sociales del deporte*. Madrid: Alianza.

Gil Calvo, E. (1988) 'Las clases de ocio de las clases ociosas', in Castilla, A. and Díaz, J.A. (eds) *Ocio, trabajo y nuevas tecnologías*. Madrid: Fundesco.

Gil Calvo, E. (1991) *Estado de fiesta*. Madrid: Espasa.

González Moro, V (1986) *Hábitos culturales en la Comunidad Autónoma de Euskadi*. Vitoria: Gobierno Vasco.

González Moro, V. (1990) *Los estilos de vida y la cultura cotidiana.* San Sebastián: Baroja.

González, J. (1990) 'Leisure, culture and the political economy of the city: case study of Bilbao', in *XII World Congress of Sociology.* Madrid.

González, J. (1993) 'Leisure Policy in Spain', in Bramham, P. et al. (eds) *Leisure Policies in Europe.* Wallingford: CAB International.

Ibar, M. and Longás, J. (1992) *Cómo organizar y gestionar una entidad de Animación Sociocultural.* Madrid: Narcea.

Instituto de la Mujer (1990) *La mujer en España.* Madrid: Ministerio Asuntos Sociales.

Instituto de Servicios Sociales (1990) *La tercera edad en España.* Madrid: Ministerio Asuntos Sociales.

Jornadas sobre integración de personas con minusvalía en actividades de tiempo libre. Vitoria: Gobierno Vasco.

Jornadas sobre la Cultura en España y su integración en Europa (1993). Madrid: Ministerio de Cultura.

Montaner, J. (1991) *Estructura del mercado turístico.* Madrid: Síntesis.

Munné, F. (1988) *Psicosociología del tiempo libre. Un enfoque crítico.* México: Trillas.

Pedró, F. (1984) *Ocio y tiempo libre ¿para qué?* Barcelona: Humanitas.

Piñuel, J.L. (1987) *El consumo cultural.* Madrid: Fundamentos.

Quintana, J.M. (1986) *Fundamentos de Animación Sociocultural.* Madrid: Narcea.

Racionero, L. (1983) *Del paro al ocio.* Barcelona: Anagrama.

Rispa, R. (ed.) (1985) *Nuevas tecnologías en la vida cultural española.* Madrid: Fundesco.

Ruiz Olabuenaga, J.I. (1989) *La descodificación de la vida cotidiana: métodos de investigación cualitativa.* Bilbao: Universidad de Deusto.

San Salvador, R. (1993) 'Ocio y Pensamiento en España. Estado de la Cuestión', in *Letras de Deusto*, vol. 57, pp. 133-145.

Secretaría General de Estudios (1991) *Equipamientos, prácticas y consumos culturales de los españoles.* Madrid: Ministerio de Cultura.

Setién, Mª.L. (1993) Indicadores sociales de calidad de vida, Madrid: CIS.

Simposium Europeo Centros Culturales en la dinamización de la ciudad (1990) Bilbao: Ayto.

Simposium Procesos socioculturales y participación. Sociedad civil e instituciones democráticas (1989) Madrid: Popular.

Toharia, J.J. (1990) 'Ocio y tiempo libre', in Elzo, J. (dir.) *Jóvenes vascos* 1990. Vitoria: Gobierno Vasco-Universidad de Deusto.

Trilla, J. (1993) *Otras educaciones: Animación Sociocultural, formación de adultos y ciudad educativa.* Barcelona: Anthropos.

Trilla, J. and Puig, J.M. (1987) *Pedagogía del ocio*. Barcelona: Laertes.

Valenzuela, M. (1987) 'Ciudad y calidad de vida', in *II Congreso Mundial Vasco*. Bilbao-Barcelona: Oikos Tau.

Zallo, R. (1988) *Economía de la comunicación y la cultura*. Madrid: Akal.

Zallo, R. (1992) *Mercado de la cultura. estructura económica y política de la comunicación*. Pamplona: Gakoa.

Zarraga, J.L. (1989) *Informe de Juventud en España*. Madrid: Mtrio. Asuntos Sociales.

Zorrilla, R. (1990) *El consumo de ocio*. Vitoria: Gobierno Vasco.

Chapter 6

Leisure Research in Belgium: No Engine of its Own

Eric Corijn and Patricia Van den Eeckhout

In most historical reconstructions of a scientific research field, the scope of the study is more or less obvious. The science is delimited either by a rather clear research object, or specific methodological perspective and technique, or is institutionally organised in disciplines, faculties and departments of a similar kind - or it combines some or all of these elements. This enables the historian to stick to accepted epistemological boundaries and reconstruct the history in terms of the 'origins' and 'development' of a contemporary activity. The history then helps in clarifying the dominant paradigm or the accepted concepts of the discipline. Historical reconstruction forms part of such clarification. At one end, the contemporary practice, stands scientific theory as the most abstract formulation of research knowledge. At the other end, the origins, stand different sources of thinking, located in a specific social context that gave rise to the stream of activities forming the scientific discipline. In well-established research activities such a method of writing the story of scientific legitimation is possible. It then seems possible to apply epistemological theory and look for phases in development of research programmes, or to search for the relation of internal and contextual influences in intellectual activities.

Writing such a story for leisure studies, which are in Belgium no more than elsewhere hardly recognised as 'sciences', is not that obvious. Leisure studies is a research field still in formation. The conceptual discussion is ongoing and there exists no common understanding of the specific object of the study. The 'problem' to be researched and 'solved' is not clearly formulated. This lack of clarity both makes detachment from common sense notions difficult and blurs the limits of the domain. A number of other elements are missing to establish leisure studies as a scientific discipline. Leisure studies prides itself on being a multi- or inter-disciplinary research field, but this does not yet mean more than that different disciplinary perspectives look at that object.   A real inter-(thus also trans-) disciplinary approach has not yet developed. As we shall see, leisure studies did not grow in the first place as a scientific activity focused on an intellectual problem of some kind, but as a technological question in relation to social policy.

This section is a first attempt to write a history of leisure research in Belgium. Except for a few activity reports of research groups and scarce bibliographies, there exists no overview of scientific knowledge in the field. The collective memory is also not fed by the existence of academic structures or networks referring to some kind of common background. Formally the Belgian National Foundation of Scientific Research has a committee on Leisure Studies, regrouping the academic researchers in the field. But the committee never meets, blocked by academic inertia and competition.

We have tried to compile a bibliography on the subject covering material since the middle of last century. Our main interest was to determine (a) how the theme 'leisure' first grew into a field of intellectual importance and (b) how it then was integrated in institutionally organised research, both in universities and special research centres. We have not looked at specific research topics, such as sports or tourism, developed as part of existing disciplines such as physical education, or regional economy. We have tried to describe how the social emergence of 'free time' influenced scientific interest and organisation.

We do not enter into conceptual discussion about free time or leisure[1], that is, we do not delimit conceptually the object of our study. This history is linked to the word 'free time' as it is used in research using that concept. We do however limit the kind of texts reviewed in this chapter. Our search is oriented to papers of some scientific or academic kind. Thus not all the literature around that theme is used . Pure political or moral texts, or more speculative or poetical approaches have been withheld. We have tried to trace the development of scientific research on that theme and refer to pre-scientific or para-scientific texts only if they can be situated at the roots of further academic and institutional developments.

An important element in the history of leisure research in the 20th century is its links to the development of a welfare state and subsequent organisation of subsidy for scientific research. Belgium experienced in the same period a fundamental state restructuring, from a unitarian to a federal state, with substantial autonomy for the national communities: the Flemish in the north and the Walloon in the south (with a very small third German community in the east). As cultural policy was one of the first to be regionalised, the development of leisure research has of course to be seen in the framework of regional differences. Schematically the north is Catholic and with a long agrarian history, while the south is social-democratic and with long-standing early industrialisation. Where the Catholic leisure discourse is concerned, we will concentrate on the situation in Flanders. These regional differences have their influence in policy-making in both parts of the country and in the type of approaches to social policy.

We will develop a story of the ways in which leisure became an object in Belgium of what is called scientific research. As we shall see, growing 'free time' in society made 'leisure' an object of systematic study, first outside, then inside established research institutes. That process of institutionalisation is marked in the format of the chapter which changes from a chronological structure to an institutional overview. As in the formation of other sciences a research problem gave rise to professionalisation and institutionalisation. The further process that can be traced in other scientific disciplines did not occur, namely the establishment of specific intellectual paradigms, which provide a conceptual frame and research agenda relatively independent of social pragmatism. This explains why 'leisure studies' is fading away with the reduction of welfare state social redistribution policies. We are conscious of the fact that this way of writing the history expresses a certain perspective on the research activity itself, but isn't that precisely one of the aims of a book such as this?

The Growing Free Time of the Working Class

The Unregulated Work Day

According to the industrial census of 1896, 55% of Belgium's industrial workers had working days of 10 hours and more. At that time the length of the working day of an adult industrial worker was completely unregulated. It remained that way until the Act of 14 June 1921 introduced the 8-hour work day. The first (non-academic) research explicitly addressing the leisure problem did not appear until the late 1920s. For the preceding period the social and leisure historian has at his or her disposal government and budget inquiries into the living conditions of the working class and several monographic and sociographic studies.

Animated by the positivist ambition to perform an empirical study of social reality (so that it might be analysed, controlled and influenced) statisticians, doctors, philanthropists, national and local government bodies undertook social inquiries in which the leisure problem, as such, only occupied a marginal position. For instance, the government inquiries into the living and working conditions of the Belgian working class, conducted in 1843/46 and 1886, paid little attention to leisure time and how it was spent. Although the investigators' concern did not focus solely on factors related to production, the interest in reproductive functions was largely limited to the elements which were considered crucial for production itself and as a result, most of the attention focused on working-class food consumption, hygienic conditions, housing and in 1886, education. Remarks referring to leisure mainly addressed the 'moral condition' of the working class in general: its precarious material situation was said to be aggravated or even caused by abuses such as alcoholism and the celebration of the Holy Monday. In the 1886 inquiry the meagre information explicitly dealing with working-class recreation was consequentially preceded by the heading 'moralité de la classe ouvrière'.

It is an indisputable fact that hardly any time or money was available for leisure. Family budget inquiries, calculating the cost of reproduction, give an indication of the limited importance of leisure in working people's lives. One has to bear in mind that they only took commercialised leisure into account and that even the latter may have been underestimated given people's reluctance to admit expenditure on 'luxuries' (Davies, 1992). A budget inquiry held in 1853 by E. Ducpétiaux[2], established that only a meagre 3.9% of an average working-class family's spending went to 'depenses de luxe', mostly visits to the pub and buying tobacco, although some managed to attend festivities or lose money in a lottery (Ducpétiaux, 1855). The actual spending on drink is in contrast with the emphasis put on intemperance in Ducpétiaux' (1843) study of the physical and moral condition of young workers. In this compilation of results of social inquiries, held all over Europe and the United States, Ducpétiaux addressed the problem of 'amusements et récompenses populaires'. He denounced the barbaric amusements of the working class as well as the apathy of those who shared his abhorrence. With his subsequent plea for sufficient leisure time and for leisure alternatives, combining recreation and education, Ducpétiaux seems well ahead of his time.

If we look at the family budget inquiry of 1891, concerning mostly well-paid industrial workers, the expenditure on leisure benefited only slightly from the increase in real wages and reached some 5.7% of the family's spending (*Salaires et budgets ouvriers*, 1892). In the inquiry itself and in the literature it engendered, it was treated accordingly. In the same year Ducpétiaux' budget inquiry was published, the traditionalist, but socially committed, Catholic French mining engineer F. Le Play presented the first volume in the series of monographic studies of working-class families *Les Ouvriers Européens*. Le Play believed that his quest for the conditions of social harmony would benefit from a personal and meticulous observation of social processes and problems. As he was convinced that the family (as well as religion) was the basis of civilisation, his empirical research of social reality focused on so-called representative examples of different types of families. Le Play aimed at a complete and thorough description of every aspect of working-class family life, the family budget at the core of the investigation. As a result, leisure (including non-commercialised leisure) was dealt with more explicitly. In the monographic study concerning a Brussels typographer more than a page was devoted to the description of leisure expenditure and activities (Dauby, 1859). Under the impulse of the Belgian admirer of F. Le Play, the Catholic historian and economist and one of the co-founders of the 'Société Belge Economie Sociale', V. Brants, other Belgian monographic studies were produced after 1886 and published in the series *Ouvriers des deux mondes* (Brants, 1906). They all devoted some text to describe workers' distractions and pastimes. The compilers could hardly disguise their approval when working-class families appeared to adapt their leisure occupations to their modest means and avoided drinking and the betting that surrounded pigeon-flying, cock-fighting, bird-singing etc. Occasionally the less commendable recreations of fellow workers were referred to with restrained aversion.

V. Brants was one of the most influential teachers of the Ecole des Sciences Politiques et Sociales which had been created (1892) in the Law Faculty of the University of Louvain (Meerts, 1992). Towards the end of the nineteenth century Catholics, alarmed by the threat of explosive class antagonism, welcomed limited state intervention to eliminate the worst abuses in the social arena: it was the ambition of the newly created school to form the future technocrats and politicians who would develop social and labour law. In Brants' very practical *Conférences d'économie sociale* students were familiarised with the modern methods of observation and investigation. One should not have the impression though that sociology as such was introduced: Brants' pragmatic adoption of the inductive method does not imply that the substance, the epistemological problems and theories of sociology, were discussed. The latter was rather the domain of the Institut supérieur de philosophie (Meerts, 1992) where one tried to find a compromise between the new science and Christian ethics (Wils, 1991). It was in this institute that the first 'genuine' courses in sociology would be introduced in the Catholic university in the late 1930s (De Bie, 1972, 1988).

Strongly influenced by Brants' and Le Play's empiricism, as well as by the methods of the 'Historische Schule', one of Brants' students, E. Vliebergh, produced several monographic studies: these were sociographic contributions, not focusing on individual working-class families but on different agrarian regions. Vliebergh's interest in the social, economic and moral condition of the agrarian population was the result of the growing Catholic concern for the sake of the endangered agrarian community, one of the strongholds of Catholic civilisation. Vliebergh, who became himself a professor at the Catholic university and who had a leading position in the Catholic league of Belgian farmers, was in his turn a source of inspiration for other sociographic contributions[3]. These studies were founded on a thorough investigation of printed and archival sources and on an extensive written and oral inquiry among village notables and others. Every aspect of the region was discussed, often from an historical perspective. The introductory chapters were mostly limited to an overview of the sources and a statement of the author's aim to describe how these agrarian populations lived and worked. Although no theoretical statements were made, the questionnaires reveal that one of the investigators' major preoccupations concerned the (moral) influence of industrialisation, urbanisation and migration on the agrarian communities. In the questionnaire quite a few questions explicitly addressed the leisure problem: what were the farmers' and agricultural labourers' favourite distractions and games? How much money was involved? What about fairs, dancing and poaching? Did people drink? and if so: where, when and what did they drink? Did people drink more than in the past and did women consume alcohol? Did people read and if so, what did they read, and how could that pastime be promoted? Were there special harvest festivities? The answers, gathered under headings such as 'genre de vie-moeurs', 'vie rurale' or 'divertissements et coutumes', often dealt with the changes leisure had undergone in the three or four decades preceding the inquiry. The authors especially emphasised the spreading of pigeon-flying and cycling.

In 1910 the English industrialist B. S. Rowntree published a sociographic study of Belgium, hoping that his survey would provide some lessons for the solution of the poverty problem in Britain. In the family budgets he collected, leisure expenditures were scarcely mentioned but, not surprisingly, the teetotaller Rowntree devoted chapters to the drink problem and to betting and gambling. Within the chapter on betting and gambling the favourite pastime of the Belgian worker, namely pigeon-flying, was elaborately described (Rowntree, 1910)

Before the First World War the Belgian worker may have had little time or money for leisure, but it did not prevent the parish priests and the Catholic bourgeoisie proposing leisure activities designed to keep the honest workers and the youngsters off the streets and out of the pubs in their scarce moments of relaxation (Van Damme, 1981; Stallaerts and Schokkaert, 1987). These paternalist initiatives ranged from choirs, theatre, brass bands and gymnastics, to pubs where one could play cards and have a drink in all decency. They were part of the church's attempt to counter secularisation (and later socialism) in a era when the impact of the church on people's lives became less self-evident. Progressive liberals, on the other hand, believing in education as a means of upward social mobility and integration of the oppressed, concentrated on the organisation of lectures and libraries and initiatives inspired by the University Extension Movement (Van Damme, 1981). Most of their activities only reached the lower middle class and a working-class elite. With the growth of both the socialist and Catholic workers' movement, the workers' organisations themselves developed initiatives to cultivate and distract their members, giving them lectures, libraries, plays, music, physical education or the mere availability of a meeting place of their own: the 'maisons du peuple' or their Catholic equivalents, which were the heart of the local organised workers' movement (Van Damme, 1981; Degée, 1986; Stallaerts and Schokkaert, 1987).

The 8-hour Day (1921)

With the Act of 14 June 1921 the working day was limited to 8 hours and the working week to 48 hours. Only industrial workers were covered by the law. Those employed in sectors where the balance of power had been to their advantage did not have to wait for this legal measure but others met difficulties in imposing its application. With the limitation of time taken up by production, the problem of working-class leisure became an important issue, although in this period it hardly led to academic research as such.

Belgian workers' organisations welcomed the restriction of working time, for which the socialists in particular had fought, but at the same time a major new concern arose: how would the time freed from production be spent? Would the benefits of increasing real wages and leisure time be brought to the pub or other forms of unworthy pastimes?

Of course, this concern was not new. We have already mentioned that since the end of the nineteenth century Catholic and socialist workers' organisations (the latter strongly influenced by the initiatives of progressive liberals) had developed activities, aimed at the cultural elevation of their members. However, the inter-war period witnessed a massification and an expansion of this educational work, either embedded in the political, social and economic workers' organisations or as the object of newly created institutions. Where the Catholic workers' organisations are concerned, one must be aware that they were co-ordinated by the overall workers' organisation Algemeen christelijk werkersverbond (A.C.W.), that organised the Catholic workers on a denominational basis.

Providing leisure opportunities for workers was not these organisations' only aim. At the same time these activities, often developed for male adults, women and youth separately, were indispensable instruments in colouring the worker's life with the spirit of organisation. As a result, the worker ought to be protected from rival ideologies or from the most alarming competitor: commercialised leisure. Where possible versions of commercialised recreation were produced and proposed as alternatives. If economic constraints prevented this strategy, controlling and regulating the members' use of commercialised leisure opportunities seemed the second best choice (Laermans, 1992).

A proactive rechristianisation of society, propagated by the church in the inter-war period, was the Catholics' source of inspiration. The effects of this so-called 'Katholieke actie' would last well into the 1950s (Laermans, 1992). Countering secularisation on every social level was one of its aims. Commercialised leisure (pubs, cinemas, dancing, sporting events) was an important target in this offensive against modernisation, materialism and moral decay (Stallaerts and Schokkaert, 1987). The socialists too, feared that the temptations of capitalist commercialised leisure might entice the workers (and youth in particular) away from the right cause (Dooms, 1983/84; Temmerman, 1978/79). Opposed to commercialised recreation, bourgeois perversions and bestial pleasures (such as alcohol abuse, betting, gambling and carnival) a socialist counterculture based on self-discipline had to develop (Degée, 1986).

Both in the socialist and the Catholic case, the youth movement in particular mobilised round these themes. Where the socialist youth movement is concerned a numerically small but not unimportant current must be mentioned: the so-called 'socialisme als cultuurbeweging', a philosophy imported from Austria and Germany through the Netherlands and whose influence was mostly limited to the Flemish part of the country (Temmerman, 1978/79). It criticised the 'embourgeoisement' of the working class, emphasising the cultivation of a socialist 'behaviour', rather than a change of social and economic structures. Its ideals of 'back to nature', 'back to the old pre-capitalist folk pastimes' and the puritan attitude towards drinking, smoking etc. were very much in agreement with the aforementioned denunciation of leisure in capitalist society (Temmerman, 1978/79; Dooms, 1983/84).

Both the socialists' and Catholics, view on leisure was of a very paternalist and moralising nature (Stallaerts and Schollaert, 1987; Degée, 1986; Depasse and André, 1931; Depasse, 1936; A.C.W. ,1922; Cool, 1932; Schmook, 1932). Left to their own devices, they argued, workers succumbed to the intoxicating and titillating temptations of commercialised leisure. The latter was only after profit and it ignored moral and educational preoccupations. And even if workers read books, attended lectures, plays or musical performances, their preference always went to the most vulgar variants. Only a working-class elite was supposed to make the 'right' choices where leisure was concerned, the others had to be educated in order to develop activities that were both morally and intellectually enriching. Apart from the necessary rest, popular education and healthy distractions (like athletics) seemed the only valuable options for filling the increasing non-working time.

In analysing the cultural preoccupations of workers' organisations, one must be careful though to distinguish between the ideals presented in the discourse and the work in the field. Despite the fact that both socialists and Catholics cherished the ideal of raising the moral and intellectual level of the masses, the impact of the activities, was often largely limited to the militants. For many members, the workers' organisations' educational initiatives took the form of either very practical activities (cooking lessons, hygiene, baby care, house keeping in general and even professional training) or merely distracting occupations (meetings in the local Catholic or socialist café and 'koffietafel', social occasions with coffee and cake) (Stallaerts and Schokkaert, 1987). Even organising the house-keeping lessons was not always an untrammelled success (Christens and De Decker, 1986).

There were attempts to combine education and recreation but their success was very modest. Temmerman (1978/79) suggests that in the local sections of the socialist youth organisation, members often only participated in the recreational activities. P. Landsvreugt, reporting on Flemish socialist workers' education in the educational organisations' periodical *Ontwikkeling en uitspanning* in November 1924, complained about the level of the local cultural manifestations. The latter seemed more interested in quantity than in quality (Degée, 1986). Hence, since the late 1920s, the overall socialist educational effort definitely concentrated on an activity that produced immediate and visible results, namely the formation of cadres and technocrats (Degée, 1986). Local initiative had to take care of the rest (Debruyne, 1975/76). In the 1930s the newly-created general educational organisation of the Christian workers' movement had the ambition to develop separate activities for the elite and the ordinary members. Reading Vanhaverbeke (1980) and Verleyen (1985) we have the impression that the former was rather more successful than the latter.

It was within the spirit of the inter-war Catholic action against secularisation and modernisation that the earliest inquiries focusing on leisure were conducted. These were not produced by academic circles but by concerned Catholics. The author of the first inquiry was a worried Antwerp catholic, A. Sledsens. Struck by the dangers of increased leisure time, he investigated the Antwerp worker's leisure in the years 1922-1926 (Sledsens, 1929). He made an inventory of institutions and organisations, even using statistical material concerning cinemas, music halls, theatres, ballrooms, public libraries, works for popular education, taxes on gambling etc. Far more interesting however, is Sledsens' colourful description of how Antwerp working-class families worked, lived and spent their leisure time. Expecting that these families, the women in particular, would show him the door if they knew what he was trying to find out, he used his position as a visitor of the charitable Saint Vincentius organisation in order to introduce himself into the families' lives. Five so-called typical families were chosen. Their income, rent and housing situation were described as well as the individual members' profession, character, morals and pastimes. Sledsens was certainly not trying to produce a neutral account of reality. He found few pastimes favourable, and he did not hesitate to make a passionate plea against the morally degrading pursuits that the families involved seemed to prefer. Potentially valuable activities like going to the movies or attending sporting events were corrupted as both were chosen because of the expected passions they might arouse, serving as a flight from daily reality.

Sledsens' views and the alternatives he proposed certainly conformed with the Catholic workers' organisations' treatment of the leisure problem, although, as far as we know, Sledsens (who was a lawyer) was not involved in them. In the elections of 1936 he stood as a middle-class candidate on the list of the Antwerp Catholic party (Van Mechelen, 1980). Sledsens too considered the worker as a weak individual that would instinctively grab at the lowest and easiest diversions, procuring instant excitement. Like the Catholic and socialist workers' organisations, Sledsens insisted that the worker had to be offered valuable alternatives, giving him the opportunity to develop his moral and intellectual abilities. Typical of the Catholic view, formulated by Sledsens and others, is the opinion that the worker ought to devote his leisure time to the cultivation of family life. A radio, for example, could incite him to stay at home after working hours. However, the virtues of family life were not to discourage him to attend the activities proposed by the workers' organisations' cultural sections. Apparently, a fragile balance had to be established between family cohesion and the workers' organisations' impact on the members' lives.

One of the Catholic organisations which was very militant in fighting the effects of modernisation, was the Catholic working youth movement (Katholieke arbeidersjeugd - K.A.J.). According to the slogan of its moral leader (J. Cardijn, a pupil of the V. Brants mentioned above) 'Zien, oordelen, handelen' (Seeing, judging, acting) inquiries were made into the living and working conditions of the Catholic working youth. In 1931/1932 the yearly theme of the investigations and discussions were the leisure occupations of working youth. A brochure titled 'For the Conquest of Leisure Time' was printed in which the negative effects of commercialised leisure (and the profits it made) were discussed as well as the fact that family and social organisations were losing control over leisure and how it was spent [4]. The working class, society and even civilisation would suffer the most dreadful fate if leisure was not used to work at one's moral, religious, social and intellectual development. The Catholic youth movement had to influence the way leisure was spent and develop alternatives which would grow into the youth's 'natural' leisure environment. Responsible youngsters were charged with the mission to inquire into the leisure occupations of their fellow members. They had to learn the questionnaire more or less by heart because those who were questioned were not supposed to know that it was an investigation. Detailed questions were asked in order to determine whether the working youngsters disposed of enough leisure time and whether they were able to find room for relaxation, religious duties, meetings. How could leisure time be extended? How was the enforced leisure of the unemployed spent? Another part of the inquiry concerned moral, intellectual and emotional life. How was the atmosphere at home? What were the housing conditions like? Did the mother work? Did he spend his leisure time at home? Did he have a steady relationship? Did he read, go to lectures, music performances etc.? Commercialised leisure occupations (cinema, dancing, drinking, sport) were the subject of a third part of the inquiry. The youngsters completing the investigation were not only asked to register the facts but they had to give their opinion concerning the adequacy of the available leisure time, the moral influence of some leisure occupations etc. The inquiry was carried out by the local sections and the results were discussed in the regional meetings of the youth movement. The archives contain some fragments of its results. However, we do not have the impression that a synthesis on the national level was ever made. This is not surprising since it was not so much the results of the inquiry which were important to the movement as the educational effect on those who had participated in its execution and discussion.

The Catholic Women Workers' Organization (Katholieke arbeidersvrouwen - K.A.V.) was also preoccupied by the increasing secularisation of society (Christens and De Decker, 1986). In 1938/39 the organisations' year theme was 'family life' and the K.A.V. felt the need to conduct a large inquiry into that matter. It particularly wanted to find out whether the secularisation of society had affected traditional Christian family values. The K.A.V. trusted the execution of its inquiry to an academic of the Catholic university: N. Devolder.

Since the turn of the century Catholic academics and sociology had an ambiguous relationship. One might say that both in the Ecole des sciences politiques et sociales and in the Institut supérieur de philosophie the value of observation and of the inductive method were acknowledged. However, circles of the Institute of Philosophy, that had always shown a keen interest in the problems of theoretical sociology, were hostile towards sociology as a 'system' with the ambition of penetrating reality by observation alone. Morals and religion, Catholic philosophers argued, could never be fathomed if one reduced them to their observable social functions (De Bie, 1988). For them, the observation of society should never be isolated from its normative counterpart: social philosophy (Devolder, 1943). Besides that, most Catholic academics identified sociology with a positivist, anti-religious and anti-clerical 'philosophy' that would undermine Christian morals and religion, replacing them by a new, lay religion without any reference to the transcendental (Ladrière, 1961). In the late 1930s some changes in the attitude towards sociology surfaced. In 1938/39 the Institute of Philosophy appointed canon J. Leclercq who had been teaching moral philosophy and natural law since 1921. Shortly after J. Leclercq introduced sociology as a part of his course of moral philosophy. The following year sociology was officially put on the curriculum, other more specialised courses followed and according to de Bie (1961) the Catholic university had one of the most elaborate sociology programmes of Europe by 1945.

The theme of the 'new' Catholic attitude towards sociology, was the conviction that one had to dispose of an exact knowledge of social reality, which in its turn had to be the result of careful and methodical observation. New was the openly declared belief in the possibility of a 'value-free' science with only one ambition: namely to describe the world as it was, and not how it should be. In 1943 N. Devolder (1943a) published a plea for a complete separation of observation and norm, of sociology and social philosophy. However this practice was not entirely new: some of the already mentioned 'catholic' sociographic studies of the turn of the century were undoubtedly going in that direction. The fact that these studies were products of an empirical current, avoiding the philosophers' theoretical debates, was certainly a precondition for their explicit attempt to 'stick to the facts'.

It was the same Devolder (1943b) who was charged with the inquiry among the K.A.V. members. A questionnaire was distributed to some 135,000 people. By early January 1939 nearly 15,000 usable forms had been returned. Devolder analysed and commented on the inquiry and Leclercq wrote the introduction. He emphasised that noble intentions were insufficient if an organisation wanted to influence and change social reality: first of all one needed an exact knowledge of the facts. The following questions were submitted to the K.A.V. members: do you need a home? why? do you enjoy being in mother's kitchen? why? which elements are bad for family life? what can be done to improve family life and what have you already done? did it help? It appears that 43% of the participants pointed to 'economic problems' (women's wage labour, unemployment, poverty) as a main cause for the deterioration of family life but that no less than 41% accused leisure occupations: an irresponsible use of cinema and radio, alcoholism and visits to the pub and filthy books and illustrations. For Devolder, this proved that the moral and cultural elevation of the family ought to keep pace with its increasing material well-being. Despite his plea for a value-free sociology, Devolder's comments on the results of the inquiry were full of explicit and implicit normative judgements. He described how commercialised leisure attracted the young worker, bored by his job, but with money of his own to spend. The result was that family members drifted apart because parents did not know how to combine traditional family values and the positive aspects of modern leisure (that is where the educational mission of the women's organisation came in). What abhorred him most was that commercialised leisure was only after money: no psychological, familial or educational needs were taken into account. Like the rest of industry, he argued, commercialised leisure created its own demand. He fell completely out of his (academic) role when he praised the strength of the heroic Flemish housewife, a beacon in the struggle against industry, film and public entertainment and when he celebrated that 'despite everything' the core of Flemish family life had remained thoroughly Christian.

We are not aware of any inquiries into the worker's leisure occupations conducted by the socialist workers' organisations. The latter seemed to concentrate on legislative work, as a means to promote the valuable use of non-working time. In contrast with the Catholics they were of the opinion that the national and local state could play an important part in this field, while Catholics saw the state's role limited to encouraging and subsidising private initiative.

In the same year the act on the limitation of working time was passed, the socialist minister J. Destrée lay the basis for the promotion and subsidising of local libraries and for the financial support of initiatives in the field of popular education. In 1922 several socialist members of the House of Representatives, led by L. Piérard, proposed the creation of a 'Oeuvre national des loisirs du travailleur'. By creating institutions for working-class leisure and by promoting private initiative in the same field, the 'Oeuvre' had to encourage the workers to spend their leisure time in a useful way and not in idle lounging. In 1929 at last, a strongly 'amputated' version of the Piérard's proposal was adopted by the legislative chambers and a 'Conseil supérieur de l'éducation populaire' was installed, an advisory commission that would mainly address problems of popular education (Bosmans-Hermans, 1979).

Its socialist secretary, Depasse, produced a descriptive inventory of the social, cultural and educational organisations that could contribute to a valuable use of the worker's free time. The council also made a thorough investigation of music and the role it could play in the elevation of the worker's cultural level. The 'Conseil supérieur de l'éducation populaire' was not the only advisory commission installed to investigate and document these matters. In the provinces of Hainaut, Liège and Brabant provincial commissions 'des loisirs de l'ouvrier' had already been created in 1919, before the 8-hour day had actually been voted in. The Hainaut province, containing a large working-class population, was particularly active in this field. Its 'Commission d'étude des loisirs de l'ouvrier' made an inventory of all the existing organisations that could play a part in the filling up of the worker's free time (Pastur, 1936). Particular attention was drawn to the problem of working-class housing. The commission was convinced that acceptable, quality housing was a crucial element in a healthy and socially valuable use of the free time. Shabby dwellings would chase the worker to the pub while attractive ones were a good basis for a strong family life. The commission organised competitions for the design of suitable working-class furniture and it financed travelling exhibitions where these were shown. Lectures were held where hygiene and good taste in the arrangement of one's home were discussed. Engravings and objects of art of which the commission approved because of their aesthetic and educational value, were sold in order to improve the decoration of the working-class house. Other sections were involved in the promotion of gardening and the breeding of small cattle, as a pastime that was healthy, useful and financially rewarding. Physical and artistic education, evening classes for adults and public libraries were also promoted.

The activities of the provincial commissions on leisure, especially the one of the Hainaut province, were discussed at the 6th conference of the International Labour Organization in 1924. This conference had put working-class leisure on its agenda. Where the problem of state involvement was concerned, the recommendations of the conference were clearly inspired by the Belgian example. The conference suggested the creation of regional or local commissions that would co-ordinate and harmonise the different efforts in the field of leisure. One of the attractions of the Belgian example consisted in the fact that these commissions were directed by the representatives of both public and private initiative (employers and workers). It was the provincial leisure commission of Liége that hosted the 'Premier congrès international des loisirs de l'ouvrier' in 1930. Despite the fact that some 300 representatives from 18 different countries participated, the number of Belgians was so impressive that the foreign visitors refused to subscribe to the conclusions because they were too much influenced by the Belgian situation. The next international leisure conference was held in Los Angeles but in 1935 the meeting took place in Brussels. The 'Conseil supérieur de l'éducation populaire' hosted the conference and organised an exhibition in which Belgian and foreign realisations in the field of leisure and popular education were presented (among them a model library, a model garden and a model living room). The Belgian involvement on the international level was certainly not limited to organisational matters. In the years preceding this conference L. Piérard, whom we already met as the author of the proposition to create a 'Oeuvre national des loisirs des travailleurs', had lobbied for the creation of a permanent international leisure commission. Despite the fact that the 1935 conference gave its principal agreement, the actual establishment was postponed. The consultative committee of correspondents that was eventually created in 1936 was unsatisfactory and therefore another international conference was held in Brussels in 1938. L. Piérard became the chairman and the already mentioned Ch. Depasse the secretary of the newly created 'l'Association internationale pour les loisirs du travailleur' whose activity would never really get off the ground (Bosmans-Hermans, 1979).

The afore-mentioned Catholic inquiries into working-class leisure and the inventories of leisure institutions, produced by the public or semi-public leisure commissions, were the only 'research' focusing on leisure. Academic research was still absent in this period. However, we find some important indications in the inquiries made by G. Jacquemyns. Jacquemyns worked at the Institut de Sociologie Solvay of the Université Libre de Bruxelles. The latter was the first Belgian university to have courses in sociology while the Institut de sociologie, established in 1901 by the industrialist Solvay, was the first of its kind in Belgium. The spirit in which Jacquemyns' inquiries were conducted, was in complete agreement with the mission he was charged with by the director of the institute, E. Mahaim. The latter had invited him to organise a 'observatoire social' in which careful and methodical observation would contribute to the objective reproduction of social reality.

In the years 1932/34 Jacquemyns made an inquiry into the family budgets of the unemployed (Jacquemyns, 1932/34). Jacquemyns was an historian but his methods of investigation were definitely those of a sociologist. By means of an impartial and accurate observation of reality, he argued, he would try to capture the social phenomenon of unemployment. The families' way of life was described as well as the material and psychological effects of their condition. For him, this was the best way to measure the influence of the crisis, the degradation of daily life and the social deterioration of those who had lost their jobs. 'Rien ne pourrait mieux nous éclairer sur la nature même du social', Mahaim stated in his foreword, 'que de le surprendre agissant sur les esprits, les maniéres d'etre et de penser'. Although it was not Jacquemyns' principal preoccupation, we do learn in a lot of cases how unemployment influenced leisure activities and expenditure. The observation of the way of life of some labourers who were still at work, provides us with a vivid picture of the industrial worker's pastime in the area of Charleroi. Jacquemyns was to follow this line of research with his investigation of daily life during German occupation (Jacquemyns, 1950). By means of 122 monographs the life style, the moral and social behaviour of working-class families was studied. In his introduction Jacquemyns praised the monographic method as the best way of penetrating the life of the families involved and he also stressed the sociologist's mission of objectivity. In the chapter 'Les loisirs, les distractions' the information found in the monographs was synthesised and the influence of the war on the spending for leisure and leisure occupations was described as well as the nostalgic memories of the quality and price of beer and tobacco before the war. In 1939 Jacquemyns published a sociographic study of social life in the mining villages of the Borinage (Jacquemyns, 1939). By means of a thorough investigation of different social environments and social processes, he would try to gather the sociologist's study material while trying to find a sociological explanation for the phenomena he observed. For too long, he argued, sociologists had made generalisations based on a limited knowledge of the facts; hence, the crisis in sociology. One had to restore contact with reality under the device 'observer et comprendre'. In the 40 pages devoted to 'loisirs et divertissements' a detailed descriptive account (occasionally augmented by some figures) was made of all the leisure opportunities available.

Paid Vacation (1936)

Since the beginning of the 1930s the reduction of the working week to 40 hours, without loss of pay, was more and more invoked as an expedient to absorb unemployment although it was rather half-heartedly defended by both the Catholic and socialist workers' movement. When the Front Populaire government complied with the French strikers' demand for a 40-hour week and paid vacation, an analogous strike movement spread to Belgium. Eventually paid vacation was conceded: according to the Act of 8 July 1936, workers were entitled to 6 days of paid vacation per year. Where the 40-hour week was concerned, a rather vague commitment was made to have it introduced in unhealthy industries (Maes and Van Rie, 1985).

While the introduction of the 8-hour working day had led to the creation of a 'Conseil supérieur de l'éducation populaire' and to an amplification of the cultural activities proposed by the workers' organisations, the introduction of the yearly vacation was followed by the establishment in 1937 of an 'Office national belge des vacances ouvriéres' and the increase of travelling opportunities and holiday resorts offered by the workers' organisations to their members. The 'Office national' took charge of the study and promoted working-class holidays and travel. First, the workers had to be educated to enjoy their leisure time, now they had to get used to the idea of travelling. Workers were supposed to consider travelling as dangerous and far from relaxing. The head of the Office, the liberal H. Janne (who had quite a few affinities with the socialist H. De Man and who was to join the socialist party after the Second World War), stated that it would not be easy 'pour faire entrer les vacances dans le style de vie des travailleurs' (Janne, 1939; Gaus, 1989)

With the introduction of the yearly vacation for workers in 1936, the subject of leisure finally made its explicit appearance on the academic forum. In 1937 a whole week was devoted to its study. It was in the Institut de Sociologie Solvay of the Université Libre de Bruxelles, organiser of the so called 'Semaine sociale universitaire', that the first signs of academic interest in the subject were shown. The aim of this meeting was to make an inventory of all the problems related to leisure and to register and make a critical evaluation of the proposed solutions. Sociologists, economists, psychologists, administrators, politicians and representatives of social and cultural organisations contributed to the conference. Among the subjects treated were the leisure of the different social classes, the economic importance of leisure (discussed by the renowned Catholic economist F. Baudhuin) and state involvement in the provision of leisure. The representatives

of the academic circles developed rather superficial analyses of the
problem, based on their own rather impressionist observations and,
once again, on the inventory of institutions and activities. G.
Jacquemyns reported on leisure in fascist Italy and the U.S.S.R. and
he managed to distinguish himself somewhat from the others by
explicitly addressing the problem of leisure, dominated by the state.
On the occasion of excursions to Antwerp and the Borinage area, the
representatives of social and cultural organisations gave an account of
the initiatives they were involved in. In the concluding remarks it was
stated that two major differences of opinion characterised the
discussions. First of all there was the disagreement between those who
were in favour of a solely recreative use of leisure time and those who
had cultural and educational purposes. Some were convinced that
folklorist manifestations and traditional games were flourishing while
the cultural and educational institutions, imposed upon the people,
were a failure. According to others, the working class was craving for
culture. If the desire to be cultivated was not expressed spontaneously,
it could be provoked and developed by cultural institutions. Finally,
there were those who believed that if the working class had a confused
aspiration for culture, the initiatives meeting these wishes had failed.
The second major point of discussion concerned the extent of state
involvement in the provision of leisure opportunities (Fuss, 1937).

The 45-hour Week

The campaign for a further reduction of working time started in 1954.
However, one does not have to wait for this debate and the actual
realisation of the demand to come across studies and inquiries where
leisure was explicitly treated. We have already discussed how in the
late 1930s sociology was officially introduced in the Catholic
university of Louvain. One of the fields developed by canon J.
Leclercq and his collaborator N. Devolder, was the sociology of
religion. In 1948 Leclercq headed the first international conference in
the field that took place in Louvain. The department produced studies
in the sociology of religion and, by extension, the familial and cultural
condition of different population groups. At the end of the 1940s, for
instance, inquiries on the cultural level of manual workers (Lagasse,
1948) and students (De Groote, 1949) were produced under the
guidance of Leclercq, director of the 'Cours pratique de sociologie'
and Y. Urbain, director of the 'Cours pratique de politique sociale'. By
means of interviews, workers were questioned about their daily life,
family and friendly relations, religious feelings, leisure etc.
Quantitative and qualitative details concerning leisure occupations
were gathered. In comparison with Devolder's 1943 account of family
relations, the report had a pronounced academic tone. Of course, it
stated that the worker chose the easiest and most popular diversions
but the fact is more registered than denounced. One does not have the
impression that one is reading the product of concerned Catholics,

although there are a lot of implicit value judgements. The emphasis put on family relations and family cohesion is one of them. The report also stresses the cultural differentiation within the working class, praising the benefits of schooling and education as a means of social mobility. The interdependence of family cohesion, education and upward social mobility is emphasised.

Leclercq and Urbain were among those who established, in 1955, the 'Centre de politique sociale' that was to become the 'Centre d'études sociales' in the same year. According to its founders, this sociological research institute was to perform scientific research in the field of social life and social problems (De Bie, 1972). Its work had to be of use to Belgian society in general and for the Catholic organisations in particular. Leclercq had contacts with the Catholic unions and employers who offered the centre financial support in the form of research contracts. Most of the research projects concerned problems of industrial sociology but in 1956/57 an opinion poll concerning the reduction of work time was undertaken by order of the Catholic union Algemeen Christelijk Vakverbond (A.C.V.). Before we look into this and similar studies, we have to discuss the mobilisation of the Catholic union for the reduction of work time.

In 1954 unions and employers had reached the principal agreement that the increase of productivity would be compensated. According to the unions, this could take the form of an increase in wages, a productivity bonus or, first of all, a reduction in work time [5]. A working week of 40 hours was put forward as the goal to aim for but both the Catholic and socialist union agreed that a transition period of a 44 or 45-hour week was inevitable. The Catholic union stressed the need for a working week of five days: this was supposed to be beneficial for family life, for the attendance of church and for the workers' participation in the educational activities organised by the workers' organisations' cultural branches. However, when it came to the implementation of the agreement, the employers appeared to have their well-known economic arguments ready to advise against it. In the months that followed the Catholic union mobilised to have its demands met. A petition campaign was launched and on three Saturdays they went on strike, claiming a 5-day working week and a minimum wage. Both the radicalisation of the Catholic and the abstinence of the socialist union can be largely explained by the political constellation of the moment. In the spring of 1954 the one and only post-war government without the Christian-democrat party (with the exception of the short-lived coalitions after the liberation) had been formed. Given the vertical lines of solidarity within the Catholic pillar, the Catholic union was more inclined to oppose the government, the more so as the government's school policy had turned the Catholic world as a whole against it. The socialist union on the contrary, was not eager to break the anti-clerical solidarity with the liberals and join the anti-government forces, not in the least because quite a few union bosses were also holding political positions. However, when the intense mobilisation round the education policy had lessened, it was the socialist union's turn to take the initiative and eventually the employers were forced to give in. In July 1956 some 53% of Belgian blue and white collar workers enjoyed the 45-hour working week. By 1960 it was almost general. It was legally generalised only on 15 July 1964. The 40-hour week, demanded for more than 30 years, is still far ahead. From 1962 onwards the unions wanted a gradual introduction of the 40-hour week, without loss of pay, by means of biennial collective agreements. In 1963 and 1966 however, they gave their preference to a third holiday week and the doubling of vacation pay. The employers and the government continued to resist work-time reduction. We will have to wait for the end of the 1960s before agreements on a gradual introduction of the 40-hour week occurred. Those of 1969 and 1970 shortened the work time by one hour. In 1972 the 42-hour week, in 1974 the 41-hour week and in 1975, at last, the 40-hour week was obtained. The struggle lasted for 44 years (Maes and Van Rie, 1985)!

It appears that the Catholic educational organisations were, once again, not at ease where the effects of the work time reduction of 1956 were concerned. This is not surprising since the 'traditional' leisure problems were emphasised by progressing secularisation and a declining impact of the moral and religious prescriptions. In 1956 the overall Christian workers' organisation's periodical *De gids op maatschappelijk gebied* devoted several articles to the leisure problem. It appears that the main themes of the Catholic discourse on leisure in the inter-war period were still prominent in the 1950s (Laermans, 1992). The devastating effects of commercialised leisure were perhaps less formulated in terms of personal corruption than as a gigantic process of massification and depersonalisation. In contrast with the pre-war period this concern not only led to sermons and pleas against some forms of leisure activities but it engendered sociological studies and enquiries explicitly addressing the use of free time. The general point was that one needed accurate and not impressionist information about social reality in order to develop a policy that would successfully control and influence it. Of course this idea was not entirely new. The inquiries of the nineteenth century, as well as the monographic and sociographic studies were produced for similar reasons. However, while the latter addressed the broad social and economic conditions of whole regions and social classes, the inquiries of the 1950s were explicitly conducted in order to register the beliefs and feelings of actual or potential members of social organisations. The fear that the organisation might lose its impact was the major motive for their execution. Although this preoccupation was already present in Devolder's K.A.V. inquiry, we do think that one has to wait until the middle of the 1950s to witness a general acceptance within the Catholic world of the idea of using the results of sociological research as a basis for the elaboration of a specific policy. The fact that the workers' organisations' bureaucracies were more and more manned by technocrats with an academic education, instead of self-taught men, social workers and priests, was of course not without importance. In the same period Devolder (1958/59) signals the very pragmatic use of the results of the sociographic studies in the field of religion. He points to another important development namely the fact that the passionate theoretical debates, full of philosophical speculations and theological apriorisms, belonged to the past: methodology and techniques had come to the foreground. This undoubtedly eased the general acceptance of sociology in the Catholic world.

As already mentioned, the Catholic union ordered the 'Centrum voor sociale studies' of the Catholic university in 1956 to conduct an opinion poll among blue collar workers in order to find out whether the generally assumed striving of the labouring masses for a reduction of work time corresponded with reality (Centrum voor sociale studies, 1956/57). One had to find out whether the workers preferred a reduction of work time or a rise in pay and which forms of work-time reduction had their approval. The motives for these preferences where equally important and in order to 'explain' them, information on the participants' personal, familial and work conditions were gathered. As the Catholic union had distinguished itself in claiming a reduction of work time, it was eager to find out whether the workers knew which union had taken the initiative in that matter. Two thirds of the participants (in which Christian union members were over-represented) gave a preference to work-time reduction, mostly with the motive that they would use the increased non-working time for resting and attending to household jobs.

In preparation of a regional congress of the Catholic worker's co-ordinating organisation A.C.W. in the province of Limbourg in 1956, an inquiry concerning the members' leisure occupations and the workers' opinion about the effects of the 5-day working week was organised. The questionnaire was elaborated with the help of two researchers of the 'Centrum voor sociale studies' of the Catholic university. Besides the inquiry, quantitative and qualitative information concerning the leisure opportunities available in the area was gathered (A.C.W.-Limburg, 1956). This was also the case on the occasion of the regional congress of the A.C.W. in the area of Turnhout in the same year (A.C.W.-Turnhout, 1956).

In the spirit of using the supposed value-free results of sociological research to adjust one's policy, the 'Centrum voor sociale studies' was charged in 1957 by the overall Catholic youth organisation 'Jeugdverbond voor katholieke actie' (J.V.K.A.) to look into the leisure occupations of the Flemish youth between 13 and 24 years old (Centrum voor sociale studies, 1957). The organisation clearly feared that Catholic youth work was losing its impact. It was not enough to have the 'right' values, one had to be able to 'sell' them to as many people as possible! If Catholic youth associations were to keep or even enlarge their number of followers, they had to find out what the youngsters were really interested in: what were their favourite pastimes? The organisations could then try to integrate these elements in their programme. It is clear that, in comparison with the pre-war period, there was a disposition to adapt oneself to social reality instead of merely trying to influence it. The K.U.L. researchers carrying out the inquiry, produced a rather 'dry and mainly quantitative report. They explicitly stated that they wanted to make a snapshot of the principal leisure occupations of the Flemish youth without inquiring into motivations and opinions. They also stressed that they had taken care that neither the questionnaire nor the execution of the inquiry contained normative elements or value judgements. A general conclusion was explicitly left out. Questions were asked about pocket money and the way it was spent. The researchers also wanted to know whether the youngsters had to give their parents an explanation for their comings and goings, their visits to the cinema and the way they spent their pocket money. Other questions addressed specific leisure occupations (with special attention to leisure spent within the family), the adherence to (youth) associations and the extent of the involvement. Apparently the researchers of the institute were unable to convince their sponsor of the soundness of their methodology (interviews), because the J.V.K.A. insisted that they would also use a questionnaire which was unfavourably regarded by the researchers since they had no control on its distribution. Between the lines you sense the irritation caused by the youth organisation's unfamiliarity with sociological research methodology.

Reading these research reports one might have the impression that the passionate pleas against modern leisure had entirely disappeared from the Catholic discourse. This was not the case, they just led a separate life. It appears that within the Catholic discourse about leisure, two distinct but interrelated lines had been drawn. In fact this process corresponded with the 'division of labour' between observation and norm, sociology and social philosophy, proposed in Devolder's plea (1943) for a value-free sociology. On the one hand, we find the academic research reports, made by order of Catholic organisations, where an effort was made to present a 'neutral' account of leisure, and on the other hand, you have the old moralising plea against the direction modern society and leisure in particular, were taking. In the latter, the mission of the working-class educational organisations was formulated. The organisations foresaw new week schedules coming into being as a result of the 45-hour week and they had a keen sense of the fact that they had to introduce their cultural activities in the workers' lives before new habits had become irreversible.

The report of the biennial meeting of the Flemish wing of the co-ordinating workers' organisation A.C.W. is an excellent example of the way moralising and sociology were combined (A.C.W., 1959). The meeting, held in 1959, was entirely devoted to the leisure problem. It appears that the A.C.W. had put its own research department to work instead of appealing to the 'Centrum voor sociale studies'. H. Deleeck and N. Van de Gracht, the latter had worked at the 'Centrum voor sociale studies', prepared an inquiry into the leisure occupations of Catholic organised blue and white-collar workers. Interviews were used in combination with time budgets. Questions were asked about working hours, the length of the journey to work, extra jobs and earnings, familial life, specific leisure occupations, relations with friends and neighbours, the adherence to associations and the extent of this involvement. The report distinguished between semi-free time and net free time. The latter was subdivided in social contacts, recreation and active occupations (hobbies, sport, further education). Time spent involved in the different leisure activities was related to status, age, education, familial situation, the professional activity of the spouse, income, housing, work time, degree of urbanization and union membership. It was published in the A.C.W.- periodical (Deleeck and Van de Gracht, 1960) but Deleeck was also present on the meeting of 1959 where he discussed the results of his investigation. In Deleeck the two tracks followed in the Catholic leisure discourse met. His speech referred to the major conclusions of his report (the family as the core of leisure occupations and the limited importance of commercialised leisure and associative life), but it lacked the 'neutral' academic tone that predominated in the published version. He added some advice for the organisation's functioning but he did not seem able to make up his mind whether he should make explicit value judgements on the 'passivity' of working-class leisure occupations or not. One can not say that the results of his inquiry were intensively used by the other speakers, they seemed to prefer to stick to their moral discourse. The fact that most of the leisure time was spent within the family, though one of the Catholic workers' organisations' goals, was even greeted with mixed feelings: the family was not supposed to seclude its members from society. Henceforth, the workers' organisations' cultural activities should address the family as a whole instead of its individual members. It is clear that the praised family values were not supposed to compete with the organisation itself!

The Walloon wing of the overall Christian workers' organisation M.O.C. met on the same subject in 1960 (M.O.C., 1960). Here the research had been conducted by the 'Centre de recherches socio-religieuses' of the Université catholique de Louvain. It was published in *Les dossiers d'action sociale catholique* (M.O.C., 1960). There had been an inquiry into the way paid holidays were spent as well as an inquiry into the workers' leisure occupations in the week days and during the week-end.

Although the moralising warnings were still explicitly present in the Catholic worker's organisations leisure discourse of the end of the

1950s, one can register some cautious changes. Confronted with the de facto influence of commercialised leisure on their members, Christian workers' organisations no longer preached mere hostility towards all forms of modern recreation. From the years 1958-1963 onwards, a critical and alert integration of the Christian in the commercialised forms of amusement seemed appropriate (Laermans, 1992). The emphasis was less on prohibition than on the need for a specific leisure education so that people would make the 'right' choices: midway between complete liberty and overprotection. The mere condemnation of commercialised leisure as a flight from daily reality, made way for some understanding: as long as the worker was denied 'human treatment' on the work floor, the evasion in the purely recreational was unavoidable (A.C.W., 1959).

Welfare Policy

The Transition to Welfare Politics

Meanwhile, at the Catholic university, not only the research institute 'Centrum voor sociale studies' became involved in leisure research but for students too, leisure and leisure occupations became topics for their graduation theses. As far as we know the first of its kind was delivered in 1955. In the same year a young lecturer was engaged at the sociology department: Frans Van Mechelen. In the sixties and seventies he would dominate both cultural policy and academic leisure research. Given the importance of Van Mechelen for both research and policy, some biographical details seem appropriate (Gaus, 1989)[6]. Flemish nationalism was Van Mechelen's major source of inspiration. He had the conviction that the Flemish people suffered from material and cultural retardation and raising Flanders' cultural level was going to be one of his major preoccupations. Van Mechelen pointed to the fact that, given Belgium's unbalanced economic and demographic development, Flanders, an area of high birth rates and low wages, functioned as a labour reservoir for the industrialised parts of the country. He denounced the exploitation of the Flemish worker who had to indulge long journeys on the train to go and earn a decent wage and he stressed the harmful effects of this mobility on family life, moral and religious standards, cultural level and on Flanders' own industrialisation. He pleaded for Flanders' economic development as the best means to restore Flemish culture. In close connection with his Flemish nationalism, Van Mechelen developed 'solidarist' sympathies: he was anti-marxist and he rejected class struggle but at the same time he denounced the workings of big capital and the parasitic bourgeoisie as one of the major reasons of Flanders' backwardness.

Since 1947 Van Mechelen has studied the mobility of labour and the development of employment in Flanders. His doctoral thesis was a monograph about labour relations and the process of integration in a foundry. Before he was appointed at the Catholic university, he worked as an expert in 'human relations' in the 'Office belge pour l'acroissement de la productivité', established as a result of the previously mentioned agreement between employers and unions concerning labour productivity. Van Mechelen was also an expert in the field of opinion polls for which he created a separate association Burop (Bureau voor opiniepeiling). We have already stated that in the 1950s the Catholic workers' organisations gradually accepted the usefulness of sociological research. Catholics with an academic background like F. Van Mechelen may well have played a crucial role in this process. Among the sociological articles published by Van Mechelen in the co-ordinating workers' organisation's periodical, we find a remarkable plea, published in 1953, for the creation of an institute of economic sociography, designed to study labour in all its aspects, that would give the actions of the Catholic workers' movement a scientific basis (Van Mechelen, 1953).

The sociologists were not the only members of the Catholic academic guild to take an interest in the leisure problem. The growing concern about the life style of youngsters (unorganised youth in particular) and the declining attraction of youth movement inspired Catholic pedagogues and psychologists to inquire into the occupations, values and pastimes of adolescents (Laermans, 1989, 1992). In 1956 Kriekemans, a psychologist and pedagogue of the Catholic university, and his assistant Cammaer started with a study centre for youth problems (Cammaer, 1967). Kriekemans had already addressed the problem of leisure education within the family in his many lectures concerning working-class leisure (e.g. Kriekemans, 1956). In 1959 this centre, attached to the Catholic university, became an inter-university entity. The centre did not address typical family, school or work problems but it concentrated on what it called 'het derde milieu': youth in its leisure time and how youngsters could be influenced along leisure activities and organised youth work. As its initial name 'Seminarie voor jeugdbeweging' illustrates, the problems youth movements were confronted with, predominated the research of the centre's first years of existence. With the help of Catholic social workers-to-be, inquiries were made concerning the attitude of 16 and 17 year olds regarding the youth movement in particular and corporate life in general. Further research emphasised unorganised youth and how it could be reached by other forms of youth work. Buyck and Cammaer (1967), two members of the centre, published a synthesis concerning leisure occupations of Flemish youth based on the results of more than 50 studies (mostly theses of social workers) made between 1952 and 1964. In the middle of the 1960s the centre started a research project round the meaning of dancing as a leisure occupation for youngsters, using interviews, written inquiries and participant observation.

The concern about secularisation that inspired Catholic leisure research, was not counterbalanced by a comparable socialist strive to dominate the free time of their members. As a result, we hardly find socialist investigations on the matter. We know of an inquiry conducted in 1957 by a workers' tourism organisation (ATB De Natuurvrienden s.d.). Questions focused on the way holidays in particular and leisure time in general were spent. Although in 1956 and 1957 the overall cultural and educational organisation's periodical *Opvoeding* devoted several articles to the leisure phenomenon, the moral panic of the Catholics appeared to be completely absent. Although the influence of commercialised leisure was occasionally denounced, one does not have the impression that the 'leisure problem' was a live issue within the socialist world.

Meanwhile at the Université Libre de Bruxelles sociologists had developed expertise in the study of public opinion. In 1945 Jacquemyns took the lead of the newly created 'Institut universitaire d'information sociale et économique' that was to publish some 40 studies of Belgian public opinion in the twenty years to come. Among the subjects treated in the first ten years, were the Belgian's reading habits, the audience of the radio programmes, the attendance of film-shows, holidays and paid vacation and travelling. Most of these subjects were treated several times. Besides the study of public opinion the sociologists of the U.L.B. started to research the impact and the audience of mass media. In the papers published by the U.L.B. 'Centre national d'étude des techniques de diffusion collective' the researcher Thoveron (1959) published what he called a synthesis of Belgian research in the field of leisure. In fact he limited himself mostly to the results of the already mentioned opinion polls and the studies of the national radio and television station I.N.R. of its own audience. Both universities, the Katholieke Universiteit Leuven and the free-thinking U.L.B. formed the first research institutes to document public state leisure policy.

Katholieke Universiteit Leuven

In 1960 the Faculty of Economic and Social Sciences of the Katholieke Universiteit Leuven reorganised its research in an Institute for Economic, Social and Political Research, of which the Study Group on Culture and Leisure Time (also called the Study group on Cultural Promotion) headed by Prof. F. Van Mechelen and U. Claeys formed one out of the seven subdivisions of the institute.

> The Study Group on Cultural Promotion owes its existence
> to the evolution of society towards a leisure society. The
> phenomenon of leisure is indeed a characteristic of our
> present-day culture.
> (An, 1973: p.16)

This group executed in 1962 the first general survey on leisure activities in Flanders commissioned by the first minister of culture in Flanders, R. Van Elslande. The leisure concept was operationalised in a negative definition in relation to work time, with a distinction between 'semi-free time' and 'real free time'. This concept was completed with a functional description derived from Dumazedier's Three D's ('délassement', 'divertissement', 'dévelopement') and a policy option in which adult education, cultural promotion and leisure were integrated. The survey revealed a real average working time of 49 hours a week (for the male employed population), 60 hours sleep a week and 30 hours free time a week, the rest being 'semi-free time' (with an average of 10.5 hours a week transport-time). The leisure activity was divided into four areas: recreation and development, social life, study and vacation. The four areas were researched in participation and frequency. Differences between sexes, status and urban-rural contexts were registered. The survey both pleaded for an increase in socio-cultural infrastructure and a form of leisure-education. This first report in 1964, was completed in 1966 with a social stratification study of leisure activities, confirming the link of range and intensity of leisure activities with educational level.

In 1967 and 1969 two other research volumes were edited. The first studied weekend activities of families in the winter 1964-1965, in which a thousand interviews were completed in a three-week period. The second reported on family and social vacation and culture consumption at the Belgian coast (Van Mechelen, 1964-1966-1967-1969). The research design fitted into a logical-empirical approach to science and was to deliver data for shaping social planning within the framework of the welfare state. Prof. Van Mechelen himself became Minister of Culture in Flanders from 1968 until 1972. The link between his policy and his research activity was stated explicitly in a colloquium organised by the KUL-research group on 10 and 11 October 1969 (An, 1969). His ministry organised a network of cultural centres and a policy of 'cultural activities brought to the people'. In that period some 'legitimation' research was completed in preparing data to document cities' requests for cultural subsidies. It formed a regular research money resource flow to build and maintain leisure research centres of which some did take the form of private companies.

This form of paternalistic 'democratisation' of culture was not only questioned in its effectiveness but was also opposed - in these last years of the sixties - as a form of 'bourgeois' cultural policy. Five years later, in its quinquennial report of 1973, the research team at the KUL openly aimed at founding a 'new approach to cultural policy'. The existence and format of popular culture had to be placed on inventory'. Until this time the concept of culture, and the cultural policy with which it was linked, were restricted to the transfer of knowledge and traditional values, which appeared in the existing forms of education and the fine arts. The democratisation tendencies of recent decades have affected fundamentally both education and culture. There has been an attempt in particular to confer a larger and richer substance to the formerly narrow concept of culture. This development responded clearly to the pressure from the progressive wing of the Christian workers' movement (Albrechts, 1969) (and the spirit of the time) which objected to the politics of democratisation of elite culture and defended another form of socio-cultural work linked to their own associative life. This in turn inspired a special interest in life and activities of associations (Billiet, 1973), initially sports organisations.

In the beginning of the eighties, the research centre in Louvain was given a second chance by the ministry of culture to execute an overall survey on leisure activities in Flanders. It was inspired by the context of economic crisis and by the changing relationship between work and non-working time. Naeyaert and Claeys signed the voluminous reports edited from 1984 onwards (Naeyaert and Claeys, 1984).

This research indicated a change of trend in leisure activities in 1980, the year that the economic crisis did influence a change in social and political context. The conclusions can be summarised as follows:

1. Media-consumption remains the main leisure activity. Only the written media suffer from the crisis.

2. The more utilitarian hobbies such as gardening, car mechanics, woodwork, etc. maintain participation levels, whereas artistic hobbies do show a clear reduction. Time-intensive but low-investment hobbies maintain their level.

3. Organised associative life is clearly reduced. Whereas in 1963 70% of the Flemish were members of at least one association, in 1983 this figure has fallen to 43%

4. Cultural participation was reducing. In three years theatre visits reduced from 36% to 22%; museums and exhibitions saw participation figures reduced from 47% to 32%; cinema from 50% to 32%. These figures were clearly determined by the first years of cuts in wages. (Afterwards these figures showed a slight recovery.)

5. Vacations and tourism became an important societal phenomenon. Between 1963 and 1980 the part of the population staying at least one week a year out of their homes increased from 27% to 57%. Three quarters of them went abroad. Between 1980 and 1983 this vacation-participation fell for the first time from 57% to 53%. The proportion of the domestic vacation increased from 29% to 37%.

The results of this survey seem to have shaken leisure research itself. Suddenly the economic crisis was introduced in the dream of the coming of a leisure society. It formed the basis of another colloquium (Claeys and Baeten, 1985) where the main context changes of the eighties were listed and subsequent reorientation of research was proposed. The discussion included a contribution from philosopher B. De Clerq where he revisited the wrong assumption of the coming of a 'civilisation du loisir' (De Clerq, 1985) . He stresses on the contrary the growing impact of wage labour and consumption pressure, thus determining all forms of leisure. He proposes a critical assessment of the notion 'labour', based on Arendt's distinction between labour, work and activity. To redefine 'free time', he argues, we have to determine what we really mean by 'freedom'. De Clerq proposes a renewed in depth discussion.

In practice two directions were taken in reaction to the dualisation of society in the 1980s, without much paradigmatic discussion. On the one hand projects were oriented to what can be called the 'crisis problems' (the unemployed, migrants, retirement, individualisation...), 'exceptions' to the scheme of the 1960s. On the other hand research followed the development of a new leisure market in areas such as tourism, recreation, sports .... Overall leisure research was reduced at the KUL, not least because the centre's director, U. Claeys, became Commissioner General of Tourism in Flanders.

Université Libre de Bruxelles

Meanwhile at the ULB sociologists took part in the period 1964-70 in the international comparative time-budget research commissioned by the social research centre in Vienna and carried out by Szalai, Feldheim and Javeau were in charge of the Belgian contribution (Javeau, 1970). In 1966, 2000 individuals made up a time budget of one day. As an international project, this research is not only very descriptive, but even ascriptive as it concentrates on the naming of activities. Moreover one can question the use of a one day 'tranche de vie' to get an insight in the overall time structure of life. The results indicated the scope of the reduction of the work time. The researchers proposed a time division in four parts: obliged time (work), constraint time (transport, buying), necessary time (sleep, eat, care) and free time.

In 1966-67, H. Janne, professor in sociology, ex-inspector-general at the Commissariaat-generaal voor Toerisme, ex-minister of education (1961-65), introduced in the magazine of British Petroleum[7] the debate of the repercussions of the changing relation between work and leisure. The author takes a critical stand towards the negative results of the new technologies and the new labour organisation. Reviewing the data of French research, Fourastié, Dumazedier but also Lismonde (1965), he discusses the moral implications of more free time for the masses and pleads for a well-construed socio-cultural policy. For him a 'leisure civilisation' can only be prepared by a 'learning civilisation', thus proposing the idea of permanent education.

In the same vein, Govaerts (1969), used the data of the time budget to study the differences between men and women. In general she underlined that an analytical difference had to be made between 'time free from work' and 'time disposable for leisure'. Especially for women, access to the latter form was restricted. As a result Govaerts insists on the importance for leisure of the access to paid labour and to education. Without really developing a separate research institute, Govaerts will develop leisure studies and will function in the international leisure studies networks.

Such work has been developed by Roselyne Bouillin-Dartevelle, a sociologist, researching in close collaboration with Dumazedier leisure practices in the French-speaking part of Belgium. In 1984 her PhD researched youth leisure practices, both with qualitative and quantitative research methods. This resulted in a typology of six categories of leisure behaviour: 'the readers', 'the eclectics', those centred around the peer-group and rock music, those oriented towards practical activities, the sports-oriented and finally those centred around television and dance. In 1991 she co-edited a report on cultural practices in the French community in Belgium. A substantial introduction situates this survey in the continuity of leisure research in Wallonia. What is striking is that the intellectual context draws solely from French sociology (Dumazedier, Touraine, Bourdieu) and this recent survey does not discuss recent developments in the field of international leisure research. It remains in the tradition of time-budget analysis and of traditional survey research. This recent book was the result of a comprehensive research project commissioned by the French-speaking regional government and delivered during the years 1983 to 86 by both the ULB and the Université Catholique de Louvain. The survey is based on a questionnaire of 3059 persons. The classification is based on a typology of eight forms of activity derived from three criteria: spatial localisation (interior-exterior), individual position (active-passive) and aim (information, expression or interaction) of the activities. In the conclusions, family life is on top of social activities and interest in public life is decreasing. Activity is more important than passivity, reflection more than creativity.

Vrije Universiteit Brussel

The French-speaking ULB gave birth in 1970 to an independent Flemish Free University of Brussels. From the start there was a leisure studies department, linked to the Institute of Physical Education. It had a clearly vocational aim. 'Leisure-agogics' provided for students in physical education in the era of growing recreational sporting, fitness and health fashions and mania about the body and body image in the 1970s and 1980s.

In 1975 a research centre headed by L. Bollaert was created. It did not build on any research tradition like the KUL or ULB research. As opposed to the 'humanistic' projects in these institutes, the VUB group was very pragmatic in its policy orientation. Early studies included participation research, and tools for shaping welfare services of commissioners. But the crisis of the welfare state was already well under way. So the centre adapted immediately to the shift of socio-cultural work towards a more market-oriented individualised service. Managerial interests in leisure business, such as marketing for the new privatised parts of the sector, were developed. The scientific know-how was subjected to both public policy research ordered by civic authorities, and private management and marketing research. The leisure studies department never did develop a clear research programme of its own.

Sports research best negotiated the turn of the 1980s, orienting itself to recreational (youth) sports organisations (under the direction of P. De Knop). On the other hand a large research project on leisure education and the school (Corijn and Theeboom, 1988), indicates the paradox of the objective decline of paid labour and the subjective increase of the interest in it. It developed a policy proposal for linking school education, socio-cultural work and leisure provision. These research results illustrate the gap between the ideological remains of welfare ideology and practical predominance of market laws: the research never did influence any practice.

The development of tourism research followed this shift towards the market. In the beginning of the eighties Bollaert and Kenis (1986) organised a Delphi-research project trying to work out a consensual model for vacation spreading with the tourist industry, the employers, the school system and public authorities. At the end of the eighties a reorientation towards vocational training in the tourist sector also influenced research projects.

Other Research Institutes

Besides the departments or leisure research groups at the KUL, ULB and VUB no real separate research groups were formed. Only W. Faché, originally teaching in Brussels, developed a research centre at the Ghent University, linked to the Education Department and oriented to youth research and cultural policy. His main research contributions were in the field of planning of cultural and educational policy. He is an active participant of the leisure studies scientific networks.

Within the universities several departments took leisure or an aspect of it as a research object: Renson on sports and popular sports (Leuven), Van Rompu on cultural participation and infrastructure (Antwerp), Versichele researched vacation figures (Ghent). The development of demand-oriented leisure research in the universities was linked to the impressive development of the state on different levels and to its regulative function.

Outside the universities two developments have to be mentioned. On the one hand the development of cultural policies created a sector of applied scientific research, partially done at universities, partially at special independent research centres like the 'Service for Applied Sociological Research' delivering legitimation research. On the other hand the growth of tourism as an important economic factor, not only fed university research but gave birth to the Westvlaams Ekonomisch Studiebureau that started publishing reports in 1963. By 1990 130 papers were published, mainly market research of Belgian coast tourism. As an ongoing link between leisure research and politics, the Van Clé Foundation started its activities in the mid-sixties. In 1973 it organised its first world congress, in 1987 the latest edition.

A Balance Sheet

What catches the eye in this description - and even more in our study of more than 300 publications - is how little critical, theoretical or conceptual research has been carried out. Conceptual discussions are absent. Most of the research pieces - like the two substantial Louvain surveys - start by stating explicitly that they are not going to use any conceptual framework. Others repeat the same bibliographical introduction, putting the operational definitions 'á la Dumazedier' in the front. One of us has dealt with some of the conceptual problems of leisure studies and argues for the need of conceptual clarification, but has remained completely marginal in the field (Corijn, 1986, 1987a, 1987b; Corijn and Theeboom, 1988).

Very few contributions reflected critically on the research methods used. Scheys (1983) published a discussion on the strategies through which non-participation is defined as a social problem. In reality most of the research is participation research as a form of market-research before policy, or impact-research after policy. Scheys argues that the presented strategies can be viewed as a consequence of the growing institutionalisation of leisure and serve the professional and commercial interests of various groups.

An even more consistent theoretical research project was set up in the centre for sociology at the VUB in a research team TOR (Tempus omnia revelat) developing a sociology of time. Elchardus (1983) published the *Ethics of the dual conception of time*, in which he derived a list of possible social meanings of time from the Parsonian four-function paradigm. Certain spheres of activity are then viewed as the result of historical developments in social meanings of time. The leading contemporary social conception of time is described as dualistic, tending to reduce social reality to two kinds of time and two spheres of activity, defined as 'instrumental' and 'gratificational'. By stressing the importance of meaning in the activity, Elchardus challenges the results of the classical time budget studies describing from the outside activities and their duration. The development of this research centre of time sociology is only marginally linked to the leisure research networks.

An even greater exception is a critical reflection on the results of research-based policy. Laermans (1992) reviews the policies of culture spreading and the democratisation ideology behind it, that funded most of the research in the Louvain research centre. He questions the theoretical validity of aiming at the 'acculturation' of the masses forced into the 'élite high culture' and shows empirically that the longitudinal comparison of the participation figures confirms Bourdieu's thesis that cultural participation has to do with education level and even more with social origin. Laermans even questions the effectiveness of the turn towards socio-cultural work, that in fact replaces the high culture of the elite by the life expertise of the middle class.

The history of Belgian leisure research can be periodised according to the growth and the importance of leisure as a social phenomenon. The free-time activities of the aristocracy or bourgeoisie in the 19th century were not of any scientific interest. Free time became a 'problem' linked to some kind of moral panic or anxiety of possible lack of social control by the elite in the time of the workers' struggle for the reduction of the work-day. The subsequent problem of 'knowledge' was situated in the field of labour relations. Leisure studies then were linked to the institutions as the International Labour Office in Genève or union intelligence. The perspective in which the research was done is related to the strategic position taken by the political-ideological 'pillars'. The Catholic workers' movement saw the reduction of the work day as an opportunity of strengthening family life and social bond in their own organisations. Their force resides in the hegemony of civil society. That is why this research is more oriented towards private initiative, service and organisation. The socialist movement of the end of the 19th century was also oriented towards the reinforcement of its own 'camp' as a counter-power against bourgeois society. Initially shorter work days were also seen as bases for organisational and political strengthening of its own pillar. In line with both the reformist turn in social-democratic politics and the Keynesian turn in capitalist economics (shaped in the thirties), what is now called a Fordist accumulation model is generalised from the forties onwards. The state became both the regulator of social integration and the place of class negotiations. The model of the welfare state was accepted both by the majority of the labour movement and the employers. Free time became essential as mass communication and consumer culture developed, permanent education and cultural integration formed part of the introduction of new technologies. Leisure studies formed part of social planning research, of the overall interest in organised well-being. It became part of academic research and official research money circuits. Most of the research practice was based on an ideological myth, the coming of the leisure society. This phase formed the focus of research, at least in its quantitative aspect.

This phase came to an end or faded away with economic and social crisis in the second half of the seventies - with massive unemployment, the deregulation of labour organisation and the introduction of new technologies and new work schedules - and the subsequent ideological shift away from the idea of a welfare state towards so-called 'free market' regulation. In reality leisure research did not easily adapt to that contextual change. Most of the research was reoriented towards private research money and market-oriented research objects. More and more the social science approach was replaced by a pure managerial economic approach, thus cutting off the branch on which it was sitting. As long as leisure was reduced to a problem of supply and demand, leisure studies naturally becomes reduced to an industrial question. The existing research centres were reduced: in the ULB the research team disappeared, in the KUL it is drastically reduced in effectiveness and no longer related to the leisure research networks, in the VUB it is losing its central interest in leisure to diversify towards more lucrative fields as tourism and sports. The strategic pragmatism of Belgian leisure research has led to a critical situation.

The most striking element of the history of leisure research in Belgium is its incapacity to lay any foundations of a separate scientific tradition. Leisure research remained immediately linked with societal and political questions. It did not use this opportunity to develop the scientific distance, by discussing theories about the object and organising separate scientific language communities. Scientific co-ordination never existed. The research groups remained isolated within their institutions and did not form a leisure research community. There was hardly any contact between the two language communities, except for some between ULB and VUB. For some time, some Flemish researchers (very few) were linked to the Dutch Inter-university Workshop. Once this workshop gave birth to the Dutch speaking Vereniging voor de Vrijetijdssector - a leisure studies association - it did not seem possible to develop the Flemish branches. With the total lack of identity, leisure research in Belgium seems to be drawn back to aspects of more traditional scientific disciplines and to pure marketing and management as far as the applied research is concerned.

Theoretically most leisure research - even the sociological - remained linked with some kind of social pedagogy, thus following the French tradition. No critical strain was formed. Most critics, both from a theoretical and from a methodological point of view, withdrew from the field and rejected any legitimation of the existence of leisure studies. Positivist empiricism was the only tradition allowed in a field, financed for social-technological research. In the prosperous years no (economic and cultural) capital was put aside to build a scientific research tradition. Nor were theory and research habits developed. With the fading of the welfare state and the increase in neo-liberal market politics, social planning was replaced by free consumption, ruled by supply and demand. Leisure studies became mere market studies, and leisure researchers were not always the best placed to execute them.

As in other countries the conventional leisure studies field more or less disintegrated and has not re-oriented towards other topics of research as 'pleasure', 'consumption' and 'popular culture'. The necessary critical bases were not developed as the researchers in the 1960s and the 1970s shared in a rather uncritical way the assumptions of the coming of a 'leisure society'. The new topics of research were developed outside the circuit of 'leisure studies'. One can think that such a reorientation of the field is theoretically more promising and interesting. But it also draws attention away from more traditional research as the labour-leisure relationship, encompassing discussion on human emancipation or the relationship between leisure and education. The changing interests have not only to do with post-modernist research styles, but also with adaptation to the recent developments in the labour market and ideology.

The leisure research boat in Belgium grew with the importance of a social problem, but it did not build a scientific engine of its own in due time. Now that economic crisis, labour flexibility and ideological shift have radically changed the social and economic context, it seems to be floating like an ill-constructed raft unable to steer the academic debate.

REFERENCES

A.C.W. (1922) *Negende Vlaamsche sociale week*. Antwerpen: Volledig Vererslag.

A.C.W. (1959) *De arbeidersstand en de vrije-tijdsbesteding. 38ste Vlaamse Sociale Week*: Kortrijk.

A.C.W-Limburg (1956) *Provinciaal congres. Verkorte arbeidsduur en vrije tijdsbesteding*: Hasselt.

A.C.W.-Turnhout (1956) *VIIIe A.C.W. congres. Zedelijk verslag door E.Janssen, Proost der sociale werken*: Turnhout.

Albrechts, J. (1969) 'De arbeiders en het kultuurbeleid in Vlaanderen', *De gids op maatschappelijk gebied*, vol. 60, no. 6, pp. 469-488.

An. (1973) *Quinquennial report, study group on cultural promotion*: Leuven, KUL.

An. (1969) *Kolloquium Planning en Kultuurbeleid*: Verslagboek, Studiegroep voor kultuurbevordering, Leuven.

A.T.B. De Natuurvrienden (no date) *Onderzoek sociaal toerisme en vrijetijdsbesteding*: Antwerp.

Billiet, J. (1973) *Verenigingsleven in Vlaanderen*, Leuven: Katholieke Universiteit Leuven (unpublished Ph.D. thesis).

Bollaert, L. and Kenis, D. (1986) *Vakantiespreideng*. Brussels: Vrije Universiteit Brussel.

Bosmans-Hermans, A. (1979) *Vijftig jaar Hoge Raad voor de Volksopleiding 1929-1979*. Brussels.

Bouillon-Dartevelle, R., Thoveron, G. and Noël, F. (1991) *Temps libre et pratiques culturelles*. Liége: Mardaga.

Brants, V. (1906) 'La part de la méthode de Le Play dans les études sociales en Belgique', in *Réforme sociale*, pp. 636-652.

Buyck, L. and Cammaer, H. (1967) *Vrijetijdsbesteding van de jeugd in Vlaanderen*. Antwerp: Documentatie-onderzoek.

Cammaer, H. (1967) 'Jeugdproblematiek' in Kriekmans, A. (ed.) *Tien jaar onderzoekswerk*. Antwerp: University of Antwerp.

Centrum voor sociale studies (1956/1957) *Opinieonderzoek bij de arbeiders betreffende de vermindering van de arbeidsduur*. Louvain: Université de Louvain.

Centrum voor sociale studies (1957) *De vrijetijdsbesteding bij de Vlaamse jeugd*. Louvain: Université de Louvain.

Christens, R. and De Decker, A. (1986) *Vormingswerk in vrouwenhanden - De geschiedenis van de KAV voor de tweede wereldoorlog (1920-1940)*: Louvain: Université de Louvain.

Claeys, U. and Baeten, E. (1985) *De Vrijetijdsmaatschappij anno 1994:* Leuven: Sociologisch Onderzoeksinstituut, Katholieke Universiteit Leuven.

Cool, A. (1932) 'Volksontwikkeling. Voor onze studiekringen. Twee schemas van lessen over den vrijen tijd', in *De gids op maatschappelijk gebied*, pp. 108-115.

Corijn, E. (1986) 'A dialectical leisure concept.' *Procedings 6th European Congress on Leisure 'Free Time in the Cities*. Vienna: ELRA

Corijn, E.(1987a) 'Marx en de relatie arbeid-vrije tijd', in Regtering, H. (ed) *Macht, Norm en Verzet*. Amsterdam: SISWO.

Corijn, E.(1987b) *Naar een real-utopie over arbeid en vrije tijd, Socialistische Standpunten*. Brussels: Vrije Universiteit Brussel.

Corijn, E. and Theeboom, M. (1988) *Vrijetijdsopvoeding en de school*. Brussels: Vrije Universiteit Brussel.(3 vols.).

Dauby, J. (1859) 'Compositeur typographe de Bruxelles', in *Les ouvriers des deux mondes*. Paris, vol. 2, 193-232.

Davies, A. (1992) *Leisure, gender and poverty*. Buckingham: Open University Press.

De Bie, P. (1961) 'L'oeuvre scientifique et pédagogique du professeur Leclercq', Louvain 1938-1961, in *Jacques Leclercq, L'homme, son oeuvre et ses amis*. Tournai, pp. 39-49.

De Bie, P. (1972) 'Jacques Leclercq et le développement de la sociologie', in De Bie, P (ed.) *Jacques Leclercq. Un homme et son temps*. Louvain: Université de Louvain.

De Bie, P. (1988) *Naissance et premiers développements de la sociologie en Belgique*: Louvain: Université de Louvain-la-Neuve.

Debruyne, G. (1975/76) *De Centrale voor arbeidersopvoeding van haar stichting in 1911 tot het uitbreken van de tweede wereldoorlog.* Ghent: University of Ghent (unpublished Ph.D.thesis).

De Clerq, B. (1985) 'Vrijtijdsmaatschappij: alternatieve idee'n en ontwerpen.' in Claeys, U. and Baeten, E. (1985) *D e Vrijetijdsmaatschappij anno 1994:* Leuven: Sociologisch Onderzoeksinstituut, Katholieke Universiteit Leuven.

Degée, J.-L. (1986) *Le mouvement d'éducation ouvriére. Evolution de l'action éducative et culturelle du mouvement ouvrier socialiste en Belgique (des origines á 1940).* Brussels.

De Groote, L. (1949) 'Un sondage sur la culture des étudiants', in *Bulletin de l'I.R.E.S.*, pp. 807-858.

Deleeck, H. and Van de Gracht, N. (1960) 'De vrije-tijdsbesteding van werklieden en bedienden', in *De gids op maatschappelijk gebied*, pp. 939-1065.

Depasse, Ch. and André, A. (1931) *L'organisation des loisirs du travailleur en Belgique et á l'étranger.* Parijs.

Depasse, Ch. (1936) 'L'utilisation des loisirs du travailleur', in *Revue du travail.* Parijs.

Devolder, N. (1943a) 'De mogelijkheid van een positieve waardevrije sociologie', *Tijdschrift voor Philosophie*, pp. 328-364.

Devolder, N. (1943b) *Volk en gezinsleven. Een enquéte door de Christelijke arbeidersvrouwengilden*: Brussel: S.L.

Devolder, N. (1958/59) 'Vijfentwintig jaar godsdienstsociologie. Van algemene sociologie over theologie naar sociografie', *Sacerdos*, pp. 11-25.

Dooms, C. (1983/84) *De Belgische socialistische arbeidersjeugdbeweging in het interbellum (1923-1940).* Ghent: University of Ghent (unpublished Ph.D. thesis).

Ducpétiaux, E. (1843) *De la condition physique et morale des jeunes ouvriers et des moyens de l'améliorer.* Brussels.

Ducpétiaux, E. (1855) 'Budgets économiques des classes ouvriéres en Belgique', in *Bulletin de la Commission centrale de statistique*, pp. 261-440.

Elchardus, M.(1983) 'De ethiek van de dualistische conceptie van de tijd', in *Vrijetijd en samenleving.* Den Haag: Stichting Recreatie.

Fuss, A. (1937) 'Loisirs et divertissements: compte rendu de la XIXe semaine sociale universitaire de l'Institut de Sociologie Solvay', *Revue de l'Institut de Sociologie*, no. 4.

Gaus, H. (1989) *Politiek-biografisch lexicon van de Belgische ministers en staatssecretarissen 1960-1980.* Antwerp.

Govaerts, F. (1969) *Loisirs des femmes et temps libre.* Brussels: Université Libre de Bruxelles.

Jacquemyns, G.(1932/1934) *Enquéte sur les conditions de vie de chaumeurs assurés*: Liége, 5 vols.

Jacquemyns, G. (1939) *La vie sociale dans le Borinage houiller* (Notes, statistiques, monographies) Brussels.

Jacquemyns, G.(1950) *La société belge sous l'occupation allemande 1940-194:*. Brussels (3 vols.).

Janne, H. (1939) 'Les vacances populaires en Belgique', *Revue internationale du travail*, pp. 202-227.

Javeau, C.(1970) 'Les vingt-quatre heures du Belge: l'enquéte belge du projet international budget-temps'. Bruxelles: Université Libre de Bruxelles.

Kriekemans, A. (1956) 'Opvoeding tot vrije tijdsbesteding in familiaal verband' in *Vrije tijdsbesteding en geestelijke gezondheid. Verslag van het congres gehouden* te Hasselt 15 april 1956 in *Bulletin van de katholieke vereniging voor geesteshygiéne*, no. 2, pp. 16-31.

Ladriéré, J. (1961) 'La sociologie, son introduction dans la pensée catholique', in *Jacques Leclercq, l'homme, son oeuvre et ses amis:* Tournai, pp. 185-205.

Laermans, R. (1989) 'Tussen beeld en enquete-formulier: ontwikkelingen binnen de naoorlogse jeugd in Vlaanderen en België', *Tijdschrift voor Sociologie*, pp. 367-410.

Laermans, R. (1992) *In de greep van 'de moderne tijd'. Modernisering en verzuiling. Evoluties binnen de A.C.W.-vormingsorganisatie.* Leuven-Apeldoorn: Garant.

Laermans, R (1993) 'De januskop van de sociale ongelijkheid', *Tijdschrift voor Sociologie*.

Lagasse, Ch. (1948) 'Niveaux et manifestations de culture chez les ouvriers de la grande industrie', in *Bulletin de l'I.R.E.S.*, pp. 833-907.

Lismonde, H. (1965) 'Loisirs et planification socio-culturelle', *Revue de la Société royale belge des Ingénieurs et industriels*. Bruxelles: SRBII.

Maes, J. and Van Rie, K. (1985) *De werkdag.De geschiedenis van de strijd voor arbeidsduurvermindering.* Antwerp.

Meerts, K. (1992) 'De personalistische traditie aan de Katholieke Universiteit te Leuven rond de eeuwwisseling', in L. Bouckaert and G. Bouckaert (eds.) *Metafysiek en engagement. Een personalistische visie op gemeenschap en economie.* Louvain.

M.O.C. (1960) 'Evolution des loisirs et promotion des travailleurs', *42e Semaine Sociale Wallonne*. Brussels: M.O.C.

M.O.C. (1960) *Les dossiers de l'action sociale catholique*, 343-359, 424-427, 451-486, 521-527, 712-724. Brussels: M.O.C.

Naeyaert, D. and Claeys, U. (1984) *Vrijetijdsbesteding in Vlaanderen anno 1983, Participatiegegeven:* Katholieke Universiteit Leuven, Leuven.

Pastur, P. (1936) 'Les commissions provinciales des loisirs en Belgique,' in B.*I.T. Les loisirs du travailleur. Rapports présentés au congrés international des loisirs du travailleur*, Bruxelles 15-17 juin 1935, 78-91.

Rowntree, B.S. (1910) *Comment diminuer la misére. Etudes sur la Belgique*: Paris.

Scheys, M. (1983) 'Kanttekeningen bij de problematisering van non-participatie', in *Vrije Tijd en samenleving*, Den Haag: Stichting Recreatie.

Schmook, G. (1932) 'De openbare bibliotheek in verband met den vrijen tijd van den arbeider', *Bibliotheekkunde*, pp. 5-8.

Sledsens, A. (1929) 'Het gebruik van den vrijen tijd door de Antwerpsche werklieden', *Beknopt onderzoek over de jaren 1922-1926.* Antwerp.

Stallaerts, R. and Schokkaert, L. (1987) *Onder dak. Een eeuw volks - en gildehuizen.* Ghent: University of Ghent.

Temmerman, E. (1978/79) *De Socialistische jonge wacht (1914-1929).* Ghent: University of Ghent (unpublished Ph.D. thesis).

Thoveron, G. (1959) *Centre national d'étude des techniques de diffusion collective* , no 1, pp. 6-46.

Van Damme, D. (1981) *Welzijnswerk en kapitalisme.* Ghent.

Vanhaverbeke, P. (1980) *Het A.C.W. en de volksontwikkeling. Ontstaan en werking van de C.V.O. 1921-1940*: Leuven: Katholieke Universiteit Leuven (unpublished Ph.D. thesis).

Van Mechelen, D. (1980) *De katholieke partij in het arrondissement Antwerpen.* Leuven: Katholieke Universiteit Leuven (unpublished Ph.D. thesis).

Van Mechelen, F. (1953) 'Toegepaste sociologie. Noodzaak en mogelijkheden in onze tijd', in *De Gids op maatschappelijk gebied*, pp. 320-328.

Van Mechelen, F. (ed.) (1964, 1966, 1967, 1969)*Vrijetijdsbesteding in Vlaanderen.* Antwerpen: Uitgeverij Ontwikkeling.

Verleyen, A. (1985) *Het ontwikkelings - en opvoedingswerk met volwassen arbeiders in het A.C.W. Een Westvlaamse invalshoek 1918-1935.* Leuven: Katholieke Universiteit Leuven (unpublished Ph.D. thesis).

Wils, K. (1991) *Het verdriet van Leuven. De reaktie op het positivisme in het Hoger Instituut voor Wijsbegeerte (1889-1914).* Leuven: Katholieke Universiteit Leuven (unpublished Ph.D. thesis).

NOTES TO CHAPTER 6

[1] In Flanders the language is Dutch and the word used 'vrije tijd'. See for a discussion the chapter by Mommaas, Chapter 4. In Wallonia the French language uses - as in English- the difference between 'loisir' and 'temps libre'.

[2] E. Ducpétiaux was the Inspector- General of the Belgian prisons and poor-relief institutions. He wrote on working-class housing, poor-relief, charity, poverty, working-class budgets, education, criminology etc. Before joining the Catholic forces in the 1850s, he was part of the progressive liberal movement in the capital in the 1840s.

[3] The contributions of E. Vliebergh, R. Ulens and L. Verhulst (seven in all) were published in the series *Mémoires. Académie royale de Belgique: classe des lettres et des sciences morales et politiques* between 1906 and 1926.

[4] Kadoc. Archief K.A.J.- nationaal voor WO II, nr. 21, 22, 23 and 36. K.A.J.-V.K.A.J. 'Ter verovering van den vrijen tijd', *Jaarprogramma 1931/32*.

[5] The following paragraph draws on a chapter from the forthcoming doctoral thesis of A. Meynen (V.U.B.).

[6] The following paragraph also draws on a chapter of the forthcoming doctoral thesis of A. Meynen (V.U.B.).

[7] In 1966 *BP Review* dedicated four issues to the discussion of the coming of the 'leisure society'. The contributions were later published in a book: *La civilisation des loisirs, Culture, morale, économie, sociologie: enquête sur le monde de demain*, Marabout Université, 1967, Ed. Gérard, Verviers. In this publication F. Van Mechelen reported on his survey of 1964 and Jean Fourastié and Joffre Dumazedier wrote the two chapters on the prospects for the future.

Chapter 7

Leisure Research in the UK

Peter Bramham and Ian Henry

There are several ways of reconstructing and representing the history of leisure research in the UK. At first blush, the task seems straightforward as leisure studies have a relatively short pedigree, belonging to the welfare state or Fordist era in the more recent post-war period. The conventional wisdom that constitutes leisure studies can be read off a variety of key texts, research reports, journal articles and conference papers. All publications have benefited from wide national and international circulations and are firmly embedded in undergraduate reading lists in a wide range of leisure courses. The extensive run of Leisure Studies Conference Papers (from 1975) and the Leisure Studies Journal (from 1983) provide rich documentary sources for the developing field of leisure studies.

There have been several overviews by authoritative figures to map out the changing field of leisure research; see Parker (1971, 1983); Roberts (1970, 1978), Rojek (1985, 1989), Green, Hebron and Woodward (1990). Indeed, the 'founding fathers' of leisure studies are themselves alive and well so that a relatively small oral history project would provide a more detailed historical narrative about the personal, professional and institutional networks behind the leisure discourse. Such a project could proceed to map out the policy contexts within which leisure studies developed as research funding agencies such as the Sports Council and the Economic and Social Research Council commissioned comprehensive state of the art reviews for leisure studies and embarked upon research projects in neglected topics during the mid 1980s (see Henry, 1984).

Such a research strategy would tend to rely upon the a history of leisure studies, mediated and reflexively produced by the dominant writers, many now professors, by the most visible academic journals and by the most successful research institutes during the past generation. As elsewhere in historiography, there is also a hidden and neglected history of leisure studies to be explored which broadens out the official version of leisure studies to survey those writers and research projects which have engaged with the topic of leisure from a variety of disciplinary backgrounds, often researching into other leisure-relevant areas, yet working not as researchers within leisure studies networks nor defining themselves as part of the leisure research community.

Writers and projects hidden from history may be teased out through detailed bibliographical surveys, both at a local and national level. Such literature research strategies rely in part upon the coding conventions of professional librarians rather than whatever hegemony the leisure studies research community can muster in any one historical period. Such bibliographical surveys and archival work into leisure topics can be organised into discrete historical periods, can locate and explore the different and contested concepts of leisure within a variety of academic disciplines, can uncover neglected leisure texts and evaluate their relevance to later generations of leisure scholars. By unearthing neglected research into leisure topics, the conventional vision of leisure studies broadens to include more marginal texts and problematics. These serve to relativise the conventional and legitimised accounts about leisure and leisure research. Such interrogation of historical sources are not innocently cumulative but rather provide a corrective to the more public well-rehearsed history of leisure research.

The history of leisure research must be more than historicism; it must be more than the collection of historical facts about the dates of important conferences, publications and research initiatives. It must transcend the conventional and sanitised histories of knowledge which often cast original writers as heroes struggling to map out contested fields of study in the face of resistance from established disciplines. Such histories are whiggish in direction as founding fathers develop theories, consolidate methodologies and data collection and so accumulate shared knowledge which becomes reified into professional networks, research centres, universities and teaching programmes.

Whether one writes the history of leisure or the history of the study of leisure in the UK, the task is doubly daunting. It is hard to gain a safe vantage point from which to survey the contested battlefield of leisure and identify the warriors who would be prepared to take sides or even define themselves as leisure researchers. Any hope of a single distinctive authoritative historical narrative is barren. There is little in the way of consensus with intellectuals, if pressed, offering different histories of leisure and leisure research. These histories provide diffident commentaries on the development of the field of study, its key writers, critical phases, institutional networks and possible futures.

All histories of leisure, whatever their sources, face common problems. First, what to include and what to omit in such a history? One response would be to write a national history of the study of leisure. This could involve examining the significant contributions made by writers to mapping the concept of leisure, developing research agendas and publishing findings for wider academic and professional communities in the UK. Certain key writers emerge, usually of transnational stature, who have had something to say about the position and role of leisure in people's lives and who have provided theoretical perspectives, concepts and research agendas which have had major transnational, national and local impacts (or at least have left significant residues of research agendas and researchers).

On the other hand, there have been many studies of leisure which have been neglected or simply ignored by later generations of leisure researchers. Many contributions come from intellectuals and artisans who would not see themselves as leisure intellectuals but their interest in leisure topics arose from other research questions around family, culture, class, policy, change and so on.

Eschewing the likelihood of ever finding a safe vantage point, what if one's vision is turned towards leisure studies rather than leisure? What constitutes leisure studies in the national UK tradition? What research methodologies, what techniques of data collection have been deployed in the UK leisure field? What disciplinary perspectives have dominated research traditions in the UK?

This chapter traces the history of leisure studies through the development of the sociology of leisure. It is this particular vantage point with which the authors are most familiar and one which has played a dominant role historically in the development of leisure studies and leisure research.

The dominance of sociological perspectives within leisure studies is no coincidence. Research into discrete leisure sectors - such as arts, sports, outdoor recreation and tourism were felt to be too specialised and somewhat limiting. Leisure researchers did not ignore the study of sport, recreation or the arts but demanded a broader field of vision. Leisure writers within these fields tackled research on topics such as sport *and* leisure or recreation *and* leisure. Leisure was not simply conceptualised as an afterthought but rather signified a demand to place particular leisure sectors and practices within holistic, spatial and sociological perspectives. This entailed relating specific leisure practices to wider social processes of class, gender, and lifestyle, whilst simultaneously engaging with policy-led research programmes. Given this broader contextual view of leisure sectors it is not surprising that leisure researchers were sociologists often finding their way into multi-disciplinary research teams. This is not to suggest that other disciplines such as economics, geography and psychology have not made significant contributions to understanding leisure: see Gratton and Taylor (1992), Patmore (1983), Glyptis (1991), Stockdale (1985) and Ingham (1986). However, a dominant theme in the national history of leisure research in the UK has been the desire to locate specific leisure practices within wider structures of legitimacy, culture and everyday life.

Dominant Traditions and Scientific Research

Within the UK academy, the orthodox account of the nature of scientific research has been provided by philosophers, particularly Karl Popper, and has been described as logical positivism. The domain assumptions of logical positivism are conventionally that the world is empirically knowable and mediated to the senses, that the social and natural sciences share a common foundation and that facts and values must be kept separate when doing research. Scientific discoveries are secured not by verification but by falsification, i.e. scientists seek to disprove their theories as their hypotheses are tested against available empirical data. Scientists are therefore encouraged to disprove their own theories and this intellectual hygiene and rigour account for the outstanding progress that scientific knowledge has made during the past generations. The growth of knowledge, secured by scientific research, ensures that scientists are increasingly able to measure, control and predict the natural world. Scientific practices, particularly via experiments, permit scientists to isolate variables and establish causal relationships between phenomena.

In *The Structure of Scientific Revolutions* Kuhn (1970) provides an alternative account of the nature of research activity within the natural sciences. As a professional historian, Kuhn argues that the conventional philosophical account offered by logical positivism is empirically inaccurate. Drawing from examples in physics (e.g. classical mechanics and quantum theory), Kuhn suggests that scientific practices fall short of the prescriptions for scientific method set out by philosophers of the natural sciences and in particular, the accounts provided by logical positivism. Kuhn argues that scientific activity operates within assumptive worlds or traditions which are shared and conventionally sustained by the scientific community within any historical period. During such time, scientific activity operates within a paradigm which offers a way of theorising about the world, a code of good scientific praxis and, most importantly, a series of puzzles or problems for researchers to solve. Kuhn uses the term puzzles to denote research problems that may be resolved within an existing paradigm, using conventional research techniques. Kuhn argues that this 'normal' research is conducted within the scientific community, whose members are socialised into, and committed to the domestic dominant paradigm.

Kuhn's account presents scientific research operating within a closed community which routinely tackles research puzzles. For Kuhn, paradigms and the socialisation of scientists into existing practices and research problems, are functional for scientific progress and development. Change is possible as the conventions for scientific practice may change and anomalies occur; these are puzzles which cannot be resolved within existing theoretical frameworks. Such anomalies may be disbelieved, acknowledged but ignored, or marginalised by the scientific community. New scientific work establishes gradually alternative explanations for such anomalies which eventually become research puzzles for the new paradigm. Scientific revolutions occur rarely when the scientific community experiences a fundamental crisis, facing incommensurate paradigms which provide different accounts of both scientific praxis and of the nature of the worlds they are trying to explain. In normal times, existing paradigms are embedded within institutional networks of research funding. Normal science proceeds both successfully and happily tackling the complex puzzles locked within the dominant paradigm.

Kuhn's analysis of normal science within the scientific community of the natural sciences has been subjected to substantial debate and criticism. Philosophers have objected to Kuhn's analysis of the nature of scientific revolutions and the character of normal science. They have pointed out the shifting meanings associated with his key terms of paradigms and exemplars, his preoccupation with the actual nature of science which rides roughshod over philosophical debates of epistemology, ontology and the driving importance of rationality underpinning the scientific endeavour to accumulate knowledge. Some writers such as Lakatos seek to reconcile the two accounts by discussing progressive and degenerative paradigm shifts. Others such as Sklair suggest that Popper outlines the charter for natural sciences whereas Kuhn is more concerned to study the functions of scientific activity within the wider society. Others suggest that these philosophers have systematically misread Kuhn and his historical concerns.

There has indeed been considerable debate about the relevance of Kuhn's account of natural scientific activity to the development of the social sciences. Nowhere in Kuhn's work is there the suggestion that his analysis is applicable to scientific developments in other disciplines outside the natural sciences.

Many feel that the structures and processes within the preconstituted world of the social sciences (what Giddens terms the 'double hermeneutic' which engage the social scientific community) renders it difficult to transfer Kuhn's arguments satisfactorily to the history of the social sciences. Nevertheless, however uncomfortable Kuhn and others feel about this, writers within the social sciences have deployed some of his arguments to understand the complexities of the developments in social science theory and research. Despite these controversies concerning Kuhn's history of the natural sciences, he does provide an interesting vantage point to make some sense of the developments in leisure research.

Rojek describes leisure research as characterised by paradigmatic rivalry and more recently (Rojek, 1993) he writes of three moments in leisure studies - the dominance of functionalism in the 1950s, the politicisation of Marxism and feminism in the 1970s and the latest critique from postmodern thinking in the 1990s. The diversity of research agendas, projects and networks of researchers make it difficult to provide an authoritative and coherent research history of leisure in the UK. Rojek's own work has been to draw on mainstream social science theorists such as Marx, Durkheim, Freud and more recently postmodern theorists such as Baudrillard and others to assess their relevance to understanding leisure in contemporary society. None of the writers reviewed took leisure as their central problematic or research topic.

To see leisure studies as a field of study with inter-paradigmatic rivalry generates a series of interesting questions

- What counts as a research tradition as a discursive formation? Do groups of researchers aspire to paradigmatic status? - Do they seek hegemonic control over the research agendas, research styles and research contracts?

- What are the main exemplars of research within leisure studies? Are they shared / valued / contested by researchers working within different research traditions?
- How is the multi-paradigmatic rivalry managed? Do researchers locate their work within a distinct theoretical tradition and ignore the work of others or do they self-consciously engage with and criticise alternative paradigms and research agendas?
- How and why do particular research agendas and exemplars of research gain ascendancy over others? What criteria do researchers use to evaluate research?
- Do policy makers and practitioners within different leisure sectors deploy the same criteria in their judgement research work? What impact does research sponsorship and funding have upon the trajectory of research projects?
- In what cultural, political and economic contexts do particular research initiatives flourish? How successful have intellectuals been as legislators for the central and local state?

A History of Leisure: Research Traditions in the UK

The history of leisure and the history of leisure research are analytically distinct. It is only in the past twenty years that there has been a concerted effort to discover the history of leisure. It seems remiss of leisure researchers not to have reflected upon their own practices. Little attention has been paid to the legacies that previous writers have left current research traditions. It is worth a lengthy quote from the work of Barnes (1982:7)

> Those who carry out research are the recipients of a culture developed by previous generations. Research cannot proceed independently of it; its acceptance, however provisional, is a prior condition for doing science. The process of research in turn modifies and develops the received culture, and in this modified and developed form it is passed onto the next generation. The work of any individual scientist has to be understood against the particular cultural background surrounding him at his point of entry into the research tradition.

Kuhn's analysis of the natural sciences and the ways in which the scientific community exercises authoritative control over the nature of normal science could provide a useful starting point for analysis.

However, it is beyond the scope of this chapter to engage in such a task rather we shall confine ourselves to examining the reasons for the absence of a history of leisure research which would construct a definitive shared history of leisure.

The reasons for the absence of a history of leisure are various. Social science research has been dominated by other research questions. Mainstream social theory has been concerned with serious aspects of social processes - those of work and the organisation of the labour process, political power and authority, religion and the family. These institutions have occupied the intellectual horizons of thinkers, which have relegated leisure to a residual category. It has frequently been conceptualised as such, usually in relation to the world of work and paid employment. Leisure was usually an afterthought, an appendage, stuck conventionally within the work-leisure couplet. When leisure has been centre stage, at the top of the political agenda, it has been enmeshed in moral panics about law and order issues, usually in relation to youth, inner-city disorders and spectator safety. Nevertheless, unacceptable leisure practices were viewed symptoms of a deeper malaise - growing secularisation, changing family relations, the dwindling authority of social workers and educationalists, the corrosive impact of television and other mass media styles, signifying violent anomic society, polarised by unemployment.

The student disorders within the late 1960s began to raise global questions about the nature and prospects for industrial capitalism. Academics began to focus on the changing nature of class relations, the restructuring tendencies of information technologies, robotics and computerisation which suggested a growing debate about the leisure society and the need for education for leisure.

It was in this atmosphere of change in the early 1970s that there was a pragmatic alliance between policy makers, educationalists and researchers. 'Leisure and the quality of life' appeared on the political agenda in the early 1970s as final element of the welfare state, as citizen's rights. Ironically, at the very time in the UK that leisure was becoming part of the welfare state in the mid 1970s, public sector funding and research came under the closest scrutiny because of changing global markets and the stagflation in the UK economy. The precise impact of public expenditure cuts and the restructuring of the state have been mapped out in detail in the political economy of welfare expenditure. This is less the case for leisure funding, although some attempts have been made to explain the support for leisure expenditure as part of a partisan compromise because of the catch-all nature of leisure policy, its stress on externalities (differentially defined by political parties) and on community development (viz. Henry and Bramham, 1986; Coalter, 1989; Henry, 1993).

It is important too to trace the location of leisure courses within the UK. Universities adhered to traditional disciplines and fields of study. The emergence of social science research within the London School of Economics (LSE) that occurred in the 1960s was in part the growth of a professionalising elite which sought to develop scientific research as a professional activity and to exclude lay practitioners and volunteer observers that were the hall-mark of the Mass Observation studies in the 1930s.

It was only with the collapse of teacher training places in the 1970s that colleges of education provided diversified degree courses and vocational qualifications. It was in the Polytechnics and Higher Education Colleges that leisure courses emerged. A crucial catalyst in this process was the need to validate new courses outside the University sector under the auspices of the Council for National Academic Awards (CNNA). The CNAA validation panels provided a crucial legitimating network for the empowerment of traditionally neglected areas of study. Leisure studies and leisure researchers within the UK were located in the most unlikely places. Sheffield, Liverpool and Edinburgh were the centres of leisure research and consultancy rather than the more traditional universities of Oxbridge, London, Durham and so on.

It was within this financially restrictive climate that a watershed occurred within the leisure studies field as the Sports Council and the Social Science Research Council jointly commissioned 'state of the art' reviews in a whole range of leisure research areas. In addition the Sports Council / Social Science Research Council (SC/SSRC) research of its own in perceived neglected areas of interest.

The Social Science Research Council had to change its title to the Economic and Social Research Council under direction from government ministers who felt unable to legitimate the social sciences with the term 'science'.

It is a question for the sociology of knowledge as to why particular disciplines and fields of study need to construct and reconstruct their own official histories. Indeed in Kuhnian terms a mature science operates within a research paradigm which generates its own historicity, mediated by research centres, sponsorship and key official texts. As some writers contend, postmodernity is a crisis essentially for the intelligentsia and their changing position within a more flexible society and what some term a post-Fordist economy. The intellectual is no longer a legislator but rather an interpreter of the postmodern condition. The comfortable status position of the intellectual within welfare capitalism becomes much more vulnerable in the late 1970s and early 1980s. The knowledge base of the welfare-state researcher, locked into contracts to accumulate knowledge for social engineering to meet needs becomes more problematic when the boundaries of state intervention in welfare, education and leisure are contested and redrawn.

Horne *et al.* (1987) point to three major strands in the emergence of leisure studies in the 1970s - the emergence of leisure professionals following local government reorganisation in 1974, the appearance of leisure studies academics and courses within higher education and the need for planners to manage countryside resources and access. This led to the formation of the Leisure Studies Association and the publication of the Leisure Studies Journal in the early 1980s. The pragmatic alliances of the 1970s were dissipated by the 1980s with the application of Thatcherite policies for the funding of research institutes, universities and Higher Education. The shifting boundaries between the central state, quangos and the local authorities were redrawn. Research consultancies in the private sector emerged drawing mainly on marketing perspectives and the public agenda was privatised into agencies, ideologically driven by the Audit Commission, which appeared in 1984. Local authorities responded to cutbacks in central state support and growing local unemployment by setting up their own policy research units and marketing sectors. Leisure in the form of enforced leisure (unemployment) became a crucial policy issue and certain local authorities saw research as a crucial resource both to evaluate their own services and to resist central government directives. In addition, other local authorities saw leisure investment as an important ingredient in urban restructuring.

Another factor in the development of leisure research was the developing critique of leisure studies as policy-led, untheorised free time studies. Throughout the 1970s and 1980s there was a growing presence of feminist research which introduced issues and questions from the women's movement and began to explore the silences in leisure research about women's experience, about access to resources and time free from serving the needs of others. Feminist research and feminist arguments began to have a more visible presence in conference themes.

Another undercurrent of criticism also came from Marxist theory developed by the Centre of Contemporary Cultural Studies which sought to locate leisure in a broader context of working class culture. There is a distinct tradition of Marxist analysis within the UK which draws heavily not only on the Frankfurt School and Gramsci but also on the works of Raymond Williams, Richard Hoggart, Stuart Hall,

Perry Anderson and Richard Johnson. This strand represents an interest in agency and cultural reproduction, with leisure as part of culture and as a site of both hegemony, struggle and resistance.

A final influence has been the growing work inspired by debates about postmodernity, drawing inspiration from such writers as Baudrillard and Lyotard. The crucial agent introducing these ideas was the journal *Theory Culture and Society* and the work of Mike Featherstone in pursuing and popularising debates about postmodernism and mass consumer culture. Featherstone was in the vanguard of a group of researchers who were part of an international leisure studies network which was fuelled by European Community funding and developments in UK higher education which encouraged the Europeanisation of courses with the single market in 1992, student exchanges and the development of joint curricula and staff exchanges.

The UK Empiricist Tradition

The histories of leisure and leisure research are remarkable by their absence. Such vestiges have been firmly embedded in what can best be described as a 'positivist empirical tradition'. The essential quest for the emerging field of leisure studies and leisure education was to categorise and measure the facts of leisure, to clear a space for a new and relevant area of research and of policy. The driving rationale for collecting such facts has been suggested by the factors outlined above - the pragmatic and pressing concerns of teachers developing new courses, policy makers at central and local levels with overall strategies to plan and a wide range of leisure professionals confronted with the need to develop and implement policy in a fluctuating environment with a wide variety of different groups. The collection of facts of participation, the knowledge of policy initiatives elsewhere, the place of leisure in people's lives, the spatial distribution of facilities, issues of access, conservation, and participation all suddenly become crucial ingredients in making sense of existing careers, developing new ones and legitimating policy initiatives. With this diverse context of pragmatic commitments, it was hardly surprising that loose alliances were formed and recast. Some were strengthened by the resistance of more traditional disciplines to the study of leisure, just as configurations of researchers within the area of leisure studies (viz. feminists and Marxist analyses) met heavy resistance from established conventional leisure studies researchers. Research Institutes won consultancies and became established experts with strong links to government quangos, central governments and local authorities, and publishers whereas others did not.

Amongst this diversity, there is a shared apologetic theme which underpins practically all leisure research. Real research is conducted elsewhere in the mainstream of academia. Leisure research is something of a diversion. For some writers leisure is simply a cruel and complex joke and they prefer to specialise in sport, tourism, media, physical recreation and education. For others, leisure provides a crucial field for research which will, if broadly categorised into wider issues of individualised and collective consumption, provide a critical site to explore the crucial debates about agency, structure and culture in advanced capitalism. Leisure offers a crucial site for testing out interdisciplinary frameworks and exploring the policy boundaries which cast people as citizens, clients or consumers of goods and services.

This overall commitment to collecting facts has been described by many as Britain's empirical tradition and its central focus has been on methodology and on techniques of data collection. Researchers have devoted little space in their writing to reflect upon the nature of the research process and the problems they have set themselves, their involvement with policy makers and sponsorship, funding and the theoretical categories they have deployed in their work and, not least, their relationship to groups of people who have been studied. This has not necessarily constituted a fundamental flaw in that they have engaged with the task of data collection, rather than being paralysed by theoretical debates. Their legacy has been a rich bed of data collection and surveys - much has been fragmented, dispersed and unpublished. This is not to suggest that leisure researchers have been unaware of theoretical issues but rather that these have been of secondary concern as they have embarked on their research projects, defining themselves as detached scientists collecting and analysing objective information about leisure forms and practices.

Whilst it is important to demarcate major phases and debates in UK leisure research, it would be contentious and self-defeating to provide a definitive chronology of leisure research. Such a project begs many relevant questions and would please no one. It would risk accusations of bias, neglect, misrepresentation, misunderstanding and omission. What does follow however, is less comprehensive and contentious. The subsequent sections illustrate distinctive research problematics and strategies, whilst simultaneously representing significant developments within leisure research. These different traditions and styles of research appear and reappear in the history of leisure research and depend upon a separate research strategy. They constitute links within a chain which supplies information towards characteristic themes scrutinised in research into leisure. In a Kuhnian sense they have been exemplars of scientific research which have a presence within the scientific community and have been replicated and have informed other research and researchers. Each research project exhibits a distinctive mixture of hard and soft data, tackles the unique and the general, faces issues of detachment and involvement, addresses the social, political and cultural issues of the day. Conversely, all have been caught within the organisational contexts of research funding, constrained by time and resources.

Surveys and Surveillance

19th Century Surveys: The Condition of the Working Class

The roots of the UK empirical tradition are buried deep within the 19th century. Many intellectuals were confident that the problems generated by industrial capitalism could be resolved by a rational scientific discourse about the social world. Royal Commissions, Select Committees of Parliament and individual reformers set out to collect systematic information about the nature of the world and how it could be moulded along scientific rational principles. At the centre of this cataloguing process were often Benthamite principles of moral philosophy, a utilitarian calculus that could be applied to any policy problem - the need to produce the greatest happiness for the greatest number of people. Politics and policies became a single scientific enterprise; the issue was one both of technique and reason. Hence, faced with the problem of Poor Law Reform, Chadwick set about collecting information about the diverse conditions and practices of providing for relief to those unemployed in both rural and urban areas. Having collected his returns from surveys to local key decision makers, Chadwick sought to present the evidence to make an incontrovertible case for utilitarian policies within the social policy field. The Poor Law was introduced (albeit with local interpretations and resistance) to distinguish between the deserving and undeserving poor and vagrants. The meagre rates of relief were based on the principle of 'least eligibility' so as to maintain work discipline, with the welfare rates approved from the centre, as part of a rational scientific project. The family lifestyles, social conditions, patterns of consumption particularly of alcohol, patterns of religious observance, previous patterns of work were major parameters for defining access to relief and social welfare. Consequently, during the 19th century the political infrastructure was fragmented into a central and local system of administration which began to monitor, survey and study the life and culture of ordinary people. Indeed, many journalists, evangelical missionaries and researchers began their quest into unknown Britain to survey the culture of the urban poor. Their approach mirrored that of British anthropology which catalogued the attitudes and behaviour of the alien cultures they encountered and destroyed as part of imperialism and colonial aggrandisement in Southern Asia and Africa.

The results of these endeavours of data collection provided the Blue Books for Marx and Engels to write about the condition of the working class. Within this genre of research were the momentous research project conducted by Mayhew (1851) *London Labour and London Poor* as well as Booth (1881) *London's Poor*. Such empirical research points out the structural determinants of poverty and unemployment. People were trapped in a family cycle of poverty, although the conventional wisdom of the time sought to explain poverty away by blaming the victim. It was deemed to be the result of individual fecklessness or work shyness, exacerbated by drink. The empirical work conducted by Seebohm Rowntree and more recently by Peter Townsend carried a critical edge to their data collection. Such work introduced the concept of relative deprivation and shifted the causal factors for an impoverished lifestyle away from the individual and more towards the structural processes of low wages and inadequate state income support for those with families and disabilities.

It is worth pausing to look at the neglected work of Seebohm Rowntree as his life and long research career epitomised the determined vitality and confidence of the UK empirical tradition. Although better known for his several analyses of poverty in York, Seebohm Rowntree, in collaboration with Lavers as his researcher, produced a unique, academic and authoritative 'social study' published as *English Life and Leisure*. The original rationale for the research was 'a detailed survey of facilities that would be needed in York to make ample provision for the satisfactory recreation of the inhabitants' (1951: xi) but the study broadened out to examine the spiritual and cultural life of the whole nation.

The scale of data collection was formidable. The first part of the book drew on some of the 975 case histories which were collected by Lavers, 'without the respondent knowing, once their confidence had been gained' (1951: xii). These were supplemented by other techniques of data collection: special enquiries into completing 'the pools' (498 people surveyed); participant observation in pubs, cinemas, evening classes, a case study of leisure facilities of a small town (High Wycombe) where both the researchers lived, and some comparative analysis of Scandinavian countries, which entailed a study visit in 1947 from Seebohm Rowntree, under the guidance of a Norwegian economist and sociologist Christian Gierlorf. The researchers also contacted and relied upon over 200 persons, both experts and non-experts, on relevant matters surrounding drinking, gambling, young people, promiscuity, cinema, religion and so on.

What was so striking about the book was not only the wealth of data and detail collected from a range of primary and secondary sources but rather the confidence that the researchers had in their task and their strong policy recommendations. The researchers had little doubt about the both the validity and the objectivity of their data collection and interpretation. Issues about making sense of, and evaluating the spiritual and cultural life of the nation evaporated because 'Our biases cancel each other out' (1951: xiv).

The structures of class, race and gender were simply not relevant, nor were their religious nonconformity and teetotalism (as both were not prohibitionists). Gambling was castigated as ethically wrong because it was a rejection of reason, civilised behaviour and attempted to gain property without effect.

In the first part of the book, the case studies are presented as unproblematic, mediated as they are by the researchers' judgement about sexuality and useful leisure. Three examples will suffice

> She is a teetotaller and non-smoker. Is of course innocent sexually, and does not gamble. She likes the radio, cinema and theatre, but her main recreation is looking after her husband.
> (case No. 16)

> Is pretty well unemployable as he is shy, stupid and filled with complete confidence in his own merit. He is mildly homosexual and this has obviously sapped his moral fibre.
> (No. 34)

> There can be no doubt about her sexual innocence. She has an exceptionally nice nature - kind and gentle and has been very well brought up. She goes to chapel most Sundays, does not gamble nor drink but has recently started to smoke. Her hobbies are knitting, cycling and playing tennis... Inexperienced but likely to make a good wife for some lucky man.
> (Case History of Under 20s No. 14)

The overall conclusions of Seebohm Rowntree and Lavers 'tour de force' were that people pursued commercialised mass pleasurable entertainment in the absence of viable and rational alternatives. They were afraid of the Americanisation of English culture, particularly through film and pornography, valuing the efforts made by the state and the voluntary sector in Scandinavia to provide rational recreations for their populations.

Mass Observation: 1930s and the Unemployed

The period 1880-1930 has been characterised as the British State confronting a series of crises with the collapse of liberalism and liberal hegemony (Hall and Schwarz, 1985:11). During this period lie the origins of collectivism, providing a crucible for the crises of 1980s and the demand to restructure the collective settlements of welfare capitalism made during the past two generations. The central problem of the 1930s was economic; the painful realignment of the UK economy with international markets and competition was exacerbated by the overvaluation of sterling on its return to the Gold Standard. The impact on regional economies within the UK was uneven with traditional primary production (particularly coal, steel) and manufacturing production (shipbuilding, textiles) facing high levels of unemployment. Research by Jahoda *et al.* into the lives of men without work explored the psychological impact of worklessness. Jahoda was an Austrian psychologist who emphasised that the structure of everyday life and mental health were secured by paid employment. She drew heavily on Freudian psychology to argue that work bound men into social reality and work-time was a crucial feature in their lives. Jahoda's analysis was insightful not only because of her work into the policy problem of unemployment but also because she was Austrian and a woman.

One recurring theme in the UK research tradition has been the substantial impact that non-English academics have made in the social sciences. The British tradition was seen by Perry Anderson (1968) to avoid global theorising about the totality of social formations. Indeed, there have been no major UK writers who have generated theories about the totality of social relationships in modern industrial capitalism. Whilst there has been a plethora of anthropological accounts of pre-literate societies there has been a reluctance to develop theories of modern industrial societies, as writers have been content to rely upon European and US frameworks. Anderson (1968) has explained this historically by the absence of a bourgeois revolution (unlike nation states in Europe) and the gradual assimilation of the industrial bourgeoisie into the traditional land owning aristocracy who maintained control over the culture, life style and the unwritten UK constitution.

Jahoda's research into unemployment in the 1930s highlighted the central importance of paid work or employment in providing a structure for people's everyday life. It provided a sense of time, of sociability and solidarity. The absence of work meant a sense of loss. The initial freedom of unemployment, the burst of euphoria, gave way to a sense of timelessness and fatalism, a tiredness of living. This enforced leisure has been re-examined by many other writers with the reappearance of large-scale unemployment in the 1980s (see Willis *et al.*, 1987; Glyptis, 1989; Seabrook, 1988).

During the late 1930s, throughout the war and well into the post-war period, there emerged an extraordinary research initiative called the Mass Observation studies. It represented the most comprehensive and detailed attempts at ethnography. Julian Huxley at the time welcomed this research as a collective self-analysis. Professional researchers such as Mark Abrams were less enthusiastic about the nature of the research and the precise quality and reliability of the data collected by these large scale studies. Mass Observation surveys were directed by Charles Madge and Tom Harrison, focusing on the working-class culture of Worktown (Bolton, Lancashire), and their holiday making in Blackpool during Wakes week. Unlike other data collectors, Harrison reflects upon the variety of research strategies at the disposal of the social scientist. He suggests seven major techniques of data collection; from surveys to participant observation. It is significant that Mass Observation deployed a whole range of hard and soft techniques of data collection - from questionnaires to participant observation, or what Harrison tellingly refers to as 'penetration'. The driving rationale of the two researchers (one a newspaper reporter, the other a poet) was to explore the collective unconscious of everyday people in industrial society.

In his preface to *The People and the Pub*, Harrison remarked upon the ease with which he gained finance in 1932-35 to explore Central Borneo and other islands in the Western Pacific yet it dawned upon him that no research had been completed in the wilds of Lancashire and East Anglia,

> Whilst studiously tabulating the primitive, we had practically no objective anthropology of ourselves, despite 'social surveys' on a statistical basis.

The precise site for this exploration and the *only* published research study from this wealth of observation and data was *The*

People and the Pub. Three other publications were planned with help from the radical left-wing publisher Gollanz. These were to be books, on politics and the non-voter, on religion and on holidaying in Blackpool. *The Pub and the People* provided an extraordinary range of data - on the spatial location of the pubs, their physical layouts, types of beer, speed of beer consumption, types of head gear, numbers of 'dry and wet' spittoons, types of ale consumed, and topics of conversations. The immense detail of everyday life was mediated by observers and photographed by Humphrey Spender. They sought to reconstruct the networks of pub culture by surveying the drinkers, the landlords and staff, the bookies, prostitutes and music makers. Mass Observation sought to document the everyday life of ordinary people, to provide a democratic and aesthetic account of culture, ordinary values and responses. Mass Observation relied upon two thousand volunteer researchers, with little concern about the validity or reliability of this fact gathering exercise.

Another strategy for data collection employed by Mass Observation were 'Panel Reports'. Those included on such panels responded to directives from Mass Observation, a house in Dover Street, the East End of London, to observe and record topics in order to document and explore, limply informed by some anthropological perspective on ritual and beliefs within everyday culture. Such panellists also were encouraged to keep diaries - usually on the twelfth day of the month and to act as covert researchers on particular topics defined by the research directors - such as jazz, dance halls, ceremonies, Christmas, gambling and so on. A review of the work of Mass Observation by Alan and Mary Tomlinson (1983) suggests that the panellists were over-representative of the intellectual middle classes and the respectable aspiring working classes. It is worthwhile noting that prospective panellists were required to send information about themselves, their reasons for wanting to work for Mass Observation, their reading habits, a description of their mantelpieces (!) and an account of the people in their lives. The wealth of data is presently stored at Sussex University and remains to be analysed. It is something of a harsh outcome for all this material; which meticulously, if unproblematically, documented the everyday life and culture of ordinary people.

British Community Studies

Mass Observation was heralded as the first community study. In addition to Worktown, the researchers also provided a detailed account of life in an Exmoor village. This rich vein of research was further developed in the 1950s and 1960s. The rationale behind such research was descriptive, ethnographic and nostalgic. Community studies constituted the rediscovery and reaffirmation of the importance of class difference. They also failed to acknowledge the central importance of women in support networks and patterns of neighbouring within people's lives. The research strategy was to live within a particular locality and to document the working, family and leisure lives of people. A major focus of this tradition of research was that of occupational communities within the working class. A series of studies of extreme occupations (coal miners, deep-sea fishermen) documented the centrality of work-relations in men's lives and how these spilt over into friendship networks in working men's clubs, and other proletarian subcultures such as pigeon racing, supporting the local rugby league team, tending allotments and angling. Parker (1971) drew upon these studies to document the oppositional nature of leisure which functioned to compensate for the dangerous, damaging manual work. Such studies were valued by later Marxist theories of leisure not simply because they focused upon the working class but because they placed leisure squarely within community and class culture rather than treating leisure simply as free time where people could make choices.

The community study highlighted the problems of doing social science research; the problematic nature of the concept of community which carried three intertwined dimensions - of place, of social networks, and of communion, a sense of belonging and critique of existing urban industrial relations. The community studies completed were diverse and the processes of working within research teams were complex and at times fraught (Bell and Newby, 1977). There have also been some damning criticisms of the failure to theorise gender relations within this genre, by the men themselves (Frankenberg, 1982). However, more recent research into patterns of neighbours and neighbouring, highlighting patterns of community care, have been more sensitive to theories of gender relations (Abrams and Bulmer, 1987).

Leisure Studies: The Founding 'Fathers'

It is difficult to underestimate the impact of the work of two writers within the UK tradition - namely Parker and Roberts. Their research work has done as much as any one else's to establish leisure as a discrete field of study but their most fundamental contribution has been the publication and popularity of student textbooks. Although their institutional backgrounds differ substantially with Roberts at the University of Liverpool and Parker at the OPCS (Office of Population

Censuses and Surveys), they share certain common roots which distinguish their analysis of leisure.

Both Parker and Roberts started from a research interest in the sociology of work and employment. It was through empirical surveys and quantitative research into the place of work in men's lives that they approached research into leisure. Both were interested in examining the influence that patterns of employment have on families and leisure participation.

Both were interested in American and European literature about leisure and the debates about free time and the coming of a 'leisure society'. Indeed, most students and academics became aware of US and European studies - writers such as Huizinga, Caillois, de Grazia, Kaplan, Kelly and so on through reading the commentaries on such texts by Parker and Roberts rather than reading the original texts themselves. This highlights an important feature in the mediation of leisure studies knowledge. English-speaking researchers have come to understand key international writers on leisure via authoritative commentaries of key texts, whereas academics outside the UK often have the opportunity and the linguistic capacity to read texts in their original language. Such readings of texts suggest something more than the accepted 'double hermeneutic' of social analysis as English texts have to be understood and analysed by academics who do not 'think' in English.

The dominance, or more accurately the hegemony, of the English language within international academic communities in part explains the dominance of US and UK research within leisure studies. Both Parker and Roberts have made substantial contributions to developing international networks and publications on leisure. Both have been committed to establish leisure as a field of enquiry rather than the more narrow concerns of sports, arts, recreation, media or tourism. Both Parker and Roberts have played leading roles on Editorial boards of academic journals such as *Leisure Studies* and *Leisure Sciences/ Loisir et Société*. Parker and Roberts have also played important roles in international conferences, as keynote speakers, plenary commentators and organisers. They have also been centrally involved with the formal institutional networks promoting international scholarship - LSA (Leisure Studies Association), ELRA (European Leisure and Recreation Asociation) and WLRA (World Leisure and Recreation Asociation). This involvement has led to a variety of international publications and collections. Both therefore can be seen to constitute the 'conventional wisdom' of the leisure studies field, certainly within the UK.

There are four major elements to such conventional wisdom which they have sought to defend. First, the centrality of the work-leisure couplet; secondly, leisure as a site for individual freedom and choice; thirdly, the focus on the *social* context of leisure, especially within the family; finally, both celebrate an essentially pluralist view of liberal democratic capitalist society and leisure policy.

Leisure and the Quality of Life: Planning for Other People

During the 1970s there was a growing interest from central and local government in the role sport and recreation facilities played in meeting people's leisure needs and quality of life. Inner cities were the sites where these arguments were explored. The Department of the Environment White Paper, *Recreation and Deprivation in Inner Urban Areas* focused on the idea of recreational deprivation, which could be objectively identified by an index of social indicators such as unemployment, housing density, income, car ownership, ethnic-minority households. Such detailed data bases offered leisure professionals one attractive strategy for tackling inner city deprivation, urban planning and community development. The major target groups for initiatives and research were the young unemployed, ethnic minorities, women - particular single parents, and the elderly. Empirical work was deemed necessary to identify the spatial distributions of users, times and distances travelled and so measure the amount of underuse by disadvantaged groups. Much research was undertaken at a local level; many user-surveys of sports and leisure facilities were unpublished but often presented as internal documents for local policy makers.

As part of a general policy thrust, the DoE commissioned research into defining leisure needs. Earlier work by the Rapoports' *Leisure and the Family Life Cycle* had highlighted the strategies that people deployed to balance the worlds of work, leisure and family. Based on their interviews with over thirty dual-career families, the Rapoports had argued that there were four major stages within the family life cycle. Each stage generated different preoccupations, interests, and resources to balance the conflicting demands of leisure, family and work. Leisure needs changed during different stages of the life cycle and personal happiness could be secured by integrating the three different planes of work, leisure and the family.

This discussion about leisure needs developed from broader debates surrounding the definition and measurement of the quality of life. Researchers had become interested in both objective measures of concept of the quality of life and the problems of aggregating subjective interpretations of people's lives. The OPCS had already conducted surveys of measuring the psychological satisfactions individuals experienced about different aspects of their lives. Mark Abrams' research in *Social Trends* 1973 measured 11 'domains' which individuals ranked on a seven point satisfaction scale. The domains chosen were Housing, Neighbourhood, Health, Job, Finance, Leisure, Family Life, Friendships, Education and Police, Courts and Welfare. The research also measured people's perceptions of the past, present and future, as well as an evaluation of their entitlement. Quality of life surveys relate primarily to marriage and family life and people score highly in these domains. The lowest scores tend to be education, housing, leisure and standard of living - the latter being a crucial determinant of the quality of life.

The DoE (1977) developed four 'experiments' in different urban areas, namely Stoke-on-Trent, Sunderland, Clywd and Dumbarton. The purpose of the experiments was to introduce locally-led campaigns to develop and increase leisure activities via the optimum use of existing resources. The Action Programmes involved a full range of sport, cultural and recreation facilities, namely, information services, transport, mobile leisure facilities, community theatre, community festivals, equipment pools, projects for young people and the disadvantaged. In all over 400 separate projects were launched under the auspices of the experiments and the guidance of Experiment Officers. The median cost of a project was £2000. The Evaluator's report presented an 'achievement factor' in all local projects of two thirds success; yet none of the areas kept the local group structures after the end of the experiment. All employed professionals from theatre, sports and community workers to develop existing talent and sometimes these professional animateurs were rejected by the local community.

This major initiative was part of a wider action government research programme designed to improve the quality of life; this had started with Education Priority Areas and Inner Area Studies. The experiments were to last two years, during the years 1973-76 and were monitored with unexceptional policy conclusions. The research programme had three parts - an assessment of what role leisure played in people's lives and the relationship between leisure and the quality of life; an examination of how local management programmes worked in practice and an evaluation of local programmes.

The main conclusions of *Leisure and the Quality of Life* (DoE, 1977) were that the immense potential for self-help in community via voluntary organisations could be secured by a variety of measures. They highlighted the need for co-operation between the state, the commercial and the voluntary sector, for increased access to facilities, resources and personnel, and for localised networks of facilities. Those who participated in the action programmes were already active in leisure and community pursuits; few additional participants became involved and no new leisure interests were uncovered.

It is interesting to compare the quality of life research with Bishop and Hoggett's (1985) report for the ESRC/SC a decade or so later. Both studies were interested in the 'voluntary sector' and the role that leisure could play in people's lives. However, the two research initiatives started from different assumptions about policy, theoretical perspectives and different value positions about the scope for government intervention. In part, these differences mirror the substantial changes in the policy and research environment in the intervening years. Bishop and Hoggett's research into the voluntary sector completed case studies of two areas: one was suburban middle class in Kingswood, Bristol; the other inner city and multicultural in Leicester. Bishop and Hoggett drew heavily on Gorz's analysis of the production and consumption of leisure, suggesting that voluntary groups organised around enthusiasms, and were essentially democratic by nature and certainly did not require professional intervention and direction. To do so would threaten the 'fragile pluralism' that characterises leisure tastes, a feature valued and celebrated by Roberts (1978).

Youth Unemployment, Race and the Working Class

Rather than the leisure revolution predicted by US optimists, the late 1970s and 1980s were a period of economic stagnation and government retrenchment in the UK. Unemployment, particularly amongst young males had become a central policy problem. Whilst politicians were talking about the 'new realism' researchers within the Centre of Contemporary Studies (CCCS) at Birmingham University were attempting to document the reality of working class culture. Paul Willis' (1977) work *Learning to Labour* encapsulated many of the research concerns and commitments of the talented groups of postgraduate researchers working under the direction of major English writers in cultural studies - Richard Hoggart, Stuart Hall and Richard Johnson. Each gave the CCCS his own unique theoretical drive, resulting in a range of publications examining leisure and culture within the structures of oppression and resistance surrounding class, race and gender issues.

Willis' work symbolises the distinctive agenda set by CCCS research. His ethnography captured the culture of resistance the 'lads' had to schooling and to dead-end work; however, his participant observation was redolent with Marxian categories of labour power, ideology, commodification and consumerism. Although letting the lads speak for themselves and for a white racist and sexist culture, Willis' committed Marxian analysis interrogated the position of young workers entering the labour market with few academic qualifications. The leisure activities of the lads were an uneven mixture of hanging about with 'nothing to do', defending territory against other groups, including the police or participating in more adult leisure patterns of going out, sexual encounters and drinking.

Although producing other readings of working class culture and subcultures, Willis' collaborative research in Wolverhampton completed in 1983 relied on more traditional methodologies (Willis, 1990). It provided an external audit of local authority services for young people and its policy recommendations were informed by a youth survey, 1% sample of 16-24 year olds living within the Wolverhampton Borough, with particular reference to the young unemployed. In the document presented to the then controlling Labour Group, Willis encouraged youth subcultures, for example black youth community organisations to write their own contribution to the overview on the social condition of young people in Wolverhampton. The final report encouraged the local state to acknowledge the broken transitions facing young people, particularly black youth, and the collective problem of unemployment. In a powerful preface and postscript to the work, Willis (1988) demanded a material democracy for young people and an enthusiastic commitment from the local state to provide a coherent and democratic youth policy (as did Corrigan's (1985) contribution to the LSA's conference on *Youth and Leisure,* with his demand for a social democratic commitment to youth work). It appeared that the enfants terribles, the radical Marxists were becoming the most powerful advocates of social democratic welfare intervention.

Feminist Research

Feminist writing has become increasing important in leisure studies research in the UK, as it has in mainstream social analysis. Two milestones for feminist analysis have been Margaret Talbot's (1979) Sports Council / Social Science Research Council state of the art review, *Women and Leisure* and Rosemary Deem's (1986) research in Milton Keynes *All Work and No Play?* The icon of leisure research funded from the same source, now named the Sports Council / Economic and Social Research Council, was the Sheffield study into women's leisure. A collaborative research team, committed to socialist feminist research, completed one of the most important research projects into women's leisure. What makes the research even more compelling was that their research strategy reflected the methodological constraints and compromises imposed on funded research projects by the UK tradition. The Sheffield study provides an interesting case study to make sense of the policy discourses within UK research.

Their starting point for research was the oppression of women and the feminist critiques of some of the conventional wisdoms forwarded by Rosemary Deem and other feminists writers in the mainstream of social and historical analysis. Given the importance of the experience of women, the research team instigated a series of in-depth interviews and group discussions with women in Sheffield to explore the dimensions of oppression in women's lives. However, the research team felt that this wealth of qualitative data would cut little ice with male policy makers so the research team took a strategic decision to complete a detailed survey in the Sheffield area (sample size =777). This part of the research was contracted out to a national market-research agency (NOP).

The research team offer some interesting insights into the management of large-scale survey techniques and the tensions that exist between 'legitimate' quantitative data and the qualitative data collected by interviews and group discussions. The fact that certain categories of women (e.g. the elderly, racial minorities and disabled) were knowingly not included in the final survey need not detain us here. The important research findings have been promulgated in various conference papers, the ESRC/SC report and the book *Women's Leisure, What Leisure?* Despite the importance and impact of the research, the main field worker failed to secure a full-time academic contract with then titled Sheffield Polytechnic, the leading researcher joined Her Majesty's Inspectorate for Higher Education and other key writers in the field of leisure and cultural studies have been dispersed into a range of faculties, schools and divisions within the Polytechnic. Nevertheless, Sheffield is still the site for innovative interdisciplinary thinking, as was signified by the staging of the LSA conference in 1992, *Body Matters*. Other writers have also problematised gender roles and the construction on masculinity and femininity within people's everyday lives (Scraton, 1994).

Postmodernism

Some social theorists suggest that the late 20th century signifies a qualitatively different era or social epoch which can be described as 'postmodernity'. Others, including those writing in cultural studies and feminist traditions, dispute the term 'postmodernity' and dismiss postmodernists as nihilistic intellectuals who have misrepresented art as life. Such critics argue that the term high modernity or late capitalism more closely expresses the condition of the 'new times' (Hebdige, 1988). However, most intellectual domains recognise the 'postmodern' and acknowledge the radical nature of contemporary changes taking place in all spheres of life. Whilst these changes are often contradictory and strong continuities with the past remain, there are, it is argued, features of a 'postmodern' society which are significantly different from a previously 'modern' era.

The issues raised by postmodern thinking and the birth of postmodernity are multi-dimensional and complex. Change permeates several spheres of life: the economic, the political, the social and the cultural. One key feature of the postmodern is difference and *dedifferentiation* - traditional hierarchies, divisions and boundaries collapse. Certainty implodes as 'all that is solid melts into air'. Divisions between high and low culture are deemed to be no longer relevant. Postmodern analysis posits 'the death of the author'. There can be no one uncontested interpretation of a book, painting, or film and therefore the intellectual have no authority to speak for 'the other', to present his/her analysis as the privileged account.

Dedifferentiation occurs within ordinary people's everyday life. For example, the organisation of both time and space becomes more flexible and fragmented as individuals deconstruct traditional patterns and reconstruct their own individual pathways and life course. Whether one looks at patterns of work, ethnicity, leisure tastes, sexuality, meal times, media consumption, life styles, holidays and so on - traditional and collective patterns have become more differentiated and individualised (Urry, 1990).

Whether one examines the economic, social, political or cultural spheres, significant shifts in experiences of leisure, life styles and social circumstances have been encountered in recent decades. Although the term 'postmodernity' derives largely from cultural experiences and in particular the language of architecture, it has been adopted as an inclusive term to incorporate major economic and social changes. Postmodern analysis presents a deep challenge to conventional wisdom about social sciences and leisure research.

> What Baudrillard, in common with other post-modernist
> writers, has done, is to show how much agency and structure
> theories rely upon established institutions, traditions,
> conventions and taken-for-granted understandings for their
> effect. These features may spring from reality but, in time, this

connection can all too easily atrophy.
Rojek (1990:19)

For postmodern theorists the links between new life styles and consumption are significant in leisure and in the formation of personal identities. Featherstone (1991) has argued that consumer culture celebrates the aestheticisation of everyday life - fashions become significant and one must live with style(s). The media endorse not products but lifestyles. Consumption then is not so much the consumption of commodities but the consumption and display of signs. Ethnographic research has recently been completed which operationalises Bourdieu's concept of cultural capital and examines service sector lifestyles in a gentrified urban setting.

Traditional techniques of social science research become obsolete as language and texts have been displaced by figural forms. For many, authenticity and real life nostalgically belong in the past but these can be represented and reconstructed in theme parks and heritage centres for tourists, not only to gaze upon but also to experience, interact and engage with. Leisure, as part of the patterns and styles of life and consumption, plays a significant role in defining people's identities, experience and consciousness. These approaches have been adopted by Hebdige (1988) in analysing developments in Britain in the 1980s, particularly in relation to popular culture and 'consumer identities'. One's life course becomes a reflexive project during which one *must* make choices and develop and discover one's self and identity (Giddens, 1991). Free-time and leisure practices provide an ideal and legitimate site for just such a quest.

Social theory about the postmodern tends to remove the everyday realities of work and leisure into esoteric debate and obscure terminology. It is destructive - critical of everything so there is no urgency to be critical any more (Bauman, 1992). Whatever their theoretical position, whether acknowledging a distinctive break with past existence or not, all recognise significant recent change and attempt to understand it. Leisure also conforms to these cumulative changes, it is increasingly commodified, individualised, diverse and flexible. Part of the debate has also involved a questioning of the nature of social theory itself. Postmodernists argue that the 'crisis of modernity' is not merely a matter of economic, political, social and cultural dynamics but is an intellectual crisis in understanding the social world. Intellectuals are no longer authoritative legislators but interpreters. The Enlightenment 'project' and its key ideas on the nature of scientific objectivity, progress and emancipation are being questioned, as just one language game. 'Open questioning' and deconstruction of knowledge are central to Lyotard's thesis, as is the rejection of the notion of objectivity in the form of grand theories or meta-narratives which he associates with 'myriad stories and fables' (Lyotard 1986).

Whether the more extreme claims of the postmodernism are accepted or not, these approaches to social theory highlight significant and recent economic, social and political changes and attempt, paradoxically given the scepticism about meta-narratives, to make sense of them comprehensively. The focus on individual consumption and its emphasis on current life styles and cultural forms ensures its importance in attempting to understand leisure in the 1990s. For the postmodernists, leisure is no longer a fixed entity, characterised by freedom or control but is fragmented, dedifferentiated and de-centred.

REFERENCES

Abrams, P. and Bulmer, M. (1987) *Neighbours and Networks*. Oxford: Basil Blackwell.
Anderson, P. (1968) 'Components of the National Culture', *New Left Review*, no. 50, July-August.
Barnes, B. (1982) *T. S. Kuhn and Social Science*. Basingstoke: Macmillan.
Bauman, Z. (1992) *Intimations of Postmodernity*. London: Routledge.
Bell, C. and Newby, H. (1977) *Doing Social Research*. London: Tavistock.
Bishop, J. and Hoggett, P. (1985) *Leisure in the Voluntary Sector*. London: Sports Council / Economic and Social Research Council.
Coalter, F. (ed.) (1989) *Freedom and Constraint*. London: Routledge.
Corrigan, P. (1985) 'So what is wrong with social democratic youth work anyway?' in Haywood, L. and Henry, I. (eds) *Youth and Leisure*. Brighton: Leisure Studies Association.
Deem, R. (1986) *All Work and No Play*. Milton Keynes: Open University.
DoE (1977) *Leisure and the Quality of Life: a report on four local experiments*, 2 vols. London: HMSO.
Dower, M. (1979) *Leisure Provision and People's Needs: Stage II Report*. London: Dartington Trust / Institute for Family and Environmental Research.
Featherstone, M. (1991) *Consumer Culture and Postmodernism*. London: Sage.

Frankenberg, R. (ed.) (1982) *Custom and Conflict in British Society.* Manchester: Manchester University Press.

Giddens, A. (1991) *Self and Identity in Modernity.* Oxford: Polity.

Glyptis, S. (1989) *Leisure and Unemployment.* Milton Keynes: Open University.

Glyptis, S. (1991) *Recreation and the Countryside.* London: Longman.

Gratton, C. and Taylor, P. (1992) *Economics of Leisure Services Management*, 2nd ed. London: Longman.

Green, E., Hebron, S, and Woodward, D. (1990) *Women's Leisure, What Leisure?* Basingstoke: Macmillan.

Hall, S. and Schwarz, B. (1985) 'State and Society, 1880-1930' in Langan, M. and Schwarz, B. (eds) *Crisis in the British State.* London: Hutchinson.

Hebdige, D. (1988) *Hiding in the Light.* London: Comedia.

Henry, I.P. (1984) 'Analysing Leisure Policy' in Bramham, P., Haywood, L., Henry, I. and Kew, F. (eds) *New Directions in Leisure Studies*, Working Paper No.1. Ilkley: Department of Community Studies, Bradford and Ilkley College.

Henry, I.P. (1993) *The Politics of Leisure Policy.* Basingstoke: Macmillan.

Henry, I.P. and Bramham, P. (1986) 'Leisure, the Local State and Social Order' in *Leisure Studies*, vol. 5, pp. 189-209.

Horne, J. et al. (1987) *Sport, Leisure and Social Relations.* London: Routledge.

Ingham, R. (1986) 'Psychological Contributions to the Study of Leisure - part one', *Leisure Studies*, vol. 5, pp. 255-279.

Jahoda, M. (1933) *Marienthal: the Sociography of an unemployed community*, (republished, 1972). London: Tavistock.

Kuhn, T.S. (1970) *The Structure of Scientific Revolutions* (2nd edn). Chicago: University of Chicago Press.

Lakatos, I. (1970) 'Falsification and the Methodology of Scientific Research Programmes' in Lakatos, I. and Musgrave, A. (ed.) *Criticism and the Growth of Knowledge.* Cambridge: Cambridge University Press.

Lyotard, J.-F. (1986) *The Post-modern Condition: an essay on knowledge.* Manchester: Manchester University Press.

Mass Observation(1943) *The Pub and The People.* London: Gollanz.

Olszewska, A. and Roberts, K. (1989) *Leisure and Lifestyle.* London: Sage.

Parker, S. (1971) *The Future of Work and Leisure.* London: MacGibbon.

Parker, S. (1983) *Leisure and Work*. London: George Allen and Unwin.

Patmore, A. (1983) *Recreation and Resources: patterns and leisure places*. Oxford: Blackwell.

Rapoport, M. and Rapoport, R. (1975) *Leisure and the Life Cycle*. London: Tavistock.

Roberts, K. (1970) *Leisure*. London: Longman.

Roberts, K. (1978) *Contemporary Society and the Growth of Leisure*. London: Longman.

Roberts, K. (1983) *Youth and Leisure*. London: George Allen and Unwin.

Rojek, C. (1985) *Capitalism and Leisure Theory*. London: Tavistock.

Rojek, C. (1989) 'Leisure and Recreation Theory' in Jackson, E. and Burton, T. *Understanding Leisure and Recreation*. Pittsburgh: Ventura Publishing,.

Rojek, C. (1990) 'Baudrillard and Leisure' in *Leisure Studies*, Vol. 9 pp. 1-20.

Rojek, C. (1993) *Ways of Escape: Transformations in Travel and Tourism*. Basingstoke: Macmillan.

Scraton, S. (1994) 'The Changing World of Women and Leisure? Feminism and Post-Feminism' in *Leisure Studies* Vol. 13.

Seabrook, J. (1988) *The Leisure Society*. Oxford: Blackwell.

Seebohm Rowntree, B. and Lavers, G. (1951) *English Life and Leisure: a Social Study*. London: Longman.

Stockdale, J. (1985) *What is leisure? and empirical analysis of the concept of leisure and the role of leisure in peoples' lives*. London: Sports Council / Economic and Social Research Council.

Talbot, M. (1979) *Women and Leisure*. London: Sports Council / Social Science Research Council.

Tomlinson, A. and Tomlinson, M. (1983) *Mass Observation Surveys: Insights into Leisure and Culture*. London: Sports Council / Economic and Social Research Council.

Townsend, P. (1979) *Poverty*. London: Routledge.

Urry, J. (1990) *The Tourist Gaze*. London: Sage.

Veal, A. (1989) 'Leisure, Lifestyle and Status' *Leisure Studies*. Vol. 8 No 2.

Willis, P. (1977) *Learning to Labour*. London: Saxon House.

Willis, P. (1978) *Profane Culture*. London: Routledge.

Willis, P. (1990) *Common Culture*. Milton Keynes: Open University Press.

Willis, P. (1988) *Youth Review*. London: Avebury.

Chapter 8

The International Perspective in Leisure Research: Cross-National Contacts and Comparisons

Theo Beckers and Hans Mommaas

Introduction

Twenty five years ago, in his famous review of leisure research, Joffre Dumazedier criticised the assumption that most societies were heading towards a vast increase of leisure time. According to Dumazedier, the sociology of leisure was the naive captive of oversimplification. To overcome this pitfall, the sociology of leisure should become a 'predictive' and a 'differential' sociology. In order to become predictive, one should:

> (...) analyse leisure time as an integral part of the total time of human activity. Thus, the real relation between leisure and other categories of time could be more clearly distinguished, and this in turn would make it possible to estimate a time utilisation schedule within the socio-economic dynamic of a given society (Dumazedier, 1969:33).

And it should be differential:

> (...) given that leisure research and policy cannot be generalised, but rather relate to a specific society, in a specific period, taking into account different real or possible conceptions of leisure in accordance with levels of economic development (post-industrial, industrial or pre-industrial) and different types of

social organisations
(Dumazedier, 1969:34).

Instead of generalisation, the sociology of leisure should concentrate on differentiation. The principal units of such a differentiation would be 'societies', i.e. national states. Their comparative organisation of leisure time would reflect their level of development.

In this contribution we want to sketch the historical formation of an inter- or cross-national perspective in leisure research. In doing so, our focus will be on (a) the rationales underlying these inter- or cross-national perspectives, (b) the content of cross-national research questions, and (c) the broader logic underlying those questions. We hope to illustrate how cross-national perspectives were originally based on the universalisation of a 'Fordist' conception/regulation of time, and a nation-based conception and regulation of culture.

Leisure exists as one of the oldest topics of social scientific research. From the very beginning leisure research was a domain of experimentation with new research methods, and was linked to various ecumenical projects. To illustrate its international orientation, two crucial periods can be pointed out. Both periods include about fifteen years of prosperous cross-border academic debate and/or research. The first period starts after World War I with the introduction in the West of an eight-hour working day and of paid holidays, and ends in the economic recession of the 1930s. The second period starts in the mid 1950s, in the midst of the physical, economic and moral reconstruction of Europe, and ends in the affluence, the consumer culture and the welfarism of the late 1960s and early 1970s. In addition, a third period can be distinguished, from the economically troublesome 1980s until the present day. This is a period which shows again a vast increase in cross-national activities, partly continuing established traditions, but partly also based on new interests and concepts, moving away from former 'conventional wisdoms', underpinning leisure research.

The Quest for Leisure 1919-1935

Free Time and the International Labour Movement

In the early twentieth century the social distribution of time had developed into an important international political issue, and the behaviour of workers in their 'spare' time had become a moral concern for many. The famous '3x8' slogan of the labour movement, claiming the daily schedule of eight hours for sleep, eight hours for work, and eight hours for leisure as a natural and proper scheme, articulated a broad social demand, in the form of a laconic time-budget. Essential to the new perspective on time was the notion of a universal labour standard (Cross, 1993:77). This notion asserted the idea of a universal right to a minimum of time, free from work.

This '3x8' doctrine had gradually emerged in the nineteenth century. When industrial employers attempted to replace the informal pace and duration of labour by a standardised intense workday, they produced, under the pressure of the international labour movement, also its mirror opposite: the demand for an equally uniform and completely unimpeded period free from work. Besides, it was discovered that the mass of workers constituted a large consumption market. In addition, entrepreneurs increasingly recognised that well-organised leisure could make a re-productive contribution to business and soften the antagonism between classes, in particular where the working classes adopted bourgeois leisure pursuits. A more rationalised and positive approach to leisure gradually replaced the traditional moral and inhibitive perspective on leisure, interpreted as a threat, to be regulated.

In 1919, the international quest for free time had culminated in the general acknowledgement in industrial Europe and the US of the eight-hour day. The Washington Eight Hour Convention of 1919 was the first project of the new International Labour Organisation, with its office in Geneva, directed by the French socialist Albert Thomas from 1919 till 1933. For Thomas the eight-hour day was both the legitimate fruit of mass productivity and a guarantee for an optimal use of labour power in a mechanical age. Thomas combined the goal of a democratisation of free time, with the quest for productivity oriented scientific management. Albert Thomas believed that through a new humanism the worker could be transformed into a new human being who could create democracy and thus peace (Beckers, 1990). In his view workers had to organise their leisure themselves, within their own institutions. He objected fascist and corporatist institutions for leisure. Due to the presumed supranational character of the interests of the working class, and, because of the international character of the labour movement, from the very beginning, the self-organisation of the worker's leisure received a strong international dimension. Independent international leisure organisations were formed in various fields like the World Association for Adult Education (1918), the Socialist Workers' Sport International (1920), the International Office for Allotments and Workers' Gardens (1926) and many others.

In 1924, Thomas devoted the meeting of the general assembly of the ILO to leisure. This was in order to commit representatives of employers, trade unions and governments to preserve the independent 'right to leisure' as an objective for international action. To prepare for that meeting, in 1923, ILO submitted a request to the governments of the affiliated nations for more empirical information on the leisure activities of workers in their country. The request yielded a large number of national reports, some of which were published in the

International Labour Review of 1924. This international interest in workers' leisure was preceded by Bevans' pioneering 1913 publication on workers' spare time in the State of New York, and followed by a long series of research projects on the same subject in, for instance, France, Belgium, Germany, the Netherlands, the Soviet Union (see other chapters in this volume). At the International Labour Conference of 1924, workers' leisure was the main subject. State representatives, employers and socialist and Christian labour unions discussed the recommendations, formulated on the basis of the national reports. The recommendations were startling in their insignificance, having no political effect whatsoever. Only the empirical material collected is valuable as the first cross-national empirical study on leisure, based on a common questionnaire. This rich source of data still awaits a more detailed secondary analysis.

Albert Thomas was no doubt deeply distressed by the political failure of the conference. He had hoped that the 1924 resolution would contribute to the salvation of the eight hour day which began losing ground as early as the 1920s. It took several more years before the ILO picked up the threads. At the first International Congress on Workers' Spare Time held in Liège in 1930, a proposal put forward by Thomas was adopted. It contained the proposition to establish an international committee at the ILO-office in Geneva, to encourage and co-ordinate the work done in different countries, to promote amongst workers 'a wholesome and judicious utilisation of their spare time'. The committee was officially installed during the second congress held in Brussels in 1935, but was doomed to passivity.

There were several reasons for this passivity. At that moment the project of the international organisation of workers' leisure had already become corrupted by the political antagonisms in Europe between totalitarian states like Italy, Germany, the Soviet Union, Portugal and Spain on one hand and democratic political systems in France, Great Britain, Scandinavia and the Low Countries on the other (Sternheim, 1938). In addition, the economic recession of the 1930s, and the increasing international competition, prevented the development of a supra-national politics of free time, but rather stimulated national solutions. In addition, during this period the notion of free time became increasingly equated with consumption or the dream of a consumers' paradise (Cross, 1993:77).[1] Related to this was the shift in the thirties from the idea of a progressive expansion of daily free time, to the packaging of leisure in weekends and annual vacations. Even the international labour movement changed its strategy from the struggle for an eight-hour working day to paid holidays. The result was that while in the United States, with the onset of the Great Depression, shorter hours became a topic of public debate (Hunnicutt, 1988:147), in Europe the idea of an international and progressive reduction of work time was discredited. The representative of the ILO in the international committee expressed the change in priorities rather clearly when, in 1934, he stated:

> What the masses have been demanding for many months is bread and not circuses, and the fundamental task now is to get the economic machine going again
> (Mequet, 1934:582)

The Scientific Management of Leisure

When after World War I the entitlement to free time was recognised, a mutual and convergent interest in the modernisation and rationalisation of leisure emerged across classes and nations. A fragile alliance of labour and humanist engineers developed. The approach to leisure developed from moral panic and repression to rational and positive action.

A clear example was the American National Recreation Association. This first professional organisation in leisure was founded in the United States in 1906 in response to urban problems like overcrowding, immigration and juvenile delinquency (Hunnicutt, 1988:109).[2] Through public recreation facilities, migrant children could be 'Americanised', juvenile misbehaviour controlled, and the natural desire of children to play given a proper opportunity. The traditional reform goals served the association well until 1910, when new goals were established, due to the leadership of social scientists, who felt that play, recreation and leisure should be planned scientifically. This reflected a broader development, also noticeable in Western Europe (Germany, United Kingdom and the Netherlands) resulting in a rationalised planning of public leisure facilities, especially in industrialised urban areas. During the 1920s, indexers of books, periodicals and newspapers not only found that the word leisure was used more often, but that it was used in different ways, especially in cross-reference with hours of work (Larrabee and Meyersohn, 1958:389).[3]

In Europe and the United States leaders of the labour movement joined hands with the leaders of the rational recreation movement. Both the labour and recreation movement, represented by leaders of the working class and of the progressive urban elite, formed part of a broader political, economic and cultural project, aimed at a 'modernisation' of the labour process.

In that sense, there is a remarkable resemblance between the ideas of Thomas, who had his roots in the labour movement, and the policy of leading scientific managers like Taylor, Ford and Philips aiming at a rationalisation and commodification of both working time and free time. For Ford and other scientific managers, but also in the eyes of fascist and national-socialist political leaders, leisure was not an antipode to work, but a means of creating new reasons to work.

Promoting leisure was the best way to foster loyalty to industrial and thus national progress. And both the Popular Front in France and the national-socialists in Germany rewarded their supporters with the right to leisure.

Victoria de Grazia (1981) has demonstrated convincingly how the combined interests of labour and capital in Italy, during the early twenties, created a fertile breeding ground for Mussolini's leisure organisation 'Opera Nazionale Dopolavoro' (OND). The approach of Italian fascism to leisure can be understood in the context of that regime's need to 'nationalise the masses' (Wilson, 1988:144). In this they were aided by two forces. One was the advance in mass communications technology, especially radio and film, which did much to facilitate the emergence of a national civic culture. The other was the emergence of what in the United States came to be called 'welfare capitalism', programmes of business-guided and -sponsored leisure activities, all designed to combat unionism, to lower absenteeism, to increase productivity and loyalty to the company. In the early days of Fordism, the paternalism of the nineteenth century was replaced by a science-based, technocratic approach to the regulation of the workers' free time, an approach the fascists encouraged and themselves employed. Now leisure was not only related to the development of Fordism on a company level, but also to the development of national welfare, economic health and political strength. At first, the fascists simply endorsed scientific management of companies like Fiat. They discovered however, that welfare capitalism worked better if what began as a private managerial operation, became more acceptable to the nation writ large, due to its public character.

The American National Recreation Association organised the first international scientific conference on leisure in 1932 in Los Angeles, at the occasion of the Olympic Games. The more than one hundred countries represented decided to hold an international recreation conference every four years, prior to the Olympic Games. The second and last conference of this type took place in Hamburg in 1936, and was organised by the national-socialist 'Kraft durch Freude' (Strength through Joy). The American National Recreation Association was present, but all socialist leisure organisations boycotted this political meeting.

Scientific Leisure Research

At that time Marie Jahoda and Paul Lazarsfeld were looking for new topics of research and like social scientists in many other countries they were thinking of studying the problem of leisure:

> One day, we told Otto Bauer that we wanted to do a study on
> leisure. He - quite rightly - smacked his tights and said: 'On
> leisure? But the problem we now face is that there isn't any work.

Why don't you study unemployment?' He drew our attention to
Marienthal.
                        (Beckers, 1990: 202).

Marie Jahoda and Paul Lazarsfeld formed part of a generation of
social academics, that developed a scientific-empirical interest for
leisure as a means to understand society. Stimulating this was not only
an increasing demand from public institutions for scientific
knowledge about leisure, but also a strong conviction amongst those
concerned, that the increase of social-scientific insight in people's
everyday life, would improve the effective formulation and rational
evaluation of public policies. In the Netherlands, Kruijt and Sternheim
are good examples of this new generation and approach (see
Mommaas in this volume). Likewise, American sociologists like
George Lundberg, and Robert and Helen Lynd stressed that leisure
was a 'modern' phenomenon, the social dynamics of which were not
yet known. Because of the fact that leisure was the time in which
people were considered to be free to experiment with their lives, they
were sure that the study of modern leisure would serve to uncover the
changing dynamics of 'modern' society. In addition, Herbert Hoover's
Committee on Recent Social Trends considered leisure and recreation
as critical areas for study (Hunnicutt, 1988:135). In Europe, the
Frankfurter Institut für Sozialforschung included leisure in its
scientific programme (Beckers, 1990).

After World War I, empirical leisure research developed gradually.
An international, yet disconnected, group of young researchers, was
interested in people's factual behaviour and in the reality of daily
leisure. A more empirical approach replaced mere contemplation. For
many social scientists leisure was an appropriate domain to test new,
more sophisticated research strategies and techniques.

The most important innovation was the application of time-
budgets. Time studies became popular in economics, sociology and
psychology. In their time-budget research, statisticians, economists
and sociologists were drawing from a respectable tradition of income
and expenditure studies on workers' families. Analogous to the early
psychological studies on the perception of duration, time-budget
studies were only concerned with studying how much time was
allocated for work, family and leisure. This information was, and still
is, used as an indicator of particular lifestyles and the quality of
peoples' lives: quality being measured by the amount of free time
available and/or spent (Adam, 1994:94).

The spread of a new rationalised outlook on time, which had
developed in the context of the industrial organisation of labour and
the social struggles between labour and capital, was further enhanced
by the introduction of chronometric time-and-motion studies in
programmes of scientific industrial management. Influential were the
works of Ferdinand Le Play, Ernst Engel and Franklin Giddings. As

far as we know Franklin Giddings, a leading American sociologist, professor at Columbia University and, as many academics of his days a Social Darwinist, was the first to use the time-budget technique. In the context of industrial capitalism, time had become money, and now money replaced time in budget analyses.

Giddings used to give his students practical assignments consisting of mass observations of individuals' behaviour through a number of days. These assignments aimed at the analysis of everyday behaviour as a function of belonging to a particular social group. One of his students was the theologian George Bevans who under his supervision did the first 'modern' piece of leisure research. In 1913 he published 'How Workingmen Spend Their Spare Time', a text based on time-budgets of workers in New York. Thus, shortly after the introduction by Frederick Taylor of time-studies in the analysis of the labour process, a similar rational calculative outlook on the use of time marks the international beginning of an academic interest in leisure.

The bulk of time-budget studies published before World War II originated in Great Britain, the Soviet Union and the United States, and quite a few in France and Germany. Other countries like the Netherlands or Belgium were only sporadically represented (Szalai, 1972:6). Time-budget data were used to measure time spent on paid work, housework, personal care, sleep, recreation, and/or the use of leisure (ibid.). The possibility of increasing free time as well as upgrading its use, were frequently discussed in early leisure research. In the 1920s and 1930s major contributions to the study of time-budgets were made in the USSR by Stroumilin, and in the United States by Sorokin (a refugee from the USSR). In 1939 Berger's intellectual classic 'Time Budgets of Human Behaviour' appeared, and in 1931-1933 Lundberg, Komarovsky and McInerney used time-budgets for the study of leisure behaviour in Westchester County. The first study on leisure in the Netherlands by Blonk, Kruijt and Hofstee (1933-1936) introduced the same method in Dutch social science research.

Although there is a considerable resemblance in the content and origin of leisure research in many 'modern' Western states - a similar rationalist interest in workers' leisure, applying time-budget analyses -, no evidence could be found of any personal links between the researchers involved in the various countries. Similar tendencies and lines of development did not generate direct international contacts between academics. Although the studies in Marienthal and Westchester seem to have had a clear impact on the Dutch study on workers' leisure, as one of the researchers revealed to one of us, there were no personal contacts. We know of only one scholar who tried to act as a cross-national intermediate: Andries Sternheim.[4]

The Democratisation of Leisure 1955-1970

Rationality and State Intervention

The real boom in leisure research appeared in the late 1950s and early 1960s. This can, amongst others, be related to the changing role of leisure in societies more and more dominated by mass-consumption, and to a welfare-oriented expansion of state-intervention in most non-totalitarian Western countries.

Optimistically, intellectual and political leaders saw leisure as part of the breeding ground for a national citizenry, enjoying the rational fruits of the Enlightenment in the form of travel, physical exercise, outdoor recreation and cultural participation. Pessimistically, they saw leisure as part of the spreading of a consumer culture, driven along by the quantitative logic of the new cultural industries, producing other-directed submissiveness and mass culture, a potential breeding ground for a new totalitarianism. In practice, Western welfare states adopted a strategy with regard to leisure, similar to Mannheim's notion of 'planning for freedom'. In his book *Man and society in an age of reconstruction* Mannheim (1935) explored a third alternative between the chaos of laissez-faire capitalism and the totalitarian control of fascism and communism. To Mannheim, planning for freedom implied the regulation of the entire institutional configuration, based on a democratically chosen plan, which guaranteed the collective freedom of society. The provision and education for leisure by the state played an essential role in such a plan. More and more leisure was defined as an individual and democratic social right. In the welfare state leisure became a citizen's entitlement, a social service to be delivered by the state, a possible corrective to consumer culture.

One discipline, inspired by changes in industrial relations, urban integration and social stratification took the lead: sociology. In the context of the post-war educational boom, and embedded in the service of the welfare state, academic sociology expanded drastically. Many of the new sociologists were convinced of the fact that increased affluence and leisure, together with the levelling of social inequality, signalled the dawn of a post-industrial leisure society. For them, the shift from a work or production-oriented to a leisure or consumption-oriented life formed a natural and even necessary element of advanced or post-industrialisation (Rojek, 1985:2; Mommaas, 1991:294). Within the context of a spreading consumer culture, scholars like Dumazedier, Friedmann, Aron, Brightbill, Riesman, Meyersohn, Wilensky, Mead and Schelsky commonly started to regard leisure as an important object of scientific inquiry. Dumazedier and many others heralded an emerging leisure society. A cultural rather than a political revolution would free workers from routine and obligation. A further radical reduction in labour time was expected to result from automation. In addition, the counter-culture of the 1960s seemed to confirm the arrival of a homo ludens and a definite shift in values. And indeed, many western nations showed an accelerated growth of leisure consumption, a spreading of middle-class aspirations, an increase of leisure facilities and programmes, of recreational space, and of leisure research and training programmes.

The welfare state tried to channel the appetites of the masses in a rational way. There was a general quest for knowledge as a foundation for rational planning, and hence for an empirical investigation of leisure. In addition, the expansion of the welfare state produced a series of new professions. These included youth work, community work, adult education and recreational work, and as a result, the first courses on leisure and/or recreation appeared in higher education curricula. On the basis of all this, in many western countries, leisure research received a higher status and priority in social sciences and gained the support of key persons and important institutions. National scientific research centres, networks, journals and projects were established and state-of-the-art reviews published.

In 1955 in Chicago, in the midst of fierce intellectual debates concerning the emergence of a popularised, market-driven mass culture, a leisure research-centre was founded under the supervision of David Riesman (Lanfant, 1974:67). Meyersohn and Denney carried out various projects on cultural participation in American suburbs, the relation between work and leisure, and the impact of mass media. In Kansas City, Havighurst investigated the social meaning of leisure. Wilensky chose the industrial region of Detroit as his area of research. In 1958 Meyersohn and Larrabee published *Mass Leisure* a compilation of papers with quite opposing viewpoints on leisure, demonstrating the momentous interest and academic acceptance of leisure research in the United States.

Another major stimulus delivered the publications from Margaret Mead, Paul Lazarsfeld, Max Kaplan and other leading scientists on behalf of the Outdoor Recreation Resources Review Commission; these were represented in 1962 to president Kennedy and the Congress. For Meyersohn this was an 'accident':

> The accident occurred when a Presidential Commission was appointed to make recommendations concerning the needs and resources of American recreation. A series of inquiries were sponsored, and 27 volumes of study reports were issued. Some of them are very valuable in providing a baseline for the charting of consumption as well as gratification of various outdoor recreation activities.
> (Meyersohn, 1969:50).

The start of the *Journal of Leisure Research* in 1969 was an indicator of the increase in the USA of a scientific interest in leisure, of the institutionalisation of the leisure profession, and of the increasing political support for outdoor recreation planning. By that time, much of leisure research was already policy inspired and relied heavily on a positivist, value-free outlook on social science. Dominant were time-budget analyses and survey methods. Hence, in 1963, Bennett Berger, in his critical state of the art review, could conclude:

> The sociology of leisure today is little else than a reporting of survey data on what selected samples of individuals do with the time in which they are not working and the correlation of these data with conventional demographic variables
> (Berger, 1963).

In a period of cold war and positivist, value-free social science, especially the time-budget method proved to be an efficient and neutral bridge between researchers on both sides of the ideological division in the industrial world.

The first critique on the role of leisure research in the 'scientific management' of society could already be heard. One point of criticism was political. Especially during the 1960s the production and consumption of leisure via the market corresponded no longer to the rationalist ideals of intellectuals and political leaders. Since leisure research developed in the public sector, little attention was paid to consumerism and market forces. Philosophers of the Frankfurt School, like Adorno, Fromm and Marcuse had criticised the commodification of culture and the way this process was reified and supported by social researchers. Cocooned in their idealistic and a-political concept of leisure, leisure researchers did not respond to this neo-Marxist criticism. Neither did leisure researchers involve themselves with the *dritte Methodenstreit*, to remain loyal to their conventional wisdom.

The second point had to do with the theoretical limitations of the way in which leisure was conceptualised and operationalised. Although some contemporary authors, like Marie-Francoise Lanfant (1974) in France, demonstrated a critical approach, this type of evaluation of the blossoming 1960s of leisure research only reached its peak in the second half of the 1980s.

As is shown in other chapters in this book, in countries like the Netherlands, France, Belgium and West-Germany, a similar development of applied leisure research can be detected. In France, for instance, Dumazedier started his CNRS-research group on leisure and popular culture in 1954 (see Samuel, Chapter 2). The work resulting from that group would have a long and profound impact on leisure research in other countries of southern and central Europe. In the Netherlands, in 1954, the Central Bureau of Statistics created a special research division which realised two pioneering projects on the leisure behaviour of the Dutch population (see Mommaas, Chapter 4). It was only a matter of time, before this increase in national research programmes would make an impact on the international level.

Cross-national Research

Until World War II, the international orientation in leisure research in most cases remained confined to a cross-national exchange of (nation-based) ideas and experiences. This occurred either in the context of international conferences and meetings, or on the basis of internationally distributed journals and books. This changed gradually after the 1950s. Not only was the cross-national exchange of information intensified, it was also addressed more directly, through unified and standardised cross-border research projects.

It is possible to relate this post-war internationalisation of leisure research to a further 'compression' of time and space, something which can in turn be linked to market forces and technological developments in transport and communication (cf. Harvey, 1989). Also of importance were developments in the handling and processing of data, enabling the management of larger amounts of information, and stimulating the use of 'modern' statistical procedures. But perhaps most significant of all was the growing popularity of so-called international-relations politics, and the related increase in the number of supra-national policy organisations which could function as new supra-national resource bases for cross-border research projects.

In the post-war era, international relations again became a major focus of attention in European as well as American geopolitics. This resulted from either a genuine ambition to abolish globally the political and economic conditions which had twice involved almost the entire world population in a war with one another, or a more selfish wish to contain the global expansion of communism and to open new markets for Western industries. In the context of this growing interest in international politics, cross-national research contacts and projects served various purposes. Sometimes they were seen as politically safe vehicles for the enhancement of cross-national cultural relations, thus stimulating a mutual understanding and exchange of ideas across the iron-curtain lowered over Europe. In addition, cross-national research could perhaps deliver the knowledge necessary for international developmental policies. A cross-national comparison of economic, political and/or cultural developments, amongst developed and developing countries, could perhaps display factors, which could trigger successful industrialisation, democratisation, and/or participation politics. In theoretical terms, the research became framed in developmental perspectives on global relations. Popular were versions of convergence and/or modernisation theory (So, 1990). Subsequently, cross-national comparative research became increasingly popular and prestigious. This even to the point where it developed into a self-reliant research-branch, with its own books, journals, departments, conferences and specialists.[5]

Within leisure research, the international orientation followed general developments (see Lanfant, 1974, whose inventory of the post-war development of leisure informs the following section). During the 1950s, leisure became an internationally recognised area of social science research, and a serious meeting ground for scholars from both sides of the Atlantic Ocean, and from both sides of the political and ideological watershed dividing Europe. Free time as the 'neutral' temporal mirror-image of decreasing labour time, and leisure as an indicator of the quality of everyday life, were well suited for the purpose of a cross-national investigation of the condition of cultures in an industrialising and modernising universe.

In 1954 a first international conference on the use of sociology in the organisation of leisure and popular education took place in Wegimont, Belgium (Lanfant, 1974:91). In 1956, Dumazedier co-ordinated a first comparative European study on leisure and culture in six cities situated in Denmark, Finland, France, the German Federal Republic, Poland and Yugoslavia. The study was launched by the Department of Social Sciences of UNESCO, which, as a non-political and supranational intermediary would play a crucial role in the early stimulation of cross-national research contacts across Europe.

On the fringes of the third International Conference of Sociologists in Amsterdam in 1956, a number of academics, interested in leisure, met (namely Dumazedier from France, Anderson from the USA, Ten Have from the Netherlands, Ossipov from the Soviet Union, and Hennion, director of the Pedagogical Institute of UNESCO). In 1957, the group formed the International Group on Social Sciences and Free Time. This occurred during a meeting in Annecy, the medium sized French city where, in 1954, Dumazedier had initiated his major project on urban leisure and culture, a project directly inspired by the Lynd's pre-war study on Middletown (Ibid: 64, 91, 114). The new international research group on leisure was again linked to UNESCO, which subsequently took over the supervision of the six cities project. In 1959, during the fourth International Conference of Sociologists in Meina, already 13 teams of sociologists and practitioners, from Western and Eastern European countries, were present (Ibid: 91). Finally, in 1965, during the sixth International Conference of Sociologists in Evian, the group was officially transformed into the Research Commission on Leisure (RC 13), a Commission of the International Sociological Association (ISA). In the first years of its existence, a major cross-national time-budget project, directed by Alexander Szalai, stimulated and integrated the group.

The use of time

It is clear that the Multinational Comparative Time-Budget Research Project, as it was officially labelled, originated within the 'modernist' mixture of developmental geopolitical and ecumenical scientific sentiments mentioned above. The project resulted from a debate, initiated by a paper, delivered by Szalai himself during the

International Conference on the Use of Quantitative Political Social and Cultural Data in Cross-National Comparison, held at Yale University in 1963. The debate focused on the lack of standardised procedures in time-budget research, enabling successful use of the method in cross-national comparative research.

As already mentioned, the popularity of time-budget research had increased tremendously after World War II. This was, among other things, stimulated by the expansion of social state intervention, and the related increase in public leisure facilities. Of particular importance, was the spreading of (public) television and the quest for data to measure its impact on everyday life and improve the planning of programmes:

> Leisure, or the lack of it, is the central theme of an incredible number of time-budget studies carried out since World War II in practically all countries where social research has reached a certain stage of development. (...) the shortening of the daily or weekly working time and the lengthening of the average life span much beyond retirement age, the long hours spent on commuting or, for that matter, on sitting before the television set, the growing need for adult education and the everlasting domestic slavery of housewives and mothers in spite of all refinements in frozen or pre-cooked food, kitchen gadgetry, laundry automation and the like - all these are factors that have contributed to making leisure a far more complicated and far more general problem than it was in a period when working people simply had to fight against impossibly long hours that left them insufficient time for even their most immediate personal needs
> (Szalai, 1972:9).

However, the specific research strategies followed, the variables involved and the classification of activities included, varied enormously. It was expected that by carrying out a series of common time-budget surveys, situated in different countries, a future standardisation would be stimulated. This would in turn stimulate the use of time-budget methods in quantitative, cross-national comparative research (Szalai, 1972:5,6).

More substantively, the project was targeted at a cross-economic and/or cross-cultural analysis of the impact of processes of urbanisation and industrialisation on (sub)urban everyday life (ibid: 10). As such, the project seems to be influenced by notions of convergence theory, which predicted a merging of free-market liberalism and totalitarian communism due to the global spreading of industrialisation processes.

In 1964, the project was adopted by the neophyte European Coordination Centre for Research and Documentation in Social Sciences (the Vienna Centre, initiated by UNESCO, and for obvious reasons closed in 1994), eager to stimulate academic cooperation across the iron curtain.

Initially the project involved eleven European research institutes from Belgium, Western Germany, France, Hungary, Poland, Yugoslavia and the USSR. In the course of time six more joined, situated in Bulgaria, Yugoslavia, Poland, Czechoslovakia, Eastern Germany and the USA. By April 1966, fifteen surveys had been carried out, situated in twelve countries. The surveys were aimed at those parts of the population, most integrated in modern industrial economy, living in urban settings.[6]

The voluminous account of the project, counting no less than 870 pages and published as late as 1972, gives a clear and nuanced evaluation of the many problems involved in developing such a gigantic standardised (i.e. 'modernist') research project.[7] In addition, the clear awareness is expressed that, due to the fact that most of the surveys were situated in and around specific urban regions, the results would not be generalisable to the level of countries as such, precluding the possibility of a truly cross-national comparison.

Reading the various accounts of the research, taken up in the publication of 1972, one can not but become acutely aware of the problems the complexity of the data must have given a group of researchers, lacking a clear integrating theoretical and/or methodological outlook on things.

On the level of the project as such, the basic conclusion is that across the various sites investigated (reaching from Peru to the USA to Germany to Russia), industrialisation has led to an important homogenisation of the temporal structure of everyday life. This homogenisation transcends vast differences in cultural tradition, and in economic and political structures (Robinson *et al.*, 1972:115). At the same time, the authors were impressed by the consistency of the amount of time allocated to specific activity-domains such as travel and the mass media. Despite vast differences in the level of technological developments, the total amount of time devoted to such activities remains the same. They are part of what is called a 'common human design' (Ibid: 144).

It is stressed that the cross-national differences that do exist are only registered around the margins of this common human design. The projection of these differences on a two-dimensional scale results in a picture, showing a remarkably resemblance to a geographical map, organised by an East-West and North-South divide. The East-West dimension relies on differences in time devoted to work, television, informal socialising, and eating and sleeping:

> It seems reasonable to think of our East-West axis in time use as arising primarily from variation in work and its social organisation on one hand, and a factor involving technological

development and consumer affluence on the other.
(Converse, 1972:159).

The North-South divide is produced by differences in time devoted to activities like resting, cooking, outdoor recreation, eating and sleeping, watching television, shopping, personal care and religion. It is suggested that the North-South divide seems primarily to be an indoor-outdoor one, reflecting differences in climate (ibid: 166).

In addition to these general conclusions, individual participants have used the material to investigate numerous other research questions, ranging from the organisation of child care in the various countries, to the impact of TV on mass media use, and the relation between educational status and the use of time. Some analyses restrict themselves to sheer description of findings, while others have aimed at the testing of hypotheses. Some deal only with a comparison of specific sites, while others have tried to formulate universal law-like conclusions, or to investigate the local impact of global diffusion processes (e.g. the spreading of industrialisation, television, or 'individualism'). As such, these various contributions deliver a striking example of the variety of ways in which not only the time-budget method as such, but also the method of cross-national comparative research can be used.[8] In the end, however, it seems to be that this variety of approaches and research questions from a heterogeneity of disciplinary, theoretical and policy interests can be held responsible for the fact that the project did not have more of an impact than it had.[9] In fact, the project would remain the only truly cross-national research project of some significance, focused on leisure, until the second half of the 1980s.

In 1968, still with the help of UNESCO, and strongly influenced by the ideas of Dumazedier, the European Centre for Leisure, Education and Culture started its activities in Prague. Apart from a number of bibliographies on leisure-research in various countries, the journal *Society and Leisure* was one of the most important products of this centre. It was the first scientific journal in the field with a strong international and comparative orientation. The American *Journal of Leisure Research* appeared one year later, but preserved till today an inner-directed, national focus. While *Society and Leisure* radiated the humanist and rationalist French tradition which linked leisure to the democratisation of culture, the *Journal of Leisure Research* had that typical empirical and positivist bias, reflecting the reduction of leisure to outdoor recreation in many Anglo-Saxon countries outside Britain (USA, Canada, Australia, New Zealand).

Leisure in a Globalising World 1980-1995

Restructuring the Frame of Reference

A third crucial period in the development of international cooperation in leisure research can be characterised by key-words such as professionalisation, fragmentation and pluralisation, and transnationalisation. At the same time that in both leisure research and leisure education stronger international links were established, conventional ideas and approaches became the object of debate. The field of leisure research became fragmented between attempts to either defend the tradition, or to adapt the study of leisure to new theoretical and societal developments.

Traditionally, leisure research has always depended heavily on direct public support, more in particular from the national state. Since the early 1980s this support has no longer been clearly evident. Reaganism and Thatcherism, the end of communism and the restructuring of the welfare state generated a transnational shift from state to market, from leisure services to leisure consumption, from democratic to meritocratic leisure. This shift also created the need for new types and styles of professionalism and placed new questions on the research agenda. The approach to leisure became more and more economic and commercial, stressing the importance of leisure in terms of consumption and the creation of employment and other benefits for the urban, regional and national economy.

In addition, the need for more and better professionals, together with a revived expectation during the early 1980s of the increase of free time and leisure consumption, generated quite a number of new programmes in higher education, especially in Western and Central Europe. Instead, in the United States, the number of leisure studies programmes decreased as a consequence of a decline in the political support for leisure service delivery.[10]

The gap between the worlds of knowledge and application, of academics and practitioners, has widened and deepened. In the United Kingdom for instance, in 1979, next to the research oriented Leisure Studies Association (LSA), a unified professional body was established, the Institute of Leisure and Amenity Management (ILAM). In the United States an organisation for leisure scholars was created, the Academy of Leisure Sciences, situated outside the traditional National Recreation and Park Association. On the contrary, the Dutch Vereniging voor de Vrijetijdssector (VVS), founded in 1989 as the successor of a network of academic leisure researchers, still claimed to bridge the gap between critical reflection and the operational use of knowledge.

The World Leisure and Recreation Association (WLRA) and the European Leisure and Recreation Association (ELRA), organised on a cross-national model, lost their significance and became footloose in relation to new directions and initiatives in leisure research. They started to represent the disputed establishment which did not prove able to incorporate or relate to new developments in social theory.

From the late 1970s onwards, within various North-Western European countries, new generations of researchers, having had their academic training in the stormy 1960s and 1970s, started to debate the self-evident neglect or one-sidedness of the post-war 'modernist' model of leisure research. This was either stimulated by the legacies of the German Frankfurt Schule, by the British neo-Marxist tradition of social history and/or cultural studies, by a revival of pre-war American urbanism or criminology, by the (re-)discovery of figurational sociology (Elias), by French post-structuralism (Althusser, Foucault, Bourdieu) and/or by English post-functionalism (Giddens). National leisure research hegemonies became subject to ongoing critique.

Of vital importance for the subsequent pluralisation of approaches were the first International Conferences of the Leisure Studies Association (LSA), organising an alternative international forum for various critical approaches (see Bramham and Henry, Chapter 7). In addition, the European Community established the ERASMUS programme, oriented towards an inter-national exchange of students of higher education, but also stimulating cross-national contacts between various leisure studies courses. Here one can point at the Programme in European Leisure Studies (PELS) in Brussels, Bilbao, Loughborough and Tilburg, and the postgraduate programme Homo Ludens in Gent. These formed additional frameworks for a trans-national exchange of new ideas and approaches. At the same time, the ERASMUS programme formed part of a broader 'Europeanisation' of a European economic, political and cultural space, also stimulating cross-border research contacts, based on new European resources.

In the midst of these new transnational links, functioning more or less independently from traditional networks like those of WLRA/ELRA and RC 13, and responding to a new wave in time-space compression (now decorated with the label of 'globalisation'), the conventional model of cross-national and comparative research gradually lost some of its self-evident character. In addition, new research groups were started, which did not use leisure as their primary point of departure. Here one could point at cultural studies, tourism studies, and at research on sports and physical education. Separate scientific communities were developed, using new channels of communication, journals and programmes.

Thus, within and outside the community of leisure researchers conventional wisdoms became challenged. Beneath all the differences involved (and yet to be explored), if one were to summarise what these alternative viewpoints had in common in comparison to the preceding models, one could point at: (1) a more theory - and history - based approach to social reality (involving the notion of the theory-dependent character of not only 'facts' but also 'methods'); (2) a firm interest in the social and/or collective dimension of leisure and in leisure as a gender and class-related concept; (3) an interest in the active involvement of people in the constitution of their leisure and in interpretive methods to analyse the 'meaning' of leisure; (4) attention for the politics and the production of leisure; and (5) a serious concern for commercial, popular and informal leisure in addition to 'public', 'serious' and/or 'formal' leisure.

Cross-National Projects on Leisure Participation

The 1980s showed a remarkable upsurge in cross-national leisure research projects. One of the organisations leading in the initiation and development of these projects was again RC 13. During the second half of the 1980s, almost simultaneously, three publications bore fruit, containing the results of two cross-national research projects. In 1987 *Trends in the Arts* was published, edited by Linda Hantrais and Teus Kamphorst, in 1989 followed by *Trends in Sport*, edited by Teus Kamphorst and Kenneth Roberts. Both projects formed part of a broader project: *Explaining Leisure Features*. In that same year, 1989, *Leisure and Life-Style* was published, edited by Anna Olszewska and Kenneth Roberts.

Explaining leisure features

Explaining Leisure Features was originally conceived as a collaborative project between the Netherlands and Hungary. However, during a meeting of the World Leisure and Recreation Association at Marly-le-Roi in 1984, the members of RC 13 invited other leisure researchers to join. Subsequently, a plan was agreed for a series of multinational studies of trends in leisure behaviour, from the early 1970s onwards:

> The main objective of the project is to contribute to the general knowledge about why people in contemporary societies adopt a particular form of leisure behaviour and to explain how and why leisure patterns change and develop.
> (Hantrais, 1987:1).

The project not only aimed at international collaborative work on leisure research. In addition, it was aimed at 'a better understanding of the peculiar features of each society through cross-national comparison' (Ibid).

In the introduction to the two publications which so far have been published of the project, the editors show themselves rather conscious about the pretensions and problems of cross-national comparative research. Taking a positivist perspective, three main problem-areas of cross national and comparative research are pointed out: the definition of research parameters (the problem of the definitions of leisure and/or culture), the lack of comparable data sets, and the management of the research (for instance, the problem of funding). Because it was obvious to the organisers that they could not meet the standards needed for a truly cross-national research project, they lowered their ambitions and gave their project the sub-title: 'a multi-national perspective'. In addition, given the diversity of the national data, it was decided not to compare detailed leisure participation figures, but to compare general participation trends. The basic research questions, formulated as guidelines for the contributors, were aimed at the deduction of world-wide trends in leisure participation, as well as at regional/cultural variations. Thus, as the editors acknowledge, the project displayed more of an inductive-descriptive, instead of a theoretical-analytic character. There are no theoretical perspectives or theory-informed research questions underlying the project, thus giving a rationale for combining research data from countries situated rather differently in historical time and global space. In addition, it is recognised that individual interests of the authors, and the varying availability of data, have seriously hampered a strict comparability. Nevertheless, the main rationale of the project as such, and the main line of reasoning followed in the analysis of the data gathered, remained perfectly in line with the basic logic of cross-national comparison. In the end the aim was to look for explanations for general trends in leisure, observed over the past two decades (Hantrais, 1987:217).

In *Trends in the Arts*, the first study of what was originally conceived as a series of studies on specific fields of leisure activities (including the arts, sport, reading, the media), eight contributions were included: from Canada, the United States and Puerto Rico, via France, Britain and the Netherlands, to Hungary and Czechoslovakia. Again, the co-ordinators show themselves acutely aware of the practical and principal problems involved in cross-national and comparative research in general, and in this project in particular.[11] However, in spite of these problems, the editors reached some interesting conclusions from the material collected (see Hantrais, 1987; Kamphorst, 1987).

The most basic one concerns the strong and often re-established correlation between people's level of education and their participation in the arts. In the past this relation has been interpreted as a causal one, based on the suggestion that 'modern' education socialises people into the general rules and complexities of artistic aesthetics (one 'learns to appreciate'). However, neither historically, nor cross-nationally does this intra-national correlation hold. Despite all the problems which are obscuring a clear comparability, so much is clear from the data, that, in all the countries involved in the project, the rise in the level of national education which occurred from the early 1960s onwards has not resulted in a comparable increase in the attendance of theatres, opera's and concert halls, or to an increasing cultural homogeneity between the various strata.[12] On the contrary, some contributors suggest that existing gaps have even widened. Neither is it the case that countries with a generally higher level of education show a comparably higher level of participation in the arts.

The alternative hypotheses, formulated in order to explain these findings (see Kamphorst and Van Beek, 1987:155; Samuel, 1987:99) point at the possible role of a person's cultural 'legacy' and of primary instead of secondary socialisation; at the fact that the school system fosters traditional cultural values, thus in a sense reproducing cultural inequalities; and at the ongoing importance of strategies of socio-cultural distinction. Cultural elitism is a 'cumulative process of exclusion':

> (...) privileged groups in society use their intellectual and
> material resources, through family socialisation, to maintain the
> distance which exists between them and other social groups
> (Hantrais, 1987:228).

Thus, the findings raise questions with regard to the general effectiveness of national public redistribution policies, while at the same time paradoxically pointing at the ongoing importance of the national dimension in the structuring of the global cultural field.

Twenty-one researchers 'representing' fifteen countries contributed to the second project, concerned with *Trends in Sport*. They ranged from New Zealand, Japan and India, to Bulgaria, Czechoslovakia, Poland and Finland, to Portugal, Italy, France, Great Britain and the Netherlands, to Nigeria, to Canada and the USA. An entire encyclopaedia of national sport trends catches the reader's eyes throughout the fifteen contributions. In the concluding chapter, the basic question is what world-wide trends in sport participation can be deduced from the material.

Less focused in relation to the arts project, several trends are notified. They include, for example, the world-wide incorporation of sport in national health policies; the world-wide domination of sports like walking, running and swimming; the overall decline in sport participation since the second half of the 1970s; the increasing domination of amateur sport by professional sport; the overall pluralisation, diversification and differentiation of types of sport; the decentralisation of sport policies and the privatisation of sport facilities; the de-formalisation and de-institutionalisation of sport; increasing consumerism and commercialisation; the increasing 'spectatisation' and 'mediatisation' of sport.

Clearly, this time, the perspective is a generalising one, searching for universal developments and universal 'laws' of explanation. When trying to account for the world-wide decline in the participation of sport, factors pointed out by various authors, of importance within their own national context (e.g. economic decline, changes in demographics), are refuted on the basis that they do not explain cross-national differences or developments elsewhere.

Leisure and life-style

Also initiated out of the 'inner circle' of RC 13 was yet another project. During the first half of the 1980s a group of authors planned to develop a joined project to investigate the implications for everyday life of the current restructuring processes, involving the economic crisis, an increase in global competition, new technological developments and the crisis of welfare politics. The central aim was not to formulate universal law-like explanations of leisure. Instead, the aim was to analyse the nation-specific effects of global restructuring processes. The expectation was that:

> (...) people's experiences of, and responses to, the changes might vary in significant ways depending on the ways of life to which they were already committed
>   (Olszewska and Roberts, 1989:i).

Initially, 'ways of life' is translated into national differences with regard to, amongst others, a society's economic performance, work ethic and level of hedonism. But in addition, the authors show themselves clearly aware of the fact that trends and their impact do not only vary between, but also within countries (Ibid: 2, 3).

Eleven authors joined the project and in the end nine countries were included, ranging from Brazil, Puerto Rico and the USA to Great Britain, France and Belgium, to Hungary and Poland, and to Japan. Together this variety was supposed to realise a global perspective on trends and reactions. The group developed a common frame of reference, not so much consisting of a common theoretical framework and a related central research question, but of a set of questions, aimed at an investigation of national responses to recent global economic and technological trends. However, in their introduction to the publication of the project, the editors have to admit that 'some (contributors) ignored the guidelines completely and no one was wholly faithful' (Ibid: 5).

As the editors indicate, given the fact that no attempt was made to develop a common theoretical framework, the various national contributions reflected not only national differences, but also differences in theoretical preferences and political interests. Besides, the contributions were based on existing material.

Also in this case, in the end, the lack of a common perspective and the variety of approaches, together with the variable quality of the data used, and the huge and complex variety of national economic, political and cultural circumstances (how to compare, for example, Puerto Rico with Japan?) has seriously hampered the possibility of a comparative analysis of the effects of global developments on national leisure participation. Some authors only pay attention to changes in the overall participation in specific leisure domains. Others have explored transformations in the social stratification of leisure participation in general. Some have presented their data and analyses as situated within a country's specific circumstances. Others present them as general facts of life, ignoring the context to which the data owe their comprehension. Some have included a clear analysis of the way in which a nation's political response mediated global economic/technological trends. Others related changes in leisure participation directly to developments in the national economy, or to changing forms of social solidarity (while only partly informing the reader about the degree to which these differences are the result of different theoretical perspectives). Some authors stressed the continuity of changes in leisure participation since the 1980s, and downplayed the effects of the economic crises (instead, e.g., pointing at the effects of the cultural revolution of the 1960s and 1970s on leisure behaviour and experience). Others stress the discontinuity of events and the effects of the crisis of the 1980s (this again without giving the reader a clear idea about how much of this is due to the perspective involved, the structure of the data used, or the nation-specific circumstances researched).

Transcending the difficulties confusing a comparative analysis, the editors restrict themselves to the identification of general trends, evolving from the various contributions. It is noticed that throughout the various countries, the growth of work-free time and leisure spending have continued. However, at the same time, governments have retreated from redistributive policies, and the increase of non-work time on one side and of income on the other, have gone to totally different groups. The economic and political problems of the 1980s have been resolved at the expense of leisure, and in the majority of countries, growing groups of people are experiencing impoverishment, with their leisure grounded back towards 'basics' (Ibid: 13). On the other hand, the 'winners' are spending more than ever before on leisure, but much of this seems to involve the conspicuous display of wealth (Ibid: 15).

The Conventional Wisdoms Questioned

The cross-national and comparative research projects, mentioned thus far, clearly reflected the traditions of leisure research generated in especially North European countries during the post-war era. Obviously, that should not come as a surprise. Despite further possible aspirations, what was at stake in most cases was not so much the formulation of independent research questions, and the development of new research models, appropriate to a trans-national or global level of integration and analysis, but rather the bringing together, but keeping separate, of existing national data sets, in sequences of cross-national comparison. At the same time, the initiative for these projects came mostly from researchers from Northern-European countries, with a prominent position in not only their national but also in the international academic leisure research community. In the mixed-capitalist North-West, as well as in the collectivist North-East, the post-war academic scene had become dominated by positivist, if not inductive-empiricist, correlational research. With regard to leisure research, that model was targeted at issues of leisure participation, investigating the time and attention different groups of the national population devoted to publicly organised leisure facilities. As such the model was based on a Fabian state outlook on social reality, relatively biased towards not only 'formal' and 'public' (i.e. 'bourgeois') culture, but also towards individual leisure 'demand'. These traditions led to the relative neglect of issues surrounding the production and/or regulation of leisure, and paid relatively little attention to the spatial, historical and collective dimensions involved.

Leisure and urban processes

One of the cross-national leisure research projects which was developed from a different perspective was *Leisure and Urban Processes* (Bramham *et al.*, 1989). The publication formed the first product of the European Consortium for Leisure Studies and Research, established in 1987. It was aimed at an investigation of urban leisure policies across Europe.

In the introduction to the book, four reasons are given for focusing on urban leisure policies. First, it is stated that, during the 1970s and 1980s, cities have exhibited the most serious symptoms of the economic, political and cultural changes that occurred. Second, urban life is seen as increasingly concerned with non-work activities, instead of with production. This as well with regard to the everyday life of the unemployed, as with regard to the conspicuous consumption of the well-to-do. Third, the need is felt to evaluate leisure policies in the light of recent attempts for 'rolling back the state'. Fourth, authors point at the much debated issue of the 'differentiation' or 'individualisation' of lifestyles, the joined effect of factors like the flexibilisation of the labour force, housing policies, the extension of education, the 'expressive' revolution of the 1960s, and the increased reflexivity in matters of aesthetics and morality. This was expected to deliver new opportunities for leisure, but also to destroy former collective forms of leisure.

The project was intentionally aimed at a comparative analysis of urban leisure policies. The central aim of such an analysis would have to be to 'deliver more generalised insights in the role of specific contexts, for instance in the shaping of urban leisure policies' (Ibid: 5). Hence, the project was more aimed at an investigation of the influence of context, instead of at a neutralisation of context. However, the editors also acknowledged that the actual material collected could only deliver the raw materials for such an analysis.

Most contributions were focused on developments within a single nation state or even a single urban locality. Besides, no common analytical framework was used in the development and/or analyses of the different cases.

The publication contains thirteen contributions, from six European countries, ranging from Greece (Athens) and Italy (Rome), to France (Lille), Belgium (Antwerp), The Netherlands (Rotterdam and Nijmegen) and Britain (London, Leeds, Bradford). The contributions are the result of both varying urban leisure realities, and of varying perspectives on those realities. Some contributions are plainly descriptive, others aimed at a more analytical approach. Some deal with urban leisure policies from a more generalised national point of view, others focus on in-depth analysis of leisure policy in a single city. Some centre around domains of recreation and sports, others on culture and consumption.

In the conclusion, the editors once again point out the embryonic status of the project. In addition they reiterate their commitment to what is called 'contextual realism', distancing their project from comparative models aimed at a universalisation of knowledge. Not a neutralisation of context is at stake, but a comparative investigation of the role of context in mediating presence and absence. At the same time, the editors stress the theory-dependent character of comparative models of research, especially with regard to the context of comparison. From a theoretical point of view, there is nothing self-evident in choosing the nation-state as a framework of comparison, nor a region, a city, or whatever socio-spatial entity. Hence the need for a theoretical rationale underlying the comparative framework chosen.

In line with this, and generalising from the cases presented, the conclusion contains an inventory of the six different roles assigned to leisure in the various leisure policy cases presented, and a model for future comparative research. The latter builds on the various time-spatial dimensions of processes identified in the (re)structuring of urban leisure policies. These include: (a) the positioning of cities or regions in (inter)national capital accumulation processes, and the (inter)national division of labour; (b) their administrative positioning in relation to the central state; (c) the relation between the local public and private sector, and (d) local styles of leisure consumption. Thus, a multi-spatial model of structuring processes is developed, making it possible to situate the various cases in their respective but interrelated time and space.

Concluding, the book questions the optimistic suggestion underlying much market-oriented leisure-based urban development policies. So much is clear from the cases, that attracting more tourists, higher income residents, conspicuous consumers or Research and Development businesses, will not in itself contribute to urban integration. If not linked to redistributive economic and cultural policies, instead of confronting urban decay, such policies might as well run the risk of merely relocating or even deepening urban contrasts (cf. Bianchini and Parkinson, 1993).

Leisure policies in Europe

It would take four years before the second product of the European Consortium for Leisure Studies and Research was published (Bramham *et al.*, 1993). The framework of cross-national comparative research suited the substantive topic of this second project rather well: at stake was a comparative investigation of national leisure policies throughout Europe. The rationale for this study was based upon the unification of the European market. Because of an increasingly free flow of capital, labour, goods and services, inner-European competition between states, regions and cities would increase, while at the same time limiting the scope and effectiveness of various forms of public intervention. A comparison of national policies on various dimensions of leisure (for example sports, tourism, culture, recreation, the media) would enhance the development of coherent European policies, and inform policy makers of the experiences of others. In addition, it was supposed to deliver information on the advantages and disadvantages of various models of national leisure policy in relation to patterns of leisure participation, and to throw some light on the variety of national responses to changing economic, political and cultural circumstances. The latter, for example with regard to (a) the increasing emphasis on market mechanisms, and (b) the shifting public importance attributed to various leisure sectors.

Nine countries are included in the project, from Russia and Poland in the East, to Greece and Spain in the South, Sweden in the North and Britain and France in the West, and with Germany and the Netherlands in the middle.

In the conclusion the editors state that the national level is not the only significant level of policy making (it is even stated that in many instances of leisure policy, the city might be a more significant unit of analysis), and that national policy making does not evolve in isolation from supra-national influences. Again, the model used is not that of the comparison of isolated cases, joined together in some sort of social vacuum in order to formulate universal conclusions. Instead, at stake is a comparison of the ways in which situated governments have mediated transnational political and economic transformations in the changing development of their national leisure policies.

The common background against which developments in national leisure policies are investigated is that of an increasingly unified European political and economic space, meeting a global restructuring of the economy, following the disintegration of the post-war global economic equilibrium dominated by the United States. Amongst others, this shift from a so-called 'Fordist' to a 'post-Fordist' accumulation *regime*, has resulted in the replacement of a former social-democratic culture of welfarism by a neo-liberalist enterprise culture (Ibid: 237). With regard to the provision of leisure, this has resulted in the shift from a social service approach (emphasising the welfare potentials of sports and recreation), to one in which leisure appears as a tool of economic regeneration (emphasising the economic potentials of culture and tourism). This over-all liberal shift in public provision ideology and leisure policy is illustrated by referring to the case studies of Britain, the Netherlands, France, Spain and Poland.[13]

The publication concludes with an analysis of the implications for leisure policies of the Europeanisation project, pointing out the tension between on one side the use of leisure (the media, heritage culture) as a tool for the creation of a common European cultural space, and on the other the use of leisure (shopping, the visual arts, cultural tourism, popular culture) as a tool for regional development.

Conclusion

There are at least three ways in which one might speak of the international dimension of research. First, one can focus on the cross-border traffic of academic ideas, approaches, perspectives, methods and concepts. Here one could investigate the interdependency between various national intellectual communities, and try to trace and explain the international hierarchy of academic standards and ideas. Second, one could pay attention to existing international research contacts, the international organisations established, and the activities undertaken. Who is leading these initiatives, what broader scientific and political interests are involved, and what sort of research agenda has developed (or not developed)? Third, one might investigate the incorporation of the international dimension in actual research projects, and have a look at how that international dimension is conceptualised and investigated, and why.

The foregoing overview of the international dimension in European leisure research concentrated in particular on elements of the latter two, i.e. on cross-comparative contacts and research. It is an incomplete overview in the sense that no exhaustive inventory has been made of all the cross-border research projects and contacts existing. Neither have we included the vast amount of single case studies which nevertheless incorporated an international perspective and dimension in their research (e.g. investigating the impact of transnational economic restructuring on local leisure provision policies). We also did not pay attention to the many cross-national research projects targeted at a specific leisure domain such as, for example, tourism, sport, the arts, the media. The foregoing was confined to major projects, *explicitly* incorporating a cross-national comparison of leisure in a more generic sense, in particular as far as the results of that comparison have been communicated through academic books (which is obviously not to claim that other studies would in any way be less valuable).

As has been exemplified above, scholars of leisure have incorporated an explicit international perspective on their topic of investigation right from the start. Underlying this perspective, there may always have been the desire to travel, to increase one's status as an 'internationally oriented academic', to meet academics from other countries involved in a research field perhaps not that common amongst home-based academics, and/or to re-establish supra-national academic relations and hierarchies. However, in addition, underlying international projects, contacts and perspectives, there have always also been various theoretical and/or moral-political programmes.

Of major importance in the pre-war period was the international labour movement. By developing trans-national or inter-national contacts, policies and organisations it tried to meet and represent the supra-national interests of the labour class, and in so doing supporting the spreading of a Fordist regulation of time. In addition, one can think of the humanist aspirations, for instance underlying ecumenical projects like those of the Olympic movement, or of the League of Nations, striving for 'civilised' inter-state relations. During the post-war period, these supra-national programmes were joined by developmental geopolitical aspirations, aimed at an incorporation of former colonies in the industrial-capitalist 'family of nations', thus expanding the US-based political and economic hegemony. More recently, there is the 'Europanisation' of Europe, aimed at the creation of the European internal market. All of these supra-national projects have in one way or another stimulated a cross-national perspective in leisure studies, be it in the form of the organisation of international conferences, of international journals, and/or of international research projects.

At the same time, from the very beginning, the cross-national contacts between researchers also have had a scientific-cognitive rationale. Here the reason to travel and to meet and discuss had something to do with the notion of science as an ecumenical project in itself, i.e. as a project involved with the task of formulating universal knowledge. From the times of Erasmus onwards, formulating scientific wisdom was about the production of knowledge, freed from the particularities ('limits') of religion, culture and/or estate; the less place and culture specific the knowledge, the more scientific it was.[14] This can be related to the claimed importance of making explicit and/or standardising research methods, enabling a replication of research projects whenever and wherever deemed necessary. It also explains the higher status of work published in internationally instead of nationally oriented journals. Last but not least, it can be related to the already older ambition for an inductive cross-cultural and/or cross-national comparison/exchange of research findings.

However, within the social sciences, from the very beginning, there has existed some ambivalence with regard to the central aim of this universalising strategy. This ambivalence relates back to contrasting theories of knowledge and contrasting comparative models used by Durkheim and Weber. On the one hand, 'universal' can stand for 'all encompassing', in the sense of covering all possible human events belonging to a certain category. Here, the aim is to establish universal laws of human conduct, an aim comparable to the presumed model of the natural sciences. But in contrast, universal can also stand for universally reproducible, in the sense of replicable, given known circumstances. This latter interpretation leaves room for other research strategies, which do not focus on the formulation of general 'laws of human conduct', capable of 'explaining' situated events, but instead concentrating on an 'understanding' of the role of context in the reproduction of social reality. Hence the differentiation between *universalising* and *contextualising* comparative strategies. Universalising strategies are aimed at a neutralisation of context. Instead of on a *negation* of context, contextualising strategies are aimed at an *investigation* of context. The aim is to examine the role of context in the mediation of presence and absence.

In addition, within both the universalising and contextualising traditions in comparative analysis, subsequent divisions did develop, in some way further reproducing the basic universal-contextual divide. Thus, within the universalising tradition, one can distinguish between more universal and more contextual versions. The first focus on the formulation of common properties among all the cases of a certain category. The second are focused on the formulation of general principles of variation between those same cases. At the same time one can differentiate more universal and more contextual versions of contextual comparison. The first are focused on the formulation of general principles with regard to the way in which cases, situated in a common context, mediate presence and absence. The second are focused on the formulation of the particularities of a certain case, in relation to other cases within the same context.[15]

The history of the international orientation in leisure research clearly reflects this plurality of approaches. In a more universalising sense, authors have been looking for common properties of leisure behaviour, among all the national data gathered. What common trends can be discovered across these data sets, with regard to the participation in sport, the arts, the media? Here the intention was to formulate universal theories of leisure behaviour. Other researchers have looked for general principles behind intra-national variations in leisure behaviour, e.g. with regard to the role of stratification factors like the level of income, labour-market positions, or the level of education. From a more contextualising perspective, researchers have tried to investigate how national/local leisure policies have mediated the global restructuring of the economy, or they have tried to investigate how the global spreading of industrialism has affected national patterns of leisure behaviour. And last but not least, authors have also tried to explain the specifics of national patterns of leisure behaviour, contrasting those to patterns of leisure behaviour in other countries/regions.

What is striking about the history of the international perspective in leisure research is perhaps not so much this diversity of perspectives as such. Much more striking is the unreflexive use made of the diversity of perspectives, i.e. the lack of attention paid to the specific models used, and the rationales underlying them. Even within one project, authors sometimes have switched rather unproblematically from one logic of comparison to the other.

What holds for the logical status of the knowledge aimed at (universal and/or contextual), also holds for the comparative framework chosen. Although the concept of cross-national comparison adequately covers the comparative framework used in most international leisure research projects (that is to say: most of the time the focus is on establishing cross-national contacts and comparisons), nevertheless, the way in which nations and/or national states figure in these projects differs considerably.

To illustrate this, one can take recourse to a classification of cross-national and comparative research, developed by Kohn (1989), based on the way in which researchers involve the nation-state in their research. The author differentiates between research in which the nation-state is treated as an *object* of analysis (the research is aimed at a cross-national comparison of the particularities of countries), as a *context* of analysis (there is an interest in tracing general features of sub-national entities), or as a *unit of analysis* (the research deals with a cross-national interest in the relation between sub-national phenomena and national characteristics).

Again, it is not difficult to trace examples of all of these models in the history of international leisure research. In most cases the research basically involved itself with a cross-national comparison in which nation states figured as *contexts* of research. The aim is a cross-national comparison of intra-national leisure phenomena (i.e. intra-national relations with regard to leisure participation, either collected on a national or on a lower aggregate level). In addition, when analysing these data, sometimes reference is made to the particularities of national states, thus including the national state as a *unit* of analysis. More recently, when analysing national leisure policies, the national state has become a more direct *object* of analysis. But again, what is striking is not so much this diversity as such, but the generally unreflexive nature of the cross-national comparative frameworks used. However, as said before, there is nothing self-evident in taking the national state as the primary element of comparison. Why not take neighbourhoods or cities, regions or cultures, climatic zones or entire hemispheres? This obviously depends on the primary research question formulated, and the underlying theoretical perspective. Most of the time the cross-national comparative structure used has remained untheorised.

Stimulated by the strong institutionalisation of leisure research in, and identification with, national social politics, together with this lack of theoretical reflexivity, international leisure research has tended to reproduce the same nation-centric bias, characteristic of post-war social research writ large (see, e.g. Tilly, 1984; Turner, 1990; Wallerstein, 1989). Within leisure research the national state was regarded as representing the most fundamental unit of social integration, such that they:

> (...) have come to see current sovereign states (projected hypothetically backward in time) as the basic social entities within which social life is conducted. (...) They have boundaries, inside of which factors are 'internal' and outside of which they are 'external'. They are 'logically' independent entities such that, for statistical purposes, they can be 'compared'.
> (Wallerstein, 1989:316)

In contrast, the recent upsurge of interest in globalisation processes has not only stimulated a growing awareness of the nationally biased nature of cross-national and comparative research, in addition, it has also produced a growing interest in so-called *transnational* research. Stimulated by the Brussels-led 'Europeanisation' of the European field of research and education, and the loosening of the ties between leisure research and national welfare state politics, following developments in media and consumption studies, also within leisure research, there is an increasing interest in processes, structures and/or institutions transcending and/or cross-cutting the nation-state system. Here one could think of research pointed at the (emerging) transnational organisation of leisure markets and/or sectors (i.e. in the field of tourism, sports, the media, consumption) at the role of European Union policies in the reproduction of leisure sectors or at the market and/or media led transnational diffusion of leisure tastes.

Obviously, this is not to say that nation-based research no longer is of any value. Instead the basic argument should be that in globalising times, there is a growing awareness of the fact that the national state is but one of several possible institutional frameworks, primarily responsible for the structuring of our leisure. Other institutional frameworks (the market, the voluntary sector, primary socialisation, the media) functioning within various time-spatial parameters (local, regional, transnational, global) have increasingly to be drawn into the analysis.

Such an evaluation of the international dimension in the study of leisure shows up the possibility of programmatic, conceptual and theoretical *gaps*. This is especially of relevance in a domain of life which has been the sustained target of cultivating strategies by national(ising) elites, but which seems likely to escape this cultivating squeeze, due to the globalising condition of today, to become entangled in the global-local nexus of a world free market choreography. An international perspective seems then nothing but necessary. That is not to say that trans- or cross-national research would be the only viable models of research. Instead, whatever the scale of the research completed, there seems to be an increasing need to situate the objects under study in their global, instead of universal, reality.

REFERENCES

Adam, B. (1994) *Time and Social Theory*. Cambridge: Polity Press.

Beckers, Th. (1990) 'Andries Sternheim and the study of leisure in early critical theory'. *Leisure Studies*, vol. 9, number 3, pp. 197-213.

Berger, B. (1963) 'The sociology of leisure', in: E. Smigel (ed.), *Work and Leisure*. New Haven: College and University Press, pp. 21-40.

Bianchini, F. and Parkinson, M. (1993) *Cultural Policy and Urban Regeneration: The West European Experience*. Manchester: Manchester University Press.

Bramham, P., Henry, I., van der Poel H. and Mommaas H. (eds) (1989) *Leisure and Urban Processes: Critical Studies of Leisure Policy in Western European Cities*. London: Routledge.

Bramham, P., Henry, I., van der Poel H. and Mommaas H. (eds) (1993) *Leisure Policies in Europe*. Oxon: CAB International.

Converse, Ph.E. (1972) 'The implementation of the survey design', in: A. Szalai (ed.), *The Use of Time. Daily Activities of Urban and Suburban Populations in Twelve Countries*. The Hague-Paris: Mouton, pp. 43-68.

Cross, G. (1989) *A Quest for Time: the Reduction of Work in Britain and France, 1840-1940*. Berkeley, CA: University of California Press.

Cross, G. (1993) *Time and Money. The Making of the Consumer Culture*. London: Routledge.

Dumazedier, J. (1969) 'Developpement of the sociology of leisure', in: J. Dumazedier and C. Quinchat (eds), *La Sociologie du Loisir. Tendances Actuelles de la Recherche et Bibliographie (1945-1965)*. La Haye-Paris: Mouton, pp. 32-37.

Godbey, G. (1994) *Leisure in Your Life: An Exploration*, 4th Edition. State College Penn: Venture Publishing.

Grazia, V. de (1981) *The Culture of Consent. Mass Organisation of Leisure in Fascist Italy*. Cambridge: Cambridge University Press.

Hantrais, L. (1987) 'Introduction', in: L. Hantrais and T. Kamphorst (eds) *Trends in the Arts: a Multinational Perspective.* Amersfoort: Giordano Bruno, pp. 1-11.

Hantrais, L. (1987) 'Conclusion', in: L. Hantrais and T. Kamphorst (eds) *Trends in the Arts: a Multinational Perspective.* Amersfoort: Giordano Bruno, pp. 217-232.

Hantrais, L. and Kamphorst, T. (eds) (1987) *Trends in the Arts: a Multinational Perspective.* Amersfoort: Giordano Bruno.

Harvey, D. (1989) *The Condition of Postmodernity: An Enquiry into the Origins of Cultural Change.* Cambridge: Blackwell.

Hunnicutt, B. (1988) *Work without End. Abandoning Shorter Hours for the Right to Work.* Philadelphia: Temple.

Kamphorst, T.J. and van Beek, A. (1987) 'The arts in the Netherlands', in: L. Hantrais and T. Kamphorst (eds) *Trends in the Arts: a Multinational Perspective.* Amersfoort: Giordano Bruno, pp. 145-164.

Kamphorst, T.J. (1987) 'Postface', in: L. Hantrais & T. Kamphorst (eds) *Trends in the Arts: a Multinational Perspective.* Amersfoort: Giordano Bruno, pp. 233-242.

Kamphorst, T. and Roberts, K. (1989) *Trends in Sports: a Multinational Perspective.* Culemborg: Giordano Bruno.

Kohn, M.L. (1989) 'Cross-national research as an analytic strategy', in: M.L. Kohn (ed.) *Cross-National Research in Sociology.* London: Sage, 1989, pp. 77-102.

Lanfant, M.F. (1974) *Sociologie van de Vrije Tijd.* Utrecht/Antwerpen: Het Spectrum.

Larrabee, E. and Meyersohn, R. (1958) *Mass Leisure.* Glencoe: The Free Press.

Mannheim, K. (1935) *Mensch und Gesellschaft im Zeitalter des Umbaus.* Leiden: Sijthoff.

Meyersohn, R. (1969) 'The sociology of leisure in the United States', in: J. Dumazedier and C. Guinchat (eds), *La Sociologie du Loisir. Tendances Actuelles de la Recherche et Bibliographie (1945-1965).* La Haye-Paris: Mouton, p. 46-52

Mommaas, H. (1991) 'De wetenschappelijke vormgeving van de vrijetijd', in: Th. Beckers and H. Mommaas (eds.) *Het Vraagstuk van den Vrijen Tijd.* Leiden: Stenfert Kroese, pp. 278-300.

Nowak, S. (1989) 'Comparative studies and social theory', in: M.L. Kohn (ed.) *Cross-National Research in Sociology.* London: Sage, pp. 34-56.

Olszewska, A. and Roberts, K. (1989) *Leisure and Lifestyle: a Comparative Analysis of Free Time.* London: Sage.

Robinson, J.P., Converse, Ph.E. and Szalai A. (1972) 'Everyday life in twelve countries', in: A. Szalai (ed.), *The Use of Time. Daily Activities of Urban and Suburban Populations in Twelve Countries.* The Hague-Paris: Mouton, pp. 113-145.

Rojek, C. (1985) *Capitalism and Leisure Theory*. London: Tavistock Publications.

Samuel, N. (1987) 'The arts in France', in: L. Hantrais and T.J. Kamphorst (eds) *Trends in the Arts: a Multinational Perspective*. Amersfoort: Giordano Bruno, pp. 87-112.

So, A.Y. (1990) *Social Change and Development: Modernisation, Dependency, and World-System Theories*. Newbury Park: Sage.

Sternheim, A. (1938) 'Leisure in the totalitarian state', *Sociological Review*, vol. 30.

Szalai, A. (1972) 'Introduction: concepts and practices of time-budget research', in: A. Szalai (ed.), *The Use of Time. Daily Activities of Urban and Suburban Populations in Twelve Countries*. The Hague-Paris: Mouton, pp. 1-12.

Tilly, C. (1984) *Big Structures, Large Processes, Huge Comparisons*. New York: Russel Sage Foundation.

Turner, B. (1990) 'Two faces of sociology', *Theory, Culture and Society*, 7(2/3), pp. 112-135.

Wallerstein, I. (1989) 'World-Systems Analysis', in: A. Giddens and J.H. Turner (eds) *Social Theory Today*. Cambridge: Polity Press, pp. 309-324.

Wilson, J. (1988) *Politics and Leisure*. London: Unwin Hyman.

NOTES TO CHAPTER 8

[1] Or as Sternheim formulated in 1938: 'Productive capacity has increased so greatly that to avoid catastrophic consequences it is necessary for the producers to become to an ever increasing degree consumers. Society's very existence depends on the continuous creation of new needs for material goods' (Sternheim, 1938:29).

[2] The American National Recreation Association was the successor of the Playground Association of America and was responsible for the foundation of the International Recreation Association in 1956 (since 1973 the World Leisure and Recreation Association).

[3] Larrabee and Meyerson discovered 51 articles and books, published between 1910 and 1919, carrying the concept of 'Leisure', and over 410 between 1920 and 1929.

[4] Elsewhere a description and analysis is given of his position and significance for pre-war international leisure studies, within the framework of early critical theory. See Beckers (1990).

[5] In 1967, Marsh published *Comparative Sociology*, which contained a bibliography of more than 1100 comparative studies (quoted in Nowak, 1989:35).

[6] In addition to the money received from the Vienna Centre and the money invested in the project by the participating institutions, the

project was sponsored by the Stiftung Volkswagenwerk in Hannover and the National Science Foundation in the United States.

[7] Mentioned are, for example, problems related to the design of the questionnaire, the standardization of classifications of activities, the selection of survey sites and the population to be surveyed, the sampling procedures and sample sizes and the procedures of data collection, data coding and data analyses (see e.g. Converse, 1972).

[8] In terms of the differentiation Tilly (1984) has made with regard to logics of cross-national comparative research, we find not only attempts at 'individualizing comparison', but also at 'universalizing comparison', and 'variation-finding comparison'.

[9] However, the material seems to have played some importance as a data resource base in various countries in Europe, until at least the beginning of the 1970s. See Lanfant (1974:92).

[10] In 1994, still over 300 colleges and universities offered courses in North America, carrying names such as Leisure Studies and Services, Recreation, Parks and Tourism, and others (Godbey, 1994:337). Maney of these programmes were accredited by the Council on Post-Secondary Accreditation through the NRPA and the American Alliance for Leisure and Recreation. Such academic programmes may be situated in a variety of departments within the university, including health, physical education, forestry, hotel and recreation management.

[11] Mentioned are, amongst others, the arbitrariness of the process whereby countries were included in the project or not, the fact that cross-national comparative research tends to downplay the importance of differences within countries, the fact that a synchronic comparison as such does not take account of the different positions of cultures/countries in historical time, the difficulties involved in the comparability of data due to the 'crazy-making' cross-national variability in operationalizing and measuring 'participation', and, last but not least, the problem of the various national definitions of 'the arts'. It is interesting to see how the various national definitions of the arts differ from one another, how the arts are demarcated from 'leisure', 'free time', 'entertainment' etc., and how this is related to the way the various national participation data are organized. This deserves a study of its own.

[12] That is, with the notable exception of visits to museums and historical monuments. The explanations given for this exception are: the easy access to an increasing number of sites; the increasing informality and flexibility they offer; their attractiveness as places for family outings and school parties (Hantrais, 1987b:229).

[13] Here, as the editors admit, some of the tension can be felt between the aim to compare the role of the specifics of local political,

economic and cultural histories in the mediation of trans-national processes, and the aim to distil common developments from single nation studies.

[14] See for instance Nowak (1989:38) who states: 'Time-space limits of validity of (...) historical generalizations are substitutes for some unknown factors, the empirical variation of which is correlated with the boundaries of particular societies, systems, or cultures - within some of which our theory "works", while in other societies the theory "does not work"'.

[15] This distinction is inspired by the model of comparative research developed by Tilly in his emblematic *Big Structure, Large Processes, Huge Comparisons* (1984:81/3). However, while almost duplicating the four positions Tilly differentiates (universalising comparison, variation-finding comparison, encompassing comparison and individualizing comparison), here, these four are presented as the result of the subsequent reproduction of the difference, from the very beginning dividing the social sciences, instead of being based on two rather formal criteria (i.e. 'multiplicity of forms' and 'share of all instances').

Chapter 9

Leisure Research in Europe: Trajectories of Cultural Modernity

Hans Mommaas, Hugo van der Poel, Peter Bramham and Ian Henry

Introduction

The aim of this book has been to bring together various histories of the study of leisure in a variety of European nation-states. In addition, a first attempt has been made to address the cross-border exchange of ideas in the European field of leisure studies. Coming to the close of the post-World War II era, it was expected that the project could encourage some reflection upon the pace and trajectory of the research field in question. This is of interest not just from the point of view of leisure research itself, but also from the more general perspective of cultural theory. Because the concept of leisure draws together in a common conceptual space a wide variety of cultural activities - from the physical to the mental, the traditional to the modern, the playful to the serious, the popular to the elitist, and the local to the global - it is a rather useful concept to study the social and cultural conflicts and interdependencies involved in the history of the formation of culture (Lefebvre, 1991; Bourdieu, 1990). In addition, this book deals with the investigative involvement of intellectuals and reformers with this cultural battlefield. This further adds to its relevance as a contribution to the history of the formation of culture during a century in which the sovereign power of the state in cultural affairs has both reached and passed its historical high point (Bauman, 1987; Toulmin, 1990). As such, it is intended that this publication delivers material for a further analysis of the historical trajectories of leisure and culture, as part of a broader theory of modernity.

The project has been organised along a cross-national comparative framework. Although this very much resulted from the same circumstances which so often force international research projects into a cross-national model, nevertheless, in a certain sense, the framework suited the topic. At least until recently, when looked upon from an institutional point of view, the domain of leisure research has first of all been organised within the framework of the nation-state system. State-based social, educational and cultural policies and nationally integrated language and publication communities, amongst others have been the factors of primary importance in shaping the map of the study of leisure across Europe.

Of course, this is not to imply that differences within, and/or similarities across, national communities would be of marginal importance. Although having had a primary influence in the structuring of the field, the national 'scale' is but one of several socio-spatial 'scales' along which leisure research in Europe has become organised. From the mid 19th century onwards, many cross-border contacts existed between academics, social reformers, social administrators and members of social movements. These contacts have played an independent role in stimulating a cross-border empirical sensibility to, amongst others, labourers' pastimes (see Beckers and Mommaas, Chapter 8).

As was hinted at in the introduction, this project took quite some time to develop. This is explained not only by reference to the usual difficulties involved in the preparation of cross-border projects - especially when these depend on the 'spare time' of researchers. In addition, the difficulties point at wider historical-institutional discontinuities, such as the current de-stabilisation of intra- and international relations in Europe, and to the many ways in which this is unsettling the position of scholars. In addition, there were factors involved which more specifically relate to the changing status of leisure research within academia. One can think here of the difficulties scholars met in reserving time for this project in an academic environment which is not only becoming more and more time-pressured and commodified, but which also seems to move away from the issue of leisure to adjust itself anew to the latest jargon in state and market institutions. Finally, there is the fact that a lot of the contributors had to prepare their contribution from scratch. Little work had been done yet on the history of leisure research, something illustrating a certain lack of self-reflexivity within the field.

Already, these factors can tell us something about the history of the study of leisure. Based on the foregoing contributions, this conclusion will elaborate that history, trying to extract common trajectories of continuity and change, as well as the cross-national variations between them. An attempt will be made, not only to evaluate general developments from the point of view of the 'professional' field itself, but also to investigate the relationship between these developments and broader institutional transformations.

As background there will be a perspective which owes a great deal to the recent theorisation by Anthony Giddens (1989) and Ulrich Beck (1986) of what they have labelled 'late' or 'reflexive' modernity. According to this perspective, we are in the midst of a transformation which takes us beyond the point of 'early' or 'simple' modernisation in the direction of a radicalised reflexivity or 'de-traditionalisation'. Both authors relate these developments to the recent globalisation of social reality, amongst others fundamentally changing the role and position of the nation-state, and of the social sciences. Besides, both authors stress the importance of analysing these events from a multi-dimensional perspective, taking into account the relative autonomous influence of administrative, legal, technical and symbolic institutions vis-à-vis the organisation of the economy and production.

The work of these authors is the object of intense debates. Of special concern are their supposed (neo-)evolutionary character, their cognitive and individualistic bias, and their over-all relation to earlier modernisation theories (see e.g. Lash, 1994; Alexander, 1995). However, this is not the place to go into these debates. For the time being, it suffices to say that we think both theories deliver useful tools to interpret the long-term developments in the study of people's pastimes. In recent times, these developments have resulted in the state of reappraisal the study of leisure appears to be experiencing. It is trying to come to grips with a new 'de-mystification' of cultural conformities and scientific rationalities, facing a period of renewed cultural doubt and uncertainty.

In line with the theoretical perspective chosen, and continuing the temporal-historical approach already used in various of the contributions, the development of the study of leisure across Europe will be analysed along three crucial periods of transformation. These are: (1) the period of the coming into being of free time as a domain of intervention and debate towards the end of the so-called 'long 19th century', (2) the emergence of leisure studies as a relatively independent field of research during the post-World War II period, and (3) the current period of reorientation and reappraisal. While these phases can be distinguished from a genealogical point of view, it is important to point out that there is an important overlap between them. 'Residues' from former formative periods are still very active in subsequent periods, and even up to the present day. At the same time it will be clear that this periodisation is primarily related to events in the North Western power centres of European modernisation. If taking a different perspective, e.g. from the East or the South, things would have looked different (although also such a perspective would have to take into account the changing power-figurations with the centre, and the related economic and cultural influences).

The analysis will follow a cross-comparative strategy which balances a focus on core developments with an interest in the nationally variable mediation of those developments. Thus various 'trajectories' or 'routes' can be distinguished within the development of the study of leisure, here interpreted as part and parcel of European trajectories of cultural modernity (Therborn, 1995).

Ambivalence of Concepts

But first a note on concepts: to begin with, it is of some importance to stress the plural and contested nature of concepts of leisure circulating throughout Europe. Due to the necessity of using a common language, this has been considerably simplified in this book. In fact, if we had had to choose a concept most closely related to the plurality of research activities represented here, that concept would probably not be *leisure* (loisir, ocio, Muße) but *free time* (vrije tijd, Freizeit, temps libre, tiempo libre, czas wolny, fritid). Although by many authors renounced as a less than useful concept because of the 'false' presumptions associated with the notion of freedom (see Rojek, 1995 for the latest in a line of critiques), when looked upon from the perspective of the lived cultures represented here, the concept nevertheless depicts a 'positive' reality across Europe.[1] Besides, when used in an historical as well as relational meaningful way, thus avoiding the pitfalls of objectivism and essentialism, it is just the notion of 'free time' which directs our attention at the historical conflicts and societal conditions involved in its formation. On the contrary, concepts such as leisure, loisir, ocio, and Muße are often adorned with idealist, classicist thought, and subsequently used to demarcate activities and qualities, regarded as more 'rightfully' or 'authentically' representing the issues at stake.

For the editors, using the concept of leisure in the title of this book had no such function. It merely, and perhaps somewhat naively, follows a common usage of words within the international academic field (compare the European Leisure and Recreation Association or the International Sociological Association's Research Committee on the Sociology of Leisure). Here its function was to bring together research which has paid attention to peoples' pleasures and/or pastimes from a more integrated point of view. This is one of the senses in which the study of leisure or free time can be said to claim its own object vis-à-vis, for instance, the study of tourism, sports or the media. In the study of leisure there is an explicit intention to take a more integrated perspective on things, e.g. to study the place and meaning of peoples' pastimes from the perspective of what Williams (1965) has typified as 'a whole way of life', or what the human time-geographer Hägerstrand (1975) has conceptualised as the daily path through time and space.

In the future, it would be worthwhile to devote some time to the astonishing ease with which the concept of leisure has been adopted by authors from all over Europe as a meaningful notion, while often being a misnomer in relation to the plural realities and research practices in their own national settings. More generally, this points at the necessity of a future cross- and transnational hermeneutic analysis of the interrelated use of concepts like free time, fun, pleasure, play, leisure, culture, education, consumption, and the like. The interdependent employment of these concepts by various groups and professions can tell us a lot about the production and regulation of meaning across Europe.

That brings us to the second concept. Although the notion of Europe was initially used here as a shorthand to situate this study, only a moment's reflection is enough to understand the problematic nature of such a use. At stake here is not so much the fact that we have not included all the possible national histories situated in Europe, or that we have not paid any attention to the question whether the studies presented here are in any sense representative of 'Europe', or denote something specifically European (for instance vis-à-vis 'American' leisure studies). Much more basic is the question of what the concept of Europe actually stands for. Does it only indicate a geographical location, or does the term also carry historical, cultural, ethnic, and/or geo-political connotations? Are we using Europe as signifying a geographical area, an economic zone, a political union, enlightened civilisation, an ethno-cultural entity, *Christendom*, modernity, bourgeois culture? As Gerard Delantly has recently stressed, the very concept of Europe does not make very much sense if something else is not excluded. And because the idea of Europe

> cannot be disengaged from the atrocities committed in its name (...) an unreflected idea of Europe is a dangerous idea.
> Delantly (1995:157)

Thus there is a necessity to make more explicit what unites the various cases represented in this volume.

This is an easy imperative to formulate, but a difficult one to fulfil without lapsing into tokenism. This book includes the histories of the study of leisure in Spain, France, Belgium, the United Kingdom, the Netherlands and Poland, written from a variety of perspectives, thus emphasising different elements. In purely geographical terms this covers a stretch of land from the South-Western part of Europe via the Mid-Western corner to the East. In political-historical terms it touches upon a variety of state formation trajectories, involving fascist and communist collectivism, and a variety of socio-democratic state models. In socio-spatial terms the stories cover a mixture of urban and rural regions and cultures. In economic-historical terms the stories include models of market and state capitalism, and of state collectivism. In terms of economic and political power, the cases represent the centre of Europe as well as its margins, and the nowadays shifting interdependencies between them. In cultural terms the cases cover regions which have long been dominated by tradition oriented and collectivist Catholicism, and regions dominated by more rational, individualistic enlightenment and/or Protestantism.

Nevertheless, despite this plurality, there is the feeling that these are not just isolated case-studies, situated in some socio-historical vacuum, but that these stories are somehow related, and that what relates them justifies the use of the term Europe and their inclusion in a common cross-comparative framework.

To begin with, in organising their work the intellectuals and professionals in these various countries involved in the study of leisure will often have situated themselves and their work in a common intellectual framework, depicted as 'European'. They have at times seen themselves as standing on the shoulders of a diverse and highly ambivalent, but nevertheless interdependent history of European or 'classical' social thought. Even the controversies between 'French' rationalism, 'English' empiricism, and 'German' idealism would not have developed, if it was not for this European socio-cultural and political space within which these intellectual strands were positioned vis-à-vis each other, and hence nationalised.[2] Even when, after World War II, in most countries in Europe, academics turned to American (i.e. 'modern') social thought, this was not without a firm awareness of a notion of importation, and of turning away from 'classical' (i.e. 'European') history (in fact re-importing 'European' social thought, which had been 'Americanised' during the first quarter of the 20th century). In addition, reproducing the notion of a European intellectual space, there were the ongoing cross-border contacts between academics from various countries in Europe within the framework of common European academic organisations, including the European Leisure and Recreation Association and others.

Second, this common intellectual space can be seen as just one element of a broader particularity, a broader 'common space of difference'. In his recent study of the developmental trajectories of European societies, Therborn (1995) has stressed the importance of this broader internal connectivity: 'providing a pronounced interdependence of the demarcated population, and bringing internal conflicts to bear upon the organisation of the whole' (Ibid: 22). This particularity is related to three factors: e.g. the endogenous character of the European modernisation process, the European kinship and family system, and the particular comprehensive industrialisation of Europe (Ibid: 23/4). According to Therborn, the more recent, 'modern' development of this interdependent space called Europe has been characterised by class struggles, and the time-spatial specific ways these developed and were 'contained'. This can be related to the many civil wars through which European modernity was produced, and to the formation of the many '-isms', the majority of which developed out of a European context (e.g. Protestantism, socialism, communism, fascism, welfarism etc.).

This is the double sense in which the cases presented here can be seen as part of a common 'European' reality or history, a shared socio-historical space of development, a common frame of reference. It is a space with rather uneven interdependencies, which often lead to contrasting reactions and trajectories, but which always in turn influences the whole. The purpose of this conclusion is to start to explore the commonalities and variations involved in the developmental trajectories of the study of leisure through this systemic socio-historical *cum* political-geographical time-space.

A last concept worth some attention is that of 'research'. It is vitally important to stress the fact that the studies brought together here are first of all concentrated on the history of the empirical investigation of people's leisure. What has not been considered, at least not in any systematic way, is the vast amount of social and theoretical commentary devoted to the topic. As has already been hinted at in various contributions, numerous intellectuals, social scientists, cultural leaders, politicians, animators, ecclesiastical representatives, and others, have paid an abundance of attention to the dangers and/or potentials engrossed in the free time of the common people. Only a fraction of them came to the point where they were actually able or willing to go out and systematically explore the realities they talked about. Because of the unevenness between actual empirical research, and the vast amount of intellectual commentary, the latter still awaits a systematic historical analysis.

However, having put 'commentary' aside for the moment, there still remains a broad area to be covered. Research can take many forms, from administrative surveys by national or local governments, to inquiries by private or semi public leisure organisations, to applied or fundamental academic research. Besides, where today, because of the dissemination of tools and methods of research, the boundaries between these various domains is becoming more fluid[3], during 'early modern' history, the situation was even more confusing. Academics, social reformers, animators, state inspectors, administrators, movement leaders, teachers, enlightened industrials all formed part of a diffuse intellectual class, with international connections, and with a lot of institutional overlap and interdependency (see below).

Given this vast plurality of forms and appearances of social research, and given the fact that a lot of this research had probably a very local or situated character, it is likely that this study has only captured a fraction of the enormous research energy devoted to people's free time activities. It is most likely that the studies included here predominantly concern those research activities which, for one reason or another, made it into the forefront of national discourse. This may sometimes be related to the pioneering approach taken, or to the innovative character of the data, but much will also have depended on the institutional settings within which the research was situated, and on the status and position of the researchers concerned. From the point of view of the historical sociology of knowledge, much still needs to be done. As a consequence, the following can only claim to be of a preliminary and exploratory character.

Early Modernisation and the Free Time Problem

The Formation of Free Time

When trying to trace the early formation of leisure as a topic of social inquiry in Europe, a few 'constitutive' moments can be distinguished. From an historical point of view, it is important to take into account the institutionalisation of that temporal zone or enclave, freed from feudal seigneurial and/or entrepreneurial bonds, and thus labelled 'free time'. It is a reality which came into existence across Europe during that so-called 'long 19th century', spanning at least some 150 years, at the intersection of industrial capitalism and the national state. Industrial capitalism was responsible for the spreading of a time-based organisation of work, and a more strict demarcation of the spheres of work and non-work. In addition, industrial capitalism was responsible for the 'urbanization', 'proletarianisation' and/or 'massification' of larger parts of the European population. The nation state legalised the labour contract, thus releasing not only work itself, but also the sphere of non-work, from pre-modern bonds: 'the master's right in the master's time and the workmen's right in his own time' (Bailey, 1978:180).

The first public 'discourses' on free time can be traced to the turmoils, panics, utopias and conflicts involved in attempts to institutionalise this new and more abstract social, spatial and temporal arrangement/division of work and non-work, moving away from traditional forms of life, governed by local perceptions, interests and interdependencies. They are part and parcel of the 'disembedding' (Giddens) by industrial capitalism of parts of the population from local-traditional forms of social and cultural integration, 're-embedding' them within more abstract, urban and mass production based living conditions. The transformation went along with periods of increasing class conflict and class organisation, concern over national/local order, and 'the social question'. To enhance labour control and labour productivity, employers aimed at a strict time-spatial segregation between the spheres of production and reproduction, banning local folklore and local pleasures as much as possible from the shop floor. At the same time, educationalists, reformers and hygienists encouraged a further gender-specific division of the reproductive sphere, propagating the division between the 'private' household and 'public' life. Everyday life became reorganised and categorised along a time-spatial grid, dominated by the abstract rationalities of industrial capitalism, in the act also producing 'free time' as a separate domain of life.

This (re)organisation of work and non work is related to a wider 19th century transformation of notions of time and space. To characterise this transformation, in his emblematic study, Kern (1983:317) has used the metaphor of the telephone wire, criss-crossing the Western World, invading private spaces and breaking down former traditional barriers of locational as well as cultural distance and togetherness. Harvey (1989) has stressed how, due to their 'shortening' of the time, the coming of the railroad and the telegraph also implied a 'compression' or 'shrinkage' of space. This broadened the spatial magnitude of ongoing class-conflicts, turning them into truly European, if not 'Western', affairs (Ibid: 235/6).[4] In addition, this intensified the competition between states and other economic units (ibid: 259), thus stimulating a further co-ordination, rationalisation and homogenisation of time and space. In accordance with Harvey, Giddens (1989:16) has typified this latter process as 'the separation of time and space and their recombination in forms which permit the precise time-space 'zoning' of social life (...)'. Increasingly, fields of activities became disembedded from the local flows of everyday life, and re-embedded within a supra-local homogenised and rationalised time-space, enabling their 'zoning' and subsequent demarcation as work, the household and 'free time'.

However, an analysis of the constitution of free time remains incomplete without also taking into account the perspective and position from which this new reality became labelled, catalogued and organised as such, and was turned into a specific object of not only philosophical reflection and political pamphleteering, but also of empirical investigation, and rational organisation and control.

At stake here is that secularised 'spirit of inquiry', carried along by what Perkin (1969:252) in the case of Victorian England has typified as the 'forgotten Middle Class'. This is a social class consisting of a wide and diverse group of professions including, amongst others, lawyers, doctors, public officers and inspectors, journalists, professors and teachers, social statisticians, philanthropists, sanitarians, educationalists. According to Goldman (1993:98) Perkin used the term 'forgotten' to stress the fact that this group of professions occupied 'a marginal place in the written history of the Victorian period, overshadowed by the commercial and industrial bourgeoisie in its wider conflict with the working class below and the aristocracy above'.[5] However divided in their specific political and denominational affiliations and intellectual ideas (as well intra- as international), this was a professional elite which saw itself as part of a community of social and cultural 'engineers', with transnational and even transatlantic links, involved in the enlightenment of national 'society' and its governance.[6] Together they inhabited and reproduced a socio-cultural space, created by the figuration of an expanding national state-bureaucracy, a gradual collectivisation of social and cultural caring systems, a growing body of voluntary associations active in hygienic, philanthropic and/or cultural-educational work, a growing field of social research institutions, and an expanding realm of higher education and science (itself becoming more 'professional' in the sense of research-oriented, turning away from scholastic traditions).[7]

It is within this diffuse social and cultural space that during the 19th century a new epistemic discourse of the Western World developed. This discourse placed both man and the human sciences at the centre of human civilisation (Foucault, 1974). At stake was a new representation of the social as the result, not of some general divine will or cosmic fate, but as thoroughly social, as the specific product of human nature, and thus, like nature itself, knowable and steerable (Bauman, 1987).[8] The interrogation of labourers' everyday life reflected the further institutionalisation of this 'modern' power/ knowledge syndrome (Foucault, 1980), in which rationality and civilisation, and scientific knowledge and planned intervention fused together to form the inseparable elements of a new 'modernised'/ 'modernising' civic culture.

At the outset, this remained a relatively undifferentiated space, with overlapping statistical-administrative, academic, socio-political, philanthropic, educational and reform interests.[9] There was a central concern with the 'secularisation of knowledge' (even amongst enlightened fractions of those religiously affiliated), and the formulation of general rational-scientific principles, useful in the advancement of the 'wealth of nations' (Adam Smith), and thus in economic and social improvement.

During the second half of the 19th century, especially around the time of the Great Depression following 1873, this diffuse realm became gradually more differentiated, with the investigation of the nature of humankind being split up into diverse specialities and disciplines (Manicas, 1987:198). Out of the general realm of political economy, there developed a 'moral' and 'political' science, and subsequently also a 'social' science, more directly interested in 'society', 'the social question' and 'national civilisation'.

This transformative figuration, consisting of the interdependent rise of industrial capitalism and class conflict, the national state and the realm of the social, points to the specifically 'modern' origin of leisure research. 'Modern' here refers to more than just the cognitive elements involved: leisure research as standing on the shoulders of a future oriented and empirically based *Weltanschauung*, whose origins can be traced back to the beginnings of the 17th century (i.e. Francis

Bacon). In a wider, institutional sense it points to the way in which both the investigative mood, and the specific object of that mood, were brought into being as part of the development throughout Europe of that unevenly interrelated set of institutions, in social theory united under the notion of the 'modern' (modernisation, modernity, *modernité*).[10]

Trajectories of Early Modernisation

The contributions to this book have presented a rather erratic picture of the 'pre-history' of the inquiries into labourers' pastimes. This is first of all related to the fact that much research work still needs to be done (there is the suspicion that a lot of information is still buried in various archives, especially with regard to the early social surveys or monographs, carried out all across Europe). In addition, the further back one goes into history, the more diffuse the relation becomes between science, research, administration and social commentary, and between 'free time', 'pastimes' and everyday life. Hence the problem of what to include in the writing of a history of the study of leisure without lapsing into a 'colonisation' or 'overinterpretation' of history, or the 'invention of traditions'. Most importantly however, this unevenness must be related to the fact that the above sketched 'modernisation' has followed quite different trajectories across the various regions of Europe, with a lot of international and inter-institutional diversity.

During the 19th century, in the North Western part of Europe, industrialisation was comparatively advanced by an earlier and more strongly institutionalised national state apparatus.[11] This can be related to a more strongly developed urban system, with already some differentiation between the political and the economic, and with a powerful economic and cultural middle class, functioning as a catalyst for the further rationalisation/nationalisation of the economy, politics, culture and the sciences. Given their more dynamic or open character, these states were more able to contain the political, economic and cultural conflicts involved in the development of industrial capitalism, amongst others due to the early development of an elaborate system of social policies.

In contrast, in other parts of Europe, until well into the 19th or even the 20th century, feudalism remained a factor of considerable political/economic importance. In relation to a strong regional aristocracy, weakly institutionalised borders, a lower level of urbanization, a relatively less powerful or more tradition-oriented middle class, a lower level of centralised integration and democracy, and an ethnic-culturally more diverse population, the institutionalisation of industrial capitalism and the 'modern' state followed a much longer and conflict-ridden trajectory.

In general terms, this seems to throw some light on the question of why early examples of a social-*cum*-empirical sensibility to the pastimes of industrial workers can be traced back to the North Western corner of Europe. However, below such a generalised picture, additional differences complicate the formulation of strict causalities.

First it is again important to point out how the relation between early industrialism and the early empirical sensibility to labourers' free time has been mediated by the interventionist middle classes, depending on their nation-specific composition, position, and ideational orientation. For instance, while both the UK and Belgium can be seen as early industrialisers,[12] nevertheless the rationalisation/modernisation of their respective socio-cultural spaces followed quite different trajectories. In the UK, rationalised social reform, and the related social empirical sensibilities, developed very early, already during the beginning of the 19th century, in the wake of the establishment of the *New Poor Law* of 1834 (see e.g. Lis and Soly, 1980; Lacey and Furner, 1993). This was enhanced by not only an urge to contain emerging class conflicts, and to regularise the labour market, but also by a strong libertarian utilitarianism, a Protestant ethic, and in particular a strong and rationalised administrative/legal system (Ibid: 23). In the Southern regions of the Low Countries, the preponderance of a tradition oriented catholic church has for a long time inhibited a fully fledged secularisation of knowledge, and a rationalisation and collectivisation of social and cultural caring systems, instead prolonging an older decentralised and particularistic system of paternal-communal care (Lis and Soly, 1980:241-6).

These divergent trajectories of the social field can be traced to the 19th century surveys of workers' pastimes. As the foregoing case studies of the UK and Belgium have shown, those in the UK were undertaken by future oriented social reformists, eager to reform the social and moral condition of industrial workers by means of state-oriented policies. In contrast, those in Belgium were paradoxically instigated by (enlightened) catholic leaders, trying to cope with a further secularisation and rationalisation of public knowledge and morality.

The Northern parts of the Low Countries present a different case again, with a well established but relatively decentralised state apparatus, an equally decentralised, enlightened philanthropic-educational infrastructure, a rather late industrialisation process (with a developmental peak around 1895-1914),[13] and on the whole, a strong denominationally segmented, but Protestant-liberal dominated society. Here a first investigative interest in workers' lives developed rather late, around 1870, in the wake of the emerging 'social question', and the establishment of the first collective social policies (Jonker, 1988:84). Until World War II, this empirical sensibility was mainly enhanced by progressive liberals and the emerging workers' movement, both favouring a centralised and rationalised social policy, both in competition, especially with catholic, but also conservative-Protestant regionalising strategies.

Second, it is important to point to the danger of seeing things from too simplistic a national-endogenous point of view, ignoring the role of trans-border contacts in the cross-national and even cross-Atlantic diffusion of social reform policies and social research interests. Several elements are of importance here.

Manicas (1987), and Wittrock (1993) after him, have stressed the central role of the German model of the 'modern' university (the University of Berlin, founded in 1810, later re-named as Humboldt Universität) in the late 19th century expansion and transformation of the higher education system.[14] With the diffusion of this model, the 'modern' 19th century university developed in a more professional and research-oriented direction, to a large extent geared towards the interests of an expanding industrial and state-bureaucracy.[15] In this diffusion process, important national and local variations did occur. Of special importance here was the difference between either the ideal of *algemeine Bildung* and basic research, or of specialised vocational training and applied research (with important differences in the public status of the professors concerned!).[16]

This can be seen as forming part of a more general 19th century pattern of cross-national academic contacts and orientations, carried along by an expanding body of journals and books, conferences, study-tours, and scientific organisations, thus presenting researchers with alternative topics and models of research. The influential cross-national family budget project, carried out around 1890 by the social statistician Frederic Le Play forms a well known example of these early cross-border contacts (see Samuel, Chapter 2 and Corijn and Van Eeckhout, Chapter 6).

In addition, also social reformers had their cross-border contacts, studying each others programmes and initiatives, thus exporting/importing ideas and approaches. Sometimes, such as in the case of the British reformer/researcher Seebohm Rowntree, this resulted in active cross-border projects, aimed at the exporting of, in this case, the family budget method as a tool of social reform (see Corijn and Van den Eeckhout, Chapter 6 and Bramham and Henry, Chapter 7).[17]

Finally, there are the many cross-border contacts established by the early international socialist and labour movement, and the way these functioned as vehicles for a cross-national diffusion of political ideas, reform programmes, and an empirical sensibility for labourers' life. The first cross-border research projects on free time can be traced to this international network (see Beckers and Mommaas, Chapter 8 and Samuel, Chapter 2).

Free Time and Issues of National Civilisation

When during the last quarter of the 19th century, in the wake of these early transformative events, workers' distractions or pastimes did become the object of some social inquiries or empirical investigations, for the most part this was not done for the sake of 'free time' as such.

Nor do these studies seem to be dominated by 'pure' academic or social theoretical interests. What was at stake was a more holistic, almost 'anthropological' curiosity in exploring and administering the *terra incognito* of the impoverished and crowded backyards of recently industrialised urban areas. Systematically and meticulously collected information about the working and living conditions of the urban-industrial proletariat was supposed to enhance the rational grounding of legal or educational measures, and to inform social disputes and the development of social reform strategies. These investigations were part and parcel of more broader strategies, aimed at the creation of a well-integrated public sphere, favouring not just production interests as such, but, more generally, national wealth and civilisation.

Overall, these early investigations into workers' lives and pastimes can best be typified as mono- and/or sociographic, inductive, empiricist, objectivist and evolutionist. Common to them are naturalist and rationalist / interventionist sentiments, whether they were based on purely administrative concerns, on the progressive concerns of enlightened liberals, socialists reformers, or confessional philanthropists, or on a more conservative urge to fight the spreading of 'modernisation' (secularisation, centralisation, rationalism, socialism, urbanisation). Characteristic is a belief in the viability and desirability of intervention and regulation (sometimes institutional, mostly educational), combined with a strong belief in the necessity to ground those interventions, and the diagnoses related, on a scientific foundation. Basic here is the ideal of a 'science of the legislator', capable of delivering the general principles, enabling an external (i.e. 'objective') diagnosis of society, thus adorning social reform with its aura of professional certainty and political impartiality (Winch, 1993)

In these studies, workers' pastimes are investigated as indicators of their moral orientation, cultural advancement and social integration (Mommaas, 1991). Hence, there is a strongly defined interest in drinking, gambling, prostitution, the frequenting of pubs, the organisation of family life, the reading of books, gardening, and the visiting of theatres, lectures and political meetings. Workers' life is evaluated against the yardstick of the enlightened lifestyle of the educated middle classes, a lifestyle regarded as definitively civilised as such. Labourers' activities are captured in a discourse accentuating/ reproducing contradictions, typical of the bourgeois *Weltanschauung*, such as those between the cultivated and the vulgar, high and low, the rational and the impulsive, the external and the internal, the active and the passive.

It would last until the post-World War I period (the late 1920s early 1930s) before free time as such became an independent object of research. In part, this is related to the post-war prevalence of neo-mercantilist state-policies, with their emphasis on economic and social intervention, and to a new phase in the expansion of the university system (this time also resulting in the sometimes rather reluctant spreading of the 'modern' social sciences[18]).

More specifically however, there is the Russian Revolution of 1917, the socialist and communist radicalism accompanying the establishment of the Weimar Republic in 1918/1919, the socialist revolution attempt in Hungary in 1919, and the march of the Red Army through Poland in 1920. All of these events point to the increasing strength of the Left in European class-conflicts, amongst others, resulting in a growing anxiety amongst national conservative and denominational elites. As a combined consequence, this period witnessed a new increase in social policies, accompanied by laws on labour conditions (e.g. the famous law on the eight hour working day, and new laws on paid holidays). In the International Labour Organization, but also amongst reformist and conservative elites, this in itself triggered a new interest in workers' free time. Given workers' expected increase in free time, was there a need for programmes which could enhance the 'quality' of that free time? Was there a need to deliver rational-enlightened alternatives to folklore culture, regarded as provincial, backward and primitive, or to the new commercial pleasures, regarded as exploitative, passive, 'quantitative'?

As Cross (1993:87/90) has pointed out, the unprecedented crisis which followed the *krach* of 1929 subsequently revitalised debates about the possibility of a further reduction in weekly working hours, thus enabling a better distribution of employment, a preservation of present jobs and industries, and a more balanced relation between production and consumption. This resulted in aims to establish the forty hour working week and/or the two day weekend. However, by this time, the international power momentum of the labour movement had passed. Besides, the issue of the reduction of labour time had lost political and economic priority within a Europe more and more entangled in problems of economic crisis and massive unemployment, fuelling economic and political antagonisms, between as well as within nations (e.g. Germany, France, Spain, Italy).[19]

Where workers' pastimes did become an independent object of investigation (examples are mentioned from Belgium, the Netherlands and Poland), research strategies mostly followed established inductive-evolutionist canons of research. However, in addition to conventional monographic and/or sociographic research projects, this period also witnessed the first use of participation statistics and of time-budget studies (see Beckers and Mommaas, Chapter 8). Building upon the application in social reform research of the family budget method, and upon the introduction in the working environment of methods of time measurement (part of Taylor's 'scientific management' approach), by the 1920s, the time budget method was discovered as a useful tool for free time research. Well known are the early time-budget studies of Stroumiline in the Soviet Union, developed with the aim of expanding 'the cultural level of the socialist worker' (cited in

Lanfant, 1972:126). These and other time-budget studies delivered a wealth of information concerning the amount of free time enjoyed by workers, the temporal structure of their everyday life, and the amount of time invested in various possible domains of activity, hence enabling a quantification and thus 'objective' comparison of workers' cultural involvement. For the most part, the results of these innovative studies were interpreted from an external, superior, or 'legislative' perspective. They are read as indications of the level of workers' cognitive edification, moral civilisation and/or social integration.

Welfare Modernism and the Institutionalisation of Leisure Research

Post-war Economic Expansion and the Social State

It would last until the post-World War II period before free time would become a relatively independent and systematic object of study across Europe, with its own specialists, courses, journals, conferences, and its own field of codifications and definitions, cross-references and debates. Although continuities do exist, it would be a mistake to see this as a natural consequence of pre-war developments. It could just as well be argued that the institutionalisation of leisure research must be explained in terms of the discontinuities which marked post-war European social reality. The study of leisure 'materialised' in an institutional and intellectual climate which differed considerably from pre-war conditions and orientations.

Based on a comparison between 1870 and 1990 of the GDP index figures of 24 European countries, Therborn (1995:133) concludes that post-World War II Europe witnessed an unprecedented period of economic growth. Obviously, national-regional differences continued to be of significant importance, notwithstanding a considerable economic convergence in the 1960s (Ibid: 195). Throughout these years, Spain, Poland, Greece, Portugal, Ireland and especially Romania can be found at the lower end of the scales, and Sweden, Denmark, Switzerland, West Germany, France and Belgium at the upper end (Ibid: 138). Nevertheless, despite continuing disparity, and despite very different economic conditions, all national economies, whether communist, authoritarian capitalist or liberal/social capitalist, experienced significant economic progress.[20]

Four transformations, of importance with regard to the institutionalisation of leisure research, can be related to this process of economic expansion. First, as Therborn himself points out, there is the spreading across Europe of mass-consumption. Based on figures of the ownership of cars and television (two crucial elements in the spreading of consumer culture), Therborn suggests that European mass consumption began 'in Sweden and Britain in the late 1950s, spread over most of the Western Continent in the 1960s, and finally reached Spain and Poland in the 1970s, and Greece and Portugal in the 1980s (Ibid: 140). This spreading of a mass-consumer market did more than just increase the leisure choice of the populations concerned. Together with the revolutionary expansion of higher education, it broadened the means of cultural reproduction, thus gradually undermining the conditions of cultural reproduction and exchange which had allowed former national/local elites to generalise their own tastes to the standard of cultural civilisation as such and hence to create a national public sphere (Thompson, 1990). Mass consumption fundamentally 'disembedded' existing national cultural classifications and relations, 'reembedding' them within globalising consumer culture, thus trivialising and differentiating former standards of taste and morality, also putting the mass/cultural condition very firmly on the agenda of public and academic discourse.

Second, mass-consumption presupposed mass-production, although not necessarily on a national basis. As a part and result of the general reconstruction of the national economies concerned, post-war Europe went through a phase of rapid (re-)industrialisation and mechanisation. In the East, still very much dominated by rural societies, the stress was predominantly on the development of the heavy industries of coal and steal and on strategies to increase productivity (Jung, 1993:196).[21] In North West Europe, post-war reconstruction became dominated by the petrochemical and electronic industries, by automation strategies and by an expansion of the service sector. Despite these differences, in both parts of Europe, industrialisation and mechanisation processes, based on conventional 'Fordist' models of economics of scale, invoked debates about the possible future quality of work. In both cases, this was no longer couched in a discourse of class and capitalism, but related to notions of 'technological civilisation' and/or 'post-industrial society'. Inspired by neo-marxist or neo-liberal critical thinking, the mechanisation and automation of work stimulated debates about potential personal deprivation, alienation and/or the 'estrangement' of 'employees'.

Third, interrelated with this debate on the *quality* of work, also the *quantity* of work became an object of consideration and concern. From the late 1950s onwards, the economies of all the countries dealt with in this volume, experienced a renewed, although rather uneven, reduction of working hours. This took the form of a longer weekend, shorter weekly working hours, and/or an increase in paid vacation. National variations depended on factors such as the composition of the national labour market, the strength of the national economy, the position of national unions, and, most importantly, the level of national state intervention (with the state mostly playing an impeding, rather than encouraging role). The reduction of working hours again began in the North West in the late 1950s early 1960s, reaching Spain and Poland in the 1970s (in the case of the latter restricted to a forty-eight hours working week and two free Saturdays each month; see Olszweska and Roberts 1989). By some, this renewed reduction of working hours evoked utopias/fears of the coming into being of a leisure society (Fourastié, 1966). Widely aired was the feeling that leisure would become more important as a domain of socio-cultural reproduction, while at the same time there was the danger that the masses would not be prepared for it (due to their lack of capacity for self-motivation), and thus fall victim to the fads and fashions of mass-consumption.[22]

Fourth, this period of economic expansion delivered the revenues, necessary for the exceptional expansion of the state's social and cultural involvement. Between roughly 1960 and 1980, all the countries presented here witnessed a unique increase in social policies, partly aimed at a stimulation of leisure activities (e.g. sports, recreation, the voluntary sector, the media, the arts, tourism), be it within very different political, financial and organisational circumstances, and based on very different political rationales.

In Franco's totalitarian Spain, in various senses the most 'traditional' of the political systems represented here, in an attempt to combat economic problems and international isolation, the 1960s witnessed a period of relative flexibility and openness (San Salvador, Chapter 5; Gonzalez and Urkiola, 1993; Navarrete, 1990; Tezanos, 1990). A change took place from a strong celebration of catholic-Castilian traditionalism in the 1950s, to a phase of relative cultural pragmatism in the 1960s. This resulted in housing subsidies, public health care and social security programmes, but was nevertheless unable to compensate for increasing social and regional inequalities (Ibid: 152). In addition, a liberalisation and subsequent expansion of the voluntary sector took place, together with the promotion of tourism, and the stimulation of the consumer market (Gonzalez and Urkiola, 1993, San Salvador, Chapter 5).

In communist Poland, in an attempt to attract Western credit, and in response to the workers' protest of 1956, there was a shift from the strict Soviet-oriented collectivist control and censorship of the 1950s to a period of 'enlightened' and thus more plural communism in both the 1960s and the 1970s (around 1968 interrupted by a period of serious economic stagnation, political crisis and anti-semitism: Jung, 1993, Kwasniewicz, 1993). Here, the state adopted an active cultural and recreation policy orientation, strongly promoting the arts, social tourism and sports. On the one hand (especially amongst social planners) this was based on models of 'communist humanism' formulated as an alternative to the 'decadence' of capitalist consumerism. On the other hand, these programmes remained to be seen as important vehicles for political indoctrination, and the creation of international prestige and local pride (Jung, 1993).

In the North West, in the liberal-capitalist Netherlands, in the course of the early 1960s, a model of welfare-statism developed, able to reconcile a collectivisation of social and cultural caring programmes with the traditional particularistic interests of a 'pillarised' society (i.e. inventing the 'subsidiarity principle'; Van der Poel, 1993). Legitimations of cultural intervention shifted from aims based on more 'totalising' or 'superior' notions of moral and cultural civilisation/ edification - hard to sustain under a political democracy, with transnational mass-consumerism permeating national socio-cultural boundaries - to aims based on more context-dependent or individualistic rationales of personal well-being, equal access, self-actualisation and cultural pluralism. Also here, there was the idea that an opening up of pre-war socio-cultural rigidities would enhance economic flexibility (Mommaas, 1996).

The 'Americanisation' of Planning and Science

Amongst social researchers and social planners, these *institutional* changes were coterminous with fundamental changes in epistemic or *ideational* orientations-*cum*-representations. By the 1960s, the social sciences were generally accepted as an important instrument in the information and justification of state intervention. However, the social sciences of the 1960s were quite different in their orientation and position from those of the preceding period.

In France, Georges Gurvitch, during World War II active in American academia, was instrumental in the creation in 1946 of the Centre for Sociological Studies, the place where Dumazedier was to start his group on the Sociology of Leisure (see Samuel, Chapter 2). Gurvitch will have expressed more broadly shared sentiments when, already in 1945, he proclaimed the coming into being of a 'Twentieth Century Sociology'. This sociology could be characterised 'by a gradual elimination of all the uncritically accepted problems that worried sociologists of the past century' (Gurvitch and Moore, 1945:v). Twentieth century sociology signalled the end of 19th century organicism and evolutionism, and of unscientific antagonisms such as those between 'order' and 'progress', or 'individual' and 'society' (sic!). The 'logic of sociological problems' seemed definitely to have superseded the 'logic of sociological systems and schools (...) which was always very superficial' (Ibid: vi).[23]

In Belgium, by the 1950s, the Catholics' orientation towards social reality in general had developed into a more 'pragmatic' or 'technocratic' direction (Corijn and Van den Eeckhout, Chapter 6). In accordance, the Catholics embraced sociology as an important fact-finder, while at the same time the Belgian sociologists themselves were striving for a more value-free approach, thus attempting to improve their status as 'modern', professional researchers. Catholic researchers approvingly noticed how theoretical debates, full of philosophical speculations and theological apriorisms, belonged to the past: methodology and techniques had come to the foreground.

In the Netherlands, during the 1950s, amongst a new generation of academics, the sociographic method came to be looked upon as part of pre-war scientific backwardness. Sociologists, seeing themselves as representatives of a new brand of 'modern' sociology, denounced the 'moralism' and 'metaphysics' of their pre-war colleagues (not withstanding the fact that a lot of these colleagues had thought of themselves as 'strong' positivists). Post-war sociologists opted for statistical research models, able to verify precisely formulated hypotheses. This was part of a plea for an overall 'professionalisation' of Dutch sociology, based on ideals of social research-*cum*-intervention, derived from American text books and sociology courses (see Mommaas, Chapter 4).

After the country had regained its independence in 1918, Polish sociology had established itself rather quickly. This was partly based on a strong cosmopolitan orientation and established expertise amongst members of the Polish 'intelligentsia', already in the 19th century very active in the importation of Western European social thought (Znaniecki, 1945). However, the rise of Stalinism after 1948 went along with the elimination of sociology from the list of official academic disciplines, identified as a bourgeois and anti-socialist science (Kwasniewicz, 1993). Sociology was only able to regain its course during the liberalisation of Polish society which followed the successful protests of the Polish workers in 1956. By that time, however, sociology had changed, from a discipline formerly dominated by academic style research (be it with a strong positivist orientation, eschewing 'metaphysical' thought), to a discipline specialised in applied science and social engineering, willing to play its role in a democratic transformation of Polish socialism (Ibid: 174). Despite the official doctrine of Marxism-Leninism, Polish sociologists were again able to develop links with Western colleagues, thus coming under the 'unprecedented influence of Western, and in particular American, sociology' (Ibid: 178).

In Franco's Spain, the dominance of catholic-Castilian traditionalism (the cultural dimension of the *Francoist Bunker*) could not prevent some ongoing interest for sociology and anthropology, especially in the regions. This interest did not restrict itself to what Salvador Giner has so colourfully typified as:

> that stupid and shameful 'sociology' - which often went by the name of 'Christian sociology' - which certain ideologists, themselves devout supporters of the regime, were trying to impose in a humiliating attempt to give the dictatorship some ideological legitimacy through the Church's social doctrine.
> Giner (1990:62/3)

Next to catholic or Christian sociology, in the 1960s, there also developed a more empirical sociology. Again, Giner relates this empirical 'phase' in Spanish sociology to an orientation to North-American models of social research. This can be related to the rise of a 'pseudo-technocratic' orientation amongst members of the powerful Opus Dei movement, aiming at an economic expansion, as well as to the contacts which developed between the Spanish government and the US Eisenhower administration, both sharing a strong anti-communism (ibid: 58).

These are just a few examples of a wider change in the social intellectual climate across Europe. At stake is a move away from 'classical', 'humanist', 'European' or 'collectivist' social thought, and a new definition of the boundaries between science and morality. By some post-war intellectuals, these pre-war 'heroic narratives' (Alexander, 1995) were at least partly held responsible for the disasters of two subsequent world-wars, while now they were becoming more and more associated with 'traditional particularism', 'metaphysical speculation' and 'cultural rigidity'. Instead orientation turns towards the US, where the social scientific climate is dominated by the realism, and scientism, but also the cultural pluralism and openness of Lazarsfeld's survey research paradigm, Merton's ideal of social engineering and 'middle range theory', and Parsons' notion of 'systematic theorisation' and societal 'modernisation'.[24]

At stake here was not just a different way of doing research. While transcending former theoretical-ideological disputes, this was a paradigmatic figuration which delivered a fresh, technocratic outlook on the internal organisation, the social role, and the professional self-image of the social sciences, together with a scientific theory (the notion of 'modernisation') legitimating its superiority. In addition, the model mirrored and in turn stimulated and justified the liberal, technocratic, democratic, and modernisation rhetoric, popular not only in the 1960s Kennedy administration (Woodiwiss, 1993), but also, by emulation, amongst administrations across Europe.

Despite the vast differences involved, overall, these changes in post-war institutional conditions and ideational orientations across Europe point towards a double development. First, from an institutional point of view, there is a tendency towards an increasingly stimulating, instead of just prohibiting, preoccupation of the state with people's pastimes, in most cases gradually taking over more and more responsibilities from the voluntary sector, starting to treat leisure and culture as collective goods. At the same time, the dominant ideational orientation moved away from former 'heroic' or 'totalising' models of cultural thinking (e.g. based on varying notions of evolutionism and organicism). Instead, ideological and scientific thinking became dominated by models of 'cultural democracy' or 'standardised individualism'.[25]

The various countries represented here can be differentiated by the different trajectories they followed through these developments. Spain and Poland experienced an early collectivisation of leisure and culture, governed by 'totalising' or 'heroic' models of cultural thinking (fascist organicism and communist evolutionism). In both systems, during the 1960s, the state started to adopt a more open or pluralist cultural stand, based on a combination of economic necessity and political renewal. In the liberal-capitalist countries in the North West, the collectivisation of leisure and culture occurred later, in an ideational context which had moved away from pre-war totalising thinking, instead being inspired by the US ideals of 'realist' welfarism, and social and cultural mobility.

Leisure and the Spreading of Culture

The spreading of mass-consumption and mass-production, the mechanisation and automation of work, the reduction and institutionalisation of work time, the increasing involvement of the state with issues of leisure and culture, the vast increase in the number of public leisure and recreation institutions and programmes, the expansion of higher education, the politics of relative cultural pragmatism and pluralism, the 'bureaucratisation' and further compartmentalisation of the social sciences, and the spreading of a more instrumental, technocratic model of social research and social planning - both mirroring one another in the structuring of objects and in the approach to social reality - all these factors in various ways stimulated not only a discourse on the quality of leisure and social inequality, but also the establishment of a specialised domain of leisure research.

Just as in the pre-war period, post-war leisure research developed within the grey zone between state intervention, voluntary work and academic research. Partly the study was based on 'strong individuals' taking up leisure as part of a great diversity of social and intellectual concerns and interests (e.g. Pieper, De Grazia, Dumazedier, Roberts, Parker). Partly there is the growing demand for policy and market research, delivering data of importance in the planning, justification and evaluation of an increasing amount of public and private leisure provision. Together these developments lead to a rather curious *melange* of approaches. On one extreme, standing on the shoulders of the older tradition of mass-cultural critique or enlightened pedagogics, there is a large variety of abstract commentaries, not very much involved with empirical analysis as such. On the other extreme, oriented towards 'modern' American based research models, there is the bleak empiricist 'head-counting', devoid of any explicit theoretical reflection.

In an attempt to summarise the large variety of topics, addressed in post-war leisure research across Europe, one could distinguish two central topics of attention. First there is the theme of the work-leisure relationship. Central here are debates around the alienation/ liberalisation of work and/or leisure, the search for conceptualisations of the work-leisure relationship (with the many hypotheses related), thoughts about the possible fusion of work and leisure (with the differentiation between the two regarded as an alienating product of capitalism), and ideas about future changes in the distribution of work time and/or free time. In general, this theme first developed as an appendix to the sociology of work and/or the economics of production. At stake was the search for factors which could enhance workers' productivity (especially in the East, see Lanfant, 1974), or which could improve the quality of work and/or leisure in post-industrial (Riesman, Bell) or technological (Ellul) society.

While at least in the beginning, this work-leisure couplet was central to the thematic self-understanding of the post-war leisure research discipline,[26] nevertheless, a different theme began to dominate the empirical research field, and to provide the young discipline with its institutional links to the growing domains of planning and administration. At stake was that broad area of research and debate commonly summarised under the label of 'leisure participation'. Here, the focus was on the uneven engagement of various segments of the population in leisure provisions (sports, the media, culture, recreation), on an investigation of leisure 'needs', the 'non-participation' of disadvantaged groups, patterns of community leisure, and on the relation between leisure participation and the quality of life. The empirical research was either based on 'simple' attendance figures, or, increasingly, on more sophisticated time budget studies. These projects could be targeted at the national population writ large, or at specific disadvantaged or 'problem' groups such as urban youth, women, a city's population.

From an academic point of view, this area of study first developed as an appendix to the sociology of culture and social inequality and/or the economics of consumption. But there were also links to debates concerning the quality of life under conditions of an increase in free time and mass-consumption, and to social educational and planning programmes (i.e. in sports, recreation, culture), involved in the project of the spreading of culture. These programmes were expected to compensate for the commercial pleasures of mass cultural consumption, and to enhance social equality and people's choice. Besides, there was an expanding private leisure sector, eager to implement the latest models of empirical research and statistical analysis in an attempt to become more professional and market-oriented. In this context, the concept of free time facilitated a more integrated study of a population's involvement in a variety of public activities, thus also enabling an analysis of the possible 'substitution effects' between them.

In terms of research methodologies, this period became dominated by the model of quantitative, correlational survey research, based on a combination of empirical-analytical and deductive-instrumental thinking. The dominant professional model was that of the social researcher-*cum*-engineer, working on the discovery of the social mechanisms responsible for the alienation of work and/or leisure, and the uneven participation in leisure. Knowledge of these mechanisms, based on the comparative discovery of correlational sequences, would enable the development of programmes targeted at a cure for the 'dysfunctionalities' within the social system.[27]

Late Modernity and the Reappraisal of Leisure

The Dissolution of Conformities

Looking back from the perspective of the 1990s, it is apparent how the relative optimism and self-assurance that dominated the post-war field of European leisure studies depended on situated conditions, less acknowledged by the researchers of that time themselves. Due to the Cold War and the subsuming of geo-politics under the umbrella of the USA-USSR polarisation, nationalism could indeed become regarded as a thing of the past, and the nation-state system as the most natural and primary source of social and cultural integration. In Western Europe, America's 'eastern frontier' (Delantly, 1995), the Cold War stimulated an unprecedented integration. This culminated in 1958 in the creation of the EEC, the introduction to a subsequent period of 'peaceful coexistence', with scientific institutions functioning as 'normalisers' of the East-West relationship. Economic expansion, although unevenly spread, stimulated the idea of the universal successfulness of Keynesian policies, with the state finally having mastered the economy and class conflicts, national as well as international. Especially in the north west, the ongoing expansion of the state apparatus, the increase in productivity and affluence, and the ongoing reduction of working hours indeed enabled the notion of free time as a sphere of life, situated outside the determinism of social or political-economic structures. Thus the 'problem of leisure' could be reduced to an educational or informational issue, soon to be dealt with by the expanding effort of research-based social-educational intervention.

However, this self-assured climate would not last very long. Already from the late 1960s onwards, a sequence of often unpredicted and sometimes paradoxical events slowly but steadily started to undermine established certainties. First, there was the so-called cultural or expressive revolution of the late 1960s early 1970s. A new generation of young intellectuals started to question the so recently established technocratic-functionalist standards of intellectual, aesthetic and moral planning and thinking. This was stimulated by the work of the *Frankfurter Schule* (e.g. Lukacs, Adorno, Marcuse), early marxist inspired UK cultural studies (Raymond Williams, Richard Hoggart), the critical philosophy of Sartre, the liberation pedagogics of Paulo Freire, the feminist work of Simone de Beauvoir, the critical psychology of writers like Laing,

Cooper and Basaglia, but also the philosophy and cultural practice of the pop-art avant-garde movement.

Following Martin (1983:81) or Woodiwiss (1993), one could debate whether the critical movements of the 1960s/1970s should be evaluated in terms of a break with preceding artistic modernity and/or welfare modernism, or as a continuation or even deepening of both. In addition one could debate whether the movements of the 1960s/1970s have to be seen as a by-product of an increase in discretionary free time and consumption possibilities, or primarily as a genuine resistance against these (or both). Nevertheless, it is clear how, in the West, the movement launched a critique on three fronts. First there was the standardised democracy of suburban middle class consumer culture, with its middle class superficiality and cultural instrumentality. Second, a critique was launched against the technocratic rationalisations of dominant 'modernisation' models of science and planning, with their emphasis on the end of ideology and class. Third, questions were raised about prevailing 'paternalistic' definitions of culture, grounding programmes of the spreading of culture.

In the late 1960s, cities across Europe (from the East to the West, and from South to North) witnessed student riots, often triggered by very local circumstances. The riots were led by a generation which had grown up in the ever growing affluence and cultural openness of post-war 'Americanised' pop-culture and mass-consumption. Confronted with increasing economic and cultural possibilities, the conventional cultural distinctions, moral codes and status hierarchies started to appear quite obsolete, if not straightforwardly ridiculous. Leisure became a sphere of cultural sabotage and militancy, a breeding place for counter-cultural activity and self-expression.

As Bernice Martin (1983:22) has pointed out, this was not just something that took place at a periphery of expressive extravaganza. Instead, a rising generation of 'cultural specialists' was involved at the centre of society, with a less spectacular version of their expressiveness rather quickly spreading out into a wider societal sphere. Amongst other things, this resulted in a more critical or left-wing inspired approach to the social sciences, criticising the hegemonic figuration of 'American' modernisation theory and empirical-analytic research (Alexander, 1995). In addition, in a number of countries this resulted in a crisis of cultural legitimations, opening up former cultural policies and distinctions.

Even in a traditionalist-totalitarian country such as Spain, more left-wing inspired versions of sociology did develop in this period, drawing attention to the ongoing importance of class-structures (Tezanos, 1990:152/3). At the same time, in communist Poland, the student riots sought a 'revisionist' turn in orthodox Marxism, and a further opening up of the academic field for Western intellectual thought (but were instead confronted with an outbreak of party-sponsored anti-semitism; Kwasniewicz, 1993:175).

However, at the same time, around the late 1970s and early 1980s, when critical thinking started to 'de-mystify' the dominant conformities of science, culture and leisure, an economic crisis gradually changed the institutional conditions within which this renewed 'de-mystification' took place. In the 1970s the post-war political-economic system started to disintegrate. This was first instigated by the problems of the US economy, trying to cope with the deficit caused by the costs of the Korean and Vietnamese wars (Woodiwiss, 1993). In the early 1970s an unprecedented increase in oil-prices forced by the oil-producing countries speeded up a latent world recession. From the 1976 onwards this resulted in a prolonged phase of economic 'stagflation' (a unique combination of high inflation, high unemployment and no economic growth) which would last well into the 1980s.

This economic crisis formed an important impetus to the rise of a new 'post-Fordist' political-economic *regime* (Murray, 1989). In an attempt to cope with this new and more open global condition, the economic sector stimulated technological innovation, speeding up robotisation, automation and flexible productivity. At the same time, making use of new forms of information and transportation technology, the economic sector flexibilised its geographical structure. Partly this resulted in a further global centralisation of economic co-ordination, while at the same time parts of the production and distribution process became globally de-centralised (Dicken, 1992). To co-ordinate this global 'reshuffling' of the production sector, new service sector functions and infrastructures were created, situated in cities which started to function as central nodes in the world economy (Sassen, 1994).

This global economic restructuring went along with a deepening of national social inequality, resulting in the so-called *two-tier* economy, with the workforce divided between a highly skilled, key-positioned core, and underskilled, flexibilised, un- or semi-employed margins (Gorz, 1989). Mediated by an increase in national deficits (itself the product of a combination of economic stagflation, an expansion of the potential workforce, the ageing of the population, and an increase in social demand) global economic restructuring also resulted in a shift from welfare to enterprise culture. While in the former, leisure is seen as a collective good, as a citizens' right; in the latter, leisure is evaluated in terms of its economic function, in terms of its function as a consumer good (see Bramham *et al.*, 1993).In addition, global economic restructuring went along with a restructuring and repositioning of urban economies, resulting in cities becoming involved in an intensified inter-urban competition, often transcending nation-state borders. The latter resulted in an increase in local government attention to the role of leisure and culture as vehicles of urban imagery strategies, economic development and urban regeneration (Corijn and Mommaas, 1995).

During the 1980s, together with the renaissance of liberal-conservative thinking, the economic crisis and the market oriented restructuring of leisure and cultural policies made the narratives of emancipation and humanist socialism, formerly underlying the critique of conventional leisure research and education, become more problematic and marginalised.

Third, and partly related to the aforementioned global economic restructuring, in the 1970s and 1980s the political map of Europe was drastically redrawn.

In the 1970s, there was the final defeat of Iberian totalitarianism, the result of a growing internal opposition and international isolation. Salazar's Portugal had its 'carnation revolution' in 1975, the same year that, following Franco's death, a constitutional monarchy was established in Spain under King Juan Carlos de Bourbon (Gonzalez and Urkiola, 1993). Spain had its first democratic elections, in 1978 followed by the formation of a democratic constitution. In 1982 the Socialist Party (PSOE) won the elections, signalling the beginning of a long and uninterrupted period of social-democratic government. However, by this time, the economic crisis did not allow for the building up of a welfare state system, comparable to what had happened in the Northern European states during the 1960s. Thus leisure was prevented from becoming an important issue on the public agenda. Nevertheless, gradually, welfare policies did develop, with leisure as one of its focuses of attention, but lacking a clear policy scheme, with related financial and administrative resources (Gonzalez and Urkiola, 1993).

Even more influential was the defeat of communism in the 1980s. Against the background of a deepening of the economic crisis and an increase of Western monetary and military-technological pressures, the disintegration of communist totalitarianism began with Gorbatchov's *perestroika* in the USSR, and the formation of Solidarity in Poland in the early 1980s, finally culminating in the collapse of the Berlin wall in 1989. This not only implied the final demise of the Cold War period, and the falling away of a major existing alternative for capitalism, it also implied the disintegration of a former political-economic and military cohesion, in the West as well as in the East, resulting in an upsurge across Europe of nationalism, fundamentalism and regionalism.

In Poland, the coming into power of Solidarity in 1989 was followed by an economic and political restructuring aimed at a further integration of Poland into the global market economy, based on the standards of the World Bank (Jung, 1993). As a consequence, a fierce market-oriented conservatism replaced the former post-communist socialism, with state policy showing itself 'openly hostile to many elements of the welfare state and its practice of subsidising various social activities, such as leisure' (Jung, 1993:205). In the West, together with the ongoing economic crisis, the disintegration of communism additionally weakened left wing political and theoretical thinking, instead stimulating a further revival of market oriented liberalism (Alexander, 1995).

Taken together, these sometimes rather paradoxical cultural, economic and political transformations fundamentally changed the institutional and ideational conditions of the study of leisure in the various countries represented here. As has been shown in the previous chapters, in the years to follow, given its still fragmented and weakly institutionalised character, leisure research found it very difficult to re-orient itself within these transformations.

The Reappraisal of Leisure

It was only by the late 1970s and early 1980s, that the impact of the critical movements of the 1960s /1970s were felt in the expanding field of European leisure research. Despite its increasing importance, during the 1950s and 1960s the study of leisure had not yet become very much involved with mainstream social theoretical development, thus playing a minor role in the critical rethinking of general social theory. When in the late 1970s, early 1980s, critical thinking began to have an impact upon the domain of leisure studies, its influence was threefold. A first object of critique was the notion of culture used within leisure research. Arguments were made for a more receptive analysis of the 'positive' meaning of popular or sub-cultural practices, also questioning the foundations of established leisure-education programmes. Second, the dominant objectivist research approach with its fixation on formal, statistical procedures, was criticised for ignoring not only the meaning people themselves attach to their leisure activities, but also the institutional preconditions of leisure as such. Third, and from a more theoretical point of view, the un-reflexive use made of notions of 'post-industrial' or 'free time society', was challenged, with its emphasis on democratic pluralism and free choice. Critics pointed instead to the ongoing importance of concepts of class and power.

The influence of neo-Marxism on the study of leisure has perhaps nowhere been as noteworthy and productive as in the UK. This must first of all be related to the role of the Birmingham Centre for Contemporary Cultural Studies (CCCS), a post-graduate research centre, established as early as 1964 by the marxist historian Richard Hoggart (see e.g. Turner, 1990). The ongoing interest of the centre in the 'lived experience' of working class cultures (and in the ideological role of the media in structuring those experiences) obviously made it focus upon issues of leisure. In 1980, this resulted in the staging of a British Sociological Association - Leisure Studies Association workshop, the initiative of a new generation of leisure researchers, eager to import critical thinking into the leisure studies field.

Representatives of 'conventional' leisure studies and of critical cultural studies exchanged arguments (see Tomlinson, 1981). In the years that followed, the influence of the CCCS would not only result in an alternative introduction to the topic of leisure (Clarke and Critcher, 1985), and in more interest for ethnographic and institutional research, but also in a growing attention to issues of class, race, and gender (albeit that the latter had to wait for a feminist critique on the neglect of women in Cultural Studies).

At the same time, the increasing importance of Cultural Studies (itself oriented towards French structuralism or post-structuralism, semiotics and psycho-analysis) signalled a broader move away from post-war American social theory, back to Europe and to 'classical' or 'grand' social thought. This represented a shift in ideational orientation which can also be traced to the domain of leisure studies. Formerly dominated by 'weak' versions of American-oriented scientism and functionalism, the research of leisure increasingly became influenced by the works of Giddens, Bourdieu and Elias.

However, at the same time that critical thinking and a renewed interest in social theory finally had some impact upon the leisure studies field, questioning the hegemony of former positivist and functionalist approaches, the economic and fiscal crisis also started to impinge upon the leisure studies research agenda.

In the first instance, still in line with a former social welfarist approach, this was noticeable in a shift in the early 1980s towards issues of unemployment and leisure. Here the central question was what influence unemployment would have on people's leisure participation, but also whether leisure could function as an alternative integrative sphere of life, comparable to work.

However, the interest in unemployment and leisure would not last very long and instead issues of consumption and tourism started to compete with former interests in leisure and cultural participation. Most important has been the shift, noticeable all over Europe, towards a more market oriented approach to leisure, moving away from former humanist, emancipatory or socialist evaluations of leisure as a collective good, instead stimulating an interest in leisure as a market product (Bramham *et al.*, 1993). This has resulted in a shift away from social and/or educational concerns, and from collective issues of leisure participation and social inequality, to more localised issues of public reach, of marketing and management, consumption and tourism (feasibility studies, quality assessment research, segmentation studies).

In addition, in the 1980s, postmodern social and cultural thinking gradually found its way to the leisure studies field. At this point one could debate the background of the postmodern turn: is this the cynical result of the frustrations of a former critical, anti-modernisation generation, faced with the marginalisation of social-democratic thought, and the increasing importance of consumption, hence trying to find a new discursive space for intellectual respectability (Callinicos, 1989)? Or is there a deeper transformation involved, such as a market-led proliferation of consumption and media possibilities, exploited and reproduced by a new generation or class of 'cultural entrepreneurs', causing a further opening up of the cultural field, a subsequent 'de-mystification' of scientific and cultural thought, beyond former modernist categories and foundations (Featherstone, 1991)?

Whatever its background, leisure studies had to engage itself with the growing influence of postmodern theory, with its emphasis on the local, on (theoretical and cultural) eclecticism, pastiche and assemblage, on choice, reflexivity and the other. Postmodern thinking further stimulated an interest in consumer culture, leading to issues of aesthetics, imagery, pleasure, desire, deconstruction, the body, identity and style.

Until this moment, the field of leisure studies has related itself rather ambivalently to postmodern thinking. Of course, from a variety of positions, cross-connections have been made and maintained (e.g. the works of Featherstone, Lash and Urry, Rojek). However, in general, these cross-connections are made by people from outside the conventional domain of leisure research, and remain on a rather general level of analysis.

Mediating the 'old' concerns (the work-leisure relationship and leisure stratification) with new circumstances (the further proliferation of leisure and consumption possibilities, the commodification of leisure, global economic restructuring, the enduring crisis of the welfare state, the postmodern sensibility for the local and the everyday, the flexibilisation of labour) some additional fields of research have emerged (although again mostly stimulated by 'outside' developments). Here one can think of research into the changing patterns and meanings of free time in the context of an enduring flexibilisation of labour relations. Second, there is the question of how changing relations of class, gender, ethnicity and age can be traced to the domain of leisure participation in a post-industrial, postmodern society. Third, the topic of the changing role of leisure and culture in urban regeneration processes reflects a further concern of leisure studies (together with the possible consequences of this in terms of changing socio-cultural and spatial relations of inclusion and exclusion). Last, there is the issue of the changing structure of public and private leisure provision, due to the transformation of the relations between the national state, local government and a globalising commercial sector.

Leisure Research at the Cross-roads?

In one way or another, all these externally induced topical changes have further added to a pluralisation of the field of study, also making the boundaries between leisure studies on one side, and consumer and cultural studies on the other, become more diffuse. The time that an interest in leisure studies could unproblematically be grounded on a collective interest in the participation of a nation's population in leisure and culture seems to be over. This can be traced to all the countries represented in this volume, however with important national variations. On one extreme, there seems to be Poland, with its frantic turn towards monetarist policies, resulting in a disappearance of leisure studies departments, and a fragmentation of the body of leisure researchers. This has been accompanied by an increase in the volume of work on leisure markets (notable in relation to consumption and tourism) taking place in the offices of consultants and promotion agencies (see Jung, Chapter 3). In Spain, leisure studies is plagued by an institutional and theoretical fragmentation. However, due to the relatively young age of the Spanish welfare state, this seems to be evaluated much more in terms of a case of development, rather than a case of decline (San Salvador, Chapter 5). In France, the status of leisure as an autonomous field of research seems to be threatened. Samuel points in particular to the competing upsurge of the topic of daily life in the new 'sociability' of postmodern society, a topic very much related to French postmodern sociology. In the UK, as Bramham and Henry report, the leisure studies field seems to be grappling with the claims of postmodernism, and with the shifts in experiences of leisure, life-style and consumption under post-industrial, post-Fordist circumstances. Corijn and Van den Eeckhout signal a drawing back of Belgian leisure studies to traditional scientific disciplines and to pure marketing and management. And in the Netherlands, at least according to Mommaas, leisure studies has to face a centrifugal pluralisation of its research field.

In a certain sense this situation can be viewed as rather ironic. At the same moment that authors working within the leisure studies research field notice a certain fragmentation or 'evaporation' of their research field, topics related to leisure (consumption, culture, pleasure, desire, tourism, sports, time-space) seem to be enjoying a large(r) popularity and interest than ever before, in terms of social awareness, professional activity, and academic significance. The question then seems to be whether and how leisure studies can realign itself to these new fields of interest, and redefine its relation to them. Ideally this should not just be a case of jumping on some theoretical/practical bandwagon, or of defending established positions. Rather what is needed, and what would seem to be more productive, is a rethinking of recent theoretical/empirical developments from the point of view of the long-term history of European leisure studies. It is our hope that this book will have succeeded in producing some material of interest for such a repositioning.

REFERENCES

Albrow, M. (1993) 'The changing British role in European sociology', in B. Nedelmann and P. Sztompka (eds) *Sociology in Europe, in Search of Identity.* Berlin / New York: de Gruyter, pp. 81-98.

Alexander, J. (1995) *Fin de Siècle Social Theory.* London: Verso.

Bailey, P. (1978) *Leisure and Class in Victorian England.* London: Methuen.

Bauman, Z. (1987) *Legislators and Interpreters: On Modernity, Post-Modernity and Intellectuals.* Cambridge: Polity Press.

Beck, U. (1986) *Risikogesellschaft: Auf dem Weg in eine andere Moderne.* Frankfurt am Main: Suhrkamp.

Bourdieu, P. (1990) *In Other Words: Essays Towards a Reflexive Sociology.* Cambridge: Polity Press.

Bramham, P., Henry, I., Mommaas, H. and van der Poel, H. (eds) (1993) *Leisure Policies in Europe.* Wallingford: CAB International.

Callinicos, A. (1989) *Against Postmodernism, a Marxist Critique.* Cambridge: Polity Press.

Clarke, J. and Critcher, C. (1985) *The Devil Makes Work: Leisure in Capitalist Britain.* Basingstoke: MacMillan.

Corijn, E. and Mommaas, H. (1995) *Urban Cultural Policy Developments in Europe.* Background Report for The Council of Europe Contribution to the World Commission on Culture and Development, Tilburg University / Free University Brussels, Tilburg / Brussels.

Cross, G. (1993) *Time and Money. The Making of Consumer Culture.* London: Routledge.

De Grazia, S. (1962) *Of Time, Work, and Leisure.* New York: Anchor Books.

Delantly, G. (1995) *Inventing Europe. Idea, Identity, Reality.* London: Macmillan.

Dicken, P. (1992) *Global Shift: Industrial Change in a Turbulent World.* London: Harper & Row.

Featherstone, M. (1991) *Consumer Culture and Postmodernism.* London: Sage.

Foucault, M. (1974) *The Archaeology of Knowledge.* London: Tavistock.

Fourastié, J. (1966) *40.000 uur; de mens in het perspectief van een verkorte arbeidstijd.* Hilversum / Antwerpen: Paul Brand.

Gellner, E. (1983) *Nations and Nationalism.* Oxford: Basil Blackwell.

Giddens, A. (1985) *A Contemporary Critique of Historical Materialism. Vol. II: The Nation-State and Violence.* Cambridge: Polity Press.

Giddens, A. (1989) *The Consequences of Modernity.* Cambridge: Polity Press.

Giner, S. (1990) 'Spanish sociology under Franco', in S. Giner and L. Moreno (eds.) *Sociology in Spain*. Madrid: Instituto de Estudios Sociales Avanzados, pp. 55-72.

Goldman, L. (1993) 'Experts, investigators, and the state in 1860: British social scientists through American eyes', in M.J. Lacey and M.O. Furner (eds) *The State and Social Investigation in Britain and the United States*. Cambridge: Woodrow Wilson Center Press/ Cambridge University Press, pp. 95-127.

Gonzalez, J. and Urkiola, A. (1993) 'Leisure policy in Spain', in P. Bramham *et al.* (eds) *Leisure Policies in Europe*. Wallingford: CAB International, pp. 149-175.

Gorz, A. (1989) *Critique of Economic Reason*. London: Verso.

Gurvitch, G. and Moore, W.B. (eds) (1945) *Twentieth Century Sociology*. New York: The Philosophical Library.

Hägerstrand, T. (1975) 'Space, time and human condition', in A. Karlqvist (ed.) *Dynamic Allocation of Urban Space*. Farnborough: Saxon House.

Harvey, D. (1989) *The Condition of Postmodernity*. Cambridge: Blackwell.

Henry, I. and Bramham, P. (1993) 'Leisure policy in Britain', in P. Bramham *et al.* (eds) *Leisure Policies in Europe*. Wallingford: CAB International, pp. 101-129.

Herbst, J. (1965) *The German Historical School in American Scholarship*. Ithaca: Cornell University Press.

Jonker, E. (1988) *De Sociologische Verleiding*. Groningen: Wolters-Noordhoff / Forsten.

Jung, B. (1993) 'Elements of leisure policy in post-war Poland', in P. Bramham *et al.* (eds) *Leisure Policies in Europe*. Wallingford: CAB International, pp. 189-211.

Katznelson, I. and Zolberg, A.R. (eds) (1986) *Working-class Formation. Nineteenth-Century Patterns in Western Europe and the United States*. Princeton, NJ: Princeton University Press.

Kern, S. (1983) *The Culture of Time and Space, 1880-1918*. Cambridge, Mass: Harvard University Press.

Kocka, J. (1986) 'Problems of working-class formation in Germany: the early years, 1800-1875', in Katznelson I. and A.R. Zolberg (eds) (1986) *Working-class Formation. Nineteenth-Century Patterns in Western Europe and the United States*. Princeton, NJ: Princeton University Press, pp. 279-351.

Kwasniewicz, W. (1993) 'Between universal and native: the case of Polish sociology', in B. Nedelman and P. Sztompka (eds) *Sociology in Europe. In Search of Identity*. Berlin / New York: Walter de Gruyter, pp. 165-189.

Lacey, M.J. and Furner, M.O. (eds) (1993) *The State and Social Investigation in Britain and the United States*. Cambridge: Woodrow Wilson Center Press / Cambridge University Press.

Lanfant, M.F. (1974) *Sociologie van de vrije tijd.* Utrecht / Antwerpen: Het Spectrum.

Lash, S. (1994) 'Reflexivity and its doubles: structures, aesthetics, community' in U. Beck, A. Giddens and S. Lash, *Reflexive Modernisation.* Cambridge: Polity Press, pp. 110-174.

Lefebvre, H. (1991) *The Production of Space.* Oxford: Blackwell.

Lis, C. and Soly, H. (1980) *Poverty and Capitalism in Pre-Industrial Europe.* Hassocks: Harvester Press.

Manicas, P. (1987) *A History and Philosophy of the Social Sciences.* Oxford: Basil Blackwell.

Martin, B. (1983) *A Sociology of Contemporary Cultural Change.* Oxford: Basil Blackwell.

McClelland, Ch.E. (1980) *State, Society and the University in Germany, 1700-1914.* Cambridge: Cambridge University Press.

Mommaas, H. (1991) 'Sociografie en vrijetijd', in Th. Beckers and H. Mommaas (eds) *Het Vraagstuk van den Vrijen Tijd. 60 Jaar Onderzoek naar Vrijetijd.* Leiden: Stenfert Kroese, pp. 51-63.

Mommaas, H. (1993) *Moderniteit, Vrijetijd en de Stad.* Utrecht: Van Arkel.

Mommaas, H. (1996) 'Modernity, postmodernity and the crisis of social modernisation'. *International Journal of Urban and Regional Research.*

Murray, B. (1989) 'Fordism and post-Fordism', in S. Hall and M. Jacques (eds) *New Times.* London: Lawrence and Wishart, pp. 38-47.

Navarrete, L. (1990) 'Academic organisation of sociology in Spain', in S. Giner and L. Moreno (eds) *Sociology in Spain.* Madrid: Instituto de Estudios Sociales Avanzados, pp. 55-72.

Olszewska, A. (1989) *'Poland: the impact of the crisis on leisure patterns'*, in: A. Olszewska and K. Roberts (eds) *Leisure and Lifestyle.* London: Sage, pp. 17-39.

Olszewska, A. and Roberts, K. (1989) *Leisure and Lifestyle: a Comparative Analysis of Free Time.* London: Sage.

Parker, S. (1972) *The Future of Work and Leisure.* New York: Praeger.

Perkin, H.J. (1969) *The Origins of Modern English Society, 1780-1880.* London.

Poel, van der, H. (1993) 'Leisure policy in the Netherlands', in P. Bramham *et al.* (eds) *Leisure Policies in Europe.* Wallingford: CAB International, pp. 41-71.

Poggi, G. (1978) *The Development of the Modern State.* London: Hutchinson.

Rojek, C. (1995) *Decentring Leisure.* London: Sage.

Rothblatt, S. and Wittrock, B. (1993) *The European and American University Since 1800.* Cambridge: Cambridge University Press.

Sassen, S. (1994) *Cities in a World Economy.* London: Pine Forge.

Scaff, L.A. (1993) 'Europe and America in search of sociology: reflections on a partnership', in B. Nedelmann and P. Sztompka (eds) *Sociology in Europe, in Search of Identity.* Berlin / New York: de Gruyter, pp. 213-224.

Smart, B. (1992) *Modern Conditions, Postmodern Controversies.* London: Routledge.

Smigel, E.O. (ed.) (1963) *Work and Leisure: A Contemporary Social Problem.* New Haven, Conn: College and University Press.

Tezanos, J.F. (1990) 'Inequality and class', in S. Giner and L. Moreno (eds.) *Sociology in Spain.* Madrid: Instituto de Estudios Sociales Avanzados, pp. 151-156.

Therborn, G. (1995) *European Modernity and Beyond.* London: Sage.

Thompson, J.B. (1990) *Ideology and Modern Culture.* Cambridge: Polity Press.

Tomlinson, A. (1981) *Leisure and Social Control.* Polytechnic, Eastbourne: Brighton.

Toulmin, S. (1990) *Cosmopolis: the Hidden Agenda of Modernity.* New York: The Free Press.

Turner, G. (1990) *British Cultural Studies. An Introduction*, Media and Popular Culture 7. London: Unwin Hyman.

Turner, S.P. and Turner, J.H. (1990) *The Impossible Science. An Institutional Analysis of American Sociology.* London: Sage.

Wiener, A.J. and Kahn, H. (1967) *The Year 2000. A Framework of Speculation on the Next Thirty Years.* Hudson Institute Inc.

Williams, R. (1965) *The Long Revolution.* Harmondsworth: Penguin.

Wilterdink, N. and de Zwaan, T. (1991) 'Nationalisme, natievorming en modernisering', in T. Zwaan *et al.* (eds) *Het Europees Labyrint.* Amsterdam: Boom / Siswo, pp. 253-271.

Winch, D. (1993) 'The science of the legislator: the Enlightenment heritage', in M.J. Lacey and M.O. Furner (eds) *The State and Social Investigation in Britain and the United States.* Cambridge: Woodrow Wilson Center Press / Cambridge University Press, pp. 63-88.

Wittrock, B. (1993) 'The modern university: the three transformations', in S. Rothblatt and B. Wittrock (eds) *The European and American University Since 1800.* Cambridge: Cambridge University Press, pp. 303-363.

Wolf, E. (1982) *Europe and the People Without History.* Berkeley, CA: University of California Press.

Woodiwiss, A. (1993) *Postmodernity USA. The Crisis of Social Modernism in Postwar America.* London: Sage.

Znaniecki, E.M. (1945) 'Polish sociology', in Gurvitch, G., and W.B. Moore (eds.) *Twentieth Century Sociology.* New York: The Philosophical Library, pp. 703-717.

NOTES TO CHAPTER 9

[1] This somewhat 'allergic' or 'puritan' response to the notion of free time, mostly negating its 'real' or 'positive' existence, could perhaps be understood as a reaction against the way the notion of free time has been appropriated by 'pluralist' forerunners, simplifying it by negating the power-relations and dependencies involved (see for the emblematic debate concerning this issue: Tomlinson, 1981).

[2] This relates to the Delantlyis notion of Europe as a product of conflict, or interdependency, rather than as the progressive embodiment of a unifying idea (Delantlyis, 1995:2).

[3] Today, SPSS (the Statistical Package for the Social Sciences) can be used on virtually any PC, academic research has become more market oriented, the private sector research market is bigger than ever before, and perhaps much bigger compared to the academic one, with increasing overlaps between the two.

[4] This made it possible for the bourgeoisie to command larger stretches of space more effectively, while also enabling the internationalisation of the workers' movement, shifting funds and strategies from one place to another (Harvey, 1989:236).

[5] This can be related to a wider debate about the background of the intervention in leisure between neo-marxist and liberal pluralist interpretations (see Henry and Bramham, 1993).

[6] See the collection of historical studies on the state and social investigation in Britain and America, edited by Lacey and Furner (1993).

[7] See Manicas (1987: Chapter 10), and, for an interesting collection of studies on the history of the European and American university system Rothblatt and Wittrock (1993).

[8] As is well known, there is, at least logically, nothing problematic about the relation between 'modern' rationalism and Christianity. God gave us nature, but it is up to us mortal souls to discover its workings and thus guard it in accordance with our religious obligations. In addition, numerous authors have pointed out the fact that 19th century Christendom can not be regarded as a medieval residue, but must be seen as the product of a re-Christianisation in the context of modernity: 'religion was internalised' (Delantly, 1995:70).

[9] With references to earlier research, Goldman (1993) points out how institutions such as the Statistical Society of London (following the formation of the Manchester Statistical Society in 1833; see Manicas, 1987:196), the International Statistical Congress (1853-1876), the American Statistical Association, the British Social Science Association (in 1857 established as the National Association for the Promotion of the Social Science, see Manicas, 1987:197) and the American Social Science Association (1865) developed out of this undifferentiated space. In 1880 the Council of the British National Association for the Promotion of Social Sciences 'included 31 peers, 48 MPs, 19 Doctors of Law, 14 Fellows of the Royal Society, and 'numerous' baronets, knights, ministers of the Church of England, professors and Fellows of the London Statistical Society' (Manicas, 1987:198).

[10] This is not the place to embark on the complicated history of the concept of the modern (see Smart, 1992; Mommaas, 1993). Suffice it to point to the work of Giddens, of importance because of his role in revitalising a multidimensional perspective on long-term societal development, freed from the evolutionism of forerunners (e.g. Weber, Durkheim, Parsons). According to Giddens (1985), what distinguishes 'modern' societies from 'pre-modern' is the 'de-moralising' or 'de-traditionalising' dynamic, brought about by the interrelated functioning of capitalism, industrialism and the nation-state.

[11] Here, we paraphrase Wilterdink and De Zwaan (1991), but also borrow from Delantly (1995), Gellner (1983), Katznelson and Zolberg (1986), Poggi (1978) and Wolf (1982).

[12] In terms of the proportional dominance of industrial employment, the UK can be called an industrialised nation from the 1820 onwards, and Belgium from 1880 onwards.

[13] In fact, the Netherlands never reached the point where industrial employment dominated the national labour market, instead in the 20th century more directly making the turn to a service society (Therborn, 1995:69). Thus, during the 19th century, the administratively well organised and urbanised Netherlands, were much less industrialised than, for example, administratively decentralised and rural Germany (Kocka, 1986:284).

[14] Manicas (1987:207) cites Herbst (1965:8) who reports that between 1820 and 1920 almost 9000 Americans entered German universities: 'Before 1870, most of them sought professional training in medicine and the natural sciences. But by 1878, students of

Geisteswissenschaften and the liberal arts outnumbered those in law and theology'.

[15] Manicas (1987:200) recalls research by McClelland (1980) pointing out how between 1873 and 1914, in Germany, around 173 new research institutes were formed as part of direct state action. The number of students enrolled in German universities more than doubled between 1870 and 1900, and nearly doubled again between 1900 and 1914. Corresponding figures in the US were increasing at at least the same rate. However, as will be referred to below, soon, the American university would outdo its exemplars (Ibid: 208).

[16] On the basis of the existing material, it is difficult to asses whether there is a relation between the type of university system adopted, and the advancement of a research interest in leisure. Given the relation between the early free time research projects and social reform programmes, one would expect that a more specialised, applied or vocational system would have been more beneficial. However, on the other hand, also an orientation on 'algemeine Bildung' and national education seems to have stimulated an empirical interest in free time. Perhaps it is better to say that each system developed its own particular interest in leisure, in one instance (e.g. Germany, Belgium, France, Spain) favouring animation and education, while in another (e.g. Britain, Holland) social engineering.

[17] See Goldman (1993) for a trans-atlantic example of the many cross-national reformist contacts.

[18] Manicas (1987:209) explains the late introduction or slow expansion of the social sciences in Europe, compared to the United States, by pointing to the presence in Europe of a professoriate, functioning as a feudal, privileged 'mandarin class', with strong links to the higher circles of government and finance, and no wish to alter its ways.

[19] See Cross (1993:90/5) for an interesting comparison of the struggle for a shortening of working hours between 1919 and 1930. Cross suggests that by 1930 the power of the international labour movement had decreased, compared to 1919, because of: (a) a lack of support from national reformists and from the 'governing classes', (b) the nationalisation of the labour movement due to an increasing inter-nation hostility and competition, (c) the fact that the German labour movement had already been destroyed by Hitler, and (d) the formulation during the 1930s of alternative economic policies (by Hobson and Keynes), pointing to the role of taxation and fiscal

policies as alternative economic instruments compared to a reduction of work-time.

20 Therborn points out that from a cross-national point of view, between 1950 and 1980 no country in Europe experienced downward mobility, only upward mobility (Ibid. 137). In trying to explain this exceptional success, Therborn mentions the possible role of the socio-economic dynamics, unleashed by World War II and its aftermath (Ibid. 137).

21 Here, 'free time' entered the research programme as a means to enhance the workers' productivity (Lanfant, 1972:128).

22 As this already indicates, there was much overlap between the three debates distinguished here. The debate around the quality of work in mass production society was linked with issues of mass culture and consumption. At the same time debates around mass culture and consumption were fuelled by prospects of an important future increase of free time as consumption time. All these debates were heavily influenced by discussions within the US, especially based on the early works of Marcuse, Riesman, Wilensky and Keniston. The works of Friedman, Ellul and Touraine, all from France, were also influential in the 1950s and 1960s.

23 These ideas are expressed in the preface to a book published in 1945, meant as an overview of the state of the art of global sociology at that time, and containing contributions addressing not only the development of sociological thought in a variety of thematic fields, but also in a variety of countries (amongst others by Ernest Burgess, Talcott Parsons, Howard Becker, Florian Znaniecki). It is interesting to see how, at this time, Gurvitch (and his editorial assistant Wilbert Moore) were still very far 'ahead' of many of their co-contributors (see Gurvitch and Moore, 1945).

24 It is important to point out how this notion of the 'Americanisation' of 'European' sociology is a shorthand description of a very complicated development. Suffice to point out (1) that what is imported from the US consists largely of formerly imported/ transformed European social thought; (2) that post-war American scientism also distinguished itself from the founding fathers of American social thought, which was itself, regarded as just as backward and traditional as European 'classical' thought, and (3) that also within post-war American social thought, deep cleavages existed between, for instance, the empiricism of the Lazarsfeld approach, the systematic theorising of Parsons and the more historical or qualitative approach of scholars like Mills and Riesman (Turner and Turner,

1990). Add to this the complexities involved in the demarcation of
'European' social thought (what about Britain? see Albrow, 1993), and
the problematic nature of the theme is sketched (see also Scaff, 1993).

[25] It is important to stress that most of the time this 'cultural
democratisation' was not primarily aimed at a public revaluation of
folk, popular and/or mass culture. Instead it was aimed at an opening
up to the national population of the hegemonic middle class cultural
domain (the domain of voluntary work, the arts, recreation, sports). If
one wants to imagine what 'standardised individualism' stands for, one
only has to think of the monolithic neighbourhoods, with their
homogenised and functional spatial patterns, erected throughout
Europe in the 1950s / 1960s. This was not only cheap, it was also a
spatial expression of a more general ideology in which ideas of 'equal
opportunity' were linked to a standardisation of life changes.

[26] Think here of the titles of important agenda-setting books such as
those of Smigel *et al.* (1963) *Work and Leisure*; De Grazia (1962) *Of
Time, Work and Leisure*; Parker (1972) *The Future of Work and
Leisure*.

[27] The correlation which dominated post-war research on leisure, the
correlation between the level of education and the level of cultural
participation, presented an emblematic case. It is interesting not only
for the way in which this correlation has figured in the antagonisms
between marxist and 'bourgeois' sociological thinking, but also
because of the way this correlation became interpreted, and turned
into both rationalisations for cultural and educational policies, and
scenarios for future developments.

Index